Global Bollywood

Global Bollywood

Travels of Hindi Song and Dance

Sangita Gopal

Sujata Moorti

Editors

University of Minnesota Press

Minneapolis • London

Published by the University of Minnesota Press
111 Third Avenue South, Suite 290
Minneapolis, MN 55401-2520
http://www.upress.umn.edu

Printed in the United States of America on acid-free paper

Library of Congress Cataloging-in-Publication Data
Global Bollywood : travels of Hindi song and dance / Sangita Gopal and Sujata Moorti, editors.
    p.   cm.
  Includes bibliographical references and index.
  ISBN-978-0-8166-4578-7 (HC, alk. paper)—
  ISBN-978-0-8166-4579-4 (PB, alk. paper)—
    1. Motion pictures—India.   2. Motion picture music—India.   I. Gopal, Sangita.
II. Moorti, Sujata
  PN1993.5.I8G54   2008
  791.43'0954—dc22   2007048983

15 14 13 12 11 10 09 08   10 9 8 7 6 5 4 3 2 1

Contents

Introduction
Travels of Hindi Song and Dance

Sangita Gopal and Sujata Moorti

Bollywood and the Artworks of Globalization

To talk of Bollywood is inevitably to talk of the song and dance sequence. For auteur Ram Gopal Varma whose work has not found global audiences, song-dance is the reason Hindi cinema fails to reach international standards, but for Aamir Khan whose 2002 film *Lagaan* (Tax) was seen worldwide, the song-dance sequence is the dealmaker.[1] If feminist independent director Aparna Sen identifies herself as someone who does not do song and dance, noted U.S.-based diasporic filmmaker Mira Nair's crossover hit *Monsoon Wedding* (2001) is an homage to the all-singing, all-dancing Bollywood flick. Frequently remarked upon by insiders and always remarkable to outsiders, song-dance occupies the constitutive limit of Bollywood cinema. It determines—perhaps unfairly but invariably—the form itself even as it frequently escapes the filmic context to inhabit other milieus. While Hindi popular cinema from the very beginning has remained committed to the song and dance sequence, filmi song and dance has been a capricious friend— frequently morphing into other forms such as Trinidadian "chutney," Greek "indoprepi," or Javanese "dangdut."

The song and dance sequence, then, is the single most enduring feature of popular Hindi cinema, although song-dance is hardly unique to Hindi film. From the earliest days of sound, song-dance has characterized the commercial product in other Indian languages including Tamil, Telugu, Marathi, and Bengali.[2] Indian films, however, are not

---

This introduction has been coauthored, and author names are listed in alphabetical order.

musicals, and the ubiquity of song and dance cannot be rendered in generic terms. Though the coming of sound heralded an era of musicals in Hollywood, almost immediately the "musical" evolved into a distinct genre even as the notion of "genre" itself became more stabilized.[3] In the early decades of sound, many world cinemas were dominated by the "musical," but to call Hindi films "musicals" because they incorporate song-dance is to fundamentally mischaracterize them.[4] As Rosie Thomas has pointed out, "by the 1930s a number of distinctly Indian genres were well established. These included socials, mythologicals, devotionals, historicals, stunt, costume, and fantasy films. As song and dance is an integral part of films of *all* genres, the term musical is seldom used."[5] Genres have evolved historically as well, thus adding categories such as the multistarrer, the horror flick, the urban film, and even more recently, the nonresident Indian (NRI) film, and "the musical."[6] These generic categories may not necessarily follow Hollywood typologies, and the misrecognition of the indigenous logic of genres leads to broad generalizations like all Bollywood films are musical melodramas. In postindependence India, with the waning of the studio system and changes in film-financing, the all-encompassing "social" became the predominant genre. The 1970s and 1980s saw the rise of the star system such that films were categorized according to stars and their preference for a certain image or thematic—an excellent example is the "Vijay" film. Amitabh Bachchan played the role of an "angry young man" in a number of films from the 1970s. This character was always called "Vijay" though the films were not linked to each other in any other way. Indian film typologies and taxonomies remain seriously underinvestigated.[7]

While song-dance is by no means the only remarkable feature of Hindi popular cinema, it is a deep structure of this tradition and crucial to the way it is described by both insiders and outsiders.[8] Thus, attempts to define an alternative cinema invariably identify the song and dance sequence as an element that must be discarded in order to bring greater realism to film. As early as the 1940s, for instance, Nimai Ghosh while formulating principles for an experimental cinema in Bengal eschewed the song sequence along with professional actors and the use of makeup as part of a new aesthetics,[9] whereas Satyajit Ray, a figurehead of the parallel cinema movement, noted, "If I were asked to find room for six songs in a film that is not expressly a 'musical', I would have to throw up my hands . . . yet six songs per film, per *every* film, is the accepted average and at no point in the history of Indian films has there been an uproar against it."[10]

Similarly, most "outsider" accounts of Hindi popular cinema are usually discursivized as an encounter with song-dance. Thus, the editor of a recent anthology on Bollywood films writes, "my own enthusiasm for 'Bollywood' film took off in a cinema in Zanzibar in 1989, watching dance scenes, gods and goddesses, averted kisses, and heroes and heroines rolling joyfully singing down the slopes of Himalayan mountain sides, in the company of an Afro-Arab audience of Swahili-speaking Muslims who understood as little of the Hindi dialogue as I, but were as effectively hypnotized, eagerly whistling the songs and debating what had been going on after the show."[11] Though the excellent collection has but one essay dedicated to filmigit, this originary scene is often repeated in myriad ethnographic accounts where the first-time viewer of Hindi film is simultaneously estranged by and attracted to the spectacle of song and dance. Moreover, this account highlights the afterlife of the song-dance sequence—its propensity to circulate outside of exhibition space and filmic contexts. Songs seem to condense and stand in for the films of which they are a part—thus, megastar Amitabh Bachchan reminisces, "I was walking down London's Piccadilly Circus when I saw this group of Kurds running towards me. (Laughs). I thought they wanted to assassinate me. But they stopped right there and started singing songs from *Amar Akbar Anthony* and *Muquaddar Ka Sikander*."[12] In this oft-repeated trope, Bollywood cinema survives for its viewer as a song or the fragments of a song, so we hear of the guide at the Great Wall who hums a tune from *Disco Dancer* (Babbar Subash, 1982) or the taxicab driver in Athens who connects with an Indian passenger over the title song of *Awaara* (The innocent, Raj Kapoor, 1951). The song fragment in these instances forges an affective relationship between strangers while serving as a metonymy for India thus raising interesting questions about film music's relationship to national culture.

Before we proceed, a note of clarification of some terminology is imperative. The epithet Bollywood as a description of popular Hindi cinema, and increasingly all Indian cinema, has been the subject of intense scholarly debate. While the origins of the terms are uncertain, some historians suggest that it was coined by fanzines in the 1970s as a "parodic and cheeky echo of the North American film industry, a mimicry that is both a response and a dismissal."[13] Thus, actors such as

Amitabh Bachchan and Ajay Devgan and noted film directors like Subhash Ghai believe that the term demeans and belittles the contributions of the Indian film industry reducing it to a subcontinental clone of Hollywood. Others suggest that the term has a more convoluted history, originating in the 1930s when a British cameraman described as Tollywood the Calcutta (now known as Kolkata) film studio located in the neighborhood of Tollygunge. Bollywood and other derivatives follow from this coinage.[14] The question of whether the term Bollywood is a pejorative or subversive description of Bombay (now known as Mumbai)-based Hindi film products remains unresolved. However, contemporary scholars increasingly use this term to describe that small slice of the industry that has gained international currency and are careful to distinguish it from the rest of Hindi cinema. We echo Madhava Prasad's insight that Bollywood is a name for this "new cinema, coming from Bombay but also, lately, from London and Canada, which has over the last ten years or so, produced a new self-image for the Indian middle classes." We use the term Bollywood instead of Hindi commercial cinema to capture the global orientation of this formation. When we refer to Hindi commercial cinema in a primarily domestic or a historical context that does not include this global orientation, we use Hindi popular cinema or some variant thereof.[15] Similarly, we use the terms filmigit, film song, or film music to emphasize the aural dimension of the performance sequence. While noting that many films, but not all, include dance, we use song and dance sequence or song-dance to highlight the visualization as it occurs in the film, in music videos, and in performance.[16]

If Bollywood, as Ashish Rajadhyaksha has persuasively argued in a recent essay, is not a new name for Indian cinema but rather a culture industry of which Bombay-based film is only a small part, our anthology demonstrates the extent to which this emergence of Bollywood as a "cultural conglomeration that includes a range of distribution and consumption activities from Web sites to music cassettes, from cable to radio," and from fashion to product placements relies on the song-dance sequence and the work it does both within and outside the film text.[17] We argue that any account of Hindi film as a dominant in Indian public culture or of Bollywood as a transnational phenomenon must grapple with the crucial role that song-dance sequence has played in such disseminations.[18] The very features that Rajadhyaksha has identified as crucial to the new formation—Bollywood—have always been a part of the production and circulation of film music. Far from being an additional element to the entertainment on offer, music is the central axis along which desire and identification are calibrated. While integral to the narrative, these sequences circulate autonomously—objects of aesthetic pleasure and promiscuous reproduction.

The essays in this anthology investigate the global reception, circulation, and transformation of Bollywood filmigit and address the semantic, narrative, and productive functions performed by the song and dance sequences. At times, these sequences serve "as a telescoped narrative,"[19] while in other instances, they deepen the emotional texture of the narrative, occasionally serving as the kernel that contains the film's message and conveys the "director's true intentions."[20] Because plots are often repetitive, these spectacles become the site for the film's encounter with historicity. As dense nodes of signification that stage the subject's encounter with change, they can easily be extracted from the diegetic environment. Noted documentarian Nasreen Munni Kabir describes Hindi film song as "the only truly original moments in a Hindi film. . . . I mean you couldn't use the songs say from *Border* and put it in another film. Everyone goes on about the 800 or so films produced in India but 790 seem to have the same story. It is mainly the music that shows fantastic new energy and originality."[21] It is here that innovations in technology, allusions to sociopolitical realities, and aesthetic experimentation are most in evidence.[22] Simultaneously, these picturizations code the inexpressible and the transgressive.[23] The dual address of the performance sequence—realist and utopic—facilitates its spread to other cultural forms and aesthetic milieus.

The traditionally heterogeneous form of manufacture of the Hindi film whereby "prefabricated parts," such as song and dance sequences, were brought together to create a final product also means that these "parts" have independent circuits of distribution, both official and unofficial. Film scholar Madhava Prasad suggests that postindependence popular Hindi cinema was not characterized by a high degree of vertical integration but rather different elements of a film were produced relatively independently and assembled during postproduction. Other commentators such as Rachel Dwyer and Gayatri Chatterjee refine this thesis. Their studies of Yash Chopra, Raj Kapoor, and Mehboob Khan suggest that these directors exercised a strong creative and administrative control over all aspects of filmmaking. The 1990s or the postliberalization period witnessed a partial shift in this production

The itinerant gaze: encounters with Bollywood in India are inscribed on everyday spaces, such as this image in a Hyderabad street advertising an optician's services.

mode. "Auteurs" such as Mani Ratnam, Raj Kumar Santoshi, Ram Gopal Varma, and Vidhu Vinod Chopra have moved toward greater rationalization of the production process. This period also saw the partially successful induction of corporate finance into moviemaking. While the impact of these changes is still unfolding, film music and the production of the song-dance sequence remain autonomous. If anything, the advent of new media, veteran lyricist Javed Akhtar contends, has led to the further disaggregation of the performance sequence in Hindi cinema.[24]

Today, film songs are disseminated on media both old and new including radio, television, gramophone records, cassettes, CDs, DVDs and the Internet, reaching vast and varied audiences within India and internationally. In fact, as scholars have argued, Hindi film songs are India's pop music.[25] Like all pop culture, it derives its energies from diverse sources and contexts, both folk and classical. It is quite literally "world music"—in the sense of always having incorporated influences from various global musics, and this hybridity has often made Hindi film song the flashpoint in debates on national culture. At the same time, the persistence of song-dance also marks this cinematic form as unique and enables its global travels. Yet, an engagement with the complex routes and roots of the Bollywood song and dance spectacle's entry into various spaces of globalization is long overdue. *Global Bollywood* attends to such lacunae in scholarship. The individual essays address the central-ity of song and dance sequences to any understanding of Bollywood cinema and its transnational reception. The anthology tracks the rich transformations that song-dance undergoes in different sites, enabling new identificatory and affective practices.

Bollywood cinema partakes in at least three circuits of globali-zation: metropolitan, diasporic, and subaltern. Let us start by looking at a 2002 advertisement that uses the Hindi film song and dance sequence as a fantasy space to libidinize Western consumption practices. A twelve-minute minimovie for Absolut Vodka entitled "Mulit" traces the invention of the mullet haircut to a barbershop in Bombay. Shot as a Bollywood song and dance sequence, it tracks the transgressive love story between a barber and a prime minister's daughter, a romance that results in the accidental invention of the "Mullet" cut which then becomes a worldwide rage in the 1980s. This short with "Indian actors" playfully foregrounds the "collision of two worlds" and allegorizes its own turn to the Bollywood aesthetic in the narrative of origins of the mullet. The shape of the Absolut bottle appears as a repeating motif in the "kitschy" Bollywood-driven mise-en-scène.[26] Here, the visual and aural repertoire of the song-dance sequence functions as a style-making device that transforms the quotidian into the exotic.[27] The success of Absolut Mulit commercial inspired knockoffs (an advertisement for the Tennant's beer that refers to the 2001 blockbuster *Kabhi Khushi Kabhie Gham . . .*) and tributes (a Spanish Coke advertisement where a waiter entertains bored guests with a Bollywood song-dance number—this advertisement became a sensation in Spain and Italy).[28] The song-dance sequence as a "detachable attraction" with its unique aesthetic and for-mal codes seems particularly susceptible to the ceaseless appropriation that marks transnational capitalism's quest for novelty.[29]

Globalization processes entail overlapping and intersecting circuits. Shifting the gaze away from the West, we find that in the global South Hindi film music functions outside commodity logic and articulates an alternative globalism. Bollywood's continued presence in places such as Latin America, the Caribbean, Southeast Asia, and North Africa must be theorized differently.[30] Songs arrived here as a part of cultural exchanges facilitated by political alliances like the Non-Aligned Movement (NAM). For instance, in Kano, northern Nigeria, an innovative form of music, *bandiri,* has become popular among Hausa youth. Singing live at public ceremonies such as weddings, or selling cassettes through local markets, bandiri singers are Sufi adepts who take love songs from popular Hindi films and change the words to sing praises to the Prophet Mohammed. However, the profane specter of the original haunts these religious remixes and hybridizes the sacral site of enunciation.[31] This new genre of sacred music relies on the cultural competence of listeners who have grown up listening to Hindi film songs. Bollywood music has enabled the emergence of an alternative modernity that is conjunctural.

Another understanding of globalization centers on the hybrid signifying and consumption practices that mobile, migrant populations introduce into metropolitan space.[32] Within the Indian diaspora, Hindi film songs play a crucial role and enable immigrants to express multiple affiliations. A 2002 academic conference on global media at the Massachusetts Institute of Technology (MIT) showcased diversity by staging a show where students collaborated with the local community. Entitled "Bollyspace," this performance rehearses the Indian diaspora's relationship to the cultural forms of the homeland at multiple levels. Mimicking the format of stage shows where lip-synching Hindi film stars reenact song and dance sequences for diasporic fans, this performance included video clips of contemporary hits that had been sequenced to resemble the Sony playstation game system. Against this video stream backdrop projected on multiple screens, second- and third-generation Indian American teenagers recoded the dating game format and opened it up to queer readings. The stage shows that Bollyspace references reflect an immigrant fan culture that draws sustenance from Bollywood's reiteration of family values, whereas the performance demonstrates that the song and dance sequence can equally register subversive identifications that challenge heteronormativity. Thus, Bollyspace simultaneously codes the first generation's fabrication of a community of sentiment through nostalgia and the second generation's selective mobilization of cultural forms to produce alternative identifications.[33] Similarly, urban club cultures in the United States and the United Kingdom have used Hindi film songs to carve a niche identity. More recently, gay pride week events in New York City have included "desi" dance events that have drawn multiethnic/multiracial crowds where Caucasians, African

Americans, Korean Americans, Japanese Americans, Africans, and others dance with desis, to a range of remixes and Bollywood songs in the original. These commercial texts and cultural practices are but a few instances of the diverse uses to which Bollywood is put in global space. In each case, music is central to Bollywood's mobility. Tracking the dissemination of Hindi film song and dance sequences along the different axes of globalization is crucial to theorizing Bollywood as a global formation.

In the essays that follow, Bollywood song and dance emerges as a contranational artifact par excellence whose world travels are enabled by this constitutive hybridity. Working from a conception of globalization that is attentive to its historical emergence and uneven chronotopes, the narrative of Bollywood's world travels that this anthology scripts complicates dominant paradigms of transnationalism that tend to read this as a conversation between the West and the rest. The reinvention of the song and dance sequence in unlikely places in the global North demonstrates the aesthetics of sampling, pastiche, and creative appropriation that mark postmodern global cultural formations. These hybrid, sampled musics are in sharp contrast to world music that asserts its ethnic purity. The category world music emerged in the 1980s as a record industry label to promote and sell non-Anglo-American pop music to Western consumers. World music conflates different forms of music from around the world into a single non-Western musical genre. Thus, even as it distances itself from mainstream consumption practices, it partakes in a subtle brand of neo-Orientalism. The label promotes artists as representative of authentic ethnic musical milieus, foregrounding only those who play traditional instruments or sing in indigenous languages. Here is a neocolonialist arrangement where the South offers raw materials while the North provides the technology to turn it into a state-of-the-art marketable commodity. However well intentioned the aims of world music promoters, it ends up reproducing the politics it eschews.[34] But this mode of citation must be distinguished from Bollywood's alternative resonance in the global South where it has historically served to negotiate questions of tradition and modernity and continues to inform identity formation even as these societies are being transformed by current geopolitical conjunctures. This anthology, thus, is always vigilant to the complicated nexus of economics, politics, historical legacies, migration, and imaginative geographies that underwrite the art works of globalization.

Cinema and Nation

It would be appropriate to look at the complex relationship between cinema and the national question before locating Bollywood song-dance in its transnational context. The film industry in India from its very inception was intimately implicated in the nationalist project. Dadasaheb Phalke, whose *Raja Harishchandra* (1913) is probably India's first feature film, viewed the establishment of a film industry in India in expressly *swadeshi* (of the country or indigenous) terms: "I decided to establish it [the film industry] on a permanent footing to provide employment to hundreds of worker-artists like me. I was determined to do my duty . . . to defend this industry even in the absence of any financial support, with the firm conviction that the Indian people would get an occasion to see Indian images on the screen and people abroad would get a true picture of India."[35] Despite Phalke's nationalist yearnings, the Indian film industry, in its early years, had a surprising international flavor.[36] Not only were Indian films routinely screened abroad, but the industry included professionals from Italy, France, Germany, Iran, and the United States. The films of Dadasaheb Phalke had been enthusiastically reviewed in England, and Phalke was offered 300 pounds and 20 percent of the profits to make films in London, but the *swadeshi* filmmaker declined. Phani Majumdar (1911–94)—director of the New Theatres' hit *Street Singer*—worked in Singapore in the 1950s and made several features for Shaw Malay Film Productions including *Hang Tuah* and a Chinese–Malay bilingual entitled *Circus*. The American cinematographer Duncan Ellis came to India as a cameraman in 1935 and stayed for seventeen years. He went on to direct several hit films in a nascent Tamil industry, and he can be credited with helping to incorporate music and comedy routines into Tamil cinema. One of early cinema's biggest stars was the Australian Mary Evans who came to India as part of Madame Astrova's ballet troupe. She first worked as a chorus girl for Wadia Movietone's *Lal-e-Yaman* (J. B. H. Wadia, 1933) and then went on to become the star of highly successful stunt films including *Hunterwali* (The huntress, Homi Wadia, 1935), *Miss Frontier Mail* (Homi Wadia, 1936), and *Hurricane Hansa* (R. N. Vaidya, 1937). Launched as "India's Pearl White," she was soon called "Fearless Nadia" by her many adoring fans.[37] Hence, Shuddhabrata Sengupta's suggestion that to talk about "Bombay or even Hindi cinema in the 1920s and 30s is premature."[38] The production base for these films was decidedly "pan-subcontinental." For instance, the Iranian filmmaker Abdolhossein Sepanta worked in Bombay and the first Iranian sound film, *Dukhtar-e-Lur*, 1932, was made in the Imperial Films Company (established 1926).[39] This internationalism in preindependence cinema was further reflected in a cosmopolitan workforce that migrated between the different film centers in Bombay, Madras (now known as Chennai), Calcutta, Pune, and Lahore. J. F. Madan who owned an exhibition–distribution empire and founded a studio—Madan Theatres—worked with Italian cineaste E. D. Liguoro and the cameraman T. Marconi.[40] Though Madan Theatres did not survive the transition to sound, Himanshu Rai's Bombay Talkies (established 1935) included several European collaborators including director Franz Osten.[41] We also notice that the industry was courting foreign markets and the finished products were targeted at audiences not only in South Asia but also in Central and Southeast Asia, Africa, and the Caribbean.

Thus, Indian film was decidedly internationalist in its mode of production and distribution. Nor did it speak with a single voice—in the silent and studio eras, regional centers such as Pune, Madras, Calcutta, and Lahore (which is now in Pakistan) rivaled Bombay as sites for film production. During the colonial era, the category of national cinema did not exist.[42] In fact, the introduction of sound strengthened vernacular cinema insofar as films began to be made in a specific language. Filmic form reflected regional differences as well—thus, Bengali cinema embraced the literary film, whereas the mythological was popular in Marathi cinema while a Gujarati studio like Ranjit Movietone specialized in domestic dramas in contemporary settings. Multilingual productions were common as well.

Historians of Indian film concur that the dominance of the Hindi commercial cinema industry began to emerge in the postindependence era when Hindi became the official "national language," thus giving Bombay an advantage over other regions. Unlike countries such as Egypt where decolonization was accompanied by a nationalization of the film industry, commercial film production in India remained in the unorganized private sector, gaining industry status and wider access to bank finance only as recently as 1998. This meant that Hindi film could, after 1947, begin to assume the shape and form of a national cinema that developed a distinct identity of its own and began to subsume regional cinema to a certain extent. In this period, the Indian film industry succeeded in establishing a domestic film product that outperformed

Hollywood nationally and successfully competed with it in certain markets abroad. Statistics published by the United Nations Educational, Scientific, and Cultural Organization (UNESCO) confirmed that in forty-eight countries during 1975, over 90 percent of film consumption depended on imports. Only audiences in the United States, the Union of Soviet Socialist Republics (USSR), Japan, and India viewed more nationally made films than foreign films.[43] Not only was this cinema domestically generated, it was also predominantly in Hindi. Although Hindi film industry's claims to the status of India's national cinema remains contested, if one used economic parameters alone, it would seem that Hindi film is unquestionably nationally dominant. Though, as the table illustrates, non-Hindi cinema production cumulatively outnumbered the mainstream Hindi film production in 2002 (and the Tamil and Malayalam industries numerically outpace the Hindi film industry), mainstream Hindi cinema is able to reassert its dominance in terms of reception and revenues. Thus, on average, each Hindi film generates more revenues than the sum of all the non-Hindi cinemas together. This economic prowess is due to the fact that Hindi films have a broader-based viewership—they are distributed in all five distribution segments within India and also enjoy a flourishing market overseas.[44]

In other words, though Hindi film has remained *one* of the many constituents that make up Indian cinema as a whole, we would be justified in describing postindependence Hindi film as nationalist cinema.[45]

Indian Cinema Revenues, 2002

Type of film	Average number of movies	Average gross collection per movie (all revenue streams), in millions of Indian national rupees
Hindi mainstream	75	220
Malayalam	93	40
Tamil mainstream	84	80
Telugu mainstream	74	80
Bengali	50	10

Note: US$1 = 48 Indian national rupees.

Source: KPMG and FICCI Report—Indian Entertainment Sector in the Spotlight, from Janina Gomes, *Internationalisation of the Indian Film Industry* (Mumbai: The Indo-Italian Chamber of Commerce and Industry, 2003).

This description would be true not by the dint of mere numbers but also because the film industry, in the words of Ashish Rajadhyaksha, "set itself up as a national industry in the sense of assembling a national market, even devising a narrative mode that has since been extensively identified as nationalist melodrama in ways that actually *precede* and even anticipate institutionalized state functioning in this field."[46] In other words, Hindi film performed the crucial political task of bringing into being a national public comprising spectator-citizens. In this role, the industry became indispensable to a state not yet fully capable of entrusting political citizenship. Chidananda Das Gupta, one of the key figures in the parallel cinema movement, acknowledges the national reach of this "mass produced film formula" produced in Bombay by dubbing it as "All India Film." In the absence of a state-supported cinema, Hindi film and its regional derivatives perform the integrating nationalist function carried out by such state institutions as All India Radio (AIR) and Doordarshan. Indeed, it can be said that the Indian state resented this mode of nation-building. The government found Hindi films, particularly the song and dance sequences, to be "debased and commercial" and established foundations such as the National Film Development Corporation (NFDC) in the late 1960s to foster and finance the production of an alternative cinema.[47]

Hindi films such as *Mother India* (Mehboob Khan, 1957) thematized the concept of a unified national identity and aspired to imagine the nation.[48] They did so, as suggested earlier, by subsuming regional talent and by perfecting forms of narration and address—most specifically, the song and dance sequence—that could transcend linguistic and cultural differences. It is well known that practitioners from the other cinemas have regularly moved in and out of the Hindi film industry and made great contributions to its development. For instance, Tamil director Mani Ratnam moved to Bombay cinema after having established his career in the South. Similarly, a number of stars of non-Hindi cinemas, such as Sridevi, have gravitated to Bombay from regional industries. The Hindi film industry's mining of pan-Indian talent has been nowhere more noteworthy than in the realm of song and dance. Music directors, singers, and choreographers such as P. C. Barua, Pankaj Mullick, S. D. Burman, R. D. Burman, Hemanta Kumar Mukerjee, Ilya Raja, Manna Dey, Geeta Roy, A. R. Rahman, Dalsukh Pancholi, Jayaprada, Sridevi, and Yesudas have had multilingual careers that were first established in regional industries before they moved to Bombay.

This steady movement encouraged collaboration, but it also created unique problems where regional language lyrical traditions had to be reworked to fit the Hindi film song style. The history of these collaborations illustrates constant negotiations between different regional cinemas to create a national product.[49] And, the use of musical numbers as a crucial ingredient of film sound no doubt enabled the creation of a common culture in a linguistically fragmented nation. " 'With the coming of talkies,' wrote a contemporary observer, 'the Indian motion picture came into its own as a definite and distinctive piece of creation. This was achieved by music'. "[50] The Hindi film song, writes Partha Chatterjee, "cut through all the language barriers in India to engage in lively communication with the nation where more than twenty languages are spoken . . . and scores of dialect exist."[51] Song and dance helps to dilute ethnocentrism, thus while most Hindi film characters are based on North Indian types, in the song-dance sequence "a female character can be seen dancing a typically Punjabi *bhangra,* and in another scene she can be seen performing a South Indian dance like the *Bharat Natyam.* So we pick and choose different things from different regions and mix them together."[52] This ability of the song situation to overcome linguistic and cultural differences and suture the fragments of the nation underscores the centrality of song to Bollywood grammar and prefigures its subsequent transnational legibility. Film music, circulated via AIR, functioned as India's popular music while one of the highest-rated programs on state-owned television, Doordarshan, was called *Chitrahaar* (Garland of images), and it comprised song and dance clips. Hindi film music enjoyed a prominence even in those markets most resistant to the Bombay film product. Film music's emergence as a "language" that overcomes barriers in communication is dramatically illustrated by Ashis Nandy's analysis of three "failed" hijackings that occurred between 1984 and 1993. In one instance, the hijackers—representatives of a separatist organization seeking to "destabilize" the nation-state through acts of domestic terrorism—forged bonds with the crew and passengers using the language of filmigit. Nandy contends that the rational language of realpolitik and journalism would read these events as "imperfect terrorism." However, if one recognizes that Indian "public life is shaped by the idiom and melodrama of the commercial cinema," one could unearth the rules of fair play, duty, morality, and restraints on violence that allowed the hijackers to amuse "tense and bored passengers" with melancholy love songs from Hindi films. The face-off between terrorist and citizen that such events represent was mediated by the shared vernacular of Hindi film song.[53] Hindi songs' ability to transcend linguistic barriers was put to use in an interesting literacy project that originated in the western Indian state of Gujarat. Segments of Indian population, illiterate or semiliterate, nonetheless know the lyrics of Hindi film songs and sing along when these song and dance sequences are played on immensely popular television shows like *Chitrahaar*. This project decided to insert same language subtitles into the song sequences to promote literacy among the viewers who already knew the words and were familiar with the meanings.[54]

Although the question of Hindi film's status as a national cinema and its investments in nationalism remains a complex one, well-known lyricist and scriptwriter Javed Akhtar's conceptualization playfully captures the relationship of Hindi cinema to the nation.

> There is one more state in this country and that is Hindi cinema . . . Hindi cinema's culture is quite different from Indian culture, but it is not alien to us, we understand it. Hindi cinema is our closest neighbour. It has its own world, its own tradition, its own symbols, its own expressions, its own language and those who are familiar with it understand it.[55]

If this relative autonomy that Akhtar identifies as a key characteristic of Hindi film has enabled it to function alongside the Indian state in assembling a national spectatorship or defining its products as national culture, we suggest that autonomy—most in evidence in film music and the performance segment—facilitates its mobility across technologies, forms, spaces, and cultures.

"All Talking, All Singing, All Dancing"

Any account of the global travels of Hindi film music must commence with Raj Kapoor's *Awaara*. This film where love overcomes class differences against the backdrop of an Oedipal struggle between an autocratic judge and his estranged son is a particularly accomplished instance of the "social"—a genre dominant in the 1950s. Although *Awaara*'s combination of realism, melodrama, narrative, and spectacle was paradigmatic of the films of this era, its sound track was truly innovative and its song picturizations outstanding, a masterpiece of the so-called golden era of Hindi film. If *Awaara* was an overnight sensation in India, it also found markets in the Middle East, Africa, the former Soviet Union, and East Asia.[56] Released in the Soviet Union as *Bradyaga* (1954), it was a cult favorite in China. Dubbed in Persian, Turkish, and Arabic, it broke box-office records in Afro-Asia and the Middle East. Its stars, Raj Kapoor and Nargis, became popular pin-ups in Arab bazaars while Russians serenaded them with songs from the films.[57] Crucial to *Awaara's* global success then was its music, particularly the title song "Main awaara hoon" (I am an innocent) and a legendary dreamscape that is in fact three separate song picturizations bracketed by a prologue and an epilogue. This scene that includes the song, "Mujhko chahiye bahar" (I want beauty), offers an excellent case study of the complex semantic, aesthetic, and affective functions of song-dance in Hindi cinema. Yet, this celebrated dreamscape that contributed in great measure to the film's popularity was not planned for in the original screenplay and was shot as an afterthought. About thirty sets were designed by M. R. Achrekar, and Madam Simki choreographed the dances.[58] Integrating narrative and lush spectacle, this scene condenses the themes of the film and prefigures the ending. At the same time, it functions as a metacomment on popular filmmaking with its amalgam of "art" and "kitsch" and marks a transition in narrative modes—from romantic realism to melodrama.[59] Through visual icons and "universal" signifiers, such as a staircase that leads in one direction to an idyllic world represented by a tower set amid fluffy clouds and in another to a hell represented by flames and grotesque statues, the sequence captures in shorthand the social gap that separates the principals and the various conflicts encountered by the hero. Its innovative use of space, perspective, and the movement of bodies visually realizes *Awaara's* critique of the existing social order as the hero plaintively cries, "Mujhko yeh narak na chahiye; mujhko phool, mujhko geet, mujhko preet chahiye" [I don't want this hell; I want flowers, I want music, and I want love], even while it relocates this critique in the individual. The reception history of *Awaara* repeatedly links the film's success to its inventive use of the performance sequences. The popularity of the sound track owes in great measure to the eclecticism of its musical borrowings which included Indian and Western classical music, Goan and Russian folk songs, and the choral style of the Indian People's Theatre Association (IPTA), a collective dedicated to revolutionary art practice. Out of these diverse elements, the director Raj Kapoor and the composing duo Shankar-Jaikishen created a very contemporary sound that captured the rhythms of modernity and enthralled spectators the world over.

This is by no means the only Indian film to be shown abroad, but the first whose popularity was largely driven by song. Kapoor's global success was replicated by Mehboob Khan whose films—first *Aan* (1952) and then *Mother India* (1957)—were distributed internationally on a scale unprecedented for Indian cinema. The success of Mehboob Khan's films owed in part to diasporic audiences. British television documentarian Kabir recalls seeing *Aan* in London. The actress Nimmi running through yellow mustard fields is one of her first screen memories. But as the production histories of *Mother India* show, the Indian government had little interest in aiding the internationalization of the film industry, and thus when *Mother India* was nominated for the Oscar in the best foreign film category, Khan had to special petition the Indian government to release foreign exchange to enable him to attend the ceremony. Kapoor and Khan's success is all the more remarkable when we consider that it occurred in the context of a newly independent Indian state inclined to provide, as we have seen above, very little support to the Bombay-based film industry.[60]

Song and dance has been tied to Indian cinema from its very start. Although a history of the media world in which Indian film arose is still an ongoing project, there is some consensus that the centrality of music,

Express your love: the famous dream sequence in Raj Kapoor's international hit *Awaara* (1951), where Raj (Raj Kapoor) and Rita (Nargis) celebrate their love.

song, and dance in preexisting popular and folk traditions in India must partly account for the persistence of song-dance in Hindi film.[61] William O'Beeman notes that in India, "vocal expression takes many forms which can be exhibited on a continuum—speech-dialogue-poetic recitation-intoned speech-song," with the result that for the spectator the distance between registers of utterance—speech/song—is narrower than in the West.[62] Cinema partially reflected enunciatory modes already familiar in popular culture. Thus, Gayatri Chatterjee, in a close reading of the opening sequence of *Sant Tukaram* (The Saint Tukaram, V. Damle/S. Fattelal, 1936), demonstrates how the use of songs in early sound cinema borrows from a popular mode of storytelling where a scroll painting is unfurled to the accompaniment of songs that reveal information about the events and figures in the paintings.[63] Although film was no doubt shaped by such traditional performance idioms, it also crucially mediated India's encounter with modernity and was, in turn, a part of the experience of the modern.[64] As such, certain forms of mass "art" and the Parsi theatre—technologically slick, urban, and produced for an emerging middle class—are the nineteenth-century forms most useful in contextualizing Bombay-based early cinema. Beginning in 1853, the Parsi theatre developed into a mobile, operatic entertainment that traversed the length and breadth of colonial and princely India and extended overseas into Southeast Asia. Its rise was simultaneous with that of other regional theatres in Bengal and Maharashtra, and it shared with them certain features—a proscenium style stage, painted backdrops, an emphasis on spectacle and melodrama, and the inclusion of song and dance. At the same time, as Kathryn Hansen argues, the Parsi theatre ushered in conventions and techniques of realism. It consolidated a "set of disparate, localized performance practices into a widely circulated pan-Indian style. With its emphasis on spectacle and song, it fostered modes of visual and aural discrimination that were linked to pre-existing forms, yet afforded new pleasures by means of technological innovations that conveyed the feeling of modernity."[65] Early cinema and theatre occupied overlapping spaces, and a play like *Indar Sabha* moved across media taking shape as a printed text, a set of recorded songs, a rare book, and finally one of the first talkies. In the early decades of silent cinema, theatres continued to dominate urban entertainment. It was only in the 1930s with the full-fledged coming of the talkies that theatres went into decline.[66]

Somnath Gupt whose work on the origins and development of Parsi theater is a classic thus summarizes the role of music in it:

> Aside from a few ghazals, the music of the Parsi theatre was classical . . . sometimes the influence of Western music was apparent. The only defect was that the song lyrics lacked deep feeling. In the beginning, dramas were written only in prose. Dadi Patel introduced the notion of opera with Benazir Badremunir, and the addiction to songs grew to such an extent that occasions of joy, deaths, wars and dialogues were accompanied by singing. These songs did nothing to advance the plot or characterization—the demand for songs increased and accordingly their commercial value soared.[67]

Gupt notes that theatrical songs were a hybrid form that included many musical influences including Western music. Songs enjoyed an autonomous following, and they were tied to certain stock situations rather than incorporated into the plot. Although Gupt's characterization of the song's (non)relation to narrative might be governed by modernist aesthetics that prizes integration, this extract provides crucial insights that help us grasp that certain characteristics of the song-dance in Hindi cinema might have been derived from the theatre.

Film historians Richard Abel and Rick Altman have suggested that silent films were occurring in an environment that was anything but silent. Rather they draw attention to the diversity of sound and sound image relations that characterize early exhibition.[68] This was clearly the case in India. Audiences accustomed to indigenous entertainment genres comprising music, dance, and spectacle demanded more than the moving pictures. Thus, even during the silent era, the screening of films was accompanied by live performances by dancing girls, jugglers, and musclemen.[69] Firoze Rangoonwala recounts, "It was finally with D. G. Phalke's *Raja Harishchandra* released on 3 May 1913 at the Coronation that the Indian feature film came into being in the fullest sense . . . And appeal it did to all kinds of spectators seeing the big success it proved. The whole was a one and a half hour show including Miss Irene Delmar (duet and dance), The McClements (comical sketch), Alexandroff (foot juggler) and Tip-top comics."[70] Well-known music director and lyricist Gulzar recalls, "In front of the screen was a pit where musicians would sit and provide live music for the visuals in the film . . . The loud music of tabla, sarangi and harmonium played very loudly [*sic*], would drown out the sounds not only of the noisy film projectors but also of the calls of roaming hawkers selling paan, beedis and lemon soda . . . The audience would send requests for their favourite songs *regardless* of the visuals and situations on the screen."[71] This audience-centered elaboration of song functioned as a parallel audio text that competed with and sometimes overtook the attractions on screen.[72]

By the 1920s, it was not unusual for a film to have a music score specially composed for it and played by a live band. Thus, the Bengali film *Bilet Pherat* (Foreign returned, N. C. Laharry, 1921) was promoted as the first Bengali film with a live "all-Bengali" band to accompany the screening. Following the tightening of censorship rules in the Cinematograph Act of 1918, songs became extremely important because they "could be passed off by word of mouth and were harder to censor than written materials."[73] A good example is *Bhakta Vidur* (The Devotee Vidur, Ranjibhai Rathod, 1921), a political allegory that included a famous nationalist song in praise of the chakra (spinning wheel—a staple of *swadeshi* iconography).[74] Songs, then, were linked to films even before the advent of sound. The first sound film, *Alam Ara* (Light of the word, Ardeshir Irani, 1931), established the use of music, song, and dance as an intrinsic part of Indian film. A period fantasy based on Joseph David's popular theatre play, it was shot on the Tanar single-system camera that recorded image and sound simultaneously and this proved a challenge for picturizing the seven songs that were a highlight of the film. Wazir Khan's recording of a wandering minstrel's number "De de khuda ke naam par pyare" (Give in the name of the Lord, dear one) was particularly popular and pioneered the use of a commentating chorus—a feature of many subsequent films.[75] Narrowly beaten to the screen by *Alam Ara, Shirin Farhad* (J. J. Madan, 1931) was a big-budget musical that proved a bigger hit than *Alam Ara*. This film recorded sound and image separately allowing for greater flexibility, and though credited with featuring as many as forty-two songs, film historians now believe that these were not song sequences proper but rather sung more or less continuously as in opera. The same is probably true of *Indrasabha*'s (The court of Indra, J. J. Madan,1932) sixty-nine songs. Both these films starred the popular singing duo—Nissar and Kajjan.[76] This profligacy was subsequently reined in, and directors arrived at a magical formula of six to ten songs per film. Song sequences, often accompanied by dance, were such an integral part of film that when the Wadias attempted to release a film—*Naujawan* (The youth, Aspi,

1937)—without any songs, audiences were so disgruntled that the producers had to include a trailer explaining the absence of song cushions.[77]

In the 1930s, Calcutta was a nerve center for innovations in film music. Music directors Raichand Boral and Pankaj Mullick and sound recordist Mukul Bose all worked at New Theatres, and they not only composed some of the most memorable songs from this era but also made great strides in recording technology. This music, as Biswarup Sen's essay demonstrates, was hybrid and comprised Indian and Western styles and instrumentation. In the music emanating from New Theatres which combined traditional instruments such as the *sitar, sarod, sarangi,* and *bansuri* with Western instruments such as the violin, saxophone, and flute, we find the beginnings of the orchestra that accompanies filmigit. Orchestration not only permitted the introduction of harmony and other coloring devices into film song, but Indian vernacular music began to be constructed, and more importantly notated, in a studied, rational basis.[78] Boral started out creating live scores for Charu Roy's *Chorekanta* (1931) and Prafulla Roy's *Chasher Meye* (The farm girl, 1931). His hallmark was *ghazal*-style emotionally charged songs with extensive string sections superbly interpreted by his protégé—the singer-actor K. L. Saigal.[79] Saigal is credited with perfecting the "crooning" style of singing with a personal, intimate vocalization that gave a conversational quality to most of his songs. Boral combined forms such as *thumri, keertan, akhrai,* and *kabigan,* continuing a tradition of fusion in the nineteenth-century Bengali popular music. He became the first musician to give background music in an Indian film—*Chandidas* (Nitin Bose, 1934).[80] The next year, in 1935, he became the first composer to bring in playback (as against direct-to-film) singing in a film released as *Dhoop Chaon* (Sun and shade) in Hindi and *Bhagya Chakra* (The wheel of fortune) in Bengali. Nitin Bose, the director, claimed that it was one of the first films in the world to incorporate this technique. His colleague at New Theatres, Pankaj Mullick, was a composer and singer-actor who also scored some very popular film tracks including *Yahudi Ki Ladki* (The Jew's daughter, Premankur Atorthy, 1933) and *Mukti* (Release, P. C. Barua, 1937). Mullick is credited with bringing *Rabindra Sangeet* (a hybrid style of music associated with the compositions of Rabindranath Tagore) into Indian film song.[81] Musicologist Ashraf Aziz claims that while Boral and Mullick laid the melodic foundation of the film song, it was Ghulam Haider—a leading composer working in Lahore—who brought a percussive intensity that has since remained a crucial element in Hindi film music. Haider and the singing star Noor Jehan worked together first in the Punjabi film *Sheila/Pind di Kuri* (Krishnadev Mehra, 1935) and introduced a vocal energy, range, and kineticism that has ever since remained a signature feature of filmgit. Haider's compositions for *Khazanchi* (Treasurer, Moti Gidwani, 1941) and *Khandan* (Family, Shaukat Hussain Rizvi, 1942) revolutionized the rhythmic components of the Hindi film song. Boral/Mullick and Haider constructed the musical blueprints for film song, bringing together melody and harmony with rhythm and percussion, but this formula— set in the 1930s and 1940s—continued to evolve through the decades, always remaining open to "new" sounds, techniques, and instruments.[82]

In the first decades of Hindi sound cinema, lyricists (and musicians) were recruited from among literary Urdu and Hindi poets including Safdar Aah, Kidar Sharma, Naksab, D. N. Madhok, and Qamal Jalalbadi. These men had already made their reputations as poets and writing lyrics for film songs was a secondary (though often lucrative) aspect of their craft. Film's location in mass culture and filmgit's status as popular music meant that film lyrics called forth a new poetics with its "own requirements, discipline, principles and effects." The film lyric had to be aligned not only to the musical composition but also to the picturization, and both these factors determined the repertoire of images, rhythm, diction, and syntax of film songs. Aziz thus identifies Shailendra, who wrote primarily for cinema, as an ideal film lyricist. Shailendra created a precise but limited range of words and metaphors that he recycled in his songs thus orienting his craft to the film-song and its specific modes of circulation.[83] While his contemporaries Shakeel Badayuni, Majrooh Sultanpuri, and Sahir Ludhianvi were more accomplished poets, Shailendra helped to codify the Hindi–Urdu song lyric. This codification—vocabulary and phrases that repeat—plays a substantial role in the cultural work that film songs perform which include their ability to create a community of sentiment and function as a vernacular. Many of these poet-lyricists including Ludhianvi were associated with Urdu progressive literature and radical theatre movements like the IPTA/PWA which in the 1940s developed close links with cinema through figures such as K. A. Abbas and Bimal Roy. In the 1940s and 1950s, the divide between socially progressive and commercial cinema was not as strict as it subsequently became and commercially successful figures like Raj Kapoor, and the Anand brothers (Dev and Chetan) had IPTA/PWA connections. The "fate" of the progressive poet struggling between art and commerce is the subject of Guru Dutt's films such as *Pyaasa* (Thirst, 1957) and *Kaagaz Ke Phool* (Paper flowers, 1959). Film critic Iqbal Masood suggests that the Hindu–Urdu lyric helped the industry cope with the trauma of partition which had a huge impact on Hindi cinema. A lyricist like Majrooh Sultanpuri nostalgically evoked the feudal Muslim world and directors like Yash Chopra intensify via Urdu lyrics, that are usually about loss, the affective qualities of Hindi film song. The deep emotionalism associated with filmigit owes in considerable degree to the nostalgia underpinning the Hindu–Urdu lyric.[84]

Though the technique of playback recording was in place by mid-1930s, this era was dominated by the singer-actor. Indeed, as Neepa Majumdar has argued, star identity was constructed in terms of the voice, the actor's "ability to make songs come alive," rather than the body, underscoring the primacy of the aural over the visual. As a fan of K. L. Saigal, a leading star of this period, wrote, "everyone of us is his fan because of his singing voice, that is all there is about him. His face is pudding-like, his hair is always badly dressed [*sic*]."[85] By the same token, a handsome actor like Ashok Kumar was mocked by fans for his poor singing voice. By the 1940s, however, the industry started using "ghost" voices, matching the actor's voice to the singer's voice though this, as Majumdar notes, created anxiety over the morality of voice substitution in terms not unlike those thematized in *Singin' in the Rain* (Donen and Kelly, 1952). The sovereignty of the song sequence might account for the rise of the playback singer. This practice where an actor on screen lip-synchs to a song performed offscreen by another artist has remained unique to Hindi cinema. The splitting of the singer-actor, then, recapitulates the double form of Hindi popular cinema where spectacle runs alongside the narrative. Indian audiences seem to have quickly reconciled the moral stakes of voice substitution, and playback singing became the norm in a dual-star system.[86] Initially, playback singers were not identified, but the immense popularity of some songs propelled these voices from anonymity into stardom.[87] Lata Mangeshkar, the superstar of playback singers who has lent her voice to over twenty-five thousand songs, first became a household name in 1949 when fans clamoring for her song "Aayega aanewala" (The desired one will come) from *Mahal* (The mansion, Kamal Amrohi) forced radio stations to credit her every time the song was broadcast. Her star identity has since eclipsed that of the actors to whom she lent her voice.

Thus, the music composer, the lyricist, the producer, the director, and the singer collaborate in the production of Hindi film music. These relationships are relatively fluid, and the mode of collaboration varies with the project. Although some directors like Raj Kapoor were very committed to the music track and tended to use the same "hit" team of composers—Shankar-Jaikishen—and lyricists—Shailendra and Hasrat Jaipuri—other directors like Yash Chopra used a wider array of composers but remained attached to same lyricist—Sahir Ludhianvi.[88] Javed Akhtar, a well-known lyricist, provides valuable insight into the processes of song-making in Hindi cinema: "we [music director and lyricist] meet and the producer narrates the story in a nutshell and tells us which is the first song he wants recorded because next month he plans to shoot the song. He will explain the situation when the song will feature in the narrative. Sometimes I write the lyrics and give them to the music director, but more often the music director plays five or six tunes and we'll select one tune. . . . For example with [A. R.] Rahman, I only write to the tune. Hindi and Urdu is not his language so it wouldn't be right if I gave him the words. . . . Sometimes what happens is that Anu [Malik] and I, or Jatin-Lalit and I sit together. I think of some line and tell them and they make the tune right then and there. When a producer comes to us, I might suggest that we play him the song in case the producer likes it. And so we all write the songs for the film."[89] So although the "situation" in the script is a starting point for the composition process, the pressure the narrative actually exerts on the music composer/lyricist varies to the extent that a "situation" might actually be created for a song composed in advance of it. This shifting relationship between song and film not only accounts for but also encourages filmgit's migrations to other media. It complicates the question of "integration" between performance sequence and narrative and illustrates how form is shaped by the always-evolving conventions of song-making and innovations in technology. In the last decade, technological advances such as satellite television and digital media are in the process of revolutionizing the mode of production described by Akhtar. Although the impact of these changes is still unfolding, the Bollywood song and dance sequence seems to be moving toward further disaggregation. This might indeed reflect, as Anustup Basu's essay suggests, the cultural logic of globalization. Akhtar whose views echo the lament of several industry folk says, "the songs in today's film cease to have a real function within the drama. The song has become a kind of perk that is offered with the film."[90] This nonrelation, as Prashant Pandey's ongoing research proposes, is further accelerated by the merging of sound recording with computer technology to create a sample and sound file–based approach to production. Pandey notes that busy singers like Sonu Nigam clock around 120 songs a month. The new technology has imposed harsh demands on the singers and lyricists. Their key for success is precision, speed, and a new kind of professionalism. Electronic recording and sending audio files through the Internet has dramatically changed the way the industry works. Thus, while legendary singer Asha Bhosle e-mailed a song from the United States, composing duo Nadeem–Shravan continue to work in Bombay while being based in London. As Pandey puts it, "music is being produced virtually on virtual interfaces."[91]

The rise of playback technology eventually rendered, as we have seen above, the singer-actor obsolete. As a consequence, the actor's body freed from the microphone became more mobile and this, in part, accounts for the elaborately staged dances integral to the spectacle of Hindi cinema.[92] However, dance was an important element of the spectacle and a thematic preoccupation even in the silent period. The Bengali film magazine—*Bangla Bioscope*—noted that the film *Andhare Alo* (The influence of love, Sisir Bhaduri, 1922) included a courtesan's dance,[93] whereas an "obscene" dance scene in *Pati Bhakti* (Human emotion, J. J. Madan, 1922) had to be censored.[94] In *Kalyan Khajina* (The treasures of Kalyan, Baburao Painter, 1925), the stunt star Master Vithal makes his debut as a dancing girl,[95] whereas *Mojili Mumbai* (The slaves of luxury, Manilal Joshi, 1925)—a film that sparked a debate on questions of morality and cinematic realism—was apparently based on the life of a real-life cabaret dancer Roshanara.[96] *Alibaba* (Modhu Bose, 1937) starring the classically trained dancer Sadhona Bose included the Abdullah Marjina dance sequence that long set the standard for film musicals.[97] This film that married Indian classical dance with Hollywood-inspired choreography owed its success in large measure to the inventiveness of the dance sequences including a "modern" dance segment. Modhu Bose's *Raj Nartaki* (Court dancer, 1941) was one of a clutch of "dance" films—noteworthy for being made in English and released in the United States.[98] *Prahaladan* (K. Subramanyam) made the same year was a Malayalam mythological featuring elaborate dances by the famed Gopinath–Thangamani duo.[99] 1948 was a stellar year for the dance spectacular. It saw the release of two classic dance films—*Kalpana*

(Imagination, Uday Shankar) and *Chandralekha* (S. S. Vasan). The former, four years in the making, and starring Uday Shankar uses traditional dance as a metaphor for the aspirations of an independent India. The choreography was specially designed for the camera—"with semi-expressionist angles and chiaroscuro effects"—and it became a model for the dream sequence in *Awaara* discussed above.[100] While this unusual film is an instance of the fusion of Indian modernism and cinema, *Chandralekha* is a film that translates the aesthetic of Hollywood Orientalism for an indigenous mass audience and represents a landmark in the "codification of a mass entertainment ideology after Independence."[101] *Chandralekha* also marks the first attempt by a Tamil studio to capture an all-India audience and its justly celebrated drum dance is perhaps one of the most spectacular sequences in Indian cinema. Choreographed by Jaya Shankar, Mrs Rainbird, Natanam Nataraj, and Niranjala Devi, it incorporates Indian and international dance forms to create the hybrid that has in recent years been called Bollywood dance.[102] Dance, like song, then, is a uniquely "filmi" formation that both inheres in classical traditions and is promiscuous in its borrowings. Though tied, per force, in the era prior to television more closely to the film than the song, dance's relationship to narrative is complex and varied. While it might indeed be used, as it is in the drum sequence in *Chandralekha* to forward the narrative or as in *Kalpana* to express history, it functions often as a means for embodying surplus meaning and transgressive desires.[103] As Rajinder Dudrah's and Sangita Shresthova's essays demonstrate, Bollywood dance imagines forms of becoming that the narrative forecloses. By the same token, dance as tradition and ritual is mobilized to create a sense of national and communal belonging as in the many "festive" dances that are a stock in trade of Hindi film. Like film song, Bollywood dance flows out of the film text to clubs in Trinidad, Lagos, Manchester, and New York; to streets in the lower class neighborhoods of Java and Mumbai and television screens in Tel-Aviv.

Alternative Cosmopolitanism

Hindi film music's global mobility owes in no small measure to its constitutive openness. Thus, Satyajit Ray, India's best-known "art" film director and no fan of commercial cinema, admired nonetheless the

Bollywood-style romance serves as inspiration for artist N. Pushpamala, who created a series of works allegorizing the popular romance with Hindi film icons. This image is from the photoromance *Sunhere Sapne* (Golden dreams, 1998) by N. Pushpamala.

"inventiveness" of Hindi film music. As a committed cosmopolitan, Ray was struck by Hindi film music's "embrace" of other musical idioms—"classical, folk, Negro, Greek, Punjabi, Cha-Cha, or anything you can think of from any part of the world."[104] If Ray's comment draws attention to Hindi music's voracious appetite for the foreign, song and dance sequences were consumed with equal rapacity by fans abroad, particularly in the global South, Greece, and the former Soviet bloc. This phenomenon was partly a political fallout of decolonization, the Cold War, and the rise of the NAM that created unexpected circuits of cultural exchange in the South.

Though a market opened through bilateral trade relations between the Socialist bloc and the NAM, such exchanges were at best, relatively minor, disorganized, and sporadic. With its multichannel distribution network, Hindi film and its music found its way to regions eccentric to the Cold War trajectory—Afro-Asia, the Arab world, Southeast Asia, and Central America. This mobility is all the more remarkable given that the Indian state hardly aided the industry in exporting its products. As Rajadhyaksha has argued, few commercial films were made with a non-Indian audience in mind and the foreign market, usually a single territory, was entirely controlled by the Government of India's Indian Motion Picture Export Corporation that was initially under the Reserve Bank of India (RBI—equivalent of the Federal Reserve) and then merged with the NFDC. Film was subject to the state policy on exports until as recently as 1992 when it was opened up to private enterprise. Nonetheless, UNESCO statistics from 1975 to 1977 show that Indian films were exported to Africa, Arab states, Trinidad, Guyana, Barbados, Burma, Hong Kong, Indonesia, Malaysia, Singapore, Sri Lanka, and Thailand.[105] Hindi film's success in these sites underscores the resonance that this cinema has in "transitional societies"[106] where "modernity competes with tradition, where urban and rural commingle in uneasy proximity, where underdevelopment meets development."[107] B. D. Garga's account of the reception of Mehboob Khan's *Mother India* (1957) in colonial Algeria confirms this insight: "Well over a decade after its release in India, the Cinematheque Algerienne was showing *Mother India* to a packed house. As I watched the film, I was surprised to see the spell a rural Indian family has cast upon a wholly Arab audience."[108]

Hindi cinema's popularity in these markets during the 1950s and 1960s, Ravi Vasudevan suggests, owes in part to its ability to distinguish itself from the Hollywood product. Hindi film retains aspects of what Tom Gunning has called a "cinema of attractions"—where the relation between performance sequence and narrative is loosely structured. It is not therefore a more "primitive" but rather a "heterogeneous" form that selectively (and whimsically) imports Hollywood norms even while remaining embedded in its historical and cultural milieu. Vasudevan's focus is not on the performance sequence though as the Ray quote above illustrates this is the place where the domestic/foreign, national/international, and local/global is most energetically negotiated. As Sen and Basu argue in this anthology, film music and song picturizations are the most mobile and open spaces within the film. These sequences greedily incorporate the new and manage the shock of modernity. If the song and dance sequence is a dense node of invention, it is also a springboard for innovation. It is not only reflective but also productive of new forms.

Film music's popularity in Greece and the hybrid genre—indoprepi—that it inspired is an excellent case in point. Greece had few cultural or political links to India. Yet between 1954 and 1968, 111

Hindi films were exhibited mainly in working-class screens throughout the country. These included Mehboob Khan's *Aan* renamed *Mangala, the Rose of India; Saqi,* released as *Rosana, the Rose of Baghdad;* and *Sikander*—a historical on the life of Alexander the Great. Between 1958 and 1962, at least one out of the thirty-five movie theaters of Thessaloniki played one or two Hindi movies per week. The "foreign" films subtitled in Greek forced people with little education to read. Their titles were changed to reflect the themes: mothers losing children, social upheaval, and other emotional topics. Thus, *Ghar Sansaar* (House and world) became *Tears of a Mother* while *Mother India* was released as *Land Drenched in Sweat* and *Mela* (Fair) became *Love Drenched in Tears.* Helen Abadzi in her groundbreaking research on Hindi cinema in Greece suggests that the blend of spectacle and melodrama that characterized the films of this period resonated among lower-class audiences impoverished and dislocated by World War II. Though middle-class audiences were mostly disdainful of the cruder pleasures of Hindi cinema, *Mother India* broke through the class barrier. The box-office success of Hindi film prompted knockoffs, and in the 1960s, Greek producers began to make films with eight to twelve songs set often in a nightclub. While this phenomenon was commercially motivated, a more substantive encounter with Hindi film music is witnessed in the emergence of indoprepi. Abadzi has uncovered an extensive archive of Greek songs inspired by filmigit. While these "covers" mostly reproduce the original tunes and musical arrangements, the lyrical content is entirely new. Abadzi provides the following figures: "From the 111 movies known to have come, as well as from others whose importation is uncertain, 105 Greek renditions were identified. Many came from the best-known movies, that is from *Awaara, Sri 420, Mother India, Ghar Sansaar, Laajwanti,* and *Aan.* Many Hindi songs engendered duplicates, triplicates, and quadruplicates. For example, "Pyar hua ikrar hua" (*Sri 420*) and "Gao tarane man ke" (*Aan*) have four renditions, "Unchhi, unchhi dunia ki divare. . ." (*Naagin*) and "Aajao tarapt hai arma . . ." (*Awaara*) have three. At least 10 others have duplicates. Of all songs, 57 (55 percent) have a great similarity with pre-existing songs; 25 (24 percent) deviate significantly from the originals, 16 (16 percent) are partial renditions, where other melodies are mixed with Hindi, and 5 (5 percent) use only some musical bars." In this genre of music, like the hip-hop remixes that are the subject of Richard Zumkhawala-Cook's essay, the original Hindi songs were "Hellenized"—speeded up and simplified. Some of these songs are remembered even today though the original contexts have almost totally disappeared. Like the Javanese "dangdut" (see Bettina David's essay), "indoprepi" was viewed as debased music catering to the rural poor refugees from Turkey and, as such, a serious threat to Greece's drive for modernization. A newspaper article sums up the middle-class outrage against Hindi film and its music: "The trouble started with the first Hindi movie that was shown . . . Today the situation is such that the Hindi cinema is the most direct competitor of the Greek cinema. Hindi movies are everywhere, and tearful Nargis is much more popular than Vouyouklaki. The drawn-out and bothersome Indian music which accompanies these sad creations also tends to become our national music. . . . Most modestly speaking, this is sinking low! It is not permissible, when we fight to stand in the geographical space of Europe to have become a spiritual colony of India . . . Except if, as we wrote in the beginning, we are now paying for the consequences of Alexander's conquests . . . But even then, the price is too high."[109] Widely condemned for being derivative and backward (it looked to the East rather than the West), "indoprepi" attracted the ire of the bourgeois popular press which claimed that Hindi songs were destroying national music. As Abadzi points out, although Arab and Turkish music were also popular, filmigit outstripped them in appeal.

If condemned in Greece for not being modern enough, in postcolonial Afro-Asia filmigit thematized modernity. Thus, as Walter Armbrust's contribution illustrates Hindi films found enthusiastic audiences in the Egypt of the 1950s—a connection that, his essay argues, has been obscured in the present. In Egypt, too, cinema had emerged as a vehicle for exploring questions of modernity and nationalism, and by the 1930s, the musical emerged as a dominant genre. Film music, which adapted Western, particularly Latin rhythms to traditional Arab melodies, brought into being a modern Egyptian sound constitutive of national identity.[110] Thus, in societies like Egypt, where song and dance plays a pivotal role in public culture, Bollywood is easily translated. "The dialogue may be incomprehensible. The story line not always clear," but the mixture of Indian and Western musical codes, as M. Shamim points out, sustains audience interest.[111]

While India might have served as an icon for modernity in the Arab world, Hindi cinema's journey to the Soviet bloc was propelled by different imperatives. The reception history of Bollywood in Russia and China reveals curious disjunctures between official policies governing the import of Hindi film and popular responses to them. In each case, the song and dance sequence is the focus of contestation. The communist state encouraged imports from its Cold War ally, India, to protect and defend the domestic film market from Hollywood. Moreover, as recent research by Richard Taylor and Maria Enzensberger suggests, the "musical" was an established form in the Soviet Union, and in the hands of directors such as Ivan Pyriev and Grigori Alexandrov, it was used to express a revolutionary romanticism.[112] Songs and dances enacted a "utopia in the here and now" and the combination of symbolic and realist registers enabled the spectator to glimpse personal success within a socialist framework. The phenomenal success of *Awaara* in the Soviet Union must be seen in the context of this already existing culture of "musicals." Alexander Lipkov suggests that in the days of "Hindi-Rusi bhai, bhai" (the brotherhood of Hindi and Russian), audiences used Hindi films subversively to challenge official ideologies. Indo-Soviet friendship was memorialized in the following song from Raj Kapoor's *Shree 420* (1955) which becomes Salman Rushdie's manifesto for postcolonial hybridity: "Mera joota hai Japani; yeh patloon Englishtani; sar pe laal topi Roosi; phir bhi dil hai Hindustani" [My shoes are from Japan, these pants are English, I wear a red Russian hat, yet still my heart is Indian].

While the idealist thrust of these melodramas seemed to subscribe to the principles of Soviet art, the location of this idealism within the individual contravened the collectivist basis of communist ideology. In turn, Indian producers lured by the lucrative Soviet market injected "proletarian" angles into films to tailor to the Soviet market, but the Russian audiences would not bite. "The Soviet Union had taken a fancy to Indian film songs and dances. The selections that followed were strictly formula. It could take care of its own propaganda."[113]

The Chinese government's official disdain for Kremlin revisionism was routed through its jabs at Hindi song which were predictably characterized as "bourgeois, decadent music that sought to undermine the moral force of their socialist republic." However, the authorities were unable to prevent the Chinese "Lata Mangeshkar" on Radio Beijing from regaling the masses with these decadent songs. Sixth-generation filmmaker Jia Zhangke's 2001 film *Platform,* set in a small border town on the remote northern province of China on the brink of the sweeping economic reforms of the 1980s, includes an early sequence of a communal screening of Raj Kapoor's *Awaara*. The comrades watch enraptured as Raj winds his way through the title song "Main awaara hoon!"

Even after the dissolution of the Soviet empire, Bollywood continues to image Third World modernity for the global South. Afghanis celebrated the ouster of the Taliban in Kabul with the screening of a Bollywood blockbuster. This incident confirms that Hindi film continues to articulate an alternative cosmopolitanism, offering a counterpoint to neotraditionalist discourses. Television networks in Indonesia, Singapore, Malaysia, Thailand, Egypt, Ghana, Algeria, and Morocco, among others, offer a staple diet of Indian cinema and half-a-dozen films are screened in regular theaters. As audiences come out of the theaters singing these songs and pop acts model themselves on Bollywood, the religious right steps up its efforts to limit the import of Hindi films. The Mufti Council of Malaysia cast Hindi films as promoting an "immoral culture" and a cult of violence.[114] If the religious right describes Bollywood in terms that reveal an affinity with global perceptions of Hollywood, audiences distinguish between the two. While reflecting the "clash of civilizations," contemporary Hindi films nonetheless offer accommodations between traditional discourses like the family and technological modernity that are more in keeping with local experiences in the global South.[115]

Diaspora of Empire

J. F. Madan and Abdulallyi Esoofally were among, the earliest movie moguls, building exhibition–distribution empires that covered a vast swathe of South and Southeast Asia, including Fiji and China.[116] Between 1908 and 1914, Esoofally traveled with a tent bioscope through large parts of the Far East including Burma, Ceylon, Singapore, and Indonesia, introducing film into these regions.[117] These theaters were the fertile grounds from which the Indian diaspora of the imperial era repeatedly renewed contact with the lost homeland, thus inaugurating what would become a primary vector for Bollywood's travels. Dispersed to different continents as indentured labor servicing the commercial enterprises of Britain, this diaspora of empire turned to cinema to revive memories of home. Film viewing also served as a pedagogical tool for instructing the second generation in the cultural mores and ethos of the mother country.[118]

Films helped these migrant populations reclaim the idea of a glorious Mother India and stage nationalist, anticolonial gestures in the complex multiracial space of the colonial diaspora. In Fiji, for instance, the indentured populations were subject to British Common Law and not allowed to practice their cultural and religious traditions; they had to live under an imposed secular order. In these circumstances, Indian mythological and devotional films, especially those based on the *Ramayana,* served as an imaginative conduit for constructing a differentiated "identity" which became the basis for political struggle.[119] A Fijian immigrant of Indian origin, film scholar Vijay Mishra poignantly recalls how Bollywood mediated his real and imagined encounters with India. "From 1930 onward . . . (the) myths of the mind began to be mediated through the projection onto the visual. In an uncanny fashion, cinema reinforced the Fiji-Indian myths of an ancient land still basking in its epic glory. At the same time, spectatorial fascination with the new-found power of the visual . . . triggered a desire for India in ways that radically transformed what until then had existed only as the fantastic clichés of our forefathers . . . I had come to India in search of a pot of gold only to find that pot had been buried deep in my unconscious."[120]

While films in Trinidad, Guyana, Fiji, and other sites in the colonial and postcolonial diaspora sustain a connection to the homeland, filmigit frequently helps immigrants create fresh ties. Thus, Narmala Halstead notes how song-dance enables a new relationship between the sacred and the secular: movie songs simultaneously supplement traditional chants at religious festivals, whereas the song-dance sequence mediates courtship rituals among the young. These sequences reappear as localized performances on television talent shows and in chutney music concerts while Guyanese children view filmi dancing as a cultural activity.[121] Such "localized" appropriations of Bollywood music are implicated in particular histories that might superficially resemble practices by diasporic communities elsewhere, but they are—in fact— shaped by the specific sites of their emergence. Thus, Manas Ray's ethnographic research among Fiji Indians in Australia suggests that their cultural practices surrounding Bollywood differ markedly from that of immigrants who come from India. These differences draw attention to the unique trajectory through which Bollywood film and its music entered the social life of the migrant in the imperial diaspora. The particular contexts of consumption determine the new cultural forms inspired by Bollywood music.[122]

Fijian *curry*, Guyanese and Trinidadian *chutney*, and Indonesian *dangdut* are all hybrid forms that like Greek *indoprepi* or Nigerian *bandiri* are the result of an encounter between Bollywood music and myriad local and folk forms. This creativity is driven, to some extent, by the "distance" between the places of origin and location. While Hindi film was an object of desire for the imperial diaspora, this longing was unreciprocated. The Indian film industry was subsidized by these overseas markets, but the spatiotemporal lag ensured that the imperial diaspora remained but a shadow spectator. Vashna Jagarnath's research on Indian filmgoing and exhibition history in Durban, South Africa, sheds light on the unsystematic nature of film exports. Indian films reached South Africa from distribution centers in London, Singapore, Beirut, Hong Kong, or the Fiji Islands, and owing to this indirect route, films were not only overpriced but the exhibitor rarely knew what items a particular shipment included. Furthermore, distribution rights were not protected in any way, so multiple exhibitors could acquire prints of the same films from different agencies. She also notes that at these locations art films including the works of Satyajit Ray were rarely known.[123]

In the contemporary era of global flows, this relationship is much more symbiotic. Advances in communication technologies and the financial clout of the Indian diaspora in the West have put in place a feedback loop, whereby the South Asian diaspora is an integral part of Bollywood's viewing publics. Thus, diasporic desires are inscribed in cinematic texts giving rise to a genre that film critics are increasingly beginning to identify as the NRI films. Rachel Dwyer notes that while Hindi films in the United Kingdom of the 1960s and 1970s were mostly screened on Sunday mornings and other off-peak times, the advent of technologies like video and then satellite television made films much more accessible to diasporic audiences who became huge consumers of Hindi cinema. By the 1990s, the industry and to a great extent the Indian state became alert to the immense revenue potential of this overseas market. Thus, Yash Chopra set up a distribution office in London in 1997 and in New York in 1998 and his banner—Yash Raj Films—is credited with some of the biggest NRI films—among them *Dilwale Dulhania Le Jayenge* (The braveheart will take the bride, 1995) and *Dil To Pagal Hai* (The heart is foolish, 1997). Though largely targeted to audiences of Indian origin, these releases frequently make it to the U.K. top ten and occasionally into the top thirty in the United States. The sound track, released in advance of the films and often accompanied by teaser visuals, is a big source of profits in the overseas markets. Played incessantly on South Asian cable channels and performed on stage by visiting troupes of Indian stars, the song and dance sequences in the NRI genre tends to be a major filmic and extrafilmic attraction.[124] As Sangita Shresthova's essay demonstrates, these song and dance sequences migrate from the screen onto the stage and become the basis for a "new" formation: Bollywood dance.

The reception history of *Kuch Kuch Hota Hai* (Something or other is happening, Karan Johar, 1998, henceforth *KKHH*)—a paradigmatic instance of the NRI genre—in South Africa and Indonesia illustrates how Bollywood's growing presence in the global North is transforming the modes through which immigrants in the South consume Hindi cinema. The first Indian film to run in an upscale shopping center in Durban for an unprecedented eight months, *KKHH* was seen by more people in Durban than *Titanic*. Thomas Blom Hansen has argued that *KKHH*'s overwhelming success was owing to the film's inscription of a "global" Indian spectator/subject—at ease in the world, effortlessly maneuvering the traditional and the modern. The film's glossy depiction of a modern, urban India belied stereotypes and engendered cultural pride among diasporic Indians. The music, in particular, inspired hysteria. Capitalizing on its success, Ela Gandhi, granddaughter of Mohandas Gandhi and now a member of parliament (MP) in the African National Congress (ANC), recorded a campaign song based on the *KKHH* title number "Kuch kuch ANC."[125] In Indonesia, as Bettina David reports, this film created a Bollywood fever that went far beyond the Javanese community (an ethnic group that has historical links to India) and this new obsession with Bollywood fostered a renewed interest in "dangdut" music that had until the *KKHH* phenomenon largely been devalued by the middle-class Indonesian culture.[126] The trend toward extravagant song picturizations, if driven to a large extent by diasporic viewers, also requires as Shanti Kumar argues new and more efficient modes of production exemplified by a conglomerate like Ramoji Film City (RFC). Shanti Kumar's essay illustrates how industry arrangements in India register these changes. As Bollywood film becomes one of India's major exports, the new interest taken by the Indian state in the industry is essentially a struggle over the meaning of national identity. Interestingly, as Bhattacharjya and Mehta demonstrate in their essay in this anthology, film music emerges as a key site in this struggle.

Reversing the trajectory of *Awaara,* the 1980 bestseller "Aap jaisa koi" (Someone like you), a song from the hit-film *Qurbani* (Sacrifice, Feroz Khan), emblematizes the manner in which contemporary transnational flows and movement of peoples complicates narratives of globalization. Composed by an Indian immigrant in Britain, Biddu, "Aap jaisa koi" not only launched the career of its teenage singing sensation, Nazia Hassan, but marked the growing influence of the diaspora on Hindi film production practices.[127] Biddu is also credited with "discovering" Indipop, which for a time competed with Hindi film music as India's premiere pop music.[128] Biddu's musical career captures the complex interlocking layers in the transnational feedback loop. His influences, which include Motown and bebop, point to the intersections between Hindi film and black musics. Zumkhawala-Cook's essay spotlights a more recent phase of this interaction. More recently, A. R. Rahman's journey from regional Indian cinema to Bollywood to the West End mirrors in reverse Biddu's itinerary.

The East–West confluences that Biddu and Rahman's Bollywood compositions tap into makes their music particularly appealing to the second-generation diaspora. Not burdened by the compulsion to memorialize the nation, this population consumption of Hindi film songs is radically different from that of their parents. Creatively cutting and mixing elements from Bollywood song and dance clips, they parse their identity as difference within discourses of multiculturalism. India functions as an imaginative horizon for urban youth culture that deploys Bollywood in hegemonic neo-Orientalist fashion and simultaneously makes it the terrain for the articulation of affect. Sandhya Shukla and Gayatri Gopinath have illustrated the manner in which these musics circulate within dance clubs to resist assimilationist drives.[129] This political charge is further sharpened in the uses of this music in gay cultures, as Rajinder Dudrah's essay highlights.

The 1990s transatlantic chart-topper, "Brimful of Asha," allegorizes the ethnic diaspora's relationship to metropolitan culture. This *Cornershop* song's references to and sampling of Bollywood music remains "undecipherable" to most fans not literate in this tradition. Yet, its canny mix of dance beats, jazz, "Asian elements," and rock makes it a poster child for the expanding horizons of Western musical tastes. *Cornershop's* cofounder, British Indian Tjinder Singh, functions as a "contact zone" in Mary Louise Pratt's memorable phrase.[130] Bollywood appears in such cultural artifacts as both legible and illegible; this doubleness constituting the dominant mode of the North's encounter with Hindi film music.

Northern exposures: Bollywood song-dance enters the West in remixed albums such as *Delia at the Bollywood Ballroom*.

Bollywood music now provides the ironic rhythm for advertisements marketing nonexotic goods such as computers, it offers a melodic contrapuntal beat for remixes and underground bands, and its aesthetic idioms structure a new narrative sensibility in Western cinema, from independent ventures such as *Party Girl* (Daisy von Scherler Mayer, 1995) and *Ghost World* (Terry Zwigoff, 2001) to Baz Luhrmann's Oscar-nominated *Moulin Rouge* (2000). As Edward K. Chan's essay persuasively demonstrates, all these texts provide evidence of "dirty consumption."

If, indeed, Hindi films have always trafficked in the global, the essays in this anthology demonstrate that it is precisely music that unmoors Bollywood from the nation and propels its global travels. A turn to Hindi film not only provincializes understandings of national cinema but an investigation of Bollywood as global cinema also offers a counternarrative to the hegemonic global form offered by Hollywood. A focus on song-dance spectacles and the parallel relation they maintain to the diegetic text also helps us rethink questions of totality and unity as they pertain to cinematic form. Insofar as these sequences are both intrinsic and extrinsic to the diegesis, they compel us to reconceptualize cinematic cartography. Finally, through its mobility, Bollywood music as trope is not only deterritorialized but also reterritorialized with significant effects. Different aspects of this argument are elaborated across a number of disciplinary sites using diverse methodological perspectives.

Technologies of Globalization

Hindi filmigit has from the very beginning been shaped by a number of global forces. Disavowed by the state during the era of Nehruvian socialism, Bollywood song and dance had attenuated spaces for circulation. The liberalization of the Indian economy coincided with the entry of new media such as satellite/cable television and these new technologies crucially altered the relationship between the state and the entertainment industry, on the one hand, and the nation and the diaspora, on the other. An exploration of the overlapping and contradictory impact that new technologies and shifts in the global political economy have had on Bollywood also draws attention to how the nation and national products are packaged in the global marketplace.

Today, Bollywood films with popular sound tracks are expected to recover between 20 and 40 percent of their costs from the sale of music rights domestically and overseas. But until as recently as 1980s, film song circulated widely and vitally shaped postcolonial modernity in India and elsewhere, but the music business itself was under-commercialized. Film music was neither widely marketed nor did it seek to create demand but was rather responsive to the "listening tastes" of its publics. The advent of cassette technology, Anna Morcom's essay "Tapping the Mass Market: The Commercial Life of Hindi Film Songs" suggests transformed film song into a commodity fully implicated in the dynamics of market capitalism. Based on extensive fieldwork including interviews conducted with professionals in the film and music industries, Morcom's groundbreaking study explores the crucial role technology plays in the circulation of film song and underscores how the industry responds to and attempts to optimize the market. As a *commercially* autonomous product, song and dance sequences become not only more spectacular but also amenable to new delivery formats such as television and, more recently, the World Wide Web. She contends that the current crisis in the music industry results from globalization and new media technologies. Illegal downloads and widespread digital piracy have forced the industry to find creative sources of revenue like film song ringtones and video shorts delivered directly to mobile phones even as digital technology is transforming the mode of production of film songs.

Film music is currently such big business that the state, as Bhattacharjya and Mehta argue, is instituting copyright and antipiracy legislation to cash in on the potentially vast commercial and cultural capital of the Hindi film song. The constitutive elusiveness of the film song and the various attempts by the state and the world music industry to manage this entity toward its own ends are the subject of their essay, "From Bombay to Bollywood: Tracking Cinematic and Musical Tours." In the first few decades after independence, state-owned media restricted the circulation of Hindi film music. But the 1990s witnessed media privatization and simultaneous transformation of Bombay cinema into a global culture industry. The state was now anxious to harness this new formation—Bollywood—toward the ends of cultural nationalism. The essay analyzes copyright legislation and antipiracy laws to show how these are attempts to define film song as a national product ready to play by the rules of global markets.

Anustup Basu's essay "The Music of Intolerable Love: Political Conjugality in Mani Ratnam's *Dil Se*" explores the aesthetic ramifications of such technological, political, and economic transformations. If song-dance sequences have always counteracted the "will to realism" that seemed to be the governing cultural principle of the modernizing state, the last decade has witnessed an intensification of this drive. Through a close textual analysis of the song-dance sequences from Mani Ratnam's *Dil Se* (From the heart, 1998), Basu demonstrates how the sequences assemble signs and visibilities from other image worlds including advertising, CNN-style reportage, fashion, and tourism. Ordered by the "indifferent" logic of "geo-televisual" production and distribution, the song-dance sequence participates in an "ecology of the unthinkable."

If Basu suggests that in postliberalization cinema, the song and dance is a Deleuzian *assemblage,* Shanti Kumar's analysis of RFC provides us with a description of the kind of apparatus in which such assemblages get produced. "Bollywood and Beyond" offers an intriguing study of a "film city," a one-stop production site in Hyderabad. The integrated mode of production of RFC—reminiscent of the studio era—has altered filmmaking practices, rewritten spatial logics, and thereby transformed the idioms of moviemaking, especially the song and dance sequences. Now, directors, irrespective of budget, can skillfully move from local spaces to exotic milieus several times within the space of a song-dance sequence. Film cities such as RFC have emerged as lucrative revenue earners whose activities are actively encouraged by the state.[131] They have altered the financial landscape of filmmaking and are now positioned to address the industry's long-standing fiscal crisis. These four essays explore Bollywood song-dance in relation to technology and state policy and analyze how current global processes are recalibrating these articulations.

Translated Modernities

The transnational travels of the song-dance sequence, its circuits of distribution, and the identifications it produced among diverse audiences occurred to a significant extent against the backdrop of the Cold War and the NAM. Though Indian cinema circulated in the transnational space of the British empire, preindependence Hindi film, as we have seen, enjoyed no preeminence as such. The south–south internationalism of this era was very different in structure and content from the market-driven globalization of the contemporary moment. Hindi popular cinema's reception in "transitional societies" needs to be distinguished from Bollywood's contemporary cachet in global consumer culture. As several essays in this anthology point out, song-dance sequences have been transformed and translated into new idioms specific to the regional contexts and helped stage particular negotiations with modernity. Simultaneously, Bollywood's contemporary global currency makes it the bearer of cosmopolitanism in the global South. As we have argued above, song and dance's ability to signal the "modern" resonates in cultures whose relation to India is at best peripheral or nonexistent enabling these cultures to solve certain "local" problems.

Biswarup Sen's essay "The Sounds of Modernity: The Evolution of Bollywood Film Song" returns us to the beginnings of Hindi filmigit to suggest that the musicological capaciousness of Hindi film music is an enabling condition for its popularity across the world, especially among non–South Asian audiences. Sen crafts a new history for Indian popular music by arguing that filmigit has not only been constitutive of the popular but its structure of feeling has always been emphatically transnational. The essay offers a rich, textured, and layered account of the popularity of particular playback singers, forms of music, and genres at different moments in Indian history. These shifts were not serendipitous but were rather the product of a series of intertwining forces that helped constitute India's different encounters with colonial and postcolonial modernities.

This worldliness permits Bollywood music to travel felicitously in many parts of the global South where it is worked upon and remixed to produce hybrid music genres such as dangdut in Indonesia. Hindi film song makes available an aural register that permits the articulation of locally grounded modernities and helps recast nations as "intimate neighbors" as Bettina David argues. Exploring the dynamic relationship between Bollywood films, its music and dangdut in contemporary Indonesia, David's essay reveals how "traditional" hybrid music forms

Starry eyed: a song-dance sequence from *Gate to Heaven* (2003), a German independent film by Veit Helmer about an interracial romance encoded in Bollywood style.

are altered by modernist responses to global cultural flows. She also explores the complicated circuits of reception of Bollywood films among the Javanese and mainstream Indonesians. Once largely restricted to, albeit a central aspect of, Javanese subculture Bollywood films as well as dangdut are now a staple of the contemporary mediascape. This has altered significantly the meanings associated with dangdut. In the 1970s, dangdut singers, not unlike *bandiri* musicians in Nigeria, had married Hindi film song aesthetic to an Islamic code of conduct to signify a modern Asian Muslim identity. Today, dangdut and Hindi film songs are being used by the urban upwardly mobile classes to signify a cosmopolitan Indonesian identity. Rather than link this new site of consumption with Bollywood's growing salience in the West, David contends that it is produced by a "cultural affinity" between Indonesians and Bollywood.

In the case of Egypt, as Walter Armbrust's essay "The Ubiquitous Nonpresence of India: Peripheral Visions from Egyptian Popular Culture" argues, this "cultural affinity" between two nations is obscured from view but omnipresent. Although official discourse in Egypt denigrates the escapist pleasures of Bollywood (the word "Hindi" is synonymous with "silly"), its historical engagement with Hindi film, its stars, and its music survives as traces in public culture. The discursive "invisibility" of Hindi film, Armbrust contends, is a symptom of a narrative of power where the primary dialectic is the one between national cinema, on the one hand, and Hollywood and Europe, on the other. Armbrust begins to reconstruct this hidden archive through exploring the image of India and the Indian film industry in Egyptian films and fan magazines. The essay focuses on two periods of exchange—the 1930s and then the 1950s—and traces a growing familiarity with Hindi film, but this Armbrust argues is a "familiarity that breeds contempt." Though the portrayal of India in the 1930s Egyptian cinema is thoroughly Orientalist, it also helps envisage the East as an alternative to Hollywood. By the 1950s, as Indian films made their entry into the Egyptian market and began to compete against the domestic product, the attitude seemed to shift and Hindi film, song-dance in particular, tended to become the axis of difference. But even here, given the importance of the performance sequence in Egyptian cinema, the response to spectacle in Hindi film was ambivalent. The song and dance sequence simultaneously authorized Egyptian dance culture and delegitimized Hindi film.

Bollywood as Commodity Form

In the previous section, we outlined the numerous ways in which song-dance participates in the emergence of vernacular modernities. Here, we explore the transformation of the song-dance sequence, and arguably the Hindi film product itself, into a valued commodity that is fetishized in the global marketplace as a difference-making device. The song-dance sequence and filmigit are consumed in various ways—as kitsch, as neo-Orientalist artifact, and as placeholder for memory and ethnic identity. Developing Dick Hebdige's distinction between two modes of appropriation, the one where ideology redefines cultural practice and the other where culture takes on the commodity form, the essays explore how these modes intersect and the overlapping spaces different consumers occupy.[132] Thus, if Bollywood song-dance appears as an "exotic" commodity to some consumers for others, it is a shared idiom for expressing marginal political identities. In each case, though, filmigit takes on a commodity form. The essays claim that this dialectic of commodification and identification is a productive one that brings into focus the ways in which audiences negotiate the different logics of the marketplace.

Edward K. Chan's essay tracks film song's reception in the United States over the last three decades to offer an account of how "liberal humanism manages social difference." The nontraditional Bollywood consumer's (NBC) encounter with film song is marked by exoticization and kitsch and needs to be distinguished from the NBC's appreciation of high-art products such as Satyajit Ray films or Indian classical music. If the consumption of Bollywood film song as "cool" reflects geopolitical inequalities inherent in the global marketplace of culture, it also underscores liberalism's inability to cope with racial difference. The centrality of kitsch in these appropriations is problematic though inevitable, but to conjure away such differences, he suggests, is equally delusional. The consumption of cultural difference is always "dirty," Chan concludes.

The current fad for Bollywood is linked to its reinvention as a "culture industry" in quest of global markets. The so-called Bollywood "look"—colorful and exaggerated—used to sell consumer goods ranging from throw pillows and ethnic skirts to interiors that looked like the homes of famous Hindi film stars is most intensely visualized in the song and dance sequences that have always functioned as advertisements for products and lifestyles.[133] Rajinder Dudrah argues that this commodified celebration of the kitschy and campy aspects of the Bollywood aesthetic is related to the use of song and dance sequences in the South Asian queer club scene in the United Kingdom and is part of contemporary mass media's fascination with gay aesthetic practices. But though South Asian queers view Bollywood kitsch as opening up a space for alternative desires, this aesthetic of excess enters mainstream culture as a trend that does not in any way disturb or challenge dominant norms but merely supplements it with some exotic color. This transformation of Bollywood camp into commodity Dudrah insists is a trivialization of the "secret" politics that Bollywood enables among queer communities in Britain.

Similarly, Richard Zumkhawala-Cook's essay illustrates the neo-Orientalist frame that governs the consumption of Bollywood film song in contemporary U.S. popular culture. Focusing on hip-hop's recent fascination with filmigit, Zumkhawala-Cook examines the manner in which artists such as Jay-Z and Missy Elliot cannibalized Hindi pop music with a carelessness that in the post–9/11 era reproduces the racist politics underpinning the United States' global hegemony. "Bollywood Gets Funky: American Hip-Hop, Basement Bhangra, and the Racial Politics of Music" points out the specific ways in which market-driven hip-hop artists use Bollywood idioms to recode prevalent fears and anxieties surrounding the Middle East and brown people. The cultural work of such appropriations is not only troubling but also vastly different from the "progressive" affiliations and identificatory practices Bollywood sound has enabled in the United Kingdom and among activist groups in the United States.

Bhattacharjya and Mehta track this history of the ongoing commodification of Bollywood filmigit by marking two temporal figurations of Hindi film song in the United Kingdom. The first occurs in the 1980s with compilations aimed at new immigrants and the Indian market. In this phase, songs from the 1950s and 1960s are marketed for their heritage value, but in later compilations, this link to an authentic nation-state is missing. Hindi film songs are now rechristened Bollywood music, and this categorization is the product of a collaboration between second- and third-generation diasporic Indians and the world music industry.

"New" Becomings

We have argued that Bollywood song and dance provides a repertoire of images, visualities, and performance idioms that articulate with local concerns at different reception sites. In the process, song and dance itself gets transformed. If Indonesia and Egypt both retain peripheral links to the Indian state, Ronie Parciack's "Appropriating the Uncodable: Hindi Song and Dance Sequences in Israeli State Promotional Commercials" is set in contemporary Israel and documents Bollywood's accidental arrival in the mediascape of a country that has no real history of consuming Hindi film. Analyzing the use of a Hindi song as a jingle for a state-run company, Parciack points out the multiple levels at which its unfamiliar music and choreography come to signify the unity and harmony the Israeli state seeks to promote. Though the linguistic and cultural references remain uncodable, the advertisements exploit this unintelligibility to effectively articulate a nationalist discourse that sutures the conflicts at the core of Israeli self-identity. Such appropriations, perhaps unwittingly, reproduce the utopic function that song and dance served in the early years of Indian nationalism. Parciack offers close readings of a series of advertisements to show how filmigit and the milieu of song-dance imagine a new destiny for the fragmented Israeli state.

While Bollywood film song in Israel functions as a commodity to signal otherness and thereby shore up national identity, in the United States the same idioms have been deployed by activists seeking to form networks of minoritarian affiliation and affect. Zumkhawala-Cook explores how South Asian DJs in the United States have organized events such as Basement Bhangra and Bollywood Disco to produce a consciously politicized environment, wherein the organizers advocate for social causes, such as police brutality against immigrants and violence against women. At these events, Hindi film song is remixed with hip-hop to create a subculture of sound that forges new affiliations and identifications. Dudrah explores one such affiliative process through a thick description of a queer night in a Manchester nightclub. He suggests that the aesthetics of excess exemplified in song-dance offers the queer spectator pleasures that a more "realistic" text might foreclose.[134] Though Hindi cinema's governing ideology is heteronormative, the song and dance sequence represents "a line of flight" that opens up a space for other desires and fantasies. He urges us to look beyond the ideology of the film text to the South Asian queer becomings that the Bollywood song and dance sequence "secretly" enables.

While queer South Asians and activists in the United States creatively use song-dance to articulate specific concerns about their own location while constructing new identities and identifications, other communities have brought into being a performance category—Bollywood dance. Both in the diaspora and in India, new sets of meanings have accreted around the elaborate dances featured in the song picturizations. Choreographed sequences often migrate from the screen to the stage, to dance halls, and to community centers. These migrations not only draw on but also radically recode the meanings that the dance had in its filmic context. A hybrid and evolving art form, Bollywood dance like filmigit has borrowed features from indigenous and folk traditions as well as transnational and Western dance forms. In the United States and the United Kingdom, Bollywood dance is not limited to staged performances but rather has become popular in aerobics classes and other "fitness" programs.[135] In each of these sites, the creative remixing of diverse performance traditions allows participants to express their affiliations to multiple cultures without prioritizing any one. This new formation is the subject of Sangita Shresthova's essay that analyzes how student performances of Bollywood dance rarely mimic the film version, rather the reel performance serves as the vantage from which diasporic youth offer an embodied display of their fractured affiliations. Shresthova's essay offers another account of the way Bollywood dance enables the immigrant body to express "secret desires."

Politics of Embodiment

The role of the body gets frequently left out of discussions of Bollywood style and its affinity with pastiche. Feminist theorists of corporeality have highlighted the ways in which gendered and racialized identities are inscribed in bodily gestures and movements.[136] Recognizing the ways in which embodied practices traffic in the field of identity politics is central to understanding how and why Bollywood song and dance sequences are mobilized in different national and cultural spaces. Bollywood dance sequences offer more than the pleasures of visual spectacle. Shresthova's essay offers an insightful analysis of how class and caste differences are registered on female bodies. Examining a single dance sequence "Dola re dola" from the film *Devdas* (Bhansali, 2001), she points out how choreography provides a temporary emancipated space where the female protagonists are able to transcend the social rankings ascribed to them in the narrative. Bodily movement allows them to express libidinal energies proscribed by heteronormative patriarchy.[137] These meanings are flattened when the same dance migrates from reel space to a performance stage. A performance of this same number by South Asian Americans highlights the racialized body. Dudrah's essay reflects on how in the space of the dance club Bollywood enables a different kind of sexual embodiment. His essay points out that queer engagements with the Bollywood song and dance sequence in nightclubs have more to do with recoding visualities and bodily movements than with performing identity. Exploring the phenomenology of the non-Indian subject's encounter with Hindi film song, Chan posits that a recentering of the body is crucial to an understanding of fan behavior; "Food and Cassettes: Encounters with Indian Filmsong" points out that the non-Indian fan's consumption of Bollywood film song is always associated with gastronomy and he explores the NBC encounter with Bollywood in phenomenological terms. Each of these essays complicates our understanding of the performative body. While Judith Butler and other theorists have argued that we "treat gender as a corporeal style, an 'act,'" the essays in this anthology illustrate that song-dance's polysemy allows it to become an integral part in identity-based body projects across continents where the performative is both dramatic and nonreferential.[138] The essays challenge the assumed fixedness of nationalist identification as well as the presumption of heteronormativity. These essays reveal that not only does Bollywood song and dance create a contact zone, but the body itself becomes a borderland where improvisational and interactive elements help reconstitute subjectivities.[139]

Bollywood at the Crossroads

As we write this, the "airtight world of Hindi cinema is breaking down" and once again mainstream filmmakers are debating a radical makeover.[140] Key Bollywood figures, such as Ram Gopal Varma and Sanjay Leela Bhansali, are querying the relevance of the song and dance sequence. Varma's *Naach* (Dance, 2004), for example, is a cinematic exploration of this transitional moment as was *Rangeela* (Full of color,

1995).[141] While this debate has gained momentum, there are historical antecedents for commercial Hindi cinema's rejection of song and dance sequences. Yash Chopra's *Ittefaq* (Coincidence, 1969) had no songs and even the wildly successful *Deewar* (The wall, 1975) had only two song-dance sequences. In the global arena, however, Bollywood aesthetics continues to inspire fashion, advertising, club culture, alternative music, and independent filmmakers. Gurinder Chadha's "homage to Hindi cinema," *Bride and Prejudice* (2004), and Mira Nair's *Vanity Fair* (2004) both included song and dance sequences.[142] Although neither of these exercises in "multiplex multiculturalism" succeeded at the box office, they incorporated Bollywood performance idioms into canonical Western narratives.[143]

In India, new technologies have accelerated the migrations of song and dance to other media even as the Hindi film product is being rapidly transformed. At least twenty television channels—many broadcast globally—feature film songs in their programming lineup, and six of these are music channels dedicated wholly to songs. Hindi filmigit continues to reach growing audiences, and film cities, such as RFC, have ensured that the song-dance picturizations grow ever more spectacular. Choreographer Farah Khan jokes that locations, from Alaskan glaciers to Egyptian pyramids, have transformed Hindi films into "another Discovery Channel."[144] If electronic technologies have facilitated piracy in the form of illegal downloads, the spread of FM radio has sharply reduced the traditional sources of revenue like cassette and CD sales. The industry is increasingly relying on the advance sale of music, satellite, and television rights to cover their investments. At the reception end, the emergence of multiplex theaters that charge exorbitant ticket prices and provide tax shelters to exhibitors has ensured that a film with an extensive multiplex release in urban centers can recover its costs in the first weekend. The long-running silver jubilees are a thing of the past.[145] These changes in the mode of exhibition are beginning to shape the content of Bollywood; universal appeal is no longer a structuring element, instead filmmakers focus on youth, urban, and NRI markets.[146] In the wake of such niche markets, the industry is turning to unconventional nontheatrical sources to recover costs, such as through the sale of cell phone ringtones. In short, the future of Bollywood film song is foretold through the shrill tones of doom and euphoria that accompanies the discourse on globalization. These tones might indeed be the surest sign that we are traveling in the empire of Bollywood.

Notes

1 Ram Gopal Varma, "Interview," *Filmfare,* March 2003, 64–65; and "The Young Turk: Bollywood's Most Respected Young Actor, Aamir Khan," *Time,* October 20, 2003, http://www.time.com/time/asia/covers/ 501031027/int_khan.html.

2 For an excellent essay on the semiotics and politics of the song and dance sequence in contemporary Tamil cinema, see Vivek Dhareshwar and Tejaswini Niranjana, "*Kaadalan* and the Politics of Resignification: Fashion, Violence and the Body," in *Making Meaning in Indian Cinema,* ed. Ravi Vasudevan (New Delhi: Oxford University Press, 2002), 191–214. Priya Jha explores the gendered national identifications enabled by Hindi song and dance sequences in two cult films from the 1970s in her insightful essay, "Lyrical Nationalism: Gender, Friendship, and Excess in 1970s Hindi Cinema," *The Velvet Light Trap* 51 (Spring 2003): 43–53. An overview of Indian film music is provided in Alison Arnold, ed., *The Garland Encyclopedia of World Music,* vol. 5, *South Asia: The Indian Subcontinent* (New York: Garland, 2000), 525–70; see especially Paul D. Greene, "Film Music: Southern Area," 542–47. For an astute analysis of the different kinds of "gazes" employed in song and dance sequences, see Woodman Taylor, "Penetrating Gazes: The Poetics of Sight and Visual Display in Popular Indian Cinema," in *Beyond Appearances: Visual Practices and Ideologies in Modern India,* ed. Sumathi Ramaswamy (New Delhi: Sage, 2003), 297–322.

3 While the industrial mode of production in Hollywood might indeed have encouraged the stabilization of genres, Rick Altman has noted that Hollywood films, at least from a commercial standpoint, are marketed as incorporating multiple genres and/or crossing generic boundaries. See *Film/Genre* (London: BFI, 1999). Corey Creekmur attempts to rethink song-dominated Indian cinema in a more international frame to suggest that the compilation of sound track-dominated American cinema of recent years might find an (unacknowledged) model in the song-dominated Indian popular cinema. See his, "Picturizing American Cinema: Hindi Film Songs and the Last Days of Genre," in *Soundtrack Available: Essays on Film and Popular Music,* ed. Pamela Robertson-Wojcik and Arthur Knight (Durham, N.C.: Duke University Press, 2001), 390.

4 Much work remains to be done on the musical as a global form. To refer to other cinemas—Egyptian or Hong Kong for instance—as "musicals" might be an equally normalizing gesture. After all, the Soviet musical was expressly promoted to compete against and provide an alternative to the Hollywood musical. As Stephen Teo in his work on Mandarin and Cantonese language musical cinema in Hong Kong has shown, this was an immigrant form of entertainment that combined motifs of Westernization with traditional Shanghainese singsong entertainment. A majority of productions, regardless of genres, featured songs that were inserted into the films karaoke style. These songs eventually became the basis for Mandarin pop. As the *chaqu* format made way for the *gechang,* songs were much

more integrated to the narrative. Similarly, the Cantonese opera film, immensely popular in the 1950s and 1960s, virtually disappeared in the 1970s as a more affluent population began to frequent the theatre while Cantopop absorbed the musical influences of Cantonese opera film. See *Hongkong Cinema: The Extra Dimensions* (London: BFI, 1997), 29–60.

5 Rosie Thomas quoted in Madhava Prasad, *Ideology of the Hindi Film: A Historical Construction* (New York: Oxford University Press, 1998), 46 (emphasis in original).

6 Though the "musical" has been around from the earliest days of sound, we refer here to a recent and very self-conscious use of this term. Ram Gopal Varma's *Rangeela* (Full of color, 1995) and Subhash Ghai's *Taal* (Rhythm, 1999) are films that thematize music and showbiz. The ascription "musical" might indeed be an attempt to make these films intelligible to a global audience bred on Hollywood genres. By the same token, from the days of early cinema, there have always been films based on the film and music industry including *Street Singer* (Phani Majumdar, 1938); *Abhinetri* (The actress, Amar Mullick, 1940); or famously *Kismet* (Fate, Gyan Mukherjee, 1943), *Kathputli* (Puppet, Amiya Chakravarti, 1957), and *Teesri Kasam* (Third vow, Basu Bhattacharya, 1966). These films often functioned as vehicles for their singing and, in the case of *Kathputli,* dancing stars—Saigal, Kanan Devi, and so on. Later examples from the 1970s would include *Abhimaan* (Pride, Hrishikesh Mukherjee, 1973) and *Parichay* (Identity, Sampooran Singh Gulzar, 1972). The 1980s saw the advent of the "disco" films such as *Disco Dancer* (Babbar Subhash, 1982) and *Star* (Dev Kumar Varma, 1982).

7 See Creekmur, "Picturizing American Cinema." See also Ranjani Majumdar, "From Subjectification to Schizophrenia: The 'Angry Man' and the 'Psychotic Hero' of Bombay Cinema," in *Making Meaning,* 238–66; Prasad, *Ideology of the Hindi Film;* and Ravi Vasudevan, "Shifting Codes, Dissolving Identities: The Hindi Social Film of the 1950s as Popular Culture," in *Making Meaning,* 99–121.

8 Lalitha Gopalan, playing off Tom Gunning's concept of the "cinema of attractions," has characterized Indian popular cinema as a "cinema of interruptions." In addition to the song-dance sequence, other conventions such as the fight sequence, the comedy fragment, intervals, and dialogues punctuate the narrative in Indian popular cinema forcing us to rethink notions of narrative totality. See Lalitha Gopalan, *Cinema of Interruptions: Action Genres in Contemporary Indian Cinema* (London: BFI, 2002); Nasreen Munni Kabir, *Talking Films: Conversations on Hindi Cinema with Javed Akhtar* (New Delhi: Oxford University Press, 1999); Gita Kapur, "Revelation and Doubt: *Sant Tukaram* and *Devi,*" in *Interrogating Modernity: Culture and Colonialism in India,* ed. Tejaswini Niranjana, P. Sudhir, and Vivek Dhareshwar (Calcutta: Seagull, 1993), 19–46; Gita Kapur, "Mythic Material in Indian Cinema," *Journal of Arts and Ideas* 14–15 (1987): 79–108; and Ashish Rajadhyaksha, "The Phalke Era: Conflict of Traditional Form and Modern Technology," in *Interrogating Modernity,* 47–82.

9 Moinak Biswas, "The City and the Real: Chhinnamul and the Left Cultural Movement in the 1940s," in *City Flicks: Indian Cinema and the*

Urban Experience, ed. Preben Kaarsholm (Calcutta: Seagull, 2004), 40–59.

10 Satyajit Ray, *Our Films, Their Films* (Calcutta: Orient Longman, 1976), 73 (emphasis in original).

11 Preben Kaarsholm, "Unreal City: Cinematic Representation, Globalisation and the Ambiguities of Metropolitan Life," in *City Flicks,* 1–25, 20.

12 "Netvamsham!" *Times of India,* July 18, 1999.

13 Priya Jaikumar, "Bollywood Spectaculars," *World Literature Today* 77 (October–December 2003): 24–29.

14 M. Madhava Prasad, "This Thing Called Bollywood," *Seminar* 525 (May 2003), http://www.india-seminar.com/2003/525/525%20madhava%20prasad.htm.

15 Key scholarly essays that debate the term Bollywood and its emergence include Jaikumar, "Bollywood Spectaculars"; Prasad, "This Thing Called Bollywood"; Ashish Rajadhyaksha, "The Bollywoodization of the Indian Cinema: Cultural Nationalism in a Global Arena," in *City Flicks,* 113–39; and Biswarup Sen, *Of the People: Essays on Indian Popular Culture* (New Delhi: Chronicle Books, 2006).

16 The song and dance sequence is also referred to as song picturizations—this term as Corey Creekmur and Neepa Majumdar have suggested emphasizes the primacy of the aural over the visual—while a film situation might "require" a song, the song is first composed and then put into images. See Creekmur, "Picturizing American Cinema," 375–406; and Neepa Majumdar, "The Embodied Voice: Song Sequences and Stardom in Popular Hindi Cinema," in *Soundtrack Available,* 161–81.

17 Rajadhyaksha, "Bollywoodization," 116. See also Amit Rai's in progress book project "Untimely Bollywood."

18 Indian cinema, in recent years, has been the topic of much critical scholarship. Key research has focused on theories of national spectatorship, the ideological work these films conduct within the nation, Bollywood's narrative modes, and the cultural and political contexts of its production and reception. These texts include Sumita Chakravarty, *National Identity in Indian Popular Cinema, 1947–87* (Austin: University of Texas Press, 1993); Gopalan, *Cinema of Interruptions;* Ashis Nandy, ed., *The Secret Politics of Our Desires: Innocence, Culpability, and Indian Popular Cinema* (New Delhi: Oxford University Press, 1998); Prasad, *Ideology of the Hindi Film;* and Vasudevan, *Making Meaning.* Recognizing the predominance of spectacle in Bollywood cinema, contemporary scholarship has been attentive to the visual style and semiotic codes of Hindi cinema. In this regard, see Rachel Dwyer and Christopher Pinney, eds., *Pleasure and the Nation: The History, Politics, and Consumption of Public Culture in India* (New Delhi: Oxford University Press, 2001); Rachel Dwyer and Divya Patel, *Cinema India: The Visual Culture of Hindi Film* (London: Reaktion Books, 2002); and Ashish Rajadhyaksha, "Neo-Traditionalism: Film as Popular Art in India," *Framework* 32/33 (1987): 20–67. Another line of inquiry has tracked the multiple modalities through which Bollywood enters diasporic space and participates in identity formation. Vijay Mishra, *Bollywood Cinema: Temples of Desire* (New York: Routledge, 2002); Rosie Thomas,

"Indian Cinema: Pleasures and Popularity," *Screen* 26, nos. 3 and 4 (May–August 1985): 116–31; and more recently, Raminder Kaur and Ajay J. Sinha, eds., *Bollyworld: Popular Indian Cinema through a Transnational Lens* (Thousand Oaks, Calif.: Sage, 2005); and Kaarsholm, *City Flicks*. Though all these studies reference the centrality of song and dance sequences to Bollywood genres, with the exception of Gopalan's *Cinema of Interruptions,* Sudipta Kaviraj's "Reading a Song of the City: Images of the City in Literature and Film," in *City Flicks,* and Brian Larkin's "Bandiri Music, Globalization and Urban Experience in Nigeria," in *Bollyworld,* few explore the centrality of song and dance. Similarly, with the exception of *Soundtrack Available,* Bollywood remains largely absent from accounts of film music. Thus, Kay Dickinson, ed., *Movie Music: The Film Reader* (New York: Routledge, 2003), has no essay on Bollywood. Though an emerging body of work examines how South Asian diasporic urban youth culture uses film music to forge new identities, the focus of these analyses remains largely local. See Sunita Sunder Mukhi, *Doing the Desi Thing: Performing Indianness in New York City* (New York: Garland, 2000); Sanjay Sharma, John Hutnyk, and Ashwani Sharma, eds., *Dis-Orienting Rhythms: The Politics of the New Asian Dance Music* (London: Zed Books, 1996); Sunaina Maira, *Desis in the House: Indian American Youth Culture in New York City* (Philadelphia: Temple University Press, 2002); and Sandhya Shukla, *India Abroad: Transethnic Cultures in US and Britain, 1947–97* (Princeton, N.J.: Princeton University Press, 2002).

19 Vinay Lal, "The Impossibility of the Outsider in the Modern Hindi Film," in *Secret Politics,* 234–65.

20 Partha Chatterjee, "When Melody Ruled the Day," in *Frames of Mind: Reflections on Indian Cinema,* ed. Aruna Vasudev (New Delhi: UBS Publishers, 1995), 51–65, 59.

21 Nasreen Munni Kabir, *Bollywood: The Indian Cinema Story* (London: Channel 4 Books, 2001), 130.

22 For an analysis of the song text's relationship to image text, see Biswarup Sen, "In Praise of Hindi Film," *Telegraph India,* October 29, 2003; and Jonathan Durr, " 'Seeing' Song in Bollywood: Landscape, the Postnational and the Song-and-Dance Sequence in Hindi Popular Cinema" (master's thesis, University of Wisconsin, 2001).

23 Richard Dyer, "Entertainment and Utopia," in *Hollywood Musicals, the Film Reader,* ed. Steven Cohan (New York: Routledge, 2002), 19–30.

24 See Prasad, *Ideology of the Hindi Film,* 29–51; Rachel Dwyer, *Yash Chopra* (London: BFI, 2002); Gayatri Chatterjee, *Mother India* (London: BFI, 2002); and Kabir, *Talking Films,* 131.

25 Sudipta Kaviraj performs a bravura analysis of a film song—"Yeh dil mushkil" (Darling, it is hard)—as expressive of Indian modernity without ever having seen the film *CID* (Raj Khosla, 1956), in which this song appears! See Kaarsholm, *City Flicks,* 60–82.

26 Can be viewed at absolut/mulit.com. An excellent analysis of this advertisement and the subtle ways in which it sells product can also be found at http://vij.com/archive/tv_ad_satires_on_india.html.

27 See Dorinne Kondo's *About Face: Performing Race in Fashion and Theater* (New York: Routledge, 1997); and Sujata Moorti, "Out of India: Fashion Culture and the Marketing of Ethnic Style," in *Blackwell Companion to Media Studies,* ed. Angharad Valdivia (London: Blackwell, 2003), 293–308.

28 Can be viewed at http://vij.com/archive/tv_ad_satires_on_india.html.

29 Bollywood fever maybe more than a passing trend. *The Oxford English Dictionary* now has an entry on Bollywood because it has become a "household name."

30 For different readings of this process, see Fredric Jameson and Masao Miyoshi, eds., *The Cultures of Globalization* (Durham, N.C.: Duke University Press, 1998); Benjamin Barber, *Jihad vs. McWorld: How Globalism and Tribalism Are Reshaping the World* (New York: Ballantine Books, 1996); and Mike Featherstone, *Undoing Culture: Globalization, Postmodernism, and Identity* (London: Sage, 1996).

31 We are indebted to Brian Larkin for this example whose work examines the imaginative world made available to Hausa Youth through transnational media flows. See his "Indian Films and Nigerian Lovers: Media and the Creation of Parallel Modernities," *Africa* 67, no. 3 (2003): 406–40.

32 Inhabiting the interstices of cultures, diasporic populations emerge as the blueprint for the global subject and enable a complex cultural dynamic. The presence of immigrants in the metropolis provides the model for identity as alterity that the nation uses to reimagine itself as multicultural. For more information, see James Clifford, *Routes: Travel and Translation in the Late Twentieth Century* (Cambridge, Mass.: Harvard University Press, 1997); Homi Bhabha, *The Location of Culture* (New York: Routledge, 1994); and Arjun Appadurai, *Modernity at Large: Cultural Dimensions of Globalization* (Minneapolis: University of Minnesota Press, 1996).

33 For recent work, see Maira, *Desis in the House;* Shukla, *India Abroad;* Anne-Marie Fortier, *Migrant Belongings: Memory, Space, Identity* (Oxford: Berg, 2000); and Paul Gilroy, *The Black Atlantic: Modernity and Double Consciousness* (Cambridge, Mass.: Harvard University Press, 1993).

34 See Timothy D. Taylor, *Global Pop: World Music, World Markets* (New York: Routledge, 1997); Charles Keil and Steven Feld, eds., *Music Grooves: Essays and Dialogues* (Chicago: University of Chicago Press, 1994); and Sharma et al., *Dis-Orienting Rhythms.*

35 Quoted in Rajadhyaksha, "The Phalke Era," 47. Phalke is referring to an indigenous cinema—one that is "authentically" and entirely Indian. Indian films constantly negotiate the foreign have always been influenced by global trends—in this sense, they can hardly be called indigenous—however, they are a domestic or—as Ravi Vasudevan puts it—a local product. See Ravi Vasudevan, "Cinema in Urban Space," *Seminar* 525 (May 2003), http://www.india-seminar.com/2003/525/525%20ravi%20vasudevan.htm; and Ravi Vasudevan, "Introduction," in *Making Meaning,* 36.

36 See Priya Jaikumar's groundbreaking work for the intertwined histories of imperial cinema. *Cinema at the End of Empire* (Durham, N.C.: Duke University Press, 2006).

37 See Ashish Rajadhyaksha and Paul Willemen, eds., *Encyclopedia of Indian Cinema*, 2nd ed. (London: BFI, 1999), 142; and Rosie Thomas, "Not Quite (Pearl) White: Fearless Nadia, Queen of the Stunts," in *Bollyworld*, 35–69.

38 Sengupta tracks the career of cameraman Dilip Gupta who shuttled between the film industries in Europe, the United States, and India as exemplifying the cosmopolitan energies of Indian cinema in its nascent years. See Shuddhabrata Sengupta, "Reflected Readings in Available Light: Cameramen in the Shadows of Hindi Cinema," in *Bollyworld*, 118–40, 122.

39 Rajadhyaksha and Willemen, *Encyclopedia*, 108.

40 Madan claimed to have worked in several Italian coproductions, but *Savitri* (1923) made by Giorgio Mannini for Cines in Rome was probably just released by Madan. But Liguoro—known in Italy for his Orientalist spectaculars—certainly directed and starred in Madan's *Nala Damayanti* (1920). With *Dhruva Charitra* (Triumph of Devotion, 1920), also directed by Liguoro with a large international cast, Madan attempted an international breakthrough. *The Times of India* noted that this film "offered directions in which a greater appeal may be made to the Westernised mind in picturing modern India." Madan also employed the Frenchman Camille Legrand who directed *Ratnavali* (1922). See Rajadhyaksha and Willemen, *Encyclopedia*, 139, 244; and Sengupta, "Reflected Readings," 123.

41 Rai's chief collaborator Franz Osten worked at Bombay Talkies with cameraman Josef Wirsching and set designer Karl von Spreti. His best-known directorial credits for the studio includes *Achyut Kanya* (The untouchable girl, 1936) and *Jeevan Naiya* (Lifeboat, 1936). Rai had first met Osten and worked with him in a European coproduction *Prem Sanyas* (Light of Asia, 1925). This Orientalist fantasy had a major release in Germany and the United States and did very well in Central Asia. Rajadhyaksha and Willemen, *Encyclopedia*, 167, 183.

42 See Alison Arnold, "Hindi Filmi Git: On the History of Commercial Indian Popular Music" (PhD diss., University of Illinois at Urbana-Champaign, 1991).

43 These data are from a UNESCO report, *Statistics on Film and Cinema* (Paris: Office of Statistics, 1981).

44 In 2002, 11 percent of Indian cinema's revenues were generated from overseas theater viewership. Most industry experts believe that Hindi films account for the largest percentage of these revenues.

45 Rajadhyaksha, "Bollywoodization," 128.

46 Ibid., 127 (emphasis in original). Elsewhere, Rajadhyaksha argues cinema's privileged location as a producer of the "national" is central to understanding the Bollywood "cinema effect" in the poststatist era. See Ashish Rajadhyakha, "Rethinking the State after Bollywood," *Journal of the Moving Image* 3 (2004): 47–90, 64.

47 Critics such as Vasudevan and Rajadhyaksha contend that parallel or art cinema that received government financing was much more statist than nationalist. It reflected and produced the realist aesthetics of a postcolonial state. See Vasudevan, "Introduction," 8; and Ashish Rajadhyaksha,

"Themes of Nationality in Indian Cinema," *Journal of Arts and Ideas* 25–26 (December 1993): 55–70. Also see Chidananda Das Gupta, *The Painted Face: Studies in India's Popular Cinema* (New Delhi: Roli Books, 1991).

48 Chakravarty, *National Identity,* 17; see also Jyotika Virdi, *The Cinematic Imagination: Indian Popular Films as Social History* (New Brunswick: Rutgers University Press, 2003).

49 Arnold, *The Garland Encyclopedia.*

50 Nanabhai Desai quoted in Eric Barnouw and S. Krishnaswamy, *Indian Film,* 2nd ed. (New York: Oxford University Press, 1980), 72. See also Chatterjee, "When Melody Ruled the Day."

51 Chatterjee, "When Melody Ruled the Day."

52 Kabir, *Talking Films,* 54.

53 Ashis Nandy, "The Discreet Charms of Indian Terrorism," in *The Savage Freud and Other Essays on Possible and Retrievable Selves* (Princeton, N.J.: Princeton University Press, 1995), 1–31, 17. We are grateful to one of our anonymous readers for pointing us to this example of film song's relation to nationalism.

54 We are grateful to one of our anonymous readers for directing us to this project. For more, see http://www.developmentgateway.org/culture/.

55 Kabir, *Talking Films,* 35.

56 http://www.screenindia.com/old/20010608/fretro.html.

57 Alexander Lipkov, "Bollywood in Russia," *India International Centre Quarterly* 21, nos. 2 and 3 (1994): 185–94. His conversations with Russian school children evocatively capture its continuing resonance.

58 http://www.upperstall.com/films/awaara.html.

59 See Chatterjee's excellent discussion of this scene in her monograph on *Awaara* (New Delhi: Wiley Eastern, 1992).

60 When Khan first conceptualized *Mother India,* he titled the film *This Land Is Mine* and targeted a global audience. Thus, he hired the Hollywood-based Indian actor Sabu Dastogir famous for Robert Flaherty's *Elephant Boy* (1935). These plans eventually fell through because of import restrictions imposed by the government. Khan released an international version of the film which was considerably shorter and the film was dubbed in Spanish, French, and Russian for foreign markets. Greece, Poland, Rumania, and Czechoslovakia were the first countries to buy the film in Europe, and the French version—entitled *Les Bracelets d'Or*—was widely screened in French African colonies. L. Goron, a French producer–financier, called Khan "the world's greatest film-maker today" and bought distribution rights for Brazil. The film found audiences in Peru, Bolivia, and Ecuador. In Africa, the film remained popular for decades. The following account of its reception is worth citing. Brian Larkin observes, "It's a Friday night in Kano, Northern Nigeria and *Mother India* is playing in Marhaba cinema. Outside, scalpers are hurriedly selling the last tickets to two thousand people lucky enough to buy seats in the open cinema in this city on the edge of Africa's Sahel desert." See Chatterjee, *Mother India;* Kabir, *Talking Films,* 12; and Brian Larkin, "Bollywood Comes to Nigeria," http://www. samarmagazine.org/archive/article.php?id=21.

61 Early films derived their narratives and mise-en-scène from existing theatrical traditions, including the Parsi theatre, a composite of the nineteenth-century British melodrama, and folk forms such as *nautanki* and *sangeetbari tamasha,* Sanskrit drama, mythologies, and Urdu performance traditions.

62 William O'Beeman, "The Use of Music in Pop Film: East vs. West," *Indian International Center Quarterly* 8, no. 1 (1980): 77–87, 82–83.

63 Gayatri Chatterjee, "Icons and Events: Reinventing Visual Constructions in Cinema in India," in *Bollyworld,* 90–117, 106.

64 Rajadhyaksha, "The Phalke Era," 51–54.

65 Kathryn Hansen, "The *Indar Sabha* Phenomenon: Public Theatre and Consumption in Greater India," in *Pleasure and the Nation,* 76–114, 76.

66 Prem Chowdhury surmises on the basis of the declining number of exhibition spaces showing Western films in urban areas that sound must indeed have had a detrimental effect on the audiences' response to Western films (with the exception of adventure films that continued to enjoy a large viewership and that were thematically described by Hollywood as "world audience films"), *Colonial India* and the *Marketing of empire cinema: Image, Ideology and Identity* (Manchester: Manchester University Press, 2000), 13.

67 Somnath Gupt, *The Parsi Theatre: The Origins and Development,* trans. and ed. Kathryn Hansen (Kolkata: Seagull Books, 2005), 182.

68 Richard Abel and Rick Altman, *The Sounds of Early Cinema* (Bloomington: Indiana University Press, 2001).

69 Rani Burra, ed., *Film India, 1896–1960* (New Delhi: Directorate of Film Festivals, 1981), 16. Someswar Bhowmik contends that the poor quality of the films circulated in tertiary rural markets necessitated this additional entertainment device. See his *Indian Cinema, Colonial Encounters* (Calcutta: Papyrus, 1995).

70 Firoze Rangoonwala, *75 Years of Indian Film* (New Delhi: Clarion Books, 1983), 30.

71 Quoted in Lalit Mohan Joshi, ed., *Bollywood: Popular Indian Cinema* (London: Dakini Ltd, 2001), 70 (our emphasis).

72 A situation not unlike that described by Abel and Altman, *Sounds of Early Cinema.*

73 Sara Dickey argues that in Tamil film, "the migration of politically-conscious stage actors, musicians, singers, music composers to the screen not only introduced political consciousness but also an aura of respectability. Singers like K.B. Sundarambal and M.S. Subbulakshmi acted during this time period." See, Sara Dickey, *Cinema and the Urban Poor in South India* (Cambridge: Cambridge University Press, 1993), 53.

74 Rajadhyaksha and Willemen, *Encyclopedia,* 244.

75 Ibid., 253.

76 Ibid., 255.

77 Ashok Ranade, "The Extraordinary Importance of the Indian Film Song," *Cinema Vision India* 1, no. 4 (1980): 5.

78 Ashraf Aziz, *Light of the Universe: Essays on Hindustani Film Music* (New Delhi: Three Essays Collective, 2003), 5.

79 Rajadhyaksha and Willemen, *Encyclopedia,* 68.

80 Ibid., 68.

81 Ibid., 154.

82 See Manek Premchand for excellent short sketches of the major composers, singers, lyricists, and arrangers. Manek Premchand, *Yesterday's Melodies, Today's Memories* (Mumbai: Jharna Books, 2003), 17–27. Also see Teri Skillman, "The Bombay Hindi Film Song Genre: A Historical Survey," *Yearbook for Traditional Music* 18 (1986): 133–44.

83 Aziz, *Light of the Universe*, 49–51.

84 See Dwyer, *Yash Chopra*.

85 Majumdar, "The Embodied Voice," 167.

86 In contrast, Hollywood invests deeply in the authenticity of the singer-performer. Audrey Hepburn was denied an Oscar for *My Fair Lady* when the Academy discovered that she did not sing her songs.

87 Majumdar identifies *Barsaat* (Rain, Raj Kapoor 1949) as the film with which playback artistes' names began appearing on screen and on records. See "The Embodied Voice," 171.

88 Yash Chopra regretted not being able to work with a very admired music director S. D. Burman because Ludhianvi would not write for Burman. Dwyer, *Yash Chopra*, 38.

89 Kabir, *Talking Films*, 105.

90 Ibid., 131.

91 Prashant Pandey, "Documenting the Contemporary History of the Making of the Hindi Film Song," http://www.sarai.net/fellowships/independent/archival-submissions/listitem.2006-04-28.5385189224/prashant-pandey-documenting-the-contemporary-history-of-the-making-of-the-hindi-film-song.

92 Choreographers were given screen credits from the 1970s. See Partha Chatterjee, "A Bit of Song and Dance," in *Frames of Mind*, 197–218.

93 Rajadhyaksha and Willemen, *Encyclopedia*, 244.

94 Ibid., 245.

95 Ibid., 246.

96 Ibid., 248.

97 Ibid., 270.

98 Ibid., 291.

99 Ibid.

100 James Joyce in a letter to his daughter said of Shankar, "He moves on the stage like a semi-divine being. Believe me, there are still a few beautiful things left in this poor old world." Ibid., 311.

101 Ibid., 310.

102 Ibid.

103 See Amit Rai, "An American Raj in Filmistan: Images of Elvis in Indian Films," *Screen* 35, no. 1 (1994): 51–77; and Dhareshwar and Niranjana, "*Kaadalan*."

104 Ray, *Our Films*, 74–75.

105 Rajadhyaksha, "Bollywoodization," 120–21.

106 Ravi Vasudevan, "Addressing the Spectator of a Third World National Cinema: The Bombay Social Film of the 1940's and 1950's," *Screen* 36, no. 4 (1995): 305–25, 306–7.

107 Priya Joshi, "Knocking on Heaven's Door: Can Hollywood's Audiences Let Bollywood In?" Unpublished paper.
108 Quoted in Chatterjee, *Mother India,* 77–78.
109 Quoted in Helen Abadzi, "Hindi Films of the 50s in Greece: The Latest Chapter of a Long Dialogue," March 17, 2003, http://helen-abadzi.sulekha.com/blog/post/2003/03/when-india-conquered-greece-hindi-films-of-the-50s.htm.
110 Walter Armbrust, "Rise and Fall of Nationalism in the Egyptian Cinema," in *Social Constructions of Nationalism in the Middle East,* ed. Fatma Muge Gocek (Albany: State University of New York Press, 2002), 217–50, 226. Robert Vitalis argues that Egypt's film industry like those of the late industrializers (Mexico, Brazil, Argentina, India, and Turkey) emerged in the shadow of Hollywood's global prominence in the 1940s. More recent influences have included karate and kung fu films, and thus the Egyptian film industry was never the pure domain for the production of an authentic national product. Robert Vitalis, "American Ambassador in Technicolor and Cinemascope: Hollywood and the Revolution on the Nile," in *Mass Mediations: New Approaches to Popular Culture in the Middle-East and Beyond,* ed. Walter Armbrust (Berkeley: University of California Press, 2000), 269–91, 271.
111 M. Shamim, "Bollywood Films Make Waves around the World," *Hindu Online,* February 25, 2001, http://www.hinduonnet.com/thehindu/2001/02/25/stories/14252184.htm.
112 Maria Enzensberger, "We Were Born to Turn a Fairy-Tale into Reality: Svetlyi Put and the Soviet Musical of the 1930s and 1940s," in *Popular European Cinema,* ed. Richard Dyer and Ginette Vincendeau (New York: Routledge, 1992), 87–99; and Richard Taylor, "Singing on the Steppes for Stalin: Ivan Pyr'ev and the Kolkhoz Musical in Soviet Cinema," *Slavic Review* 58, no. 1 (Spring 1999): 143–59.
113 Barnouw and Krishnaswamy, *Indian Film,* 160.
114 However, militants in Iraq during this current Gulf War told the Indian government that they wanted film stars to act as hostage negotiators. See Faisal Devji, *Landscapes of the Jihad:* Militancy, Mertality, Modernity (Ithaca, N.Y.: Cornell University Press, 2005).
115 This constitutes a civilizational distinction, in Nandy's terms. See his *Secret Politics.*
116 Burra, *Film India,* 10; and Barnouw and Krishnaswamy, *Indian Film,* 66, 69.
117 Rajadhyaksha and Willemen, *Encyclopedia,* 95. Burma is now known as Myanmar and Ceylon as Sri Lanka.
118 Narmala Halstead, "Belonging and Respect Notions vis-à-vis Modern East Indians: Hindi Movies in the Guyanese East Indian Diaspora," in *Bollyworld.*
119 Manas Ray observes that because in "Hindi films nation is imagined in familial terms, the physical distance between mainland India and Fiji did not interrupt this work of the imagination." See Manas Ray, "Chalo Jahaji: Bollywood in the Tracks of Indenture to Globalization," in *City Flicks,* 140–82, 160.

120 Vijay Mishra, *Bollywood Cinema: Temples of Desire* (New York: Routledge, 2000), x.

121 Halstead, "Belonging and Respect," 264–65, 276.

122 Manas Ray, "Bollywood Down Under: Fiji Indian Cultural History and Popular Assertion," in *Floating Lives: The Media and Asian Diasporas,* ed. Stuart Cunningham and John Sinclair (New York: Rowman and Littlefield, 2001), 136–84. See also Tejashwini Niranjana, *Mobilizing India: Women, Music, and Migration between Trinidad and India* (Durham, N.C.: Duke University Press, 2005).

123 Vashna Jagarnath, "The Politics of Urban Segregation and Indian Cinema in Durban," in *City Flicks,* 211–22.

124 Kabir, *Talking Films,* 160.

125 Thomas Blom Hansen, "In Search of the Diasporic Self: Bollywood in South Africa," in *Bollyworld,* 239–60, 250–52. This essay demonstrates how Bollywood intersects with contemporary South African race politics. Unlike in other African countries, South African blacks have traditionally stayed away from Hindi film. This is largely a consequences of the cultural politics of the apartheid regime that strictly practiced a "divide and rule" policy that limited cultural interactions between ethnic Indians and blacks.

126 For a searching analysis of the characteristics of the NRI genre, see Sudhanva Deshpande, "The Consumable Hero of Globalized India," in *Bollyworld,* 186–203.

127 The song reached number one in the Brazilian charts. http://www. loadofold.com/boots/biddu.html.

128 http://news.bbc.co.uk/1/hi/world/south_asia/3856487.stm.

129 Shukla, *India Abroad;* and Gayatri Gopinath, "Bombay, U.K., Yuba City: Bhangra Music and the Engendering of Diaspora," *Diaspora* 4, no. 3 (1995): 303–21.

130 Mary Louise Pratt, *Imperial Eyes: Travel Writing and Transculturation* (New York: Routledge, 1992).

131 George Iype, "If It's Animation, It Must be India!" rediff.com, March 16, 2005, http://www.rediff.com/money/2005/mar/16spec1.htm.

132 Dick Hebdige, *Subculture: The Meaning of Style* (London: Methuen, 1979), 92–99.

133 Rajadhyaksha, "Bollywoodization."

134 Nandy, *Secret Politics.*

135 Chhavi Dublish, "Indian Dance Routine Wins Over US," BBC News, September 8, 2004, http://news.bbc.co.uk/1/hi/world/americas/ 3634040.stm.

136 Elizabeth Grosz, *Volatile Bodies: Towards a Corporeal Feminism* (Bloomington: Indiana University Press, 1994); and Iris Young, *On Female Body Experience: "Throwing Like a Girl" and Other Essays* (New York: Oxford University Press, 2005).

137 Gayatri Gopinath, *Impossible Desires* (Durham, N.C.: Duke University Press, 2005); and, "Untimely Bollywood."

138 Judith Butler, "Performative Acts and Gender Constitution: An Essay in Phenomenology and Feminist Theory," in *Writing on the Body: Female*

Embodiment and Feminist Theory, ed. Katie Conboy, Nadia Medina, and Sarah Stanbury (New York: Columbia University Press, 1997), 401–17, 404.

140 Pratt, *Imperial Eyes,* 6–7.

141 Kabir, *Talking Films.*

142 See "The Trailblazer," *Time,* October 20, 2003, http://www.time.com/ time/asia/covers/501031027/int_varma.html.

143 Subhash K. Jha, "Bride and Prejudice Is Not a K3G," rediff.com, August 30, 2004, http://in.rediff.com/movies/2004/aug/30finter.htm.

144 Manohla Dargis, "Mr. Darcy and Lalita, Singing and Dancing," *New York Times,* February 11, 2005.

145 "Bollywood Ending," *Sight and Sound,* June 2003, http://www.bfi.org.uk/ sightandsound/feature/9/.

146 Multiplexes that constitute 2.3 percent of the screens in India account for 21–25 percent of total grosses for all Hindi films. See Namrata Joshi, "Houseful (but Kitne Aadmi the. . .?)," *Outlook,* June 27, 2005, 59–60.

147 Industry insiders estimate that a film with superstar Shahrukh Khan would earn between 40 and 45 percent of its earnings in the diaspora which together with the urban audience would comprise over 75 percent of the film's revenues. See Joshi, "Houseful."

Part 1

Home Terrains

1. Tapping the Mass Market

The Commercial Life of Hindi Film Songs

Anna Morcom

Since the coming of sound in 1931, virtually all commercial Hindi films have contained songs. It is estimated that fifteen million people visit the cinema everyday in India and the inclusion of songs in films is seen as being essential to tap the full potential of this immense market.[1] If films are a big business and songs are indeed essential to the commercial potential of films, then we may presume that film songs themselves have considerable commercial power. What is the nature of the film songs' commercial power, and how is it related to or independent from Hindi films? Do songs sell films or do films sell songs? Songs are currently used to market the parent films, but how are the songs themselves marketed? How has the commercial life of film music been affected by the advent of cassettes, videos, compact discs (CDs), video CDs (VCDs), digital video discs (DVDs), satellite television, and the Internet? This chapter explores these questions through an examination of the technologies of distribution, marketing, and profitability of film songs during four periods:

- The first few years of sound film
- The early 1930s to the mid-1980s: the gramophone era
- 1980s–2000: the cassette revolution and the spread of commercial television
- 2000 and beyond: from boom to bust

An examination of these four periods charts how the variables of audience taste, technology, business enterprise, and markets have played roles in the vast expansion of film and film song audiences. The ensuing relationships of product, technology, and marketing strategies also shed light on the multimedia nature of both films and film songs and their complex and shifting relationship to each other.

There is little published material on this subject; this study is thus based almost exclusively on fieldwork, including interviews with a number of members of the music and film industries[2]. An investigation of this kind is hindered by the fact that no official figures regarding the sale of audio rights or volume of music sales are available. These figures are seen as a trade secret and film financing is also riddled with illegal or "black" money. In the absence of official figures, producers and others are able to talk numbers up or down for tax purposes or to bolster their image or run down someone else's. The figures presented in this chapter therefore cannot necessarily be taken as reliable, but they give a sense of relative scale.

The First Few Years of Sound Film

Film songs have existed in Hindi sound films since they began in 1931. Though the recording industry was well established in India by 1931 and radio was in existence from 1927, Hindi film songs, though popular, were not at first made into gramophone records or played on the radio.[3] This suggests that film songs were not yet conceptualized as a separate entity, but were rather viewed as an integral part of the film. Also, until the advent of magnetic tape around 1950, which enabled songs recorded on the film sound track to be transferred to gramophone records, film songs had to be re-recorded for release on gramophone record.[4] Producing gramophone records of film songs may therefore not have been a technologically viable option, and a record of a song was necessary to play it on radio. The recording industry had not yet established a relationship with the film industry, let alone the level of corporate conglomeration found today.

In this period, it can therefore be said that film songs had no commercial life separate from the parent film, because they did not exist as an autonomous commercial product. Songs became popular through oral transmission as people learned and reproduced them in new contexts after hearing them at the cinema. Though music contributed significantly to the commercial success of films, it was just one of the many aspects of the parent film.

The Early 1930s to the Mid-1980s: The Gramophone Era

Film Songs on Gramophone Record

The first records of film songs were made in 1932, according to record collectors Narayan Multani and Suresh Chandravankar.[5] Initially, not all songs from a film used to be recorded, but by the late 1940s, all songs were released on a gramophone record almost always by HMV, a company that enjoyed a near monopoly on recording in India.[6] Songs were initially produced on 78 rpm records, with one song on each side, and then from the late 1950s on 45 rpm [also known as extended plays (EPs)], with two songs on each side, and from 1964 on long playing (LP) records.[7] With 78 rpm and 45 rpm records, songs were sold as individual items. It was only with LPs and, later, cassettes that an entire film sound track could be packaged as a whole, which also consolidated the relationship of the songs and the parent film.

The size of the gramophone record market was very limited in the early days, but gradually grew, achieving momentum in the 1960s and the 1970s. This was due to increased record-pressing capacity, the availability of 45 rpm records and LPs in addition to 78 rpm records, presumably an increase in the ownership of record players, and the growing popularity of film songs. In the 1970s, the arrival of the music company Polydor also introduced the first real element of competition to the market. Compared with the 1950s and 1960s, when the sale of a few thousand 78 rpm records was considered a "very very big hit,"[8] by the early 1970s, twenty-five thousand units was considered a "good sale."[9]

Other factors also inhibited the commercial exploitation of film music. HMV had problems in supplying the demand for records. V. K. Doobey explained:

> We were never efficient enough to be able to supply a super hit at any time. The material used to come from Calcutta, and the transport, you couldn't airfreight that because it would be too expensive on the cost of the thing, so they would come by train or by lorries, trucks, so the distribution and manufacturing was never as efficient as it is today. Today the factories are efficient. It's a very huge factory today, very modern, and lot of airfreighting is done also. We charge so much of money on a compact disc that a few rupees on airfreight can easily be absorbed because the profitability is very high.[10]

It is said that until the 1960s, when capacity significantly increased, HMV catered more to A-list producers or to films that were already hits. Until around the 1970s, it was difficult for producers to get their songs printed on LP. Rajkumar Barjatya of Rajshri Productions commented that it was a "privilege" to get songs printed on LP by HMV and that "a hundred pictures came out in a year, but only a few films' LPs were made,"[11] a situation clearly frustrating for all but the producers of the most successful films and indicative of the limitations of gramophone technology. HMV's record-pressing capacity gradually improved, and by the 1970s, it was far easier to get records printed, even on LP.

Increasing audience demand bore witness to the growing popularity of film songs, and they came to constitute a larger and larger proportion of record sales in a market that was anyway expanding. By 1940, film music dominated HMV's record sales.[12] Film music grew to about 70 percent of HMV sales by the 1960s and has remained at about this level up till the present day.[13] Polydor recorded about 50 percent film music until after the introduction of cassettes, when this rose to about 70 percent, where it has remained up until the present day.[14]

Initially, 78 rpm records of film songs were released after the release of a film when it was known if the film/song was a success or not, the major criterion for the commercial success and, to a significant but lesser extent, the popularity of the film songs.[15] However, as film songs gained ground in the 1940s, they began to be released "shortly before" the film's opening.[16] This prior release of songs to promote the film appears to have escalated by the 1960s. Rajkumar Barjatya recalls that the songs for Rajshri's earliest films such as *Dosti* (Friends, 1964) were released six to eight weeks before the film. However, LPs were issued after the release, when it was established that there was a large demand for the music.[17] It was only with the widespread availability of cable and satellite television in the 1990s that the release of songs three months or more prior to the film became the norm.

The Marketing of Film Songs in the Gramophone Era

Until the late 1980s and early 1990s when television became widespread, fueled by the new commercial cable and satellite channels, there was no marketing as such of film songs, as V. K. Doobey stated, "The film, the success of the film, promoted the song itself."[18] The *commercial* success of film songs has always been primarily dependent on the success of the parent film. On the whole, a hit film means hit music and a flop film means flop music. This is still the case today, apart for exceptional songs or sound tracks.[19] The film itself was promoted through posters, trailers at the cinema, lobby cards, and advertisements in magazines and increasingly through the prior release of the music.

In addition to the parent film, however, film songs were also widely popularized, although not officially advertised (that is, through buying airtime), through radio, being played before and after the release of the film. As other chapters in this volume show elsewhere, during the period when Hindi film music was banished from the airwaves, listeners from India simply tuned into Radio Ceylon, with the program *Binaca Geet-mala* becoming a rage.[20] Hosted by Amin Sayani, this program initially took the form of a competition where people would write in to guess the top song. *Binaca Geetmala* got nine thousand letters in the first week and sixty thousand within six months.[21] Sayani was, in his own words, "a wreck," trying to cope with all the mail, so they changed the format.[22] The song lineup was now determined by combining the sales figures from fourteen shops all over India with listener requests. This show was so influential in promoting films and film songs that producers and music directors would send in thousands of bogus requests for their own songs to manipulate this forum for their own commercial ends. The show format had to change several more times in order to stop corruption. The *Binaca Geetmala* story is a testament to the extraordinary popularity film songs achieved and the key role played by radio. This phenomenon demonstrated just how important songs had become to producers as an unofficial and free way of advertising films. This period also coincides with what is widely recognized as the "Golden age" of film songs, with what are seen as the most beautiful melodies and richest lyric poetry, and a group of outstanding singers: Geeta Dutt, Lata Mangeshkar, Asha Bhosle, Mukesh, Mohammad Rafi, and Kishore Kumar. Hence, film song at this time was fueled by response to what was perceived as the enhanced quality of the product at this time.

The *Binaca Geetmala* affair also clearly demonstrated how government policy attempting to "improve" audience taste was defeated by a commercial formula from outside of India responding to popular demand. This anticipates the far more extensive commercialization that has occurred in India since the beginnings of liberalization in the 1980s as India somewhat grudgingly started to move towards a market economy.

The Commercial Profitability of Film Song
in the Gramophone Era

Although film songs had achieved tremendous popularity, at this stage, their popularity had not been exploited commercially, as Chopra states, "music did not translate into money."[23] The commercial value of songs inhered in their ability to promote the film. Thus, the kind of money producers could make from songs was described to me by Rajkumar Barjatya as "nothing much"[24] or "peanuts."[25] Until Polydor came into existence, HMV was effectively the only music company. Producers therefore gave or "donated," as Sehdev Ghei sarcastically put it, the song rights to HMV, who would make records and give the producer a 10 percent royalty. Until about the 1960s, even if a song became immensely popular, low sales volumes meant that royalty returns were minimal. By the 1960s and 1970s, with market expansion, producers might have got fifty thousand to one hundred thousand rupees of royalties from hit music.[26] Though good money in those days, these figures are tiny compared to current revenues, despite the music market crash of 2000.

Though film songs were a social and cultural phenomenon of enormous proportion, in commercial terms, they were insignificant compared to the film. Overall, this era demonstrates a creeping realization on the part of producers that film songs could earn them money directly. During this era, where there was little commercially driven promotion of film songs and distribution technology was limited, the role of audience taste had greater relative importance than in the cassette and television era, where economic reform and technological developments presented immense potential for growth.

1980s–2000: The Cassette Revolution and the Spread of Commercial Television

The Impact of Cassettes

The advent of cassettes in India paved the way for realizing the commercial potential of film music on an unprecedented scale. First, cassettes revolutionized the music industry in terms of the size of the music market and the quantum of music sold. As Manuel describes, the cassette industry "expanded exponentially" in the early 1980s:

> Sales of recorded music—almost entirely cassettes by the late 80s—went from $1.2 million in 1980 to $12 million in 1986, and to over $21 million in 1990. . . . By the late 1980s, Indian consumers were buying around 2.5 million cassette players annually (while the entire number of phonographs in the country is estimated at well under one million).[27]

Second, cassette technology revolutionized the industry by decentralizing it and introducing real competition, as small producers entered the fray, first pirating legitimate recordings and later buying audio rights for themselves.[28] Competition emerged not just in the form of more music companies, but also in the form of other styles of popular, mass-mediated music, such as *bhajan, ghazal,* and a myriad of local styles. According to Manuel, the overall market share of film music dropped from 90 percent to less than 40 percent in the new expanded market.[29] However, the overall sales of film music still expanded enormously. The proportion of film music of HMV, now Saregama, to total sales also remained more or less constant at around 70 percent.[30] This expansion meant that producers were making small fortunes from the sale of their audio rights as opposed to the "peanuts" they previously earned. This remains true even after the crash of 2000. It has made the music business a very high-risk and high-reward one. With such large amounts of money involved, the risks involved in film music are not just financial. Gulshan Kumar, the former boss of T-Series, and the single individual most responsible for the revolution in the Indian film music business, was assassinated in 1997. Piracy has also become a problem: as much as 80 percent of the official market in the late 1980s and in 2000, around 40 percent.[31]

Other more profitable forms of music and film commodification have come into existence since the 1980s: video, CD, VCD, and DVD. However, unlike the Western market, in India, cassettes still dominate. According to an article in *Screen* on April 13, 2001, there were an estimated sixty million cassette players and four million CD players. In 2000, the Indian music industry (official and pirate) sold "an estimated 210 million music cassettes and 13 million CDs." Since the crash, CDs have increased to 15 percent of the market, but the overall volume of sales has fallen some 60–70 percent.[32] While the Internet was seen as fairly insignificant to the music industry in 1999–2000, it is now cited as the major cause in the music sales slump because of illegal downloads.[33]

The Marketing of Film Songs in the Cassette Era[34]

Another dramatic change occurred due to the marketing potential opened up by the spread of commercial television in the 1990s. The advent of cassettes has, it can be argued, democratized music production, giving greater power to consumers; however, television opened up an effective marketing avenue for shaping consumer demand. This era has, therefore, seen significant shifts in the dialectic of audience taste and technological possibility and the resulting commercial profitability, popularity, and cultural presence of film songs.

We saw that in the gramophone era there was no official marketing of the film songs. However, the early 1990s witnessed marketing initiatives that promote film songs. Television offered a marketing venue for combating the increase in competition that followed the cassette revolution. Harish Dayani, then vice president of marketing at HMV, explained:

> Radio as a medium has some limitations, that you only hear, but you don't see, whereas in India the medium has always been largely the audio-visual medium, which is cinema. . . . From the audio-visual medium if you only market through the audio medium then it has got . . . limitations.[35]

Television began on an experimental basis in 1959. By 1980, it only reached 15.2 percent of the population in the form of the state network known as Doordarshan. Government initiatives extended television during the 1980s, but Doordarshan still ran for only a few hours a day.[36] Programs such as *Chitrahaar* and *Chaya Geet,* which screened songs from noncurrent films, became immensely popular but did not contribute to advertising upcoming releases. Television advertising started in the late 1980s, and in 1992–93, Doordarshan's monopoly ended with the entry of Star TV, soon followed by other commercial cable channels.[37]

Film music promotion through television did not take off until around 1994. The new cable channels, along with video, were initially seen as a threat to the film industry, for they poached on middle-class audiences, who preferred to watch films at home than go to theaters, which became increasingly run down and disreputable.[38] It was

Rajkumar Barjatya of Rajshri Productions who first viewed television as an opportunity rather than a threat and began the now standard practice of making trailers, combining clips from the film and the film songs. Thus, in the words of Harish Dayani, "the marketing of music actually started in a professional manner . . . whereby you take part of the film and use that to promote your music."[39] The songs had always been an important part of publicizing the film. With television, the film could be used to market the songs, which would in turn market the film. Harish Dayani continued:

> The marketing of music took I would say some amount of lead in terms of not only promoting the music but thereby also promoting and creating the awareness for the film. And that is how the gap between the release of the music and the release of the film started, I would say about 6/7 years ago.[40]

Although the practice of releasing music in advance of the film had begun in the gramophone era around 1950, it was not released as far in advance of the film as it is now. Now, "teasers," showing a few clips from the film, and trailers of thirty, sixty, and ninety seconds are released about one month prior to the sound track and about four months in advance of the film. These may be made by the producer or the music company, but will always involve a joint collaboration. This multimedia form of marketing and distribution has led to increasing conglomeration between the film, music, and television industries. Many music companies have gone into film production as audio rights have become so expensive (see the section on profitability), and in a similar vein, television companies have more recently begun to move into film production; *Gadar—Ek Prem Katha* (Uprising: A love story, Anil Sharma, 2001), for example, was produced by Zee Telefilms.

Advertising is widespread, with "teasers" and trailers for music of forthcoming films saturating television and radio. Songs also get played on music channels such as MTV and Channel [V] and various television shows show song-picturization clips. The songs selected tend to be the most "commercial": romantic, melodious numbers, particularly duets, which will be popular with television audiences. Although music channels promote songs and the film, they are not official sources for advertising because producers do not pay for airtime. Rather, a symbiosis develops: "Music channels want music content and music companies want their albums to be promoted through music videos."[41]

Music is the single most important marketing device for the film, and the opening a film receives is in direct proportion to the revenues from the sound track.[42] In much rarer cases, runaway hit songs can make a film a hit that would otherwise probably not have been. "Ek do teen" (One two three), through its catchy and folk-like simplicity, and "Choli ke peeche" (Behind the blouse), through its outrageousness, are generally viewed as instrumental to the success of *Tezaab* (Acid, N. Chandra, 1988) and *Khalnayak* (The Villan, Subhash Ghai, 1993), respectively. Although the film songs promote the film, they themselves rely on the film for their promotion, because they are advertised through trailers on television that use clips from the film.

The marketing of film songs and films is difficult to distinguish. Trailers using the film songs and visuals from the films are produced by the music company to promote the music, and the music, as it gains ground in the popular culture, promotes the film. However, about a month after the release of the audio and a month before the release of the film, "teasers" and trailers advertising the film are screened.[43] Like the music trailers, the film trailers combine film songs in the sound track with images from the film. Both the music trailers and the film or "theatrical" trailers promote the music and the film. It is only a slight shift in emphasis that distinguishes one from the other. The music trailers use one of the songs in the sound track and usually images from that song picturization and sometimes montages from other parts of the film.[44] Overall, they concentrate on romantic visuals, which are seen as the most conducive to songs.[45] This is especially clear in the case of action films, where romantic subplots tend to dominate audio trailers, posters, and cassette sleeves. This strategy is very circular. The songs of such action films are marketed through the romantic scenes. However, these romantic subplots may be included in the film only to capitalize on the commercial potential of songs. Such "serious" films that are "forced" to tag on songs for mass audiences include *Satya* (The truth, Ram Gopal Varma, 1998) or *Mrityudand* (Death sentence, Prakash Tha, 1997).

In contrast, the theatrical trailer and posters that build up to a film's release begin to open up more of the film, often gradually over a series of trailers and posters.[46] They may include dialogue, dramatic scenes, and actors other than the romantic duo. It is only the text or the announcement (if radio) on the trailers or posters that clearly distinguishes music and film trailers/posters from each other. The music trailers feature the name of the music company, because the music company pays for the music promotion and the film producer for the promotion of the film. Although there is more active promotion of film songs, and indeed films, now than in the gramophone era, the songs and the film both drive each other and are symbiotically connected. Songs are the main means to market the film and secure it a good opening. Yet the songs themselves have only really been marketable since the advent of widespread television, which allowed for the use of clips from the film to advertise the songs. One way to untangle the dynamics between films and film songs, at least on a commercial level, is to examine the (unofficial) statistics for the sale of film song rights and their relation to the success of the parent film. The figures are from interviews from 1998 to 2000—just before the crash in the music market that saw sales fall around 60–70 percent—and relate it to cassette sales, around 95 percent of the market then.

The music company would normally begin by putting seven hundred thousand to one million cassettes in the market.[47] The total cassette sales from star-cast films were anything from about a million cassettes to about seven million or up to twelve million in exceptional cases (not including piracy, currently around 40 percent). So, how big a role did the film play in determining whether film songs sell one million or twelve million copies (or comparable volumes in the postcrash market)? Apart from exceptional cases, the music sales are quite limited before the release of the film. Mukesh Desai of T-Series explained:

> If the songs are good, if the visuals are good, people take it up. . . . The sales go up to certain stage. . . . About [how much] is very difficult to say, [400,000], [500,000], [600,000], [700,000] possibly.[48]

It is then the release of the film that determines whether the sales will tail off at around a million or whether they will go up to four, five, six, or even ten or twelve million. Mukesh Desai continued:

> And then once the film is released, if the film is appreciated, then the sales zoom up, then it goes up to [1.5, 2, 2.5, 3, 4 million].[49]

Ramesh Taurani of TIPS explained in percentage terms the sales of music before and after the release of the parent film. For an averagely successful film, the sales would be 50/50. For a hit, they would be "40/60, 40 before release, 60 after release." For a super hit, even more would sell after the release, "then it must be 20/80, if it's a super duper

Publicity shot from *Dil To Pagal Hai* (The Heart is Crazy, Yash Chopra, 1997) which in prerelease sold a record-breaking five million copies of the audio.

hit." However, if the film is a flop, then it will be more like 100/0; in other words, sales will just about cease after the film is released.[50]

The success of the film is so crucially linked to music sales that it is only in very rare cases that music would have sold over a million or a-million-and-a-half copies before the film's release. *Dil To Pagal Hai* (1997) was an exception, selling five million copies before the release of the film, which was a big hit, and then three million after. Similarly, it is

Audio poster for Yash Raj Films' *Fanaa* (2006).

only in exceptional cases that the music would have sold more than one or two million if the film was a flop. The best-known examples of this are *1942—A Love Story* (Vidhu Vinod Chopra, 1994), which sold over three million copies,[51] and *Dil Se* (From the heart, Mani Ratnam, 1998), which is estimated to have sold around three to four million copies.[52]

While the flop film, hit music phenomenon is extremely rare, the converse, where a film is a hit but the music is a flop, is virtually unheard of.[53] In other words, once a film becomes a hit, the music will sell and become a hit even if it was not particularly popular before the release of the film. The music for *Hum Aapke Hain Koun . . . !* (Who Am I to you?, Sooraj Barjatya, 1994), one of the most successful Hindi films ever made, was not a big seller until the release of the film. The film was a megahit and sold about twelve million cassettes.[54] Had the film flopped, this number would have been more like a million. Despite the vast increase in the scale of music sales and the centrality of songs to the formal marketing of films, music still remains very much dependent on the film for its success. As music director Milind puts it:

> Very good music and if the film fails, your music goes nowhere, and very bad music and if your film is a hit, your music is a big hit [*sic*]. . . . The music is like a child and the film is like a mother.[55]

The reasons why film music is limited in its appeal without the film has to do with the musical style of this genre, which is linked to the cinema and often "gapped"[56] or full of "add-ons,"[57] incomplete or disjointed without its dramatic and visual dimension. Film songs are all written for cinematic situations, and the composition process is guided by the director, who explains the film story and song situations to the music director and lyricist in "sittings," giving often extensive details on characterization, mood, location, and the timing of shots and actions, all of which have implications for the choice of musical style and structure. Depending on the demands of the narrative and the degree of drama the director wishes to express at the level of music, some songs are more "situational," that is, have more drama manifest in the music (sometimes with extensive use of background scoring techniques) and seem incomplete without the visual sequence, and some have higher "audio value," that is, retain a strong song idiom independent of the film context. A famous example of a highly situational song is "Yeh dosti" (This friendship) from *Sholay* (Flames, Ramesh Sippy, 1975), which contains so much situational, backing-score style music to accompany the antics of the heroes Jai and Veeru that it is substantially edited for the audio version. A good example of songs with a high audio value are those from *Dil To Pagal Hai*. In the title song, for example, even though four characters are singing, this is not expressed at the level of music. Instead, only two voices are used; hence, the song remains a more conventional love duet.[58] The limited appeal of film music without the film is also related to the fact that film music is usually consumed in a way that is related in some way to films.

Also crucial to the consumption of film music is the fact that the market for music independent of a film is far smaller than the market for films. *Made in India* (1995), the superhit pop album by Alisha, for instance, sold "only" 1.5 million cassettes.[59] All Jagjit Singh's *ghazal* albums reliably sold around four or five hundred thousand cassettes.[60] These albums are thought of as highly successful, yet they sold only about as much as a flop film album would have at that time. Before the release of the film, film songs are limited to a "music-only" market, although the expectations of the coming film, its stars, and so on help expand its scope slightly. However, as the film is released, the film songs become a full-fledged part of the film rather than just an audio phenomenon, albeit one buttressed by images or expectations from the film. In this way, they access the immense market of Hindi films. If the film is a flop, neither the film nor the film songs achieve the full potential of this market, as few people see the film. Furthermore, a bad film can put people off the music. However, if the film is a hit, the songs ride on this success, reaching far into the vast market of Hindi films.

To call film songs "Indian popular music" is somewhat misleading, particularly in the context of the understanding of pop music in the West.[61] It must be emphasized that the audiovisual relationship of film songs and nonfilm pop songs (Indian and Western) is fundamentally different: film songs are always written around a narrative and come into being in a dramatic and visual context, whereas pop songs are written first and the video that often follows might have a mininarrative but is not a stand-alone item. In India, the nonfilm, "music-alone" market itself has only been able to achieve the amount of reach it has done due to television, which made it possible to produce songs with a visual component (pop songs, *ghazals,* and other genres) through the addition of videos, which can then be presented alongside film songs and can begin to compete with them.

The Profitability of Film Songs in the Cassette Era

The profitability of film songs has changed dramatically as a result of the cassette revolution and professional marketing. Polydor had begun paying producers money up front for their audio rights in the 1970s, but this was adjusted against royalties. T-Series, however, the most important new cassette company, started paying producers for rights, and as Mukesh Desai said (before the crash in 2000):

> slowly the producers have realized the price which audio rights could get, and slowly from peanuts of 20,000 and 25,000 and 50,000 royalties, prices have today gone up to [tens of millions], [20 million], [30 million], [50 million], [70 million], you keep hearing.[62]

Prices escalated wildly till the crash in 2000. Ramesh Taurani of TIPS stated in March 2000, just before the crash, that TIPS bought film audios for anything from ten to hundred million rupees and a producer was rumored, in the peak of the boom, to have been offered hundred and fifty million rupees.[63] While it must be emphasized that these are not official figures, they give a sense of the level the sale of film music rights reached. Although most payment is up front, royalties have not totally disappeared. HMV still offers producers royalties of approximately 10 percent, but this is adjusted against the up-front payment and kicks in after the break-even point.

In the gramophone era, when songs were mostly sold after the release of the film, HMV had a good idea what the market demand for a particular song would be from the response to the film and the song's success on radio shows like *Binaca Geetmala*. The producer would get paid in exact proportion to sales. In the cassette era, however, computing the price of audio rights is far more speculative. The price is negotiated and paid on the anticipation that the film will be a hit, making this a risky business.[64] Furthermore, film music is the only type of recorded music that is not produced by the music company itself. As Harish Dayani said, "it is film music where we pay the maximum amount of money and have no control on music, whereas in all other areas we have total control on the music."[65]

How does the music company then ensure that it stays in business? Because the commercial potential of music is aligned so closely to the success of the film, price is set by the estimated quality and projected success of the film rather than the estimated quality of the music alone. Thus, more value is ascribed to the track record of the film's producer, director, and star cast than to the music director, lyricist, or singers, although these latter figures are important. Hence, the audio rights of albums by the same music director can sell for vastly differing amounts. Ramesh Taurani explained:

> I don't go by music director . . . see, Rahman was there in *Thakshak* also, but you know, I won't tell you the price, but what rate *Thakshak* has sold the audio rights, four times more *Taal* has sold. Then Rahman is there in both the films. So that doesn't make any difference.[66]

The prices paid for the *Taal* (Rhythm, Subash Ghai, 2000) versus the *Thakshak* (Snake, Govind Nihalini, 1999) audios were justified, as *Taal* had vast audio sales and would have been very profitable and *Thakshak* was commercially a flop, and the audio company probably did not do much better than break even at best.

The film producer oversees the making of the entire film and is ultimately responsible for its success or failure, hence the emphasis given to the producer's track record in the pricing of the audio rights. The director is responsible for the artistic side of the making of the film, and also, in association with the choreographer and art director, the picturizations of the film songs. As explained above, directors also play very active roles in the actual composition of the music, guiding the music director with the proposed song situations and making many suggestions. In film music, therefore, it is not just a matter of the music director being talented; what is more important is that the director should know how to "extract" their talent.[67] An established producer can take a new music director and get a decent price for the audio, but the converse is not true.[68] The star cast, and in particular the hero, because the Indian film industry is a hero-dominated one, is also an important factor. For example, in June 1999, Harish Dayani stated that if Shahrukh Khan is in the film, then the audio "becomes [30 million or 35 million rupees], if it is Salman, probably a little less, if it is Akshay Kumar then it is [10 million rupees], it depends."[69] The music company will also look at the entire team involved in the film. If a given producer, director, music director, or star cast have previously worked well together in the past, this adds value by increasing the odds of a future hit.

The importance of the music director, lyricist, and singers relative to that of the producer, director, and star cast, and also art director and choreographer, has been further reduced in recent years because of the increased visual consumption of film songs. Mukesh Desai explained:

> See, earlier, melody or good music, people used to hear music. They used to hear music and judge for themselves. Today things are different. . . . the normal general public . . . are all hooked to the television, . . . the promotional things which is shown on the TV, people see that, and they see the face value, "Oh it's Shahrukh, oh that movement is good, the girl is good, OK, we'll buy the audio."[70]

In India, the star status of playback singers is on the whole far less than that of the heroes and heroines, and also the nature of their stardom is very different, and largely unglamorous.[71] While this is not a new phenomenon, because film songs have always been visually and dramatically conceived and consumed, the television era heightens the role of spectacle in song picturizations, including stunning locations, glamorous clothes, and elaborate choreography. Although the music company aims to recover costs by sound track sales prior to release, in order to make a good profit,[72] the film needs to be successful.[73] In the present depressed music market, however, there is more the hope just to break even with a successful film.

2000 and Beyond: From Boom to Bust

While new trends in the Indian music industry are ongoing, there has been a significant crash in the last few years and a definite divide between the pre- and post-2000 industry in terms of sales volume and profitability for producers and music companies alike. Film producers may be offered anything from nothing to thirty million rupees for film audios, compared with ten million minimum to hundred or even, allegedly, hundred and fifty million pre-2000. The crash might be seen as a corrective to the bubble in the film audio market caused by price escalation during the long boom and fierce competition between music companies of the 1990s, and prices may recover to some extent. However, there has been a large drop in sales volumes, with the post-2000 market standing at around 30–40 percent of the pre-2000 market. A significant factor has been the increase in music piracy, in particular illegal downloads from the Internet using MP3. However, increase in audiovisual consumption has also been cited, leading to a dwindling number of consumers who want to buy audio-only products, that is, film song sound tracks on cassette or CD.[74] Ironically, the television-led audiovisual era that was so key to the boom in film music through its tapping of film music's audiovisual nature has played a role in its downfall, ultimately leaving the audio-only product behind. Box office returns and sales of film products have not suffered such a setback. One way in which music companies are now trying to combat disappointing sales is through selling music on DVD, purchasing visual as well as audio rights from the film producers, and attempting to catch up with the new listening habits.

The crash appears also to be fueling the trend to media conglomeration with which the audiovisual era began. We are seeing music companies diversify extensively: Saregama is now moving into film production, home video (marketing Warner Brothers, Universal, and BBC films in India), and theatrical distribution as well as music DVDs. Ringtones have also become an important income stream for music companies and film producers. The low prices that music companies are offering film producers is also leading big film producers to open in-house music companies; Yash Raj Films recently launched Yash Raj Music to market and distribute the audio for *Veer-Zaara* (Yash Chopra, 2004) after being offered a disappointing price for it from music companies. Yash Raj also cited a lack of enthusiasm to market film music effectively as a reason to create an in-house company, as music companies scrimp and save on marketing budgets amid low profit margins, which further contributes to low sales.[75] The basic pattern for the marketing of music, however, has remained the same.

Although songs have always been vital to the success of Hindi films, it took some five or six decades for their potential to be realized in commercial terms; although the market has taken a hard knock since 2000, film songs still have a commercial value now that they did not have in the gramophone era. The key factors have been the expansion of the music market, first through the increase in the pressing capacity of gramophone records and then far more significantly through the advent of cassette technology, the increased competition in the music industry, itself very much a result of the advent of cassette technology, and the spread of television in the early 1990s.

While film songs have become more important in commercial terms, they have done so within a symbiotic relationship with films. In commercial terms, film songs and films are two sides of the same coin. The film has remained the stronger partner, even through the music boom from the late 1980s to 2000. The dependency of the ultimate success of film songs on the success of the parent film is something that has changed little over the seven decades of Hindi sound film. Film songs have commercial power, but only when coupled with a Hindi film. This symbiotic relationship of films and film songs is reflected in the increasing corporate conglomeration of different media in the Indian entertainment industry, where "tapping the synergy between the film and television media is the key to the long-term viability of both" in the opinion of industry experts.[76] While the future shape of film music as a commercial product is at present uncertain, the ability of film songs to survive and adapt to a constantly changing media environment does still appear to center around their multimedia, audiovisual nature, and interdependence with the cinema.

Notes

This essay is based largely on chapter 5 of my book *Hindi Film Songs and the Cinema*, SOAS Musicology Series (London: Ashgate, 2008). I am grateful to the editors of this volume, Sangita Gopal and Sujata Moorti, for their many insightful comments.

82 | ANNA MORCOM

1 Rachel Dwyer, *All You Want Is Money, All You Need Is Love: Sex and Romance in Modern India* (London and New York: Cassell, 2000), 96.

2 Peter Manuel discusses film music in the context of the emergence of new forms of popular, recorded music in India following the advent of cassettes, *Cassette Culture: Popular Music and Technology in North India* (Chicago: University of Chicago Press, 1993). See also Ashok Mittal, *Cinema Industry in India: Pricing and Taxation* (New Delhi: Indus Pub. Co., 1995). There is no study I am aware of that focuses on the commercial life of film songs.

3 The first recordings were made in 1902. See Gerry Farrell, "The Early Days of the Gramophone Industry in India: Historical, Social and Musical Perspectives," *British Journal of Ethnomusicology* 2 (1993): 31–53; Manuel, *Cassette Culture*, 39.

4 See Alison Arnold, "Hindi Film Git: On the History of Indian Popular Music" (PhD diss., University of Illinois at Urbana-Champaign, 1991), 114–19; and V. K. Doobey, vice president of A & R at HMV from the 1950s to around 1995/6, interview, March 11, 2000.

5 Interview, March 6, 2000; Joshi cites 1934 in his "A Concise History of the Phonograph Industry in India," *Popular Music* 7, no. 2 (1988): 147–56, 150.

6 Arnold, "Hindi Film Git," 115; and Michael Kinnear cites an estimate of a total of around five hundred thousand 78 rpm records issued by HMV, The Gramophone Company, India, and around thirty thousand titles by competitor companies. The 78 rpm record continued up till 1970 according to "Sound Recording in India: A Brief History," 2003, http://www.bajakhana.com.au/Sound-rec-Ind-3D.htm (accessed June 2000).

7 Manuel, *Cassette Culture*, 38.

8 Doobey, interview.

9 See Anupama Chopra, *Sholay: The Making of a Classic* (New Delhi: Penguin Books, 2000), 52.

10 Doobey, interview.

11 Interview, June 30, 1999.

12 Manuel, *Cassette Culture*, 39.

13 Doobey, interview.

14 Lisa Goyhil, Universal Music, UK, personal communication (Polydor is now owned by the Universal Music Group).

15 In chapter 6 of *Hindi Film Songs and the Cinema*, I undertake a preliminary study of the popularity of film songs—as opposed to their commercial success—relative to the success of the parent film on the basis of countdown charts from three Web sites and the *Binaca Geetmala* yearly top twenty charts from 1953 to 1982.

16 Arnold, "Hindi Filmi Git," 116.

17 Interview, June 30, 1999.

18 Doobey, interview.

19 This is discussed in more detail in the section on marketing of film songs in the cassette era in this chapter.

20 See Chapters by Biswarup Sen and Mehta/Bhattacharjya for more on how the state attempted to control Hindi film song.

21 Interview, April 14, 1999.
22 Ibid.
23 Chopra, *Sholay,* 51.
24 Interview, June 30, 1999.
25 Sehdev Ghei, distributor for Yash Raj Films, interview, June 9, 1999; and Mukesh Desai, chief executive of the music company T-Series, interview, March 7, 2000.
26 Ibid.
27 Manuel, *Cassette Culture*, 62.
28 Ibid., 3–4.
29 Ibid., 63. Film music has remained at a steady 70 percent for HMV (now Saregama) releases and has climbed from 50 percent to 70 percent for Polydor (now Universal) releases since the advent of cassettes.
30 Doobey, interview; and Sanjeev Kohli, chief executive officer of Yash Raj Films and former employee of HMV, interview, June 28, 1999.
31 Desai, interview, March 7, 2000.
32 Kulmeet Makkar, vice president of sales and marketing, Saregama, interview, January 25, 2005.
33 Ibid. The International Telecommunication Union cites 16.6 million Internet users in India in 2002, 159 per 10,000 of the population, compared with 159 million in the United States, 5,514 per 10,000 of the population (http://www.itu.int/ITU-D/ict/statistics/at_glance/Internet02.pdf).
34 To contrast with the way film song is marketed internationally, see Bhattacharjya and Mehta
35 Interview, June 15, 1999.
36 Rachel Dwyer, *Yash Chopra* (London: British Film Institute, 2002), 107.
37 Ashish Rajadhyaksha and Paul Willemen, eds., *Encyclopaedia of Indian Cinema, New Revised Edition* (London: British Film Institute; New Delhi: Oxford University Press, 1999), 92.
38 Dwyer, *Yash Chopra*, 108.
39 Interview, June 15, 1999.
40 Ibid.
41 *Screen,* April 13, 2001.
42 Avtar Panesar of Yash Raj Films, UK, interview, August 20, 2001.
43 Ibid.
44 Sometimes only montages from the film are used, with the actual song picturization completely absent from the "teasers" and trailers, thereby "whetting the audience's appetite to see the song in its entirety" and drawing them to cinema halls, a ploy used by Rajkumar Barjatya for the promotion of *Hum Aapke Hain Koun . . .!* (Who am I to you) in 1994 and also by Yash Raj for *Dil To Pagal Hai* (The heart is foolish) in 1997; Dwyer, *Yash Chopra,* 177.
45 Desai, interview, March 7, 2000. The question of which emotions are deemed most suitable for songs in Hindi films is explored in my "An Understanding between Hollywood and Bollywood? The Meaning of Hollywood-Style Music in Hindi Films," *British Journal of Ethnomusicology* 10, no. 1 (2001/02): 63–84.

46 Panesar, interview.
47 Ramesh Taurani, owner of the music company TIPS, interview, March 31, 2000.
48 Desai, interview, March 7, 2000.
49 Ibid.
50 Taurani, interview.
51 The highly popular music director of this film, R. D. Burman, died before the release of this film, which may have also helped the music sales.
52 Dayani, interview, June 15, 1999.
53 In commercial terms, music very rarely is a hit if the film is a flop, but individual songs may achieve considerable popularity regardless of the film. See note 10 above.
54 Barjatya, interview, June 30, 1999; and Dayani, interview, June 15, 1999.
55 Interview, March 3, 2000.
56 See Nicholas Cook, *Analysing Musical Multimedia* (Oxford: Clarendon Press, 1998), 105.
57 Utpal Biswas, music director, interview, March 3, 2000.
58 The production process of film songs and the balancing of narrative demands and audio value in songs are described in my forthcoming article "'A Musical Screenplay': Narrative and Hindi Film Song Composition." See also my "The Visual and Dramatic Dimensions of Hindi Film Songs," *International Institute for Asian Studies Newsletter* 26 (2001), for a brief description of the situational, multimedia nature of film songs, and chapter 3 of *Hindi Film Songs and the Cinema* for a more detailed analysis of cinematic components of film song style.
59 Kohli, interview, June 28, 1999.
60 Dayani, interview, June 15, 1999.
61 For a different account see Biswarup Sen's essay in this volume.
62 Interview, March 7, 2000. See Manuel, *Cassette Culture,* 67–69, for a discussion of the role of T-Series in the cassette revolution.
63 Interview, March 31, 2000.
64 Desai, interview, June 15, 1999; and Dayani, interview, March 7, 2000.
65 Interview, June 15, 1999.
66 Interview, March 31, 2000.
67 Ghei, interview.
68 Desai, interview, March 7, 2000.
69 Interview, June 31, 1999.
70 Desai, interview, March 7, 2000.
71 See Manuel, *Cassette Culture,* 48. Neepa Majumdar discusses this albeit unglamorized "aural stardom" of Hindi playback singers in "The Embodied Voice: Song Sequences and Stardom in Popular Hindi Cinema," in *Soundtrack Available: Essays on Film and Popular Music* (Durham, N.C.: Duke University Press, 2001), 171–78.
72 Taurani, interview.
73 Dayani, interview, June 15, 1999; and Desai, interview, March 7, 2000.
74 Makkar, interview.
75 Kohli, interview, January 27, 2005.
76 Shedde, *Times of India,* June 20, 2001.

2. The Sounds of Modernity

The Evolution of Bollywood Film Song

Biswarup Sen

Popular music in the Indian subcontinent is unique because it consists almost completely of *filmigit,* that is, songs originally featured in the movies. This equivalence serves as a basis for this present essay; in what follows, I propose to trace the history of popular music as it evolved within the context of Bollywood film and to examine the role that this music has played in delineating the contours of colonial and postcolonial modernity. Such an inquiry confirms *filmigit*'s centrality as a constitutive site of the popular and brings to light its capacity for constantly reinventing itself in response to the demands of the contemporary. This achievement, I argue, is made possible by the very nature of the music. Bollywood song is the product of a practice that has been characterized by a radical openness to externalities and a consistent engagement with cultural production elsewhere. This strategy has led to the creation of an astonishingly rich and vibrant art whose aesthetic force derives from its radically heterogeneous nature. Incorporating musical styles from the world over, *filmigit* possesses a structure of feeling that is emphatically transnational. Bollywood song, along with Bollywood film, is thus an art form that not only functions as an expression of Indian modernity but at the same time exceeds the limits of the nation-state and contributes to the making of global culture.

Indian popular music entered the modern era in the early years of the twentieth century with the arrival of gramophone technology. The impetus behind these early recordings was the growing awareness, on the part of colonial entrepreneurs, that the market for Indian recorded music was likely to be very profitable. Thus, John Watson Hawd, the Gramophone and Typewriter Company's agent in Calcutta (now known as Kolkata), wrote frantically to his superiors in London on the

85

advantages of entering the recording business in India, even while asserting that "The native music is to me worse than Turkish but as long as it suits them and sells well what do we care."[1] The Company responded to Watson's pleas and the very first commercial recordings of Indian music were made on November 8, 1902, under the supervision of Fred Gaisberg, a seasoned veteran who had already conducted similar recording trips in Germany, Hungary, Spain, Italy, and Russia. This historic session utilized the services of two *nautch* girls named Soshi Mukhi and Fani Bala and included bits from the popular theater shows of the time. In spite of his considerable exposure to different modes of music making, Gaisberg turned out to be no more enlightened than his colleague at the gramophone company. He was self-reflexive enough to observe

> We entered a new world of musical and artistic values. One had to erase all memories of the music of European opera houses and concert halls: the very foundation of my musical training was undermined

He nonetheless could not refrain from voicing his disapproval of Indian music at large:

> Our first visit was to a native "Classic Theatre" . . . quite arbitrarily there was introduced a chorus of young *nautch* girls heavily bleached with rice powder and dressed in transparent gauze. They sang "And Her Golden Hair Was Hanging Down Her Back" accompanied by fourteen brass instruments all playing in unison. I had yet to learn that the oriental ear was unappreciative of chords and harmonic treatment and only demanded the rhythmic beat of the accompaniment of the drums. At this point we left.[2]

Gaisberg's reaction typifies the condescension with which colonial discourse treated objects of native culture, but what is of greater interest in the present context is his deafness to what was really at stake. Constrained by certain fixed notions of culture and musical performance, Gaisberg remained unaware that he was privy to a special moment. The "*nautch*" that he so derides is in fact far more than an unwieldy concoction of sounds, consisting as it did of classical narrative interrupted by gaudily-dressed chorus girls, of Indian voices accompanied by brass instruments, and of English lyrics sung to a "rhythmic beat"; it must be read instead as a daring attempt to fuse the disparate and the contrary into a new synthesis. What Gaisberg hears as a clumsy and somewhat embarrassing rendition of an English vaudeville number[3] is, in fact, a paradigmatic event that would serve as a template for the future.

Indian popular song has, over the decades, remained as hybrid and heterogeneous as those first recordings overseen by Gaisberg. This is made abundantly clear by the recent fracas surrounding the work of music director[4] Bappi Lahiri. As is common knowledge, Lahiri became a cause célèbre when a lawyer on his behalf filed suit in a Los Angeles court seeking to halt sales of *Truthfully Speaking*, a rhythm and blues album recorded by the band Truth Hurts. The suit, which named the famous hip-hop producer Dr. Dre as a defendant, claimed that one of the tracks on the album—the top-ten hit "Addictive"—had lifted four minutes of a tune composed by Lahiri without prior permission.[5] The situation here was full of irony, for the alleged victim of plagiarism in this case had enjoyed a notorious reputation as a "master plagiarist" himself. Summing up Lahiri's career, a columnist on the Web site musicindiaonline said:

> In the '80s, Bappi's fortunes took a turn for the better, albeit with the help of straight lifts like "*Hari Om Hari*" (*Pyaara Dushmun*), "*Mere jaisi haseena ka dil*" (*Armaan*) and disco numbers like "*Rambha ho*" (*Armaan*), "*Disco station*" (*Hathkadi*) and "I am a disco dancer" and "*Koi yahan naache naache*" (*Disco Dancer*). Known as the Disco King at his peak, the poor man is generally considered the Master Plagiarist.[6]

Such a characterization was undoubtedly a response to the fact that these "lifts" were blatant and easily identifiable—thus it is widely held that "Hari Om Hari" ("Lord O Lord" from *Pyara Dushman*, A lovable enemy, Sagar, 1980), for example, was an exact copy of "One way ticket" by Eruption, and that "Koi yahan naache naache" ("Someone dances here" from *Disco Dancer*, Subhash, 1982) was directly lifted from the Buggles's historic song "Video killed the radio star." Many other commentators have shared this take on Lahiri. Thus, Peter Manuel, author of the influential work *Cassette Culture*, notes that "The amount of plagiarization within film music has greatly increased since the early 1980s . . . by far the leading offender, and the primary butt of criticism, has been film-music director Bappi Lahiri."[7] These damning charges have, however, had little effect on Lahiri himself. Reminded by an interviewer that he was equally guilty of "stealing," the composer defended his acts of appropriation:

> I have lifted tunes occasionally—just like any other Indian director. But I haven't stolen an original piece and made a video out of it. For, this constitutes an infringement of copyright. Even SD Burman, RD Burman, Shankar-Jaikishen and Laxmikant-Pyarelal have lifted tunes

from the Beatles, Tequila and others. The trend was set even before I was born. So, it is unfair to accuse me. Anyway, we don't have any original composers today. Music directors ape RD Burman and me.[8]

The enormous success that Lahiri has enjoyed suggests that the listening public at large has been equally unconcerned by questions concerning artistic originality. Producers were clearly undeterred by his reputation; his services were so much in demand that he wrote One hundred and eighty songs in one calendar year, getting his name included in *The Guinness Book of World Records* in the process. His work has elicited a passionate following all over the globe: Arthur Mullokondov, a young Uzbek man, knows every single Lahiri composition by heart;[9] the score he wrote for *Disco Dancer* received China's Gold Award for music; and he is a legendary and inspiring figure for diasporic Indians. DJ Rekha, organizer of the cultish Bollywood Disco night in Manhattan, writes

> I always wanted to do a night focused on filmi music, but it wasn't till last spring that the words Bollywood Disco popped into my head. It all made sense. The music of Bollywood that I was most in love was the disco sounds I grew up on—Helen, Qurbani, Amitabh and of course Bappi Lahiri.[10]

The sentiments expressed by these fans make superfluous the doubts regarding Lahiri's artistic integrity and ought, instead, to stimulate us into thinking along different lines. Lahiri's extraordinary popularity suggests that much like Soshi Mukhi and Fani Bala, he signifies the entire tradition of Indian popular music. To encounter *Disco Dancer* or *nautch* music is to touch upon a node in a vast network of inflows and outflows where west meets east, classical fuses with the popular, and folk becomes mass. Such a juncture represents a musical entity that has no specific geographic location or historical origin and connotes a musical practice that is shamelessly promiscuous in its borrowings, nonchalant in the way it combines forms, unconstrained by rule or dogma, and exuberant in the multiplicity of its productions. It is to this truth that Lahiri points to when he asserts that "The trend [of lifting tunes] was set even before I was born."[11] "Bappi-nautch" points to the world of music created by composers such as Pankaj Mullick, O. P. Nayyar, Shankar-Jaikishen, R. D. Burman, Biddu, A. R. Rahman, and Bally Sagoo and by singers such as K. L. Saigal, Mohammed Rafi, Geeta Dutt, Lata Mangeshkar, Kishore Kumar, Alisha, and Apache Indian.[12]

To adopt "Bappi-nautch" as a trope for Bollywood *filmigit* has crucial methodological consequences in that it argues for a notion of the popular quite different from that used in traditional accounts. Most theories of cultural production have worked with a two-tiered model: aristocratic or "high" culture at the top and mass or popular culture at the bottom. Whatever the political implications of such a diagram—some see the popular as the primary site of capitalist manipulation, others think of it as a repository of revolutionary action—the popular is in either case sharply distinguished from high cultural forms and thought of as a distinct domain of cultural practice. It is my claim that such a "vertical" model is quite inappropriate for the purposes of understanding popular music in India, as well as explaining its spread at the global level. As "Bappi-nautch" would suggest, it is far more useful to think of Indian popular music as constituted by lines of "horizontality": export and import, imitation and emendation, sampling and remixing, Hindu and Muslim, desi and *firangi,* and durbar and *tamasha.* Such a recipe, we shall see, finds its most perfect expression in the case of Bollywood film music.

The field of contemporary Indian music can be said to consist of three major genres—Bollywood, classical, and folk. The two latter traditions have played a major role in the making of film music—one need only to think of a song like "Chalte chalte" ("As I journeyed" from *Pakeezah,* Pure heart, Amrohi, 1971) or "Chaiyya chaiyya" ("Shake it" from *Dil Se,* From the heart, Ratnam, 1998) to realize their importance as sources of style and inspiration. However, they are not constitutive of the popular; neither tradition, in its current incarnation, is capable of the play with otherness and difference so crucial to modernity and its expressions.[13] That is why, as the history of modern Indian music demonstrates, both these forms lost the battle for the heart of the masses in spite of sustained efforts to popularize them. The origins of what is now termed "classical music" can be traced back to Amir Khusrau (1253–1325), supposedly the inventor of the sitar, and perhaps to an even earlier era of Hindu temple singing. In more recent times, classical music became institutionalized through the *gharanas* and was largely supported by the rulers of princely states such as Gwalior, Indore, Mysore, and Patiala. The princely states were abolished soon after independence, and the role of patronage passed on to the central and various state governments. Over the course of the twentieth century, the practice of classical music became synonymous with "high" culture: concerts were typically staged at the most prestigious venues, its performers were feted with the highest level of governmental awards for the arts, and the form gained international recognition and respect through the efforts of figures such as Ravi Shankar and Yehudi Menuhin.

Given its reputation, it is not surprising that classical music would become one of the main pillars of official postcolonial culture. The Indian government that came into being after 1947 saw itself as an arbiter of popular taste; part of its self-proclaimed mission was to create a healthier and "higher" national culture by exposing the masses to the treasures of the country's cultural heritage. The country's geographical vastness and its large illiterate population made radio the most obvious medium for this project. As Dr. Balkrishna Vishwanath Keskar, the minister of information and broadcasting in the early postindependence years put it:

> The object is to encourage the revival of our traditional music, classical and folk. The Radio is fulfilling that task for the nation and I can say with satisfaction, that it has become the greatest patron of Indian music and musicians, greater than all the princely and munificent patronage of former days.[14]

Keskar's enthusiasm for classical music was accompanied by a condescending and dismissive attitude toward film music, which, according to him, appealed to no one "except for raw and immature people like children and adolescents."[15] Under his tutelage, the All India Radio (AIR) developed a list of seven thousand "approved" classical artists, and he saw to it that classical music comprised fully half of all the music broadcast on national radio. Keskar, however, was not destined to win the culture wars. Unable to digest the AIR's stern diet, the listening public defected to Radio Ceylon, a commercial radio station whose broadcasting policy was far more in tune with consumer demand. In the end, the government bowed down to popular taste and set up a new channel designed to disseminate "popular music and light entertainment." Started in 1957, Vivid Bharati would soon become the nation's most popular radio channel, bringing to an end Radio Ceylon's brief but significant period of broadcasting glory. This episode in broadcasting history demonstrated the limits to imposing culture "from above." Keskar's vision was fundamentally flawed in that it did not foresee the impracticality of using a nineteenth-century musical form as the vehicle of modernity, and, as it turned out, no amount of governmental patronage could enable classical music to become truly popular music. Folk music would have a similar fate, though for a very different set of reasons. Like its more prestigious counterpart, folk music too played a significant part in the evolution of modern Indian music. It is widely acknowledged, for example, that the music of the Bauls[16] was a deep source of inspiration for Bengal's most famous songwriter. Tagore would incorporate so many Baul themes in his compositions that a literary scholar would describe him as "the greatest of the Bauls."[17] We could read Tagore's use of Baul material as an opportunistic act of appropriation; he was, after all, a *bhadralok* from Calcutta whose only contact with the "folk" was in the capacity of administrator for his family's extensive estates in East Bengal. But, it could be also argued that by "lifting" Baul tunes in the manner that he did, Tagore was implicitly making the point that this music, magnificent in its own context, was too far removed from modern concerns to be truly popular and could find a wider audience only when repackaged as *Rabindrasangeet*.[18] In other words, folk music may be too intimately connected with the context of its production to be able to function as a popular art form. This is demonstrated, somewhat unwittingly, in Edward O. Henry's exhaustive field study of Bhojpuri music.[19] The genres he describes are all intimately connected to specific life practices—thus, *sohars* are sung exclusively by women when a boy is born, whereas *khari biraha* (field hollers) are sung exclusively by men of the cow-herding and sheep-herding castes. But folk song proves inadequate in the face of modernization. As Henry dispassionately observes:

> The All-India Radio station in Varanasi transmits a considerable amount of music including classical Hindustani, folk and popular music. Popular music, *consisting largely of film songs,* is enjoyed more by the younger people. Young men sing snatches of it to each other on their evening rambles around their village, and boys and girls alike make up their own verses to film song tunes.[20]

Popular culture cannot, it seems, arise out of local forms; it requires the universalizing import of Hindi film songs. And though, according to some detractors, that music is "a curious and somewhat bizarre blend of East and West,"[21] which "is not so much Indian as a form of commercial hybridization from various sources,"[22] it is to *filmigit* we must turn to in order to understand the role of music in modern India.

As is well known, with the introduction of sound, songs became an integral part of Hindi filmmaking. In the studio era (roughly the 1930s through the 1940s), Hindi film music directors—as well as actors, directors, and technical crew—were exclusively contracted to particular employers. Thus, New Theatres used Raichand Boral, Timir Boran, and Pankaj Mullick; Prabhat employed Govindrao Tembe, Keshavrao Bhole, and Master Krishnarao; and Bombay Talkies relied almost exclusively on Saraswati Devi. The music composed by these resident directors tended initially to be derivative of older forms: songs were usually composed in the light classical *ghazal* form; they often used the standard *dadra* meter; and they were usually accompanied by instruments such as the tabla, the tanpura, and the harmonium. The Bombay studios tended to be more conservative in the matter of musical taste mainly because their musical directors had a more classical bent. Saraswati Devi,[23] for example, had trained under Pandit Vishnunarayan Bhatkhande and took great pains to ensure that every musician who worked for her had mastered at least one traditional instrument. Consequently, most of the work she did for Bombay Talkies was very classical-influenced. The Prabhat trio—Tembe, Bhole, and Krishnarao—was also similarly inclined, though their music also showed the influence of Marathi folk music and Urdu *ghazals* and *qawalis*. New Theatres would produce its share of classical-based songs—K. L. Saigal's *thumri* "Babul mora naihar chuttal jaye" (from *Street Singer,* Majumdar, 1938) was a national hit—but the studio also promoted an environment for musical experimentation that involved an engagement between eastern and western traditions. Musicians from Calcutta were responsible for most of the innovations that would give Hindi film music its distinctive identity. Pankaj Mullick used Tagore's western-influenced compositions in his film scores and incorporated the vibrato, a western vocal technique, into his songs. Raichand Boral brought western instruments such as the organ and the piano into the film orchestra and was also responsible for introducing new musical techniques—his score for the film *Vidyapati* (Bose, 1937) is the very first instance of the use of chords and of western harmonic principles. The fertile interplay between different musical practices enabled New Theatres to create a uniquely modern sound that musicians elsewhere were unable to duplicate. The studio's personnel were fully aware of this distinction—when music director Anil Biswas moved from Calcutta to Bombay (now known as Mumbai), he was afraid he would be unable to find accompanists familiar with western instrumentation and so took with him four musicians who were proficient in the cello, the piano, and the Spanish and Hawaiian guitars.[24]

There was thus, in the decades of the 1930s and 1940s, an "invasion" of indigenous Indian music by western-influenced Bengali music making. As a recent chronicler of early Indian film music observes:

> Boral, the man who experimented with music forms and orchestration and made wonderful music, laid the foundations for the next batch of composers. Calcutta was a happening place in the 30's. And to give meaning and depth to Boral's talent and pioneering efforts, conditions in the city were just right: a refined and permissive New Theatres boss is B. N. Sircar, state-of-the-art recording studios and equipment, singers like Saigal, Kanan Devi, Pankaj Mullick, K. C. Dey and Pahadi Sanyal . . . there were also other great composers in Calcutta at that time: Pankaj Mullick again, Kamal Dasgupta, Timir Baran & Asit Baran, and many more. This combined with a discerning and cultured population made the whole effort a great success.[25]

The material and cultural conditions in Bengal made it an ideal place for the creation of modern Indian song. The music of the North Indian heartland was a little too traditional to appeal to a rapidly modernizing population; in the words of one writer, "the only music available to the masses was either the devotional music of *kathas, kirtans* and *bhajans* or the quawwalis, mushairas, or shennnais."[26] That explains why music from Calcutta proved so irresistible to listeners across the nation and why other regions quickly adopted the stylistic innovations first introduced at New Theatres. Thus, the softer style of singing for the microphone developed in America by singers such as Whispering Jack Smith and Bing Crosby was made popular by K. L. Saigal and soon became standard practice; orchestras expanded considerably to include western instruments such as violins, violas, cellos, pianos, organs, and drums; and the dramatic throaty style practiced by women vocalists coming out of a culture of mehfils and *nautch* singing gave way to a narrower, more restrained vocal style developed first by Nurjahan[27] and perfected then by Lata Mangeshkar.

In her illuminating study of Hindi film songs, Alison Arnold posits that the years 1931–1955 marked a dynamic and revolutionary period in the historical development of the Hindi film song. In this period, music directors worked creatively toward establishing an identifiable art form, which became national in character. According to Arnold, this

Three pioneers of modern sound and dance: Asha Bhosle, Helen, and
R. D. Burman. Courtesy of Saregama.

goal was largely met by 1955; since then, the Hindi film song, she
claims, has remained fundamentally unchanged. There is certainly
much substance to this point of view. As we saw earlier, many of the
stylistic features associated with the present-day Hindi song were
already in place several decades ago. Many of the major playback singers
of the postindependence period—Manna Dey, Hemant Kumar, Talat
Mahmood, Mohammed Rafi, Mukesh, Kishore Kumar, Geeta Dutt,
Lata Mangeshkar, and Asha Bhosle—had all started recording as
early as the 1940s, while composers such as Naushad, O. P. Nayyar,
S. D. Burman, and Shankar-Jaikishen had all established themselves
by the mid-1950s. However, to argue that Hindi film music reached
its zenith by the end of the 1950s is to overlook the enormous impact
that the music of the late 1960s and 1970s would have had on the culture as a whole.[28] Anyone conversant with this period will know that

songs such as "Roop tera mastana" ("Your beauty is intoxicating" from *Aradhana,* Worship, Samanta, 1969), "Mera samne waali kirki me" ("At the window across from mine" from *Padosan,* Neighbor, Swaroop, 1968), "Dum maro dum" ("Take a hit" from *Hare Rama Hare Krishna,* Hail Rama Hail Krishna, Anand, 1971), and "Yaadon ki baraat" ("The procession of memories" from *Yaadon Ki Baraat*, Hussain, 1973) had an impact well beyond that of the typical hit number. These songs proposed radically new versions of pleasure, sexuality, and desire: they celebrated the body by invoking new styles of movement, liberated the voice from the constraints of formal singing, and brought into play an accelerated notion of being. In short, they redefined the meaning of modernity. The "second revolution"[29] in Hindi film song is invariably linked with the names of Kishore Kumar and Rahul Dev Burman. This remarkable duo not only set the standards for a new generation of musicians, they also created what is arguably the most popular body of music to ever emerge from Bollywood film. The Kishore–RD[30] era is of enormous significance because it constituted a liminal moment in the history of *filmigit*—marking the end of the "golden age" and initiating a new paradigm of music making that is still in place today. The music of the golden age, as we have seen, emerged from a blending of western styles and traditional Indian forms. This synthesis, it can be argued, had reached its limits by the mid-1960s and was no longer adequate to the times.[31] The age required a different music, one that was faster, louder, and more direct. Such a sound could not emerge within the confines of a dominant style;[32] it required the agency of those unafraid to challenge and break with tradition. Both Kishore and RD would prove to be ideal candidates for this task. Born Abhas Kumar Ganguly into a professional Bengali family that lived in Khandwa, Madhya Pradesh, Kishore Kumar was the youngest of four children.[33] His oldest brother, Ashok Kumar, was an established film star by the time Kishore reached his teens; it was natural therefore that Kishore, an aspiring singer, would move to Bombay to pursue his career. Working initially for Saraswati Devi's chorus at Bombay Talkies, Kishore established himself singing solo playback for Dev Anand in the film *Ziddi* (Stubborn, Latif, 1948). The pairing was not entirely fortuitous—Kishore's voice was a perfect match for the cocky, light-hearted urban characters that Dev Anand helped to popularize. This association would last until Kishore's death, but in spite of hit songs in Dev Anand's movies and in films where Kishore himself played the hero,[34] "he could not make it to the top. Rafi was there and there were other great singers delivering excellent songs much of the time, like Mukesh, Talat, Manna Dey and Hemant."[35] Kishore's real breakthrough came in 1969 when, as columnist Siddhartha Dey observes, he

> took the giant leap when S. D. made him sing "Roop tera mastana" . . . and "Mere sapno ki rani" ("The queen of my dreams") in *Aradhana*. The whole nation was enthralled by his sensual vocals . . . after that, there was no looking back.[36]

That Kishore had to wait more than twenty years to become a superstar was not a matter of chance; he was, quite literally, far ahead of the times. Only when modernity had assumed a specific form could his voice begin to resonate with that of the "whole nation." It is somewhat of a mystery as to why Kishore would become a superstar so late in his career. The answer may lie, paradoxically, in what most would see as a serious lacuna in his musical education—of the male playback singers of his generation, Kishore was the only one who had received no instruction in classical music. Among his "competitors," Rafi[37] had trained under Bade Ghulam Ali Khan,[38] Manna Dey was trained by his uncle, the renowned K. C. Dey, and both Mukesh and Mahendra Kapoor were well versed in light classical music. Kishore, on the other hand, was entirely untutored, causing him to be often neglected by musical directors—songwriter Kalyanji's[39] comment that his skills lay more in "mimicry than in technique" was typical of the musical establishment's reaction to his singing style.[40] Yet it was precisely this lack of "skill" that proved to be Kishore's strongest selling point. Singers too well grounded in traditional music could, by the middle of the 1960s, no longer market their style of vocal delivery. To take the most obvious example, the great Mohammed Rafi, whose more classically inflected songs from the same period are masterpieces of execution,[41] proved insipid and inadequate when singing playback for Shammi Kapoor, who more than any other actor in the 1960s symbolized what it meant to be "modern."[42] Rafi's sedate and languid voice evoked an earlier world of courtly sophistication and never quite fit the accelerative images of modernity it was supposed to correspond to: the figure of Shammi Kapoor frenetically driving up the hills in *Kashmir Ki Kali* (Flower of Kashmir, Samanta, 1964) or gyrating madly to woo his lady love in *Junglee* (Beastly, Mukherjee, 1961). This failure signaled the end of an era in Indian music. As Manek Premchand dramatically observes:

> His voice soared high in the sky and his voice often took us up there to those dizzy heights. Thus, did the skylark's light soar high for some twenty years. Then when it eventually came down at the end of the 60s it was because trends had changed. After this he was no longer No. 1.[43]

The man who would inherit the title of "No. 1" was well equipped to give a voice to the changing times. As his brother Ashok Kumar perceptively observed, "Kishore's voice hits the mike, straight, at its most sensitive point—and that's the secret of his success as a singer without peer!"[44] It was precisely this raw directness and the up-tempo acceleration in his singing style that made Kishore Kumar, along with Rahul Dev Burman, the ultimate symbol of modernity. The classic songs in *Aradhana* were composed by S. D. Burman, but it would be Kishore's work with the latter's son that would guarantee his immortality.[45] RD had worked from a very early age as assistant to his father and had trained for a while under the classical maestro Ali Akbar Khan. Yet, like Kishore, he was not burdened by the dictates of tradition. As he observed about himself:

> I don't say I am a knowledgeable man when it comes to raags. I don't say I tried to do so and so song in Raag Darbar or attempted some difficult raag in another song. Whatever comes to my head I compose.[46]

This pragmatic attitude enabled him to make inspired decisions—experiment with combs and spoons for rhythm, utilize Bhupinder's guitar for classic numbers such as "Dum maro dum" and "Chura liya hai tumne" ("You have stolen me" from *Yadon Ki Baraat*), and introduce the electric organ in songs like "O haseena zulfe wali" ("Oh beauty with luscious hair" from *Teesri Manzil,* Third destination, Anand, 1966).[47] RD's weak bonds to the classical tradition thus enabled him to absorb the most disparate of influences and create an utterly contemporary sound. In the words of one commentator, "In many . . . ways, seen from the standpoint of Hindi cinema, he defined the music in the last third of the century."[48]

The work of two "untrained" musicians would usher in a new age in Indian popular song. The Kishore–RD sound—with its multicultural influences, its frenetic pacing, its youthful exuberance, and its upbeat rhythms—represented a complete rupture with the music of the "golden age." The revolution ushered in by Kishore and RD meant that henceforth *filmigit* would be far more influenced by developments in the global music scene. RD had redefined Indian song as a response to western pop and rock of the 1960s. By the end of the 1970s, however, disco had replaced rock as the cutting edge in international sound. Indian music directors were quick to respond to this new trend; Bappi Lahiri's *Disco Dancer,* released in 1982, was a smash hit that established him as one of the leading figures in the industry. Lahiri would come to be known as the Disco King, but that title may have rightfully belonged to Biddu, undoubtedly one of the more remarkable figures in the history of Indian popular music. Hailing from Bangalore, Biddu played in a Rolling Stones-influenced pop group before deciding to immigrate to Britain in the late 1960s.[49] While passing through Beirut, he happened to hear the Four Tops' hit song "Reach Out I'll Be There."[50] It was the first time he had ever heard black music, and it is a testament to Biddu's musical intelligence that he became an immediate convert to its rich beats and rhythms. After arriving in Britain, Biddu worked ordinary jobs—once as a chef at the American Embassy—and in time managed to save enough to rent studio time and release his first single. That record did not do much, nor did subsequent releases; most of them were produced by small labels and sold in the region of five thousand copies. In 1974, Biddu was looking for a singer to record a lush ballad called "I Want to Give You My Everything" written by Steve Weiss, the man who also wrote Glen Campbell's classic "Rhinestone Cowboy." Biddu recruited Carl Douglas, a transplanted Jamaican singer he had got acquainted with a year earlier. The Weiss song was intended to be the A side of the disc and Biddu asked Douglas if he had something to record on the B side. As Biddu recalls

> He rattled off about four to five songs . . . one had the lyrics for Kung Fu Fighting. Since it was going to be a B side I said 'Fine, we'll have a song called "Kung Fu Fighting."' So I started working out some melody for it. Nothing was taken very seriously . . . We put a lot of "hoos" and "haas!" like someone giving a karate chop.[51]

The public took the record very seriously indeed—"Kung Fu Fighting" topped the charts in both Britain and America, eventually selling an astonishing nine million copies. What followed was a remarkable saga of return. Approached by Feroze Khan to compose the score for *Qurbani* (Sacrifice, Khan, 1980), Biddu decided to try his hand at composing for

Hindi films and recruited a fifteen-year-old Pakistani girl Nazia Hassan who was living in Britain to be his lead singer. Hassan's rendition of the song "Aap jaisa koi" ("Someone like you") was a smash hit and was followed by *Disco Deewane* (Mad for disco), an album charted in fourteen countries and became the biggest Asian pop record until that time.[52] The team comprising Biddu, Nazia, and her brother Zoheb replicated the *Disco Deewane* success with three further releases: *Star* (1982), *Young Tarang* (1984), and *Hotline* (1987). Biddu would go on to adopt a series of new protégés, each of whom achieved phenomenal success under his musical guidance: Shweta Shetty with the Johnny Joker LP in 1993, the superlative "Made in India" by Alisha Chenoy (1995), Shantanu and Sagarika Mukherjee's "Naujawan" (1996), and Sonu Nigam and Sansara with "Yeh dil sun raha hai" and "Habibi" in 2000.[53] It would not be an exaggeration to say that Biddu almost single-handedly invented "Indipop," a genre that today accounts for more than 10 percent of the Indian music market. His immense legacy constitutes the third moment of modernization of Indian popular music. While the musical experimentations of New Theatres and then of R. D. Burman pulled strands of western musicality into the domain of Indian music, Biddu's strategy was a little different: he combined international and Indian sounds into a totally new form, thus pushing Indian music in the direction of a more global sound.[54]

No single artist within Bollywood symbolizes this global dimension better than India's current musical hero: A. R. Rahman. Born into a musical family—his father K. A. Shekhar worked as a conductor in Malayalam movies—Rahman started learning the piano at the age of four. His father's death when he was nine put the family into penury, and as a mere child of eleven, he joined a local troupe as a keyboard player. He was soon playing with stars such as Zakir Hussain and Kunnakudi Vaidyanathan and eventually obtained a scholarship at the Trinity College of Music at Oxford University to study western classical music. After returning to India, he was associated with various troupes as well as with local rock bands and then had a five-year stint in the advertising industry, during which time he composed over three hundred jingles! His big break came when the noted film director Mani Ratnam hired him to compose the score for *Roja* (1992). Rahman's compositions for that film—which included the hit song "Tamizha Tamizha"—took the music world by storm.[55] In the next few years, Rahman would write the music for several blockbuster films—the sound track for *Bombay* (1995) alone sold more than five million copies. Since then Rahman has virtually defined Hindi film music, as the noted director and lyricist Gulzar says, "He is a milestone in Hindi film music. He has single-handedly changed the sound of music in the movies."[56] A combination of factors has contributed to Rahman's astounding success. He is acknowledged universally as one of the most technologically savvy composers in the country. The recording studio he started in 1989—Panchathan Record Inn—has developed into one of India's most well-equipped and advanced recording studios; unlike most Indian composers, he prefers to create on the computer rather than on tape, and he has collected one of the most comprehensive sonic libraries in Asia.[57] This technical expertise gives his music an unusually contemporary feel, as Gangai Amaran, the well-known South Indian composer-singer observes, "Rahman's music is of the computer age. It is digital but intelligent, not just noise."[58] His amazing fluency in several musical languages enables him to create a synthesis that can appeal to a vast domestic audience. Zakir Hussain, the tabla maestro, argues that Rahman's popularity has much to do with his eclectic training.

> He was barely 19 years old then but had mastered many different styles of music—western classical, jazz, rock and Carnatic. He knows the public pulse and has given the public a very intelligent combination package. This reminds me of R. D. Burman. These guys made it possible to bring together all elements of world music.[59]

Rahman's stature as the premier musical director working in Hindi films today is further consolidated by his immense appeal to international audiences. His many fans abroad include ex-Talking Heads David Byrne and the producer Andrew Lloyd Weber who commissioned Rahman to compose the music for *Bombay Dreams*. Weber explained his choice by saying:

> I think he has an incredible tone of voice. I have seen many Bollywood films, but what he manages to do is quite unique—he keeps it very much Indian. For me as a Westerner, I can always recognize his music because it has got a rule tone of voice of its own (sic). It's very definitely Indian, yet it has an appeal which will go right across the world. He will hit the West in an amazing kind of way; that is, if he is led in the right way. He is the most extraordinary composer who is still true to his cultural roots, and deserves to be heard by an international public.[60]

Eclectic and multicultural, plugged in to worldwide modes of music making, cognizant of a variety of traditions though beholden to none— A. R. Rahman is the perfect advertisement for Bollywood *filmigit* today. And like Bappi Lahiri and the *nautch* girls before him, he too reveals for us *filmigit*'s essential nature: plural and open-ended, hybrid and multiple.

As we have seen, Bollywood music has repeatedly been energized by individuals and movements that have crossed musical boundaries to create new forms capable of expressing the impulses of a changing modernity. The music directors who worked at New Theatres synthesized elements of folk, classical music, and *Rabindrasangeet* as well as the techniques of western melody and instrumentation to give Hindi film music its unique form. Some decades later, the modern song was reinvented by two maverick personalities who were largely self-taught and outside of the musical establishment. Kishore and RD were able, by virtue of their marginality, to plug themselves into a global circuit of energies and forces and forge the sound of modernity in the late 1960s and the early 1970s. The paradigm of open-ended music making they established would make possible a cross-cultural synthesis evident in the work of artists such as Biddu and A. R. Rahman. If, as the other chapters in this volume so vividly demonstrate, Bollywood film music has had a huge and enthusiastic reception among a wide range of cultures and peoples, that popularity must be due, in part, to *filmigit*'s worldliness.

Notes

1   Gerry Farrell, "The Early Days of the Gramophone Industry in India: Historical, Social and Musical Perspectives," in *The Place of Music,* ed. Andrew Leyshon, David Matless, and George Revill (New York and London: The Guilford Press, 1998), 59.
2   Ibid., 59–61.
3   This song "And Her Golden Hair Was Hanging Down Her Back" was featured in the musical *The Shop Girl* (produced at the Gaiety, November 24, 1894); sung by the leading man Seymour Hicks, it was a huge hit all over Britain. The song was originally American and had been brought over to Britain a few years earlier. http://math.boisestate.edu/gas/british/shopgirl/pope.html.
4   In India, composers of movie scores and songs are most commonly known as "music directors."
5   See Richard Zumkhawala-Cook's essay in this book.
6   http://www.downmelodylane.com/bappilahiri.html.

7 Peter Manuel, *Cassette Culture* (New Delhi: Oxford University Press), 144.

8 "Straight Answers," *Economic Times of India*, February 16, 2003.

9 http://www.talentworld.biz.

10 http://www.salaamtheatre.org/bollydisco2003.html.

11 See Lahiri's quote cited earlier.

12 Some of these artists, Alisha or Apache Indian, for example, are not strictly Bollywood, but their music cannot be understood without taking Bollywood music into account.

13 The popular, far from being derived from these older traditions, comes into being by *deviating* from them. Consider the following set of songs recorded by the popular singer Mukesh in the 1950s—"To Keha Agar" (Composer: Naushad [Music Director, hence MD], Film: *Andaz,* 1949), "Tere Duniyan Mein" (Roshan [MD], *Bawre Main,* 1950), "Awara Hoon" (Shankar-Jaikishen [MD], *Awaara,* 1951), and "Suhana Safar" (Salil Chowdhury [MD], *Madhumati,* 1958). The first two are strongly classical in compositional style and presumably appealed to connoisseurs of the form. "Awara Hoon" and "Suhana Safar," both major hits, are clearly far more eclectic in style.

14 Erik Barnouw and S. Krishnaswamy, *Indian Film,* 2nd ed. (New York: Oxford University Press, 1978), 210. For another perspective on this essay, issue, read Morcom's essay.

15 Ibid., 212.

16 The Bauls were originally a sect of mendicants concentrated in the remote district of Birbhum, who earned a living by traveling from village to village, performing at *melas* and other festive occasions, and receiving alms for their singing.

17 Charles Capwell, *The Music of the Bauls of Bengal* (Kent, Ohio: The Kent State University Press), 25.

18 This term (literally "the music of Rabindranath") refers to the entire corpus of Tagore's compositions. It also, in a loose way, connotes a style of singing and a musical sensibility.

19 Edward O. Henry, *Chant the Names of Gods: Music and Culture in Bhojpuri-Speaking India* (San Diego, Calif.: San Diego State University Press, 1988).

20 Ibid., 20, emphasis is mine.

21 David B. Reck, "India/South India," in *Worlds of Music,* 2nd ed., ed. Jeff Tood Tilton et al. (New York: Schirmer Books, 1992), 213.

22 Reginald Massey and Jamila Massey, *The Music of India* (New York: Crescendo Publishing, 1976), 78.

23 Saraswati Devi was the adopted name of the Parsi singer Korshed Minocher-Homji. Manek Premchand, *Yesterday's Melodies, Today's Memories* (Mumbai: Jharna Books, 2003), 90.

24 Arnold E. Alison, "Hindi Film Git: On the History of Commercial Indian Popular Music" (PhD diss., University of Illinois at Urbana-Champaign, 1991), 232.

25 Premchand, *Yesterday's Melodies,* 18.

26 Hameedudin Mohammed, quoted in Alison, "Hindi Film Git," 265.

27 Nurjahan was the premier female singing voice of Bollywood during the decade of the 1940s. She migrated to Pakistan in 1947 and went on to enjoy huge success in Pakistan as a film and television personality. (See Premchand, *Yesterday's Melodies,* 69–73.) Her departure would leave Lata Mangeshkar as the undisputed queen of Indian melody.

28 I am thinking here of the work of such directors as Laxmikant–Pyarelal, Kalyanji–Anandji, Rajesh Roshan, and, of course, R. D. Burman.

29 The first revolution occurred in the 1930s when Hindi film music developed its distinctive style. See my discussion of New Theatres.

30 In India, Rahul Dev Burman is commonly referred to as "RD."

31 See the discussion on Mohammed Rafi and Shammi Kapoor given later in this essay.

32 The dominant style—the work of Naushad or SD—was melodic rather than rhythmic and almost courtly in its restraint.

33 Being born outside of Bengal made Kishore a "probashi" (in Bengali, "one who resides abroad"). This may have contributed to the fact that, in spite of being a national icon, Kishore was never accepted by Bengalis in the way local sons like Hemant Kumar or Manna Dey were.

34 These include *New Delhi* (Segal, 1956) or *Chalti Ka Naam Gadi* (That which moves is a car, Bose, 1958).

35 Premchand, *Yesterday's Melodies,* 266.

36 Siddhartha Dey, "The 24-Carat Magical Voice," *Screen,* October 17, 2003, http://www.screenindia.com/fullstory.php?content_id=6371.

37 Mohammed Rafi (1925–1980) was by most accounts the leading male singer in the 1950s and 1960s.

38 Perhaps the doyen of all classical vocal singers in the first half of the twentieth century.

39 Member of the famed songwriting duo Kalyanji–Anandji.

40 Dey, "The 24-Carat Magical Voice."

41 Consider songs such as "Baharo phul barsao" ("Flowers rain outside" from *Suraj,* Sun, Rao, 1966), "Yeh mera prempatra padhkar" ("Having read my love letter" from *Sangam,* Union, Kapoor, 1964), "Mere meheboob tujhe" ("My love, to you" from *Mere Mehboob,* My love, Rawail, 1963), or "Chahoonga mei tujhe" ("I will want you" from *Dosti,* Friendship, Bose, 1964).

42 For a fascinating analysis that compares Shammi Kapoor to Elvis Presley, see Amit Rai, "An American Raj in Filmistan: Images of Elvis in Indian Film," *Screen* 35, no. 1 (Spring 1994): 51–57.

43 Premchand, *Yesterday's Melodies,* 353–54.

44 Dey, "The 24-Carat Magical Voice."

45 Sound tracks from films such as *Padosan, Amar Prem, Hare Rama Hare Krishna, Yaadon Ki Baraat,* and *Sholay.*

46 http://www.panchamonline.com/.

47 Premchand, *Yesterday's Melodies,* 444.

48 Ibid.

49 http://www.answers.com/topic/biddu-1?.cat=entertainment.

50 http://www.alwynwturner.com/glitter/biddu.html.

51 Fred Bronson, *The Billboard Book of Number One Hits* (New York: Billboard Publications, 1988), 385.
52 The record featured Nazia's brother Zoheb and can justifiably be described as India's first pop record.
53 http://music.aol.com/artist/biddu/biography/1120940.
54 This strategy of fusing global and Indian music would also be the basis for diasporic musical forms such as bhangra and chutney.
55 http://www.india4u.com/.
56 http://gopalhome.tripod.com/arrbio.html.
57 http://www.india4u.com/.
58 http://gopalhome.tripod.com/arrbio.html.
59 Ibid.
60 Ibid.

3. From Bombay to Bollywood

Tracking Cinematic and Musical Tours

Nilanjana Bhattacharjya and Monika Mehta

Writers from Marx to Haraway and Appadurai have shown how emergent technologies introduce possibilities to create new forms of social relations. In the case of Bollywood sound tracks, in particular, emergent technologies of music have acquired the power to call into question that national form of belonging, without which the Indian state cannot do. Why do these sound tracks have this power? Because in a very concrete and specific sense they operate as "capillaries," through which ideas of national belonging are circulated, consumed, and reproduced, sometimes in radically different forms. Sound tracks circulate through and delineate a domain that by definition evades the reach of the law, up to and including the censorship laws that have long attempted to harness Indian film music to the project of Indian nationalism or at least nationhood.

In the era of globalization, the Indian state and the world music industry compete to regulate film music and Indian national culture. The advent of liberalization to some degree requires that the state reterritorialize diasporic communities as national communities; yet the new musical technologies and techniques—for example, remixing in both a musical and a national sense—prove simply too decentralized, private, and undetectable to regulate. The state has thus far attempted to turn its weakness into strength, by positioning certain technologies such as radio, film, and television at the heart of the nationalist project. Furthermore, the state has tried to regulate film music directly, through the enforcement of copyright laws, and indirectly, through laws regulating technologies such as radio, film, and television.

Yet even as the state attempts to recapture technologies of music in order to reproduce Indian national identity in the face of globalization, the market forces that initially emancipated film music from service to the national form increasingly constrain the very liberation they were intended to encourage. By pigeonholing Indian film sound tracks in terms of ethnic authenticity, these same market forces—as exemplified in the world music industry's commodification of the sound tracks— now limit the potential for new social relations implicit in the globaliza- tion of Indian film sound tracks via new technologies of music.

Since its inception, Indian film music's potential to transgress polit- ical, economic, and geographic boundaries has forced the state and the commercial film and music industries to negotiate its slippery character. Is this unique to Indian film song?[1] As the Indian film industry—more specifically, the commercial film industry located in Bombay (now known as Mumbai)—has gained state and industrial recognition, its sound tracks' "unofficial" popularity and consumption have increased. While transnational audiences have consumed Indian films and songs since the 1950s, a palpable shift has occurred in both the production and the consumption of Bombay films in the late 1980s and 1990s. We focus on the emergence of the term "Bollywood" as an important site for examining this shift.

As Ashish Rajadhyaksha has commented, "Bollywood" does not simply refer to the Hindi or even Indian film industries. Rather, it is a "more diffuse cultural conglomeration involving a range of distribution and consumption activities from websites to music cassettes, from cable to radio."[2] In short, "Bollywood" is an industry, a product, and a brand name, all three of which are nourished by the diaspora. As we track film music's elusive travels, we chart how differential relations among the state, the commercial film industry, the world music industry, and their audiences transform Bombay cinema into Bollywood.

Whereas the first half of our chapter investigates how the Indian state uses film music to define its own citizens and national identity, the second half demonstrates how the world music industry questions and reformulates these definitions to propose its own vision of an India freed from its moorings in the nation-state. Traditionally associated with the distribution of "foreign music" within Western markets, the world music industry since the early 1990s has competed against the Indian nation-state and India-based distributors to claim South Asian diasporic audiences and Western mainstream markets. Bombay music's transformation into Bollywood is further manifested in film music's development into a product whose patterns of consumption define a radically different notion of citizenship, one that includes South Asian diasporic audiences, and to some extent, world music consumers.[3]

Postcolonial State and Film Music

After independence in 1947, the newly formed Indian state undertook the task of nation-building. Hoping to participate in this task, the film industry requested that the government confer the film industry legitimate status, which would make available the infrastructural and credit support that the economic policies had already promised for other industries.[4] However, the "developmentalist" Indian state had no time for such frivolous pleas. After all, in the international arena, a flourishing film industry would not sufficiently exhibit the Indian state's commitment to development; the state thus reserved its economic aid for projects such as agriculture and heavy industry, which more explicitly led India toward the goals of progress and development.

Having already denied industry status to the commercial film industry, the state proceeded to define the film industry's products as luxuries and imposed heavy taxes on them. In addition, the state emphasized commercial films' dangerous potential to corrupt so-called Indian culture. In the Constituent Assembly Debates, one member stated, "I think that the greatest injury is being done to the nation by the cinematograph."[5] Another member lamented, "these cinemas are doing a great injury to our old treasure of music, poetry and art."[6] Soon after, during the Rajya Sabha Debates in 1954, commercial films were blamed for the nation's steadily declining moral standards.[7] Furthermore, on separate occasions, both Jawaharlal Nehru, the prime minister of India, and Dr. Rajendra Prasad, the president, underscored commercial cinema's wide influence and the state's need to regulate this via the institution of censorship.[8] In India, colonial administrators had introduced the idea of film censorship. The postcolonial state's decision to retain this institution compels us to reconsider its simultaneous bywords, independence and liberation.

Many Indian citizens were also concerned by the pernicious effects of cinema on the public, and thus they advocated for greater control and surveillance. For example, in 1954, thirteen thousand women from Delhi presented a petition to the prime minister demanding that the government curb the "evil" influence of films, which they viewed as condoning their children's truancy from school and promoting precocious indulgence in sexual activity and other vices. Responding to this petition, Prime Minister Nehru stated:

> Films have an essential part to play in the modern world. At the same time it is true that any powerful medium like motion pictures has a good effect and a bad effect. We have to take care therefore that we emphasize the good aspect of it.[9]

Why did the national government, which refused to censor art and literature, view the very medium of cinema as requiring censorship? We suggest that by casting cinema as morally suspect, the state could undertake the role of moral guardian of the nation—and the petition from the women in Delhi substantiates this. As a technology, film could be reproduced, it could travel and reach mass audiences; moreover, it could expose these audiences to new experiences and shape new ideas of citizenship. These possibilities generated the state's anxieties about this medium; in regulating this medium, the state was forced to acknowledge that film rivaled the state's claim over its own citizens.

All India Radio and Music

The debate on film music should be situated in this larger context of mass entertainment and anxiety about the reach of a particular technology. Surprisingly, given the centrality of music in Indian cinema, neither colonial nor postcolonial governments have ever designated specific laws that regulate the content of film music; the only laws that apply to music have instead focused on intellectual property rights (that is, copyright and piracy). As a result, the content of film music has been subject to the state authority only indirectly through other laws regulating other industries and technologies such as cinema, radio, cable television, and satellite television. Music's ability to escape direct state censorship means that an institutional history of censorship of film music per se cannot exist, but it also dictates that attempts to censor music aim repeatedly at the technologies associated with music rather than aiming at the music itself. In short, film music's unique ability to escape the direct purview of the state has enabled its considerable facility to circumvent state scrutiny and, in turn, to circulate as well as reproduce via various technologies.

The infamous All India Radio (AIR) incident where Dr. B. D. Keskar, the minister of information and broadcasting, described film music as "cheap and vulgar" and drastically reduced their radio broadcasts confirms music's significance as a vehicle for national ideology, as well as technology's role in enabling the circulation of music and, by extension, national ideology.[10] In referring to this incident documented elsewhere in this volume, we would highlight the following two points: First, film music's extraction from film has enabled it to travel independently via underregulated technologies. Second, music's ability to circulate beyond the state's control has compelled the state to compromise its own position on national culture and negotiate that process of definition with its citizens and the film industry. When B. D. Keskar in his attempt to "purify" the airwaves banned film music from the state-owned AIR, Radio Ceylon, which depended upon advertisements, mainly from American companies, increased its Hindi music programming. Once the Indian public discovered that they could listen to film songs on Radio Ceylon, they shifted their radio dials, effectively turning away their allegiance from AIR, and the Indian state. If the state intended AIR to create a link between the government and its people and to assist in producing a national community with the state at its helm, then it was clearly failing in this task. Most Indian listeners were of course unaware that their tuning into Radio Ceylon constituted a form of resistance to the Indian state; they simply liked listening to film music, and Radio Ceylon provided this pleasure. The state was not only in danger of losing its citizens but also tax revenue. The state may have also resented that an Indian product, namely Hindi film music, could be used to advertise products and thereby prove lucrative for agents outside India. Eventually, the state caved in and in 1957 inaugurated two new shortwave stations in Bombay and Madras that would broadcast film music; these broadcasts were subject to the monitoring of a screening committee.[11] Furthermore, in the battle to define national culture, this episode demonstrates how the Indian state and the elite had to negotiate with the larger public and the film industry. This would be the first of many occasions when the Indian state would struggle to negotiate its control over mediating technologies that undermined its authority over the nation's subjects.

New Technologies and the Rise of the Music Industry

The 1970s witnessed the advent of yet another potentially undermining technology, namely, cassettes. Since independence, the Indian state had pursued economic policies that protected national industries; due in part to these policies, cassette technology did not reach India until the mid-1970s. Economic policies thereafter encouraged the proliferation of cassettes across India. In 1978, the government implemented more liberal economic policies to address "slow growth in the economy and the increasing dissatisfaction of middle-class consumers."[12] Then, during the 1980s, the Indian state reduced import tariffs on cassette technology,[13] which in turn increased the affordability and accessibility of cassettes. This flourishing new technology had an impact on both music and film industries.

An example of the impact of cassettes is clearly demonstrated by the rise of Gulshan Arora and the creation of the company T-Series. The innovative Arora exploited a loophole in the Indian copyright laws that enabled him to produce and market countless cover versions of His Master's Voice (HMV) classic songs. Indian copyright law permits previously recorded songs to be released in new versions and arrangements if the original song is over two years old and if one pays the original owners a small advance and 5 percent of the royalties. In practice, neither the advance nor the royalties are enforced. Left to their own volition, most companies have opted to grant, at the most, a nominal amount to the original music composer. By the mid-1980s, the repeated exploitation of this loophole not only ended the hegemony of HMV and Polydor but also broke the stranglehold that a few singers such as Lata Mangeshkar, Asha Bhosle, and Kishore Kumar had on the film music industry. New companies and singers entered the market, creating competition.[14] While in 1990 only five companies had devoted themselves to the film music business, by 1993 over thirty companies were active in this field. Furthermore, these mushrooming music industries emerged as major financiers of commercial films. In this new avatar, the music industry has played a powerful role in the production and distribution of films and film music.[15]

A letter written to the Ministry of Information and Broadcasting about the circulation of the "vulgar" song "Choli ke peeche kya hai" ("What is behind the blouse?")[16] draws attention to the industry's new role. In the letter, Pandit Gautam Kaul, a concerned citizen, enumerates the adverse effects of the growing music industry:

> Recording of songs are completed even before the film goes into production and recording companies, without waiting for the release of the film, exploit the songs as investments. It is also noticed that there are some cases now where the songs of a movie announced for production proved immensely popular and the film remained unknown even after its release. There are possibilities that a full album of songs can be

The song "Choli ke peeche kya hai" ("What is behind the blouse?") in
Khalnayak (The villain, 1993) incited heated debates on Indian culture.

released, and the film may never be made. In such cases, the songs
would be given nomenclature as "private songs."[17]

For Kaul, these practices of production and distribution of film songs
warranted immediate attention because they were circumventing state

scrutiny. He therefore suggests that the state demand that producers submit film songs to examining committees[18] before their release and that the state create new offices to certify private and film music and thus regulate the burgeoning music industry.[19]

The practices of production and distribution that worried Kaul have, however, existed since the inception of the playback technique in 1935 and the implications that accompanied it: "The effects of using the playback technique were manifold . . . the songs could be recorded in advance, for publicity purposes, on discs to radio broadcasters and the commercial market just prior to a film's premiere."[20] As these practices were not new, we must consider why they generated such anxiety at this juncture. We suggest that Kaul's letter should be situated within the context of economic liberalization that enabled the entry of new technologies in India and created porous and uncertain national as well as cultural borders. With the advent of liberalization in the 1990s, the Indian state, already grappling with recently introduced video and cable technologies, now encountered another formidable adversary, satellite television. To regulate the circulation of video, in 1984, the Indian state amended the Cinematograph Act of 1952 to require that videos, like film, be submitted for certification.[21] However, as late as the early 1990s, the government lacked any mechanism to monitor these videos and films' broadcasts via their programming on cable and satellite television, both technologies that provided viewers easy access to films and programs prohibited by the state. As cable and satellite television stations easily breached state authority, state censorship appeared superfluous. Thus, in recommending that the government practice censorship on film music, Kaul unwittingly demonstrates how such technologies, namely cassettes, cable television, and satellite television, reveal the limits of state authority.

Defining and Protecting "Indian Culture" in the Era of Liberalization

Immune to state censorship, cable and satellite television could communicate potentially subversive or, as Kaul feared, vulgar messages.[22] In the early 1990s, the failure to regulate cable and satellite television encouraged the wide circulation of a number of "vulgar" songs such as the aforementioned "Choli ke peeche kya hai" from *Khalnayak* (The villain,

Subhash Ghai, 1993); "Sexy, sexy, sexy, mujhe log bole" ("People say I am sexy, sexy, sexy") from *Khuddar* (The Self-respecting one, Iqbal Durrani, 1993); "Meri pant bhi sexy" ("My pant is sexy") from *Dulaara* (The loved one, Vimal Kumar, 1994); and "Sarkayleo khatiya jara lage" ("Bring your cot closer, I am feeling cold") from *Raja Babu* (His lordship, David Dhawan, 1993). Each of these songs incited vociferous debates on the incursion of debilitating alien cultures on Indian values and tradition through the Trojan horse of film music. The song "Choli ke peeche kya hai" was nearly censored, and the songs "Sexy, sexy, sexy, mujhe log bole" and "Meri pant bhi sexy" were in fact censored. The Central Board of Film Certification (CBFC) asked the producers to replace the word "sexy" in these songs.[23] Although "Sexy, sexy, sexy, mujhe log bole" was eventually re-recorded as "Baby, baby, baby," every private television channel continued to broadcast the "sexy" version.

As a state-run institution, AIR initially banned these songs, a futile move since private television channels aired them, where they achieved massive popularity.[24] These incidents reveal that although the opponents of "vulgar" Hindi film songs could petition for a ban on Doordarshan (state-controlled television) or AIR, they had no control over cable and satellite television. The Indian state's own concern about the "growing menace" of television, coupled with pressure from organizations such as the Centre for Media Studies, the National Commission for Women (NCW), and the Parliamentary Standing Committee, led to the enactment of the Cable Television Networks Rules in 1994 and the Cable Television Networks (Regulation) Act in 1995, both of which attempted to regulate the influence of cable and satellite programming.[25]

The heated censorship battles of the early 1990s reflect anxieties of the state, the film industry, and the citizenry in resolving the following questions: How could the state reestablish its authority? How would the film industry compete with new forms of entertainment? How would the social fabric change due to both the quantity and the quality of entertainment available? How could India protect its culture and traditions from the onslaught of Western culture and values represented in films, sitcoms, and soap operas shown via satellite television? The debates surrounding these issues were largely exacerbated by a fear of unregulated technology. As economic liberalization destabilized territorial borders, these debates over film music symptomatize the attempt to define and affirm a desirable form of Indian identity by marking its cultural borders.

The most recent debates on "vulgar" music videos from 2003 revisit the issue of Indian values and highlight the portability of music. On November 27, 2003, the Minister of Information and Broadcasting Ravi Shankar Prasad announced that all films, trailers, and music videos shown on all television channels now had to earn a "U" certificate (unrestricted exhibition—appropriate for those under the age of eighteen)[26] from the CBFC.[27] This directive was aimed mainly at cable and state television. Later, the Ministry also announced its formation of the Broadcasting Regulatory Authority to monitor the "growing vulgarity" on television channels.[28]

Although the Indian state has been very concerned about the content of cable and satellite television programming (that is, television shows and films), the pretext for Prasad's announcement was in fact a long and heated debate on music videos. The specific video that sparked this debate was the remix version of "Kaanta laga" ("A thorn hurt [me]").[29] Released in February 2003 as a remix on the DJ Doll album,[30] "Kaanta laga" was transformed into a "provocative" music video by the chartered accountant–mass communication duo, Vinay Sapru and Radhika Rao. The video centers on a young woman, clad in low-riding jeans that offer a glimpse of her thong underwear, as she gyrates to the music, reads a men's adult magazine, and attempts to seduce her boyfriend. The song and the music video were a critical and commercial success. By December 2003, two million units of the album had been sold; in addition, the video received awards from Channel [V], the Zee Music Awards, the Screen Videocon Awards, the MTV Music Awards, and the Bollywood Music Awards.[31]

Although the sales records indicate that many enjoyed listening to and viewing these videos, some members of the Vishva Hindu Parishad (VHP),[32] Prasad, and Anupam Kher (the chairperson of the CBFC) were not among them. Members of the VHP stormed the stage of a show in Vadodara, calling dancer Shefali Jariwala's performance "vulgar." They stopped the show.[33] Similarly, the information and broadcasting minister of the BJP government was so disgusted by the video that he requested satellite channels to "voluntarily" remove it from their programming. Fearing punitive action, many satellite channels complied.[34] However, the video circulated widely, especially via the Internet. Ironically, the video in question had in fact been given a "U" certificate by the Delhi Certification Board. The regional officer who certified the video was punished for not understanding and adhering to the censorship "rules" and was summarily transferred from the Delhi Censor Board office.[35]

Multiple anxieties regarding the state's inability to control media technologies and the onslaught of "Western culture" surface in the controversy over "Kaanta laga." This debate echoes 1990s discussions on censorship, "Indian values," and "Indian culture." In these debates, the question of sexual ethics reemerges to reveal that sexuality, in particular female sexuality, is central to constituting Indian national identity.[36]

Although the concerns of the debates in the 1990s and the new millennium resemble one another, the debates in the 1990s were primarily conducted within the territorial boundaries of the Indian state. In contrast, contemporary debates unfold both within and beyond these boundaries. The Internet, in particular, has enabled the Indian diaspora to emerge as a new and important voice in these debates. The "Kaanta laga" controversy was widely discussed on the Web with respondents from India, the Netherlands, the United States, the UK, and so on writing in.[37] As the Internet enabled the Indian diaspora to participate in these debates, it also (re)constituted members of the diaspora as Indian nationals. Since new technologies help recast the nation as a deterritorialized entity, by the same token the state's attempts at regulating film music represents a move to reterritorialize hybridized diasporic subjects as a pure national community.

Copyright, Piracy, and Globalization

Like the state, the Indian Music Industry has also been concerned about mushrooming technologies, including digital video discs (DVDs) and digital music on the Internet. Although these new technologies have enabled the growth of music industries, they have also facilitated piracy, which poses a significant threat to the industry. Due to the lax enforcement of copyright laws, cassette piracy has been documented as earning more money than "legitimate companies." In the 1980s, the Indian Phonographic Industry, which was formed in 1936 to defend the rights of phonograph producers, pressed the government to implement stricter copyright laws and to combat piracy. In 1984, as part of these efforts, the government amended the Copyright Act to require that cassettes include the name of the producer on their covers. Although this amendment did decrease piracy slightly, it did not eradicate it; informal music industries continue to flourish. Since the advent of liberalization in the 1990s, the Indian Music Industry (formerly known as the Indian Phonographic Industry) increased its efforts to curb piracy and enforce copyright laws.[38] According to the Indian Music Industry:

> Cassettes sales of pirate recordings in 1997 were estimated at 174 million units with a value of some 83 million Dollars making India the World's third largest pirate market in volume and sixth in value. Pirate sales in India account for nearly 30% of total unit sales.[39]

In order to underscore the importance of instituting stricter laws, the industry draws attention to the amount of revenue that the government loses due to piracy:

> Government suffers as pirates do not pay taxes. It is estimated that piracy results in loss to the exchequer to the tune of some Rs. 190 millions in Sales Tax, Excise duty and Income Tax, in 1997.[40]

In the mid-1990s, the Indian Music Industry hired many former police officers to head its antipiracy operations. It was also faced with the task of monitoring another illegitimate practice related to piracy: the burgeoning remix industry. Even as it attempts to address these problems on its own, the Indian Music Industry has continued to lobby the government to implement stricter laws.

In response to this pressure as well as the forces of the global market, the Information and Broadcasting Ministry announced in March 2003 that it would change the Copyright Act of 1957 to eradicate some loopholes. In particular, the Ministry agreed to review the Indian Music Industry's request to delete the section in the Copyright Act of 1957 that permits the production of songs' cover versions.[41] Furthermore, the Ministry agreed to implement a new regulation to control optical disc piracy that obligated manufacturers to apply for licenses, register at the Ministry, and use source identification codes.[42] It was hoped that the decisions to "reduce excise duty on pre-recorded CDs would help curb piracy."[43]

How do we make sense of this proliferation of legislative rules at a time when the state was pursuing divestment in so many other ventures? Sassen notes, "Global markets in finance and advanced services partly operate through a 'regulatory' umbrella that is not state centered but market centered."[44] These markets, she explains, make "new claims on national states to guarantee the domestic and global rights of capital" and "national states respond through the production of new forms of legality."[45] Understood in this context, by granting film the status of an industry as well as pursuing efforts to curb piracy, the Indian state has sought to accomplish two tasks: first, to harness the enormous export potential of commercial films and music, and second, to tailor the film and music industries to international standards by transforming the mechanisms of production and marketing. We argue that by pursuing policies that bring an "unorganized" and "informal" sector of the economy under its purview, the state is actively attempting to (re)inscribe its authority over national culture in the context of globalization.

The recent efforts by the music industry and the state to reinforce copyright and curb piracy should be situated in the context of the pressures exerted by national and global markets. To identify itself as a worthy contender in the global market and to present India as an attractive, low-risk site for foreign investment, the Indian state and the music industry are compelled to join forces and eradicate piracy. The process of defining and then policing piracy creates another opportunity for the state to act and thus reinscribes its authority. By instituting rules against piracy, the state ensures that it profits from music sales. Moreover, through the process of regulation, the state has defined its mission to produce "good cinema," and "good music," simultaneously attending to the global market and to reproduce the Indian nation.[46]

Marketing "India"

While the Indian state seeks to project its vision of Indian "culture" both within and beyond the territorial boundaries of India, it has a powerful competitor in this task, namely, the "world music" industry. The world music industry exerts a disproportionate influence in distributing Bollywood music as a "foreign music" to be consumed by Western and diasporic audiences. The visibility accorded by the world music industry's distribution of Bollywood music amid leading European and American music retailers appeals to the Indian state's desire to penetrate and participate in Western markets.

Most of this music retains its original form and, in purporting to represent "India," establishes its ethnic authenticity. Appealing to Orientalist stereotypes, the world music industry sometimes repackages

Bollywood as a kitschy, dated, and amusingly inscrutable novelty. But this repackaging does not erase the products' claim as an authentic representative (and vehicle) of Indian culture, for as Simon Frith has noted, the world music industry markets exoticism explicitly to its Western audiences. The world music industry finds that marketing a sense of "truth" and "innocence"—supposedly lost within the realm of mainstream popular music—proves very powerful.[47]

Thus, although world music products may provide detailed notes on the cultural context of Bollywood, they simultaneously imply that it offers something more naïve and authentic than Western pop.[48] Thus, the industry first locates Bollywood film music within a wonderful, baffling, inaccessible world and, in doing so, contradicts the Indian state's attempts to brand itself as a modern, technologically savvy superpower. Furthermore, the marketing strategies associated with world music often interfere with the Indian state's efforts to claim and govern diasporic subjects. In the diaspora, the world music industry can redistribute and redefine Bollywood outside India to the extent that its products often replace more conventional paths to learning about and understanding Indian culture—particularly in the absence of any official state narrative governing popular culture.[49] The government does not yet consider the vast corpus of Indian film music a legitimate documentation project in itself. Film music's lack of sponsorship relates partly to the anxieties discussed earlier that concern its ability to represent national culture in a respectable light. This anxiety is also fed by film music's incorporation of "modern" or "Western" musical elements—a practice that compromises its Indianness.[50]

The lack of a state narrative on popular culture is filled by the world music industry, which performs a crucial pedagogic function in bringing Bollywood recordings to international audiences and diasporic subjects. Although world music's audiences may include American and European listeners interested in music "from other cultures," that is, the typical "world music" demographic, its audiences also include second- and third-generation diasporic South Asians and their parents. Through its distribution of Bollywood music, the world music industry mediates all these audiences' relationship to Indian culture, past and present. A Fijian Indian taxicab driver in Brisbane outlines a layman's understanding of Bollywood's potential as an educational tool for diasporic youth below:

Previously, I used to encourage my children to see documentaries on India. I do no more. These people can't show even Taj Mahal without

> showing beggars, a few lepers, flies and all that. They can't resist that temptation . . . So for entertainment, you have Hindi films. The songs, the dance, the stories, glamour—all those things that the [children] can talk about with their other Indian friends . . . My friend, India—like all our countries—can only go down and down but Hindi films will prosper. Such is the logic . . . You may call these films fantasy but it is a better way of knowing, I mean seeing, India than those documentaries.[51]

Most significantly, as the world music industry refashions Bollywood into an altogether new product, it reterritorializes (quite literally) the realm of Bollywood and relocates the site of its production from India to the diaspora, well beyond the realm of the Indian state.

Prologue: "Movie Mahal" and Golden Voices from Bombay (not Bollywood)

To trace Indian film music's distribution on world music recordings and its progressive reterritorialization of the Indian state's borders and authority, we offer a brief survey of selected recordings of Indian film music available via the world music industry. We begin with one of the earliest reissues of Indian film music on a British-based label in 1990—a three-volume compact disc (CD) set, *Golden Voices from the Silver Screen: Classic Indian Film Soundtrack Songs from the Television Series "Movie Mahal."*[52] As the title suggests, the songs were associated with the television series, "Movie Mahal," whose forty-nine episodes were shown on Channel 4 (British Independent Television) during the fall of 1987.[53] The recordings appear to have been intended as both a thoughtfully compiled, spin-off keepsake for the series' viewers, and a more easily accessible product for British audiences, since the distribution of film songs, at that time, was limited to British Asian shops and mail order outfits.

Paul Oliver's comments demonstrate the series' appeal to both British mainstream and South Asian diasporic viewers; his allusion to "Indian custom" establishes the program's ethnic authenticity via its retention of "native" qualities:

> The sights which the series offered were at times threatened by the tight definitions of Indian custom . . . Even if the colour was sometimes too lurid, the settings too opulent, the fantasy too obvious, the eroticism too suppressed, the acting too mannered for most viewers

Cover of *Golden Voices from the Silver Screen: Classic Indian Film Soundtrack Songs from the Television Series "Movie Mahal,"* volume three.

(and these are observations which do still apply), those who persisted in watching over breakfast chapattis had an introduction to the South Asian/Western crossover.[54]

Oliver points out elsewhere that the program emphasized songs from the 1950s, but the selections reissued in *Golden Voices from the Silver Screen* draw the majority of their selections from films of the 1950s and 1960s; they also include only a few selections from the 1970s and a single song from 1981. The unidentified author of the liner notes to volume three of the series has criticized more recent music, which was not included:

> Many of the songs being written now are criticized for their lack of melody and for the mediocrity of the lyrics. While it is generally acknowledged that there has been a decline in quality, the actual interesting film songs will never stop.[55]

The volumes thus assume a particularly conservative stance that is unapologetically nostalgic; nevertheless, these volumes, partly for the "quality" of the songs they include and partly for their status as a collectors' item, remain one of the most popular reissues of Indian film music.

Golden Voices from the Silver Screen's liner notes appeal to both the seasoned film viewer and an outsider; it includes a general introduction to the culture surrounding Bombay film music, but it also offers more specific information related to each selection. For instance, each volume lists typical information, such as the songs' titles and singers, and the films from which the songs are taken. But the notes also list the record industry identification number of the film sound track, the album, the film composer, and the lyricist. Furthermore, each selection is accompanied by a short description including the following: genre (*ghazal, bhajan, qawwali,* and so on), stylistic influences (snake-charming folk traditions, cabaret, Punjabi, Latin American, and so on), historical trivia, and, in some cases, how the music relates to the drama onscreen. Through these latter details, especially, the songs are firmly relocated within their filmic context.

Although the songs appear in most cases in their original form, licensed from the Gramophone Company of India, the notes accompanying "Chalte chalte" from *Pakeezah* (The pure one, Kamal Amrohi, 1972) sung by Lata Mangeshkar (on volume two) reveal the following modification of the original recording:

> Indian film soundtrack music has its own unique sound quality defined by its use in cinemas. For your purely [*sic*] listening pleasure we have removed certain [sic] of the harsher elements of the sound, while still retaining the atmosphere of the original. Therefore do not adjust your amplifier unduly.[56]

American and European listeners often describe Lata Mangeshkar's voice as particularly "cutting" and "harsh," especially in comparison with her sister Asha Bhosle's voice. However, as the distinctive syntax above suggests, this modification of the recordings' final mastering (or at the very least, the person explaining the modification) issues from a South Asian source, whose words may or may not be directed toward a South Asian audience.

The visual images on the volumes also suggest that they are marketed to a consumer more informed and familiar with Bombay film culture than the average "world music" enthusiast. The volumes include stylized portraits of playback singers Asha Bhosle, Mohammed Rafi,

Geeta Dutt, Mukesh, and Lata Mangeshkar. Although film music fans would probably recognize these singers' images, unseasoned listeners would need to consult the inside of the booklet to identify them.

Golden Voices from the Silver Screen also marks the transition between Indian (Hindi) film music, aimed at the Indian market and newly arrived British Asian immigrants, and "Bollywood." *Golden Voices from the Silver Screen* maintains the songs' filmic context and, more specifically, its status as an Indian cultural product entrenched within the Indian nation-state. In the next section, we examine more recent recordings that divorce the film song from both its filmic context and an exclusively Indian identity.

Glitz, Glam, and Kitsch: Bollywood for Insiders, In-betweens, and Outsiders

With the release of *Dil Se* (From the heart, Mani Ratnam 1998), *Kuch Kuch Hota Hai* (Something is happening, Karan Johar, 1998), and *Taal* in the late 1990s, Bollywood movies achieved a new level of commercial success in the South Asian diaspora; these films all broke "top-ten" mainstream box office records in Britain and many other markets outside India.[57] These releases were followed by the first large-scale reissue of Bollywood music on British, American, and European labels. We ascribe their emergence to the new visibility of "Bollywood" outside India and the recognition of the brand's commercial potential in Western markets.

One early release of this type is *I Love Bollywood* (2001).[58] Its notes provide some technical information, but adopt a much livelier, more humorous style than the more "educationally minded" notes accompanying *Golden Voices from the Silver Screen*. They concentrate on the spread of the "Bollywood" phenomenon and, in so doing, question the site of Bollywood music's production. The notes' authors appear to have resided in Britain for most if not all of their lives. Their comments are rooted in nostalgia, but this nostalgia is more fashionably evoked within the context of British Asian and South Asian culture's new visibility within Britain, and it attempts to project a more multicultural and cosmopolitan identity reflective of its immigrants.[59] Balinder Kaler, one author, is described as somebody who "saw her first Hindi film on her fathers [*sic*] knee at five years old but had to wait twenty years to see her first blockbuster in a Bombay cinema." The other author, Stephen

Armstrong, "on his first trip to India . . . picked up amoebic dysentery and a love for Hindi films."[60] Their notes draw attention to the inaccessibility of Bollywood films in the past and its current mainstream popularity in Britain:

> In the old days, of course, back in the 1980's and early 1990's, you could only catch glimpses . . . The odd poster in a corner of town. A video shop with Hindi titles. Maybe three minutes of a song on some late night BBC2 or Channel 4 "ethnic" programme. Now the music and the images of Bollywood are everywhere—from Basement Jaxx videos to Missy Elliott songes and mainstream cinema like Elizabeth and Moulin Rouge. The conventions of Bollywood—the aesthetic of the industry—are becoming an artistic currency in every avenue of popular culture.[61]

The authors write from an insider's perspective that appeals not to an older generation familiar with classic singers from the 1960s and 1970s, but to a listener steeped in South Asian diasporic life and contemporary British and American popular culture. This album therefore appears to be marketed to a British audience, as well as to a younger second-generation South Asian audience in Britain brought up and exposed to Indian culture through networks sometimes entirely independent of the Indian state's control.

"Made in Britain"

The recording, *The Rough Guide to Bollywood,* issued by the popular Rough Guide travel guide series, follows the label's numerous other world music recordings in including an introduction written by an "expert." In this case, however, the "expert" chosen is not an academic scholar of Indian music, but the renowned British Asian Bhangra DJ, DJ Ritu. DJ Ritu in her introduction explicitly situates Bollywood from the outset within her own experiences as an Asian person growing up in Britain, which defined her relationship with Bollywood music. She remembers being taken to small, "grubby" places as a child to see Bollywood movies and buy Bollywood records; she then rejoices that her "English India is no longer a secret," but "an experience . . . to share with everybody."[62]

The notes to the individual songs provide slightly more technical information than those found in *I Love Bollywood,* but carry a similar tone. These notes describe the songs' contexts within Bombay film and Bollywood culture, but also, when relevant, within British popular culture. The compilation notably includes more songs from recent films, including *Kuch Kuch Hota Hai,* and films from the 1970s. DJ Ritu's collaborator Sagoo, however, distances himself from these:

> [I] can look back at the '70s and appreciate that decade for producing magical music directors like R. D. Burman—we included six of his songs—and Khayyam, who's not a prolific composer but someone who produced quality work as in *Kabhi Kabhie.* There is a train of thought that says the golden period of Hindi film music is the '50s[...]; however, when dealing with an album that is meant to appeal to an international audience, the choice of music needs to be able to cut across continents, language barriers and personal prejudices.[63]

In order to appeal to a mainstream audience, Sagoo admits forgoing his own preferences—music from the 1950s—for those of Bollywood, whose songs he believes appeal to the widest market: the South Asian diasporic market and the world music market.

We now turn to a compilation of Bollywood songs issued by Outcaste Records in the wake of Bollywood's popularity in the British box office. Cofounded by DJ Ritu and Shabs in the mid-1990s to produce work by innovative British Asian musicians, Outcaste Records has never been a typical "world music" label. Label manager Shabs's comments on the first *The Very Best Bollywood Songs* album underscore this commitment to the British Asian community:

> Growing up as an Asian person almost anywhere in the world means you would have spent some time either watching Bollywood films or singing along to some of the fantastic songs and catchy melodies produced by this amazing industry.[64]

Shabs's comments present the album in familiar diasporic terms, already articulated by DJ Ritu, his former colleague.

Ironically, it is John Lewis, the world music editor for *Time Out* in London, who provides the most extensive introduction to *The Very Best Bollywood Songs* (2001).[65] Lewis adopts the characteristic voice in which non-Indians describe Bollywood—a "zany" pastiche that intermittently drops references to British pop culture:

> It's that unmistakable [*sic*] sound of Bollywood. Thundering drum patterns. Clattering zithers and shrill-voiced, fuzz-toned vocalists who wrench every ounce of soul from the music. Gorgeously orchestrated string sections where a hundred violins glide up to a shrieking crescendo in strict unison, distorting the paltry amplification like Hendrix teaming through a Marshall Stack. Ramshackle recording studios creaking at the edges as their EQ meters are pushed to the limits. A bit like Jamaican Dub.[66]

Lewis conjures an absurd, cacophonous landscape—a typical "world music" fantasy. He describes an exotic music unintelligible (and potentially distasteful) to refined (Western) ears, a ridiculously eclectic music that defies logic and any attempts at restraint. Produced in primitive "ramshackle studios creaking at the edges," within a backward India rather than a more-modernized urban studio, this music satisfies the world music consumer's first desire, namely that of (ethnic) authenticity.

Lewis attempts to distinguish himself as a more sophisticated listener, however, in the following comment:

> Just as Westerners exoticise India, Indian film is equally happy to exoticise the West. Gora aficionados of "world music" might care about authenticity, but India's cinema-goers couldn't give a damn— every imaginable stylistic genre is thrown in without any care for its provenance.[67]

Incorporating Hindustani parlance such as "filmi" and "Gora" as his own, he distances himself from typically ignorant "world music" listeners who clamor for cultural purity and establishes his own authenticity as a "Bollywood insider." Lewis thus may be interpreted as appealing to an audience "in the know" who includes the diasporic South Asian listener communities but to an audience largely unfamiliar with Bollywood films.

Reclaiming Bollywood and Its Legacy

The Music of Bollywood, issued in 2002 by Universal Music International, also markets itself toward British consumers and South Asian diasporic audiences, but conveys an altogether different image of India. Also in three volumes, this particular compilation arrives in an expensively produced digipack, with many full color photographs of a South Asian fashion model dressed in an exquisitely embroidered Benarasi sari and adorned with jewelry and glittering henna; the photographs are indistinguishable from those typically associated with South Asian wedding and other fashion magazines. On the model's photographs are superimposed smaller images of the earlier and more "lurid" album covers associated with the songs included in the compilation; their diminution ensures that the covers' "retro" imagery does not compete with the model in the foreground.

While the extravagantly dressed model identifies India as the site of venerable tradition, the notes accompanying *The Music of Bollywood* situate Bollywood film's origins (and thus, presumably, India's engagement with modernity) in 1899 when "Hiralal Sen and H. S. Bhatavdekar started making films in Calcutta and Bombay."[68] These movies were of course silent, but the mere mention of this early date serves to legitimize the overall history of film production in India. The notes later concede that "Bollywood was really born with the advent of sound," with the release of *Alam Ara* (directed by Ardershir Irani) on March 14, 1931, at the Majestic Cinema in Bombay. *Alam Ara* included several songs whose popularity apparently, according to the notes, initiated a trend with other filmmakers.

This early advent of modernity in India along with the album's opulent presentation more closely conforms to the glamorous, luxurious, wealthy, and technologically savvy image that the Indian state would prefer to project. It counteracts the image of poverty and technological backwardness suggested by John Lewis's "ramshackle studios with creaking floors." Furthermore, Universal Music's narrative claims that the early advent of Bollywood itself materialized with the emergence of sound in the Indian film in 1931. Eschewing chronological categories to mix together songs from different time periods, *The Music of Bollywood* constructs a narrative that contradicts Ashish Rajadhyaksha's earlier periodization of Bollywood in the 1990s. Universal Music's adoption of the term "Bollywood" is most likely strategic, for after the late 1990s "Bollywood" has become an effective brand that may be channeled to market all of Indian film.[69] As *The Music of Bollywood* adopts the term, it revises the history of Indian film industry to legitimate the Indian film industry's status as a global industry, with global networks as established, powerful, and extensive as those of Hollywood itself.

Reproduction and Redefinition

The German-produced album *Doob Doob O'Rama: Filmsongs from Bollywood*[70] brings together many of the issues raised in this chapter and thus serves as an appropriate conclusion. The cover image reproduces a brightly painted film poster depicting a woman (Vijayantimala) frozen in terror by the cobra before her. One opens the cover to reveal a photograph of Madhuri Dixit on its reverse side; if one flips the photograph of Dixit over, one encounters a nonsensical collage that combines a gentleman sitting on the windshield of a car as a smiling woman sits on the headrest of the front seat, elephants wandering in the background, and haphazardly superimposed Tamil labels that allude to cryptic political slogans. The CD itself is printed with a crudely printed image of the Hindu goddess Meenakshi, encircled by Tamil text that identifies its origins in the renowned Meenakshi temple in Madurai, Tamil Nadu. The cover's backside reveals the original source of the woman and cobra cover image—as a detail on a billboard in the background of a crowded street scene. Large signs in Bengali (and English) text identify the buildings below as the Dhaka Ayurvedic Pharmacy; a street sign directs us to the trams traveling toward Park Circus and Sealdah Station—recognizable only to a few as central destinations in Kolkata, West Bengal.

The songs on *Doob Doob O'Rama* are all indeed "Bollywood songs," stemming from their expected point of origin, northern India, and sung in Hindi. But the German producer who combines images of Madhuri Dixit, South Indian iconography, and a Bengali street scene defines another Bollywood, which may take place in Bombay, but can also take place in Madurai, Kolkata, and possibly Dhaka— all locations that transcend Bombay's linguistic and, more significantly, cultural borders. This repackaging of Bollywood for a Western audience thus divorces Bollywood from Bombay and its Hindi moorings to an altogether new location.

This move deepens in significance if we consider Ganti's observation that Bombay is the only city where the language of the film industry does not conform to the languages of the region: "Gujarati and Marathi being the dominant languages of the region." Furthermore the fact that cinema in Hindi [had] developed in multi-lingual Bombay rather than in the Hindi speaking north, [already] disassociated Hindi films from any regional identification and gave it a "national" character.[71]

This new move to "Bollywood" seeks to give the Hindi film an international character—one with few if any ties to a specific physical location.

As the Hindi film and its music travel from Bombay to "Bollywood," they reconfigure the political boundaries recognized and controlled by the Indian state. Bollywood music's journey from Bombay, to Madurai, to Kolkata, and finally to Bonn—where the album was "produced"—tracks Bollywood as it infiltrates the globalized marketplace to reproduce India and its likeness for these authors and elude the control of the Indian state.

Notes

1   While both music and the visual image can be circulated via various technologies and circumvent state authority, music is more "slippery" because it escapes the jurisdiction of most laws that focus on the visual image.
2   Ashish Rajadhyaksha, "The 'Bollywoodisation' of the Indian Cinema: Cultural Nationalism in a Global Arena," in *City Flicks: Cinema, Urban Worlds, and Modernities in India and Beyond,* ed. Preben Kaarsholm (Roskilde: International Development Studies, 2002), 95.
3   See Néstor García Canclini, *Consumers and Citizens: Globalization and Multicultural Conflicts* (Minneapolis: University of Minnesota Press, 2001).
4   In 1998, the Indian state recognized film as a legitimate industry.
5   Constituent Assembly (Legislative) Debates, April 8, 1949 [quoted in Aruna Vasudev, *Liberty and Licence in Indian Cinema* (New Delhi: Vikas Publishing, 1978), 78].
6   Ibid.
7   Rajya Sabha Debates, November 26, 1954 (quoted in Vasudev, *Liberty and Licence,* 107–8).
8   For Prasad's address, see *SIFCC Bulletin,* November 1954 (quoted in Vasudev, *Liberty and Licence,* 108–9). For Nehru's thoughts on cinema, see *Film Seminar Report* (Delhi: Sangeet Natak Akademi, 1956), 111–12.
9   *SIFCC Bulletin,* August 1954 (quoted in Vasudev, *Liberty and Licence,* 107).
10 G. C. Awasthy, *Broadcasting in India* (Bombay: Allied Publishers, 1965), 51 (quoted in Vasudev, *Liberty and Licence,* 78). See also Biswarup Sen's and Anna Morcom's essays in this volume.
11 Ibid., 213–14. While the committee might have been formed and existed for a short period, later reports of AIR do not show the existence of this committee. See http://mib.nic.in/information&b/AUTONOMUS/RADIO.htm and http://www.allindiaradio.org/.

12 Peter Manuel, *Cassette Culture: Popular Music and Technology in North India* (Chicago: University of Chicago Press, 1993), 60–1.

13 Peter Manuel, "Popular Music in India: 1901–86," *Popular Music* 7, no. 2 (Summer 1988): 173.

14 See "Study on Copyright Piracy in India," http://www.education.nic.in/ htmlweb/cr_piracy_study/cpr4.html.

15 M. A. Mannan, "Hitting the Right Notes," *India Today,* November 30, 1993, 50–3.

16 See Monika Mehta, "The Khalnayak Debates: What Is Behind Film Censorship," *Jouvert: A Journal of Postcolonial Studies* 5, no. 3 (2001), for a detailed analysis of censorship debates related to this song.

17 Pandit Gautam Kaul to Shri Bhargava, May 19, 1993. Kaul's letter was one of the two hundred letters that the Central Board of Film Certification received regarding the song "Choli ke peeche kya hai." This letter was a part of a larger concern about the cultural impact of economic liberalization.

18 Examining committees certify films.

19 Shakti Samanta, letter to Shri Brij Sethi, June 25, 1993.

20 Terry Skillman, "Songs in Hindi Films," in *Cinema and Cultural Identity: Reflections on Films from Japan, India, and China,* ed. Wimal Dissanayake (New York: University Press of America, 1988), 150.

21 See the 1984 amendment on videos, http://www.nfdcindia.com/copyright. html.

22 Mehta, "The Khalnayak Debates."

23 Shohini Ghosh, "Feminists Engage with Censorship," *Screen,* July 18, 2003, http://www.screenindia.com/fullstory.php?content_id=5020. CBFC told the director of *Dulaara* to replace the word "sexy" with "fancy."

24 Ibid.

25 The Cable Television Networks Rules, 1994, http://www.nfdcindia.com/ copyright.html.

26 The category "U" was first instituted by colonial administrators and subsequently maintained by the postcolonial state.

27 The Central Board of Certification is located in Bombay; there are eight other regional boards located in various parts of India. In order to obtain certification for a film, the film producers or their staff members must first file an application at one of the boards.

28 "Monitoring Ministry," *Cable Quest: Satellite Broadcasting, Cable Television, and Broadband Magazine,* http://www.cable-quest.com/monitoring.htm.

29 The original version of "Kaanta laga" can be found in the film *Samadhi* (The memorial Prakash Mehra, 1972), music director: Laxmikant–Pyarelal. "Behind the raunchy numbers," http://www.hindisong.com/Profile/ Profile.asp?ContentID-453.

30 Harry Anand, *DJ Doll Remix* (Mumbai: T-Series, 2003), CD.

31 Utpal Borpujari, "Big Leap for 'Naughty' Duo," *Deccan Herald,* August 31, 2003, http://www.deccanherald.com/deccanherald/aug31/ent9.asp.

32 The VHP is the cultural arm/police of the Bharatiya Janata Party (BJP).

33 "VHP Stops 'Vulgar' Show by 'Kaanta Laga' Girl," June 2, 2003, http:// headlines.sify.com/2160news1.html.

34 "India: Local Channels Play It Dirty," *Asia Media* (from *Times of India*), December 3, 2003, http//www.asiamedia.ucla.edu/article.asp?parentid=5388.

35 Aparna Joshi and Hetal Adesara, "Television Censorship: Is Anyone Keeping a Watch?" November 4, 2003, http://www.indiantelevision.com/perspectives/y2k3/censor.htm.

36 Selected references: Partha Chatterjee, *The Nation and Its Fragments: Colonial and Postcolonial Histories* (Princeton, N.J.: Princeton University Press, 1993); Zoya Hasan, *Forging Identities: Gender, Communities, and the State* (Delhi: Kali for Women, 1994); Radha Kumar, *The History of Doing* (Delhi: Kali for Women, 1993); and Kum Kum Sangari and Sudesh Vaid, eds., *Recasting Women: Essays in Indian Colonial History* (New Brunswick: Rutgers University Press, 1990).

37 See http://www.ndtv.com/mb/messagethread.asp?topicid=474&tablename=Music and http://nt5094.live-hosting.com/jammagbbs/postedcomments.asp?festival=Kaanta%20Laga%20video.

38 See http://www.indianmi.org/about_us.htm.

39 "Piracy," http://www.indianmi.org/music_piracy.htm.

40 Ibid.

41 Sudipto Dey, "Planning a Remix? Check the Law," *Economic Times,* November 6, 2003, http://economictimes.indiatimes.com/cms.dll/articleshow?msid=270724.

42 "I & B to Tighten Disc Piracy," *Economic Times,* March 13, 2003, http://economictimes.indiatimes.com/articleshow/43843436.cms.

43 Ibid.

44 Saskia Sassen, *Globalization and Its Discontents* (New York: New Press, 1998), XXVII.

45 Ibid.

46 Monika Mehta, "Selections: Cutting, Classifying, and Certifying in Bombay Cinema" (Ph.D. diss., University of Minnesota, 2001), 194–205; and Monika Mehta, "Globalizing Bombay Cinema: Reproducing the Indian State and Family," *Cultural Dynamics* 17, no. 2 (2005): 135–54.

47 Simon Frith, "The Discourse of World Music," in *Western Music and Its Others: Difference, Representation, and Appropriation in Music,* ed. Georgina Born and David Hesmondhalgh (Berkeley: University of California, 2000), 307–8.

48 Ibid.

49 Although the Indian government established the Sangeet Natak Akademi in 1947 as the national body to preserve and promote the performing arts, the organization's focus on "traditional" cultural forms excludes the government's recognition of Indian film music. See Shubha Chaudhuri, "Aspects of Documentation and Mass Media. A Viewpoint from India," in *World Music, Musics of the World: Aspects of Documentation, Mass Media, and Acculturation,* ed. Max Peter Baumann (Florian Nötzel Verlag: Wilhemshaven, 1992), 235.

50 Ibid.

51 Fijian Indian taxi driver, Brisbane, 1997, quoted in Manas Ray, "Bollywood Down Under: Fiji Indian Cultural History and Popular Assertion,"

in *Floating Lives: The Media and Its Asian Diasporas,* ed. Stuart Cunningham and John Sinclair (Lanham, Md: Rowman & Littlefield Publishers, 2001), 136–84, 136.

52 *Golden Voices from the Silver Screen: Classic Indian Film Soundtrack Songs from the Television Series "Movie Mahal"* (London: GlobeStyle Records, 1990), CD.

53 Ibid.

54 Paul Oliver, "Movie Mahal: Indian Cinema on ITV Channel 4," *Popular Music 7,* no. 2 (1988): 215–16, 215.

55 *Golden Voices from the Silver Screen.*

56 Ibid.

57 Satinder Chohan, "When Holly Met Bolly," *Guardian,* December 2, 1999.

58 *I Love Bollywood: 15 Classic Tracks from Bollywood's Greatest Songs* (London: Manteca World Music, 2001).

59 M. Leonard, *Britain TM: Renewing Our Identity* (London: Demos, 1997).

60 *I Love Bollywood.*

61 Ibid.

62 *The Rough Guide to Bollywood: The Glitz, the Glamour, the Soundtrack* (London: World Music Network, 2002).

63 Errol Nazareth, "Sample This: Hooray for Bollywood," *Eye,* July 3, 2002, http://www.eye.net/eye/issue/issue_03.07.02/thebeat/sample.html.

64 Shabs, "Liner Notes," in *The Very Best Bollywood Songs* (London: Outcaste Records, 2001).

65 Ibid.

66 John Lewis, "Introduction," in *The Very Best Bollywood Songs.*

67 Ibid.

68 *The Music of Bollywood* (London: Universal Music International, 2002).

69 Rajadhyaksha, "The 'Bollywoodisation' of the Indian Cinema," 95.

70 *Doob Doob O'Rama: Filmsongs from Bollywood* (Bonn, Germany: Normal Records, 1999).

71 Tejaswani Ganti, *Bollywood: A Guidebook to Popular Hindi Cinema* (New York: Routledge, 2004), 12.

4. Bollywood and Beyond

The Transnational Economy of Film Production in Ramoji Film City, Hyderabad

Shanti Kumar

A city within a city, Ramoji Film City (RFC) claims to be the largest, most comprehensive, and most professionally planned film production center in the world. Located in South India (geographically quite far from the Bombay film industry), RFC is considered by many industry experts to have surpassed the size and facilities offered at Universal Studios and other major film studios in Hollywood. With more than seven thousand five hundred employees working in twenty-nine departments, RFC has the capacity to accommodate the production of twenty international films at any one time and cater to at least forty Indian films simultaneously.

Located one hour's driving distance (approximately 40 kilometers) from the twin cities of Hyderabad and Secunderabad, RFC is also a tourist site with more than two thousand five hundred visitors every day. RFC's Web site, www.ramojifilmcity.com, describes RFC as a one-stop facility that "can offer the best of pre-production, production, and post-production facilities for any kind of film or television show."[1] According to publicity materials, RFC can provide any locale, whether it is a Japanese or a Mughal garden, an Arizona desert, or well-known tourist attractions such as the Taj Mahal in Agra, the Hawa Mahal in Jaipur, or the Golden Temple in Amritsar.

Of course, the synthetic reproductions of prominent cultural landmarks and popular tourist attractions at RFC are not "real." Yet since the cultural landmarks at RFC are made to appear as exact replicas of the real ones, they cannot be considered fake (either in the sense of being unrealistic for the tourists or the spectator who look at them). Instead, the creations at RFC must be understood in terms of what Jean Baudrillard has defined as hyperreal constructs—simulations of reality that appear as "real" as the real things themselves.[2] In this Baudrillardian sense, the cultural creations and recreations at RFC participate in the capitalist production of vast synthetic spaces that can be used by any filmmaker from anywhere in the transnational entertainment industry. Promoting RFC as "the land of movies," publicity brochures promise "an out-of-the-world experience" for visitors and entice filmmakers with a "splash of color and charm" in diverse indoor settings and outdoor locales. Notwithstanding these heady promises, what makes RFC a unique phenomenon in India is that filmmakers can make an entire film—from preproduction and production to postproduction—in a single location.

Since its opening in 1997, six foreign films and over five hundred Indian films in languages such as English, Hindi, Kannada, Telugu, and Tamil have been produced at RFC. *Maa Nannaki Pelli* (My father's wedding) was the first Telugu film shot entirely at RFC in 1997. The first Hindi film shot in RFC was *Bade Miyan Chote Miyan* (Big guy, little guy David Dhawan) in 1998. I closely analyze its song and dance sequences to demonstrate how filmmakers are tapping into RFC's one-stop shop of outdoor locations and indoor studios to produce hybrid mediascapes. In this essay, I argue that RFC represents the rise of a new global vernacular in Indian cinema that is inflected with regional variations and local traditions even as it seeks newer markets around the world.

Arjun Appadurai uses the term mediascape to describe the diversity of media images that is constantly produced and reproduced by new media technologies in a rapidly globalizing cultural economy.[3] Appadurai's formulation provides a useful framework for examining how the production practices at RFC have emerged at the intersections of global, national, and local flows of media and popular culture in South India. By foregrounding the song and dance sequences in *Bade Miyan Chote Miyan,* this essay underscores the ways in which RFC is giving shape to a new transnational economy of film production in India, even as it is influenced by the traditional codes and conventions of Indian cinema.

The Making of a Reel Estate

RFC is the dream project of Cherukuri Ramoji Rao, the owner of the Eenadu media group in the South Indian state of Andhra Pradesh. The

Eenadu group is one of the largest media conglomerates in South India, and Ramoji Rao's business empire consists of several English- and Telugu-language periodicals, including the widely read newspaper, *Eenadu*; a multilingual satellite television network, ETV; a film distribution banner, Ushakiron Movies; and a financial services group, Margadarshi.[4]

A well-known film producer and director in the Telugu film industry, or Tollywood as some fans call it, Rao recognized that filmmaking in India is a rather tedious and expensive venture because the production calendar can often be interrupted by unpredictable weather, unreliable electric supply, inappropriate set designs, and inflexible star schedules.[5] Realizing that a more reliable environment and a well-organized production schedule could dramatically reduce the time, the cost, and the resources required to make a film in India, Rao set to develop the one-stop RFC.

Planning for RFC began in 1991, and Rao acquired a barren stretch of 2,000 acres in Anjapur village, on the outskirts of Hyderabad. The RFC mandate for planners was a complex one: to create a film city that was flexible enough to cater to every filmmaker's needs and wishes, but also authentic enough to give every viewer a "realistic" feel of the diverse shooting locations.

According to RFC spokespeople, its unique selling point is that "a producer can walk in with a script and walk out with the canned film."[6] By offering the entire gamut of services necessary for producing a film, RFC has introduced the concept of "turnkey packages" in India at a time when many of the major film studios in Mumbai are content to offer only shooting floors. Pulapaka Ramesh, RFC general manager, explains that the turnkey packages are determined by "locations, number of people, type of stay, type of food, transportation, lighting and other equipment and number of days."[7] After Rao introduced the concept of turnkey packages for the Indian film industry, other studios in South India, such as the MGR Film City in Chennai, have started to offer similar one-stop services.

RFC officials also claim that the RFC has the largest number of outdoor locations and the biggest indoor studios in Asia. There are over one hundred and fifty gardens in RFC, which, along with the large and small indoor studios, provide filmmakers many options for shooting a variety of song and dance sequences. This rationalized technique of using the synthetic locales of RFC to shoot all the song and dance sequences in one

Sets for song-dance sequences at Ramoji Film City.

place for the sake of economic efficiency and scheduling convenience is quite novel in Indian cinema, where the traditional mode of producing song and dance sequences involves shooting in a variety of scenic locales from all over India or, sometimes, from around the world.

Recognizing the importance of diverse outdoor locales for the production of song and dance sequences in Indian cinema, Rao expended considerable resources in the landscaping, design, and layout of the gardens. Because the soil in the rocky Deccan plateau lacks the fertility to cultivate the plants and trees needed, red and black soils were imported. The gardens are laid out in distinct patterns to give a film director the creative flexibility to shoot one sequence in the Swiss Alps or the Arizona desert and turn the cameras and the crew in a different direction to shoot another sequence in Kashmir or in Mysore. For instance, the Two-in-One garden appears like the famous Mughal gardens from the outside and resembles the Brindavan Garden in Mysore from the inside. Similarly, the Arizona garden when filmed against a setting sun resembles a desert in the southwestern region of the United States. Shangri La gardens have been designed to create a view of trees and flowers that are always in full bloom. By naming the gardens as "Shangri La," Rao and his associates were creating a mythical city of eternal life in the rocky terrain of the Deccan plateau, but also hoping to attract the attention of foreign filmmakers to the turnkey package concept.

By bringing global, national, and local filmmakers together to the outskirts of Hyderabad and catering to their diverse modes of film production, RFC has led the way in engendering a new cinematic optics in India that I define in relation to what Homi Bhabha, following Jacques Derrida, has described as the "techno-tele-media apparatuses" of acceleration and dislocation.[8] What is "accelerated" by the techno-tele-media apparatuses of this new cinematic optics is the ability of the users "to 'access' a range of materials and material cultures" with unimaginable ease.[9] What is dislocated "is therefore, a sense of ontology, of the essentiality or inevitability of being-and-belonging by virtue of the nation, a mode of experience and existence that Derrida calls a *national ontopology*."[10]

To find an optic framework that is adequate to articulate the rapid acceleration and dislocation of national ontopologies that Derrida outlines in rather spectral and schematic terms, Bhabha recalls Walter Benjamin's analysis of the photographic camera in a much-cited essay, "The Work of Art in the Age of Mechanical Reproduction." Specifically, Bhabha focuses on the camera as a media innovation of the 1860s that introduces, what Benjamin calls, "unconscious optics" through "the resources of its lowerings, liftings, its interruptions, and isolations, its extensions and accelerations, its enlargements and reductions." According to Benjamin, the camera is a radical innovation because its technologies of representation, such as the enlargement of a snapshot, provide a more precise rendering of what is visible yet unclear to the naked eye and, in the process, reveal "entirely new structural formations of the subject."[11]

Bhabha finds that this optical unconscious is now being rapidly accelerated and dislocated by media innovations at the dawn of the twenty-first century. By juxtaposing Benjamin's description of the camera's optical resources of acceleration and Derrida's deconstruction of the radical dislocation of national ontopologies by the techno-tele-media apparatuses of our time, Bhabha invites us to think of a new "media temporality" that shuttles in a double movement to make "*at once* contiguous, and *in that flash*, contingent, the realms of human consciousness and the unconscious."[12] Similarly, in the movement between the rapid acceleration and dislocation of the national ontopology in Indian cinema, I seek to articulate a new optics that has been introduced by the techno-tele-media apparatuses at RFC as they destabilize "that we deem to be familiar, domestic, national and homely" in India today.[13]

Among the techno-tele-media apparatuses that are available to global, national, and local filmmakers at RFC are forty shooting floors, ranging in size from 20 feet by 30 feet to 135 feet by 210 feet. The smaller shooting floors consist of a variety of permanent indoor settings such as a bedroom, a living room, or a kitchen, which are often used not only by film directors but also by ETV for the production of in-house television serials. Some of the larger shooting floors are often used to create elaborate settings for song and dance sequences. The largest shooting floor, called BSF 3, has been used in several Hindi films and other regional-language films to produce elaborate song and dance sequences. As we shall see in the next section the case of *Bade Miyan Chote Miyan*, the large shooting floor is particularly useful to recreate the "aura" of an outdoor locale.

RFC spokespeople proclaim that if a film director or a television producer requires something that is not readily available with the set-construction division, Maya can create the required set. Spread over an area of 300,000 square feet, Maya (the Sanskrit word for divine magic) employs over one thousand carpenters, sculptors, and craftspersons who can transform an art director's creative ideas into cinematic reality. The furniture division, Harmony, also has a pool of carpenters and artisans who are trained to build furniture and decors for "Indian," "Chinese," "European," or "American" set designs. If a filmmaker needs a ready-made prop, RFC hosts Parade, the prop-supply division, which houses a wide variety of objects from the most mundane to the exotic.

As the creative designs and the constructed spaces of Maya and Harmony blur traditional distinctions of the outside and the inside, or the foreign and the domestic, simulations of real-life objects appear authentic in the "reel life" of cinematic frames created at RFC. The defining element of these simulated "real-life" objects is the cut or an imaginary rupture that, as Appadurai reminds us, creates a disjuncture between cinematic frames, even as it erases their differences to construct a seamless narrative that appears more real than the offscreen reality it seeks to represent. Using the cinematic resources that Maya and Harmony provide, a filmmaker can create "authentic" simulations of real-life objects, events, and places that appear glamorous and fantastic to viewers, even as they remain plausible and compelling for the mediation of everyday discourse.

Officials at RFC claim that international producers can save up to 40 percent of the production costs if they use the simulated outdoor locations, indoor studios, and the other support services in the film city.[14] If the same filmmaker also uses the postproduction facilities, the savings could be as high as 50 percent of the total costs in a comparable studio in Europe or North America. In the past, foreign films were made in India only if the story was centrally about Indians, as in the case of Richard Attenborough's *Gandhi* (1982) or David Lean's *A Passage to India* (1984). However, in recent years, several foreign films, such as *Centipede* (2004) directed by Gregory Gieras, *Crocodile 2: Death Swamp* (2002) directed by Gary Jones, *Nightfall* (2000) directed by Roger Corman, *Panic* (2001) and *Quicksand* (2002) directed by Sam Firstenberg, and *In the Shadow of the Cobra* (2004) directed by Ted Nicoloau, have been produced in RFC.

Although most of the foreign films shot at RFC so far have been low-budget, B-grade movies, Rao plans to coproduce big-budget films with well-known directors and producers in Hollywood. In March 2001, the director–actor duo of Sam Firstenberg and Michael Dudikoff produced an American film entitled *Quicksand* entirely at RFC. The film was shot on a budget of 3.7 million dollars in a four-week schedule. *Quicksand* is set in a military base in Arizona, and the filmmakers used the outdoor locations and sets at RFC to recreate the military base in a synthetic Arizona desert landscape. Firstenberg acknowledged that lower production costs combined with a highly skilled technical workforce at RFC induced him to make his film entirely in India.[15]

In this sense, Rao's vision of developing the film city as a transnational studio to attract foreign producers is in line with Hyderabad's growing reputation as a popular center for the "outsourcing" of hi-tech skills in the increasingly globalized South India. However, I would argue that the complex articulation of global, national, and local mediascapes at RFC cannot be understood merely in terms of the "outsourcing" debate in the information technology industries. The software industry is already a booming business in South India, and the Hi-Tech City in Hyderabad has run into serious competition from other equally capable contenders like Bangalore—often called the silicon valley of India. While there is a healthy rivalry between these two South Indian cities in the information technology sector, there has been hardly any discussion of their role in the global entertainment industry. The entertainment industry is a multimillion dollar enterprise worldwide, but the Indian share in the business is minimal, to say the least. In this context, the film studios of Hyderabad, led by RFC, have done well to gain a "toehold" in that market. Although officials at RFC are reluctant to divulge the figures, industry sources estimate that the production and postproduction costs in RFC are about ten times lower than a similarly equipped studio in Hollywood.[16] However, to go beyond the "outsourcing debate," it is important to remember that a fierce competition is also raging *within* the Indian film industry as the Hyderabad-based Telugu film industry is seeking to compete with the national hegemony of the Hindi film industry, which has traditionally been based in Mumbai. Moreover, filmmaking is cheaper in Hyderabad than in Mumbai by about 30–40 percent; so, many Hindi filmmakers are looking toward RFC as a more economical, efficient, and convenient location for shooting their films.[17] *Bade Miyan Chote Miyan* (1998) was the first Hindi film to be produced almost entirely at RFC; since then, other producers and directors in Hindi cinema and other regional-language cinemas (such as Bengali, Kannada, Tamil, and Telugu) have been lining up at RFC. In the next section, I closely analyze the song and dance sequences in *Bade Miyan Chote Miyan* to examine how the many hyperreal locales and synthetic studio settings at RFC have been creatively integrated into what is commonly known as the Bollywood style of filmmaking in Indian cinema.

The Place of Song and Dance Sequences in a Hindi Film

Audiences who are unfamiliar with the codes and convention of Hindi cinema often find it difficult to make sense of song and dance sequences that, they believe, are inserted rather arbitrarily into a film's narrative. Even among audiences who are avid fans of the so-called Bollywood style of filmmaking, there is a great debate on whether song and dance sequences are unique assets or great detriments to the further growth of Indian cinema. However, according to scriptwriter Anjum Rajabali, one can better understand the crucial role played by song and dance sequences in Hindi cinema by examining their placement within the narrative of a film. Rajabali describes the various narrative functions of song and dance sequences in Bollywood films in the following terms:

1. Introduction: Singing your hellos…. While it is possible to create a scene that will reveal the hero's character, many times, it is more interesting and more enjoyable particularly in love stories to use a song for the purpose….

2. Thunderbolt: When a character falls in love instantly, intensely, uncontrollably a song can convey his unique madness very effectively....

3. Beyond forbearance: Often, a situation reaches a point of unbearability for a character. However ... to prolong that situation for dramatic purposes, for the tension to get underlined and to make the viewer stay with this agony (or ecstasy) of the character, a song is an excellent way to do that.

4. Ah relief! In an action film or a dramatically intense film, songs not only provide a welcome relief from the relentlessness of the conflict but, by taking you away just long enough from it, increase your enjoyment of the thrill of the action that ordinarily strikes you.

5. A parallel narrative: Interestingly, with some love stories particularly, one can almost tell the story just with the aid of songs, even if you take all the dialogue and action scenes away....

6. Can't say it? Sing it! Songs serve the wonderfully useful purpose of beautifully expressing sentiments which would've sounded vulgar or ridiculous or self-consciously awkward in dialogue.

7. Transition: Western films usually use montage to convey the passage of time. In India ... we use a song, which can also show the passage of emotions, of growing up, of transformation.

8. What's grammar without punctuation? For the structurally conscious writer, songs ... can help to mark the ends and beginnings of movements, acts, sequences. They take you through a mood change smoothly, allowing fresh issues to emerge in the story, without tripping your gears.[18]

Although Rajabali's eight-point list is by no means exhaustive, I have quoted at length from his essay because it provides subtle insights into the much-misunderstood role of song and dance sequences in the narrative conventions of Hindi cinema. By providing specific examples from several Hindi films across the decades, Rajabali demonstrates how and why the song and dance sequence is "a useful aid" to tell a story well and to "enhance the viewers' enjoyment of the same."[19] It would be almost impossible to find a single film in which the song and dance sequences perform all eight narrative functions described by Rajabali. But in every Hindi film with song and dance sequences in it, some or most of the narrative functions described by Rajabali are fulfilled at least in part. In *Bade Miyan Chote Miyan*, for instance, the narrative consists of several song and dance sequences, which appear to fulfill several important narrative functions.

DVD cover for *Bade Miyan Chote Miyan* with Amitabh Bachchan as Bade Miyan (above) and Govinda as Chote Miyan (below).

Billed as the "Biggest Entertainer" of 1998 and directed by David Dhawan, *Bade Miyan Chote Miyan* brought together, for the first time, two of the biggest superstars of Hindi cinema, Amitabh Bachchan and Govinda—that too in dual roles. The story of *Bade Miyan Chote Miyan* revolves around the antics of two friends, Arjun Singh (Amitabh Bachchan) and Pyare Mohan (Govinda), who are police officers. Arjun's sister, Seema (Raveena Tandon) and Pyare are in love, but her brother does not approve of the relationship. Much to his consternation, he finds Pyare and Seema dancing in a park, singing to each other, "Kisi disco mein jaayen…" (Let us go to a disco).

"Kisi disco mein jaayen…" has some innovative choreographic moves and playful lines to showcase the renowned dancing abilities of

Govinda and Raveena. Although it is a typical Govinda/Raveena tandem performance, this song and dance sequence also helps to advance the story by revealing to the audiences that Arjun is no longer merely suspicious but knows for a fact that his sister is in love with his partner, Pyare. While Udit Narayan serves as playback singer for Govinda, Alka Yagnik sings for Raveena in this song and dance sequence. In terms of its narrative function, "Kisi disco mein jaayen…" enables Pyare and Seema to sing about their love for each other and also to let Arjun know about it without getting into an ugly confrontation. Thus, "Kisi disco mein jaayen…" seems to perform two general functions that Rajabali describes in the above-cited passage: of enhancing the emotional effect of a melodramatic situation and of resolving emotional tension by skillfully combining music, song, and dance with small doses of comic relief.

Meanwhile, a villainous figure named Jorawar enters the narrative. Jorawar, who is attempting to rob diamonds from a museum, realizes that a policeman is hot on his trail. Jorawar kills the policeman who trails him and subsequently kills a woman (Divya Dutta) who is an eyewitness to this murder. But there is yet another eyewitness, Neha (Ramya Krishna), who is a close friend of the dead witness. The distraught Neha tries to contact Pyare Mohan over the telephone because her friend mentions Pyare's name before dying. But due to a mix-up of identities, Neha mistakenly believes that Arjun is Pyare. Pyare colludes with this misidentification and pretends he is Arjun, while the real Arjun protects Neha from Jorawar's thugs.

As the story unfolds, Neha falls in love with Arjun, even as he appears to be rather cold to her advances. Determined to win Arjun's heart, Neha takes him home and performs a seductive song and dance sequence, "Dhin tak dhin…." Halfway through the sequence, Arjun tries to flee from the house, only to run into Neha, who is now seen dancing in a park. The setting for the park is, once again, in RFC where Neha is seen dancing with a group of dancers gathered in front of a large fountain that is shaped to resemble a large and very ornate water jug, an object which is promoted by RFC tour guides as a major landmark. As Neha continues her pursuit of Arjun in the park, the two sing and dance their way through many of the other RFC gardens. With Arjun continuing to resist Neha's advances, Pyare joins them in the song and dance and tries to convince his friend to stop protesting so much.

"Dhin tak dhin…" is probably more of a limerick than a song, with Jasbinder Narula and Sudesh Bhosle as playback singers. Although some audiences may find the setting for "Dhin tak dhin…" rather unrealistic or excessively crude in the way in which the hero–heroine romance is sexualized, it is important to recognize that the song and dance sequence enables Neha to woo Arjun in an extremely uninhibited way by speaking about her love without transgressing prescribed gender roles. Moreover, in the context of this essay, "Dhin tak dhin…" is noteworthy in that it creatively blends some of the outdoor locales and indoor studios at RFC into a seamless narrative.

Another song and dance sequence that uses the extravagant mediascapes at RFC is "Deta dil jo re…" (I give you my heart). With the "historical" locations of RFC serving as backdrop, "Deta dil jo re…" seeks to create—in rather ahistorical terms—a romantic atmosphere for the two lead pairs by drawing on popular imaginations of the shared pasts and of Islamic and Hindu Rajput cultures (as symbolized by replicas of the Mughal fort and Hawa Mahal palace at RFC). "Deta dil jo re…" begins with the two heroes (Arjun and Pyare) trying to convince the two heroines (Neha and Seema) of their undying love. But the two heroines are in no mood to listen after finding out that Arjun and Pyare had lied to Neha about their true identities. While the two heroes are dressed identically in their police uniforms and leather jackets, the two heroines are adorned in intricately embroidered traditional dresses that blend well with the ornate architecture in the background. Although the police uniforms and the leather jacket of the two heroes may seem rather anachronistic in the historical settings of the fort and the palace, the narrative conventions in Indian cinema have always allowed actors—particularly the male lead characters—to fashion their identities through a pastiche of the modern and the traditional, the Western and the non-Western. The seemingly postmodern conventions of pastiche in Indian cinema are most clearly visible in song and dance sequences that are more often than not located in outdoor contexts.

In *Nationalist Thought and the Colonial World*, Partha Chatterjee argues that the nationalist elites in colonial India fashioned their sense of identity by clearly demarcating their roles in the public and private spheres of life.[20] While in the outside world, Indian men would often wear Western clothes in recognition of the colonial authority of their British masters in the public sphere. But when inside the home, Indian men would wear their traditional clothes as a way to assert their sense of authority and control in the domestic sphere of life. Women, on the other hand, would always wear traditional Indian clothes both in the public and in the private spheres. The reason for this gendered distinction, as Chatterjee explains, is that the British saw Indian women solely in terms of their domestic roles in the home and, therefore, not under the purview of colonial authority in the public sphere. Indian men also identified with the British categorization of gender in public policy and saw women only in terms of their traditional roles in the domestic sphere.

Although the colonial distinctions of the public and the private spheres have become rather blurred in the postcolonial context, traces of this legacy can still be found in the representation of gendered relationships in Indian cinema, particularly in the song and dance sequences. Therefore, in *Bade Miyan Chote Miyan*, when Arjun and Pyare chase Neha and Seema through the corridors and around the courtyards of the palace and the fort in "Deta dil jo re…," the men go through several costume changes, but the women do not change their traditional attire for the duration of the song. In one segment of the song, the two men are shown wearing colorful matching jackets (with Arjun in blue and white and Pyare in red and white), while in another segment they are identically dressed in equally colorful Rajasthani costumes, complete with traditional headgear. While the two heroes are busy cajoling and pleading with the two heroines, they are joined by a group of traditionally dressed male and female dancers who appear in the background the chorus. Halfway through the song and dance sequence, the two heroines relent a bit and join in the singing and dancing more willingly. By the end, they reconcile, and the lovers' tiffs are settled with a kiss.

With both the lead couples firmly establishing their romantic relationships through the requisite song and dance sequences, and the mistaken identities of the two heroes all cleared up, the story takes yet another twist just before the intermission. Two small-time crooks enter, Bade Miyan (played by Amitabh Bachchan in a dual role) and Chote Miyan (played by Govinda, also in a dual role). The arrival of the two crooks as central characters in the film's narrative is highlighted by the title song "Bade miyan to bade miyan…," which is set in the "chor bazaar" (thieves' market or black market) section of RFC.

This song and dance sequence begins with a group of male and female dancers performing in front of a large audience. Bade Miyan and Chote Miyan, who are seated as the guests of honor, appear very pleased as groups of female dancers, dressed in traditional colorful clothes, gyrate in front of them. As the camera zooms in on the action, a group of women rush toward the two heroes and drag them to join in the song and dance. Wearing identical sets of kurta–pajama and waist coats, Bade Miyan and Chote Miyan sing together, "Some love us, some offer us their lives, but all who see us say, Bade Miyan is the big guy, and Chote Miyan is equally divine." The last part of this line—"Bade Miyan to Bade Miyan, Chote Miyan subhan Allah" (Bade Miyan is the big guy and Chote Miyan is oh, so divine")—is the catchy refrain for the rest of the song, even as the location for the dance shifts, rather abruptly, from outside the shopping center to an indoor shooting floor.

Inside a discotheque-like setting, Bade Miyan and Chote Miyan arrive in majestic fashion, not in a horse-drawn chariot but in a cycle rickshaw. The rickshaw is slowly drawn to the center of a dance floor, where a group of women, dressed in miniskirts or colorful pants and shirts, are performing in the backdrop. Bade Miyan, wearing dark glasses, is dressed in a suede-colored suit with black stripes, while Chote Miyan, also wearing dark glasses, is equally colorful in a bright sky blue suit. Once again as Bade Miyan and Chote Miyan break into song and dance, they are ably supported by a group of male and female dancers singing the catchy refrain, "Bade Miyan to Bade Miyan, Chote Miyan subhan Allah."

Once again, without explanation, the location shifts from the discotheque to a traditional *kotha* (or a brothel), where Bade Miyan and Chote Miyan are dancing with a group of colorfully dressed courtesans and singers. Adding color to the already colorful setting of the *kotha*, Bade Miyan is dressed in a purple Sherwani suit, while Chote Miyan is dressed in a bright orange Sherwani suit. In the background are imposing walls with intricate carvings found in the Mughal section of RFC which, as discussed earlier, also appear in the song, "Deta dil jo re…."

While serving as the title song sequence for the film, "Bade Miyan to Bade Miyan…" also serves the narrative function of creating a transition into the second half of the film by introducing the two crooks as central characters just before the intermission. In addition, "Bade Miyan to Bade Miyan…" helps to foreground one of the key elements of the comedy genre that Dhawan uses with exaggerated effect throughout the film—the act of doubling. With Udit Narayan singing for Govinda 2 and Sudesh Bhosle lending his voice for Amitabh 2, "Bade Miyan to Bade Miyan…" not only marks the beginning of the second act for the two male protagonists in their dual roles, but also doubles the viewing pleasure for the avid fan by featuring the two heroes in identical costumes, singing identical lines with identical dance steps.

In keeping with the central theme of doubling everything to the extreme, there are two song and dance sequences that appear twice in the film. One of these songs, "Deta dil jo re..." features the two heroes (Arjun and Pyare) and the two heroines (Neha and Seema) together in one version. In the second version of the same song, the two heroines take a lead in the singing and dancing, while Bade Miyan and Chote Miyan (who are mistaken for Arjun and Pyare) are relegated into supporting roles. In the first version of "Deta dil jo re...," Amit Kumar and Udit Narayan sing for Amitabh and Govinda, while Anuradha Paudwal and Kavita Krishnamurthy serve as the playback singers for Raveena and Ramya Krishna. In the second version of the song, Alka Yagnik replaces Anuradha Paudwal as the playback singer for Raveena, while Sudesh Bhosle lends his voice for Amitabh. The other song and dance sequence that has two versions in this film is "Assi chutki nabbe taal...," with Udit Narayan singing for Govinda and Sudesh Bhosle singing for Amitabh. While the first version of "Assi chutki nabbe taal..." is the longer and the more complete one, the second version is much shorter and comes toward the end to mark the conclusion of the film.

The second half of the film is built around the theme of doubling, and a comedy of errors ensues as the two cops (Amitabh 1 and Govinda 1) are constantly mistaken for the two thieves (Amitabh 2 and Govinda 2). When Bade Miyan and Chote Miyan commit a crime, the police commissioner (Anupam Kher) suspects that Arjun and Pyare are the perpetrators of the act. To add to the confusion, when actress Madhuri Dixit (playing herself) seeks police protection from criminal elements in the Hindi film industry, Arjun and Pyare are sent to look after her.

But, Bade Miyan and Chote Miyan get there before the policemen do and try to protect Madhuri from a group of men who are playing the bad guys in a film being directed by David Dhawan (playing himself). Although Madhuri clarifies that the chase sequence is just part of a film shooting, she mistakenly identifies Bade Miyan and Chote Miyan as the two policemen sent to protect her. As Madhuri's protectors, they are given star treatment on the sets of Dhawan's film and get to see her shooting a song and dance sequence, "Makhna...." Not satisfied with the lucky break that brought them so close to the reigning superstar of Hindi cinema, Bade Miyan and Chote Miyan slip into a fantasy where they are part of the song and dance sequence that Madhuri is performing for Dhawan's film. What follows is a fast-paced bhangra dance tune set to a Punjabi folk song (with Alka Yagnik singing for Madhuri and Amit Kumar and Udit Narayan lending their voices as the playback singers for Govinda and Amitabh, respectively). The song and dance sequence "Makhna…" thus performs the narrative function of, what Rajabali calls, "the thunderbolt." It is as if Bade Miyan and Chote Miyan are so struck by her beauty that no words or dialogue could adequately express their sense of awe. "Makhna…" thus serves the narrative function of enabling both Bade Miyan and Chote Miyan to visualize their fantasies of romancing the superstar of Hindi cinema by inserting themselves into a song and dance sequence with Madhuri.

At the end of the "Makhna…" song and dance sequence, fantasies are brought crashing down to reality when Bade Miyan and Chote Miyan try to flirt with Madhuri after the film shooting. She angrily throws the two men out of the film set and complains to the police commissioner about their inappropriate behavior. Since Madhuri believes that the two men who misbehaved with her were the cops sent to protect her, Arjun and Pyare are reprimanded by the police commissioner.

Later in the film, Arjun and Pyare find themselves in more serious trouble when Bade Miyan and Chote Miyan steal the fabled Kohinoor diamond from the exhibition room in full view of surveillance cameras. When the police check the surveillance video, they believe that Arjun and Pyare are the perpetrators of this crime and place them under arrest. Meanwhile, Seema is captured by Jorawar and taken as a prisoner in his den. Now, Bade Miyan and Chote Miyan must come to her rescue, and the rest leads to a Bollywood ending with the song and dance sequence "Assi chutki nabbe taal…" providing a lighthearted narrative closure to the film.

The convoluted storyline and the confusing twists and turns in the film make *Bade Miyan Chote Miyan* a comedy of excesses often seen in Indian cinema. But Dhawan weaves in well-placed jokes and catchy one-liners with crisply choreographed song and dance sequences throughout the film. Music director Viju Shah sets the songs to a fast-paced beat that works well to showcase the renowned dancing abilities of the leading stars in the film, Govinda and Amitabh Bachchan. The lyrics for the songs, written by Sameer, lend to the physical comedy, and the playful dance sequences that fans have now come to expect not only from stars like Govinda and Amitabh but also from directors like Dhawan.

For instance, a reviewer at planetbollywood.com gives *Bade Miyan Chote Miyan* a 9.0 out of 10 and opines that the film certainly lived up to the expectation of being "The Biggest Entertainer of the Year" in 1998. "I was cracking up out loud almost every 2 minutes or so," confesses the reviewer and writes, "The story is nothing new, but it's the direction, the screenplay and the performances that make the film worth watching."[21] Another reviewer at planetbollywood.com gives the music for *Bade Miyan Chote Miyan* 8 out of 10 and suggests that the song and dance sequences in this film "should figure along with the better scores in David Dhawan movies." Even as he concedes that the music of *Bade Miyan Chote Miyan* is "a good distance from good music or even melodious music," he asks, "Would anyone want to hear that in a David Dhawan movie?"[22]

There are, of course, several Indian films where one can find an excessive number of song and dance sequences that have very little or nothing to do with narrative progression or character development. Therefore, it is not surprising that many audiences and film critics are turned off by song and dance sequences when they are inserted rather gratuitously into the cinematic narrative. However, one can find an equally large number of Indian films where song and dance sequences are beautifully woven into the narrative to portray situations and emotions that cannot be expressed by words alone. In such cases, the song and dance sequence performs a significant narrative function of enhancing the story through an aesthetic sensibility that is more poetic than prosaic. In the final section that follows, I describe the narrative function that song and dance sequences serve in comedic films like *Bade Miyan Chote Miyan* and examine how studios like RFC provide directors like Dhawan with newer resources to creatively manage audience expectations in more effective and cost-efficient ways.

Abhilaksh Likhi of *The Tribune*, who places Dhawan in the pantheon of the great directors of the 1990s, argues that box-office hits like *Bade Miyan Chote Miyan* are examples of Indian cinema "at its versatile best."[23] Dhawan's comedies of excesses do well at the box office due in large part to the director's ability to weave the formulaic conventions of Bollywood into a creative style that is both entertaining and convincing to millions of audiences. Central to the cinematic language of Dhawan's comedies of excesses, such as *Bade Miyan Chote Miyan*, *Biwi No. 1* (Wife no. 1, 1999), or *Haseena Maan Jayegi* (The beautiful girl will agree, 1999), is "a colorful kaleidoscope" of everyday events in which ordinary people find themselves in extraordinary situations. For these common folk—who are no mythical super heroes—the only way out of trouble is to be on the look out for an uncommon chance event that may help resolve the situation (or if things go badly, lead to other even more extraordinary situations).[24] Therefore, in *Bade Miyan Chote Miyan*, when ordinary policemen or common thieves devise some overly dramatic schemes to extricate themselves from extraordinary situations, their exaggerated actions do not appear unconvincing to millions of everyday people.

Similarly, when Bade Miyan and Chote Miyan or their policemen doubles, sing and dance their way out of every troublesome situation that comes their way, audiences recognize that the elaborate dance steps, the fast-paced songs, the colorful costumes, and the extravagant locations are the "defining characteristics" of a popular cinematic language that was perfected by master directors like Manmohan Desai in the 1970s and 1980s and has been refashioned since the 1990s by newcomers like Dhawan.[25]

In this process of refashioning the comedy genre for a new generation of audiences, Dhawan has been rather self-reflexive in paying homage to, and parodying, the films and filmmakers that came before him and also in poking fun at himself and his earlier work in subsequent films. After completing the shooting for *Bade Miyan Chote Miyan* in 1998, Dhawan has continued to use the extravagant locales at RFC in films such as *Anari No. 1* (Novice no. 1, 1999), *Coolie No. 1* (Porter no. 1, 1995), *Jodi No. 1* (Couple no. 1, 2001), and *Dulhe Raja* (The bridegroom is king, 1998). What makes RFC an alluring location for directors like Dhawan—who are very self-reflexive both within and across their films—is the ability to economically choreograph a song and dance sequence in any or all of the gardens and later change the look of the fountain, the layout of the street, the facades of the buildings in the streets, or the shape of the multidimensional pond to create a totally different locale. This ensures that no location will become jaded from repeated exposure, even in a single film, as we have seen in the case of *Bade Miyan Chote Miyan*.

The pliant plasticity and the infinite malleability of indoor studios and outdoor locations at RFC also allows filmmakers to make use of them in many films such as *Anari No. 1*, *Coolie No. 1*, *Jodi No. 1*, and *Dulhe Raja*. Since all of these films were directed by Dhawan, shot at RFC, and featured Govinda in the leading role, the obvious self-reflexivity in this mode of filmmaking becomes an added attraction for fans of superstars like Govinda to create a cross-referential index of the various locales at RFC and feel like they are part of an inside joke that only a select few can really understand.

Some of the outdoor locales and building facades in RFC are clearly recognizable to fans when they are rather stereotypically marked as "North Indian," "South Indian," "Western," or "Japanese." In the "North India" section of the film city, for instance, there is an exact replica of the ancient fort city of Fatehpur Sikri near Agra. There is a replica of the Taj Mahal too, but it can be easily converted to resemble a mosque with a backdrop of a crescent moon at night. Similarly, a building with a front elevation that resembles the Golden Temple in Amritsar, Punjab, has a rear elevation that looks like a shopping center. These facades can be changed or removed quickly because they are built using plaster of paris. So, if a director wishes to blow up the shopping center for a film sequence, an explosion can be created in such a way that the facades explode but the underlying structure of the building remains intact.

In the creative juxtaposition of the rocky realities of the Deccan landscapes in Hyderabad with the cultural fantasies of recreating transnational mediascapes in India, RFC produces what Appadurai has described as the global vernaculars of electronic capitalism.[26] Occupying a strategic location between the national and the transnational, the electronic vernaculars produced by the techno-tele-media apparatuses of RFC are sufficiently localized to cater to the cultural affinities of regional communities and are adequately standardized to provide a global marketplace to media producers, advertisers, and sponsors.

Therefore, I argue that the global vernaculars produced at RFC are not merely about the creation and recreation of physical places. Instead, as I have shown in this essay, the hyperreal mediascapes in RFC also participate in the creation of a new optics in Indian cinema—that I have defined in terms the techno-tele-media apparatuses of simulacrum—which can be used by any filmmaker from anywhere in the transnational entertainment industry.

The synthetic spaces produced by the transnational economy of film cities are plastic and pliant matrices which, as Appadurai reminds us, work to construct a seamless narrative of places and events that appear more real than "reality" itself. However, in mapping the cultural implications of the global vernaculars engendered by film cities, the questions one must ask are not about the historical authenticity or fakeness of any particular location, building, or place. Instead, as I have argued in this essay, one must examine these fantasy spaces of RFC in terms of the changing realities of the global entertainment industry and interrogate the connections between the old and the new that are emerging through the intersections and in the interstices of the national and the transnational in film and television productions.

Notes

1 Quoted on RFC's Web site: www.ramojifilmcity.com
2 Jean Baudrillard, *Simulacra and Simulation* (Ann Arbor: University of Michigan Press, 2000).
3 Arjun Appadurai, *Modernity at Large* (Minneapolis: University of Minnesota Press, 1997), 1–23.
4 K. Suresh, "Reel Estate Tycoon," *Advertising and Marketing,* November 15, 1998, 46–50.
5 "Tollywood" refers to the Telugu-language film industry based in the state of Andhra Pradesh in South India. The name "Tollywood" is derived from the concept of naming the commercial film industries in India in relation to the commercial film industry of "Hollywood" in the United States. Although it was first used in the context of the Bombay-based Hindi film industry (Bollywood = Bombay + Hollywood), the concept was soon extended to define other Indian-language cinemas such as Tollywood (Telugu cinema), kollywood (Tamil cinema), and Mollywood (Malayalam cinema). The naming of the Telugu film industry as "Tollywood" serves a dual function for fans and media critics alike: it enables them to compare and contrast the commercial success and popularity of their native film industry in relation to the global might of Hollywood and it also helps them to draw distinctions and parallels between the regional clout of Telugu cinema and the nationalist appeal of Hindi cinema.
6 Suresh, "Reel Estate Tycoon," 46.
7 Quoted in ibid., 48.
8 Homi K. Bhabha, "Preface: Arrivals and Departures," in *Home, Exile Homeland,* ed. Hamid Naficy (London: Routledge 1998), vii–xii.
9 Ibid., ix.
10 Ibid (emphasis in original).
11 Benjamin quoted in ibid., xi.
12 Bhabha, xi (emphasis in original).
13 Ibid.
14 Kryztoff de Breza, "Ramoji Film City Woos World," http://www.rediff.com/entertai/2002/may/29ram.htm.
15 Stanley Theodore, "International Quality at Cheaper Cost: Hollywood Magic to Be Woven in Hyderabad," *The Statesman,* March 25, 2001, http://web.lexis-nexis.com/.
16 "IT Effects: Cyberabad Emerging Specialist in 3D Animation," *Financial Express,* May 13, 2000, http://web.lexis-nexis.com/.
17 Ibid.
18 Anjum Rajabali, "A Song and Dance about Everything," *Cinema in India* (April–June 2003): 60–65. see Anustup Basu's essay in this anthology.

19 Ibid.

20 Partha Chatterjee, *Nationalist Thought and the Colonial World: A Derivative Discourse?* (London: Zed Books, 1986).

21 Aniket Joshi, "*Bade Miyan Chote Miyan*: 9.0 out of 10.0." http://www.planetbollywood.com/displayReview.php?id=032906024956.

22 Sunder, "*Bade Miyan Chote Miyan:* 8.0 out of 10.0," http://www.planetbollywood.com/music/bmcm.html.

23 Abhilaksh Likhi, "90s' Cinema: Slick, Frothy, Wholesome," *The Tribune* (Sunday Reading Section), August 22, 1999, http://www.tribuneindia.com/1999/99aug22/sunday/head1.htm.

24 Ibid.

25 Ibid.

26 Appadurai, *Modernity at Large*.

5. The Music of Intolerable Love

Political Conjugality in Mani Ratnam's *Dil Se*

Anustup Basu

We Never Sing and Dance in Real Life

Mani Ratnam has said in an interview that his 1998 Hindi film *Dil Se* (From the heart) failed at the box office because the song and dance sequences obstructed the pace of the narrative.[1] Indeed, except for the "Ay ajnabi tu bhi kahin" ("Oh stranger, you too from somewhere") number, which keeps floating into the diegesis as a longing message on All India Radio sent out by the hero to his mysterious and evanescent ladylove, all the other musical segments in the film take place in virtual registers of time and space beyond the direct control of a realist narrational logic. In Ratnam's diagnosis, it becomes clear that he sees these spectacular and ceremonial departures as achieving a *thickening* of time that, in this case, ran contrary to the lean, chronometric unfolding of the thriller format. They impeded and often arrested what is seen to be a basic *dialectical* imperative of cinema of this genre, by which statements, visibilities, and happenings have to interact with each other as part of a breathless, heuristic procession. The song sequences, therefore, were seen to disrupt, to an intolerable degree, a course of "meaningful" narration. Ratnam's concern is undoubtedly shared by quite a few filmmakers of the past and present who have worked with popular Indian cinematic idioms.[2] The question here is strictly not about whether it is artistically desirable to have song and dance sequences punctuating the flow of narration. Rather, it pertains to a notion of propriety and measure—at what point do the musical insertions stop being complimentary spectacles, assume a life of their own, and begin to destroy a basic integrity of storytelling? This reckoning, in a general way, pertains to an industrial dispensation of the medium and a concomitant "modern" privileging of the *realistic narrative* as supreme intellectual and ethical instantiation (as opposed to the "affections" of the pageant, the ritual, or the ceremonial/ carnivalesque spectacle).

Lalitha Gopalan has insightfully read commercial Indian cinema as one of "interruptions," where "song and dance sequences work as a delaying device; the interval defers resolutions, postpones endings and doubles beginnings; and censorship blocks the narrative flow, redirects the spectator's pleasure towards and away from the state."[3] Along with these digressive impulses, "Indian popular films are equally invested in assuaging the discontinuity accompanying these cuts by resorting to generic logic."[4] Gopalan's formulation can be linked, in a formal sense, to the basic typologies of Hindi film narration identified by Ravi Vasudevan—the iconic, the tableau, and segments of realist continuity.[5] Seen in these terms, the interplay between the eminent (as in iconic stasis), the immanent (as in tableau), and the dialogic (as in linear realist narration) sets up a dynamic and complex unfolding of meaning in cinema, in which the camera oscillates between a secular navigation of an uneven historical world and the presentation of a static, depthless façade of an epic cosmology.[6] According to Vasudevan, as far as mainstream Hindi films are concerned, the formal ideological challenge in this oscillation between the epic and the modernist–realist codas of expression lay in securing the graduated dominance of an urban, educated middle-class subject position in the final count.[7] In formal terms, it would mean strenuously establishing a normative of "scientific" storytelling as a baseline of aesthetic value, by which different modes of the cinematic (the song and dance and the *darsanic* encounter with the iconic figure) would be judged in terms of their differential and deferential relations with realism. It is only from such a grid of value, one that sets up a clear hierarchy between the two historical roles of cinema— the pictures of life in the works of the Lumières gaining aesthetic precedence over the cine magic of George Méliès—that one can pronounce the song and dance to be an "interruption" in the first place.[8]

Scholars such as Tom Gunning and Miriam Hansen have suggested that early cinema in the west had developed along many potential lines of social usage before they were erased or overcoded by a corporatist– taylorist mode of big studio production and a style of melodramatic realism and continuity editing.[9] In the annals of Indian cinema, more specifically in relation to the song and dance sequence, we notice a similar historical process of aesthetic reformation and normalization.

For instance, in early experimentations with the technology of sound, narration in films like *Indrasabha* (The Court of Indra, J. J. Madan, 1932) or *Kalidas* (H. M. Reddy, 1931) unfolded musically, in the form of what Bhaskar Chandravarkar has called "songlets" of short duration, rather than through the now-dominant mode of dialogue-based propositional realism.[10] Ashoke Ranade has suggested that these lyrical formations were a continuous rather than an "interrupting" principle of expression, perpetually in between the poles of tune and dialogue, emanating from oral expressive cultures.[11] It would therefore be gratuitous to say that *Indrasabha* had seventy-one songs; instead, the entire sound track of the film can be considered to be a singular, constitutive body of musical narration, in which interacting lyrical assemblages were interspersed by stylized voice incantations.

The gradual suppression of this comprehensive melodic impulse, the streamlining of an often radically experimental interface between traditional forms and technology, and a cultural abjuration of genres of attraction and magic (like the Phalke and Prabhat mythologicals and the Wadia stunt films) subsequently created a nationalist aesthetic clearing for various modes of "narrating the nation."[12] The various contesting strands of cinematic realism in postindependence India—from the epic melodramatic register of the Bombay film (inaugurated by the studio products of Bombay Talkies) to the Indian People's Theatre Association (IPTA-inspired socialist realism in the early Raj Kapoor or Bimal Roy, the liberal humanism of Satyajit Ray, or the state-sponsored developmentalist realism of the 1970s (the Films Division documentaries and Shyam Benegal) were largely prompted by a general aspiration for a western-style cultural modernity that could be "homed" in the new republic and also be affiliated to an internationalist ecology of postwar development.[13] The status of the song sequence—as a signature of the variegated folk-agrarian roots of Indian film—has always been a tenuous one in this overall field. It has shifted between being a marker of indigenous cultural specificity to a formalist obstacle that had to disappear or transcoded in a gradualist process of *becoming* modern.[14]

However, there is an increasingly growing body of recent critical evaluations—both journalistic and academic in nature—that would forward a transposed perspective: Indian popular cinema is "not yet modern" because it is already *postmodern*. That is, as a postpolitical/posthistorical contemporary, the song sequence can actually be seen to impart commodity value to the film as a signature of ethnically

differentiated "Bollywood," just as a specialized style of martial arts choreography does to Hong Kong action flicks or, in terms of high art, magic
realism to a terrain of Latin-American fiction. In the transnational free
market, the song sequence, seen as such, can thus emerge as a free-floating,
eminently consumable *eccentricity* in the smooth space of planetary
capital. The point, of course, is not to be simply for or against categories
such as modernity, postmodernity, pastiche, or realism. It is to refrain
from using them as *categorical essences* and championing and denigrating
them as such. In the next few sections, I will try to demonstrate how such
concepts, along with anterior ones such as folk culture, tradition, or Indianness, can be mobilized in tandem, as packets of knowledge, information, spiritualist myths, spectacles, or affects, to create fluid-mosaic
movements of power as information in our global temporalities.[15] As a
matter of fact, we can argue that liberating the postulates that we identify
with the modern (equality, rights, citizenship, and so on) or, for that matter, an invented tradition from a Hegelian burden of a singular history
can in fact release their transformative potentialities.

The Question of Geotelevisuality

Increasingly, in an age of borderless electronic publicity, the mode of production of song sequences is being informed by imperatives of
autonomous, segmented distribution.[16] These episodes regularly appear as
self-sufficient television software much before the actual film is released.
They also continue to have an independent shelf life in video, cable, and
digital video disc (DVD) circuits, not to mention the huge audio-
products industry, long after the film completes its theatrical run. These
thus often seem to detach themselves from relations of fidelity to the
filmic whole and follow what I will call an "indifferent" logic of "geotelevisual" production and dissemination. In being aligned with "other" image
worlds of the travel documentary, the designer apparel, figurations and
statements of lifestyle, a transnational idiom of advertisement, and technologies of the self of various kinds, the making of song sequences are
often partially or completely separated from notions of "value" derived
from a founding act of narration. Simply put, such sequences can arrive
without any causal relation to the story or its composite milieu; they can
invoke bodies, spaces, and objects that can arrive from any visual universe
whatever. In accommodating them, the narrative economy of cinema only

assembles with, without acquiring an imperial command over, a global plenitude of the musical–televisual image. It is not that such interregnums have no relation whatsoever with the propulsive drive of narration; rather, the relation is usually a *disjunctive* one. That is, they impart precisely those transformative energies pertaining to desire and fantasy that characters cannot purchase from their milieus and cultures cannot draw from their locations. In these sequences, the figure of the village bumpkin or *dehat* can thus instantaneously transform into that of the dancing music–video artist or the transnational tourist or reveal a mythical comfort with different aspects of geotelevisuality—urban technologies, lifestyles, weapons, or images of aspiration and fantasy.

By the expression *geotelevisuality* we mean, in a basic sense, the projection and reception of images, sounds, and words through worldwide distances, across territorial, cultural, linguistic, and religious frontiers. This also means ceasing to consider such borders as static and positive demarcations; geotelevisuality, as a matter of fact, is indistinguishable from the historical nomadism of these very borders. Inasmuch, it has nothing *essentially* to do with the instrument called television. Rather, geotelevisuality, in various technical forms, through graduated measures of priestly and monarchical mediation, has always been a primary task of human beings trying to read their godless universe. It is in this primary sense that the postcard or the telescope can be considered to be geotelevisual, just as our contemporary items such as the television, the geostrategic satellite, or the Internet are. In the continental, primarily Germanic philosophical tradition of the west after Kant, this perpetual commerce between the local and the global assumed a particular form pertaining to a desire for a "totality" of worldly knowledge. In perhaps the most memorable twentieth-century political articulation of this philosophy in the hands of the Hungarian Marxist Georg Lukács, this ambition for a "world historical" consciousness was attached to a notion of international revolutionary praxis.[17] It is in this spirit that Fredric Jameson forwards his notion of "cognitive mapping" as an effort on part of the denizen of the postmodern, "postindustrial" city (now bereft of Lukács' proletariat, which has increasingly been relegated to the "Third World") to navigate and connect the bits and bytes of information beamed to her into a workable worldview.[18] In the age we have designated as one of information, what is being witnessed is an unprecedented intensification of such planetary traffic, in agglomerates of intelligence (of points of view, "facts," statistics, advertisements, shifting indexes, fashions, cultures, tastes, "quizdoms," animated databases, and so on) beyond the finitudes of human subjectivity or consciousness. One can also say that our occasion is also distinguished by the fact that information, as capital itself, is taking over all apertures of geotelevisual exchange, as part of an overall production of social life in itself. It is precisely in this sense that one can say that while geotelevisuality did not come into being in our occasion, it is in the present dispensation of connectivity and finance capital that it has been *informationized*.[19]

Increasingly, flows of geotelevisual information seem to radically transform configurations of "tradition" or the indigenous "self" without measured, "organic" procedures of synthesis or mediation.[20] The interchange between a cinema of the "self" and the shock and welter of planetary information that we see in the Indian context of the 1990s is part of a dynamic process no longer devoted to producing the book of the world. Rather, what is created, from moment to moment, is an amorphous mass of fragments (information that is cinematic or cinema that is informatic) where the particle signs of the engulfing global mingle indeterminately with those of the now uprooted and fanning out local. More than warring "self-other" diagrams of human subjectivity, what becomes immanent thereby are movements of a transnational "database intelligence," where random images of desire, terror, and ideology float into and depart from each other.

The song sequences are the usual, but not the only vehicles for geotelevisual excursions. In Kuku Kohli's 1995 mafiosi thriller *Haqueeqat* (Reality), the main characters are a mob-hit-man-turned garage mechanic and a young, impoverished music teacher. Almost the entire action takes place in a Mumbai city slum. However, the "dream"-based song sequences featuring the couple and their fantasies are set in Alpine Switzerland, with both of them dressed in designer western suits. In Vimal Kumar's 1997 film *Tarazu* (Scales), Caribbean bodies arrive from an ontic source (a Deleuzian any space whatever) beyond the milieu of the story and are set to music with the lead pair on a sea beach. In *Jamai Raja* (Son-in-law) (A. Kondandarami Reddy, 1990), the feudal melodrama involving the overbearing mother-in-law and the newly wed couple is interspersed by nonobligatory digressions, by which a sphere of private, nuclear desires (precisely that which is foreclosed by the joint-family narrative) becomes immanent in a fantasy setting of Sergio Leone-style spaghetti westerns. A similar escape takes place in Shankar's *Jeans* (1998), where the couple, imperiled by traditional prohibitions, is temporarily rendered afloat and free in a space of international travel featuring the seven wonders of the world in the sumptuously shot "Ajooba Ajooba" (Wonder! wonder!) number. In Shankar's *Nayak* (Hero, 2001), a song sequence depicting the conflict between the hero's public role as chief minister and his private duties toward his girlfriend takes place in a digitized setting of snakes and ladders. This remarkable episode ends with a series of shots showing the protagonist in the traditional attire of Hindu kings, presiding over a military march-past and a show of arms of medieval European knights in full armor.

Nonnarratological travel, or import of visual insignia of "foreignness," is not new to the formal dynamics of Indian cinema. Shakti Samanta's 1969 film *An Evening in Paris,* for instance, promises a romance with the European city itself (the "evening" refers to spectator and not narrative time). The film, however, moves freely from Paris through Switzerland and Germany and stages its climax near the Niagara Falls in North America. Hence, in suggesting that contemporary Indian mainstream cinema has developed a special geotelevisual character, what we are drawing attention to is only an intensification of such transports, by which the arrival of signs, the vectorization of bodies into any spaces whatsoever can happen instantaneously, without procedures of being sanctified by a dominant national culturalist ethos.[21] The latter practice involves a priestly monitoring of movements both inside and outside the geopolitical nation-state that we see in classical postwar Indian cinematic narratives of the 1950s and 1960s, generically characterized by Prasad as "feudal family romance."[22] Travels within the nation in such films are largely interiorized into a grand domestic conversation of the nation with itself, by which the *landness* of the land passes from a geographical aesthetic into a political concept. Similarly, forays into foreign shores in classical Hindi cinema are usually possible only after traditional rites of passage by which professional compulsions or touristic and libidinal desires are properly attached to the universal interests of the feudal joint family. The couple in Raj Kapoor's *Sangam* (Confluence, 1964) can go to Europe and its playground of urban desires only after marriage, with their bodies all the time being encurved by stipulations of tradition: the honeymooning twosome never kiss in public; white people in the background do. The rebellious Shammi Kapoor's star persona of the 1960s becomes possible only when the dancing Elvis Presley-like apparition is ethically rooted in the indigenous community. The alien attributes of his body are thus cast as *naturalistic* signs of libidinous eccentricity that is eventually cured by traditional coupledom as in *Junglee* (The wild one,

Subodh Mukherjee, 1961). Else it appears as feigned madness in the face of deep conspiracy in *Rajkumar* (Prince, K. Shankar, 1964) or *Teesri Manzil* (The third floor, Vijay Anand, 1966). It is the same graduated aesthetics of "exposure"—of an India-in-the-world—that we see in narratives of patriotic love in Manoj Kumar's *Purab Aur Paschim* (East and West, 1970) and patriotic espionage in Dev Anand's *Prem Pujari* (Love worshipper, 1970) and Ramanand Sagar's *Aankhen* (Eyes, 1968).[23]

We can contrast such classic images of becoming modern through a calibrated "internationalism" of bodies and insignia with some contemporary cinematic moments featuring what we can call, for the moment, a dedomesticized, metropolitan circuit of images. In a sequence in David Dhawan's *Chal Mere Bhai* (Let us go brother, 2000), the hero starts driving a car in a busy street in Mumbai; by the time he stops, the car is in a Swiss landscape, where the next development in the story takes place. We call this form of transfer "informatic" geotelevisuality precisely because it does not allow for any naturalistic anchoring of signs. If that were the case, the Swiss landscape could cinematically participate in the determined milieu of Mumbai only through a procedure of selection, enframing, semiotic ordering, and familiarization under the perspectivist control of the realist narrative. This is how, to take a stray example, London's Pinewood Studios and other English locations cinematically *become* tropical Vietnam in Kubrick's *Full Metal Jacket*. In Dhawan's film what we see instead is a transnational image machinery that creates "glocal" assemblages of desiring bodies, vectorized time-space modules, and lifestyle ideas in a manner by which these sets can "zap" instantaneously from dust to snow, from the tropical maritime shores to the Alps, from signatures of Third World poverty to a profusion of western consumerism, and from a host of brown bodies in the background to a host of white bodies in the background. Here, cinematic movement presents a virtuality that is out of bounds of the old city and its limited scenarios (it never snows in Mumbai); it is an immanent advertisement of a metropolitan state of being and its planetary imagination.

The Musicality of *Dil Se*

In Ratnam's 1998 film, Amar (Shahrukh Khan), a city-bred, educated radio journalist, meets Meghna (Manisha Koirala), a mysterious woman at a train station when he is on his way on an assignment to the politically turbulent northeastern part of India. He keeps bumping into her and falls hopelessly in love with her. What Amar does not know is that Meghna is part of a terrorist outfit affiliated to a secessionist movement in the northeast and is being trained to be a suicide bomber.[24] Most of the song sequences that accompany this dramatic unfolding of events and revelations are "free indirect" visual consolidations of an overall environ of sublimity, terror, and desire. They give birth to a world that is either contiguous to the defined milieu of the narrative or informs the latter indeterminately. The musical interludes appear to take bodies out from the breathlessness of Ratnam's political thriller from time to time and allow them to respire in and imbibe energies of a certain "outside" (of naturalism and of consumerism). This is where figures leave "characters" behind and incubate in an ecology of the unthinkable. The visual and aural flows that we see in the sequences are not fully amenable to specific contours of subjectivity, neither that of the new age city slicker male reporter nor that of the marginalized woman turned human bomb. Such episodes can be called *assemblages* in a Deleuzian sense. Assemblages are wobbly, diffuse, but pragmatic combinations of statements, affections, bodies, sounds, rhythms, and visibilities that come together and disperse constantly. [25] They are variegated pulses of semiotic energy that have a cinematic life of their own and can be commanded by narrative logic, anthropological imaginaries, and propositional statements or queries (what exactly do these MTV-type rituals mean?) only in retrospect, as "afterthoughts" of storytelling.

The "Chaiya chaiya" (Come let us go) sequence takes place at the beginning of the film, immediately after Amar's first, fleeting encounter with Meghna at a railway station on a dark and stormy night. It begins with a discontinuous cut to the top of a train moving under a clear sky and in broad daylight. The top of the moving vehicle becomes a utopian space for anthropological spectacle, ethnic chic, and folk bodies—all combined and set to techno rhythms. The hero dances with a host of people in spotless rural attire and a comely belle whose rustic form is magically animated by an urban impelling of music. Such an assemblage of camera perspectives (ethnography, heritagism, and so on) is a recurring feature in many Hindi film musical interludes featuring North Indian peasant bodies, Goan fishermen, or tribal figures. In such situations, the camera assumes both an urban, anthropological "look" (by which the city historically has read the country) and a perspective that incorporates such bodies into a metropolitan, posthistorical arcade of "ethnic" diagrams. The bodies of peasants, fishermen, or tribals thus become figurable (as dancers inseparable from the dance) at that interstice between the home and the world, at once inside and outside the cinematic city. The anthropological distancing of their forms and settings, as objects of "discovery" and study, is offset and inseparably recombined with a vision that redresses them as part of the city's fascinated romance with itself and its projected outside.

The "Chaiya chaiya" sequence, from a top-angle, panoptic position, injects a thickened cluster of signs into the otherwise linear continuum of the narrative, hailing in a different world of desires. It provides a godly urbane look into an "India" passing through a peaceful interregnum that comes *between* activities of urbane journalism and those of infranational armed conflict. The sequence allows for a momentary incursion of health, when the camera momentarily assumes a seemingly *normal* task of a museumic-spectacular translation of various life functions of the world. It is precisely this normalcy that the subsequent narrative will "shock" the camera out of. A transnational techno rhythm, in assemblage with the melodic strains of an indigenous Sufi tradition and Urdu poetry, occupies the figures of ethnically dressed peasants and fruitsellers, luminously absolving them of the dirt and grime of labor. There are, of course, two sides to this feature that can be said to be a general tendency of not only Indian popular cinematic forms, but also the myriad commerces of planetary communication. On the one hand, they destroy certain priestly pieties of the "local," affecting perverse contaminations and desacralizations. On the other, they can also remove from the picture the *agon* and historicity of difference (the imperial career of capital, the international division of labor, and so on). The multiple emissions of a global electronic database that are beamed from the skies always interact in a complex manner with memories of the earth. Faced with such a mélange of formations, we perhaps need to refrain from fortifying and protecting *dictated* edifices of tradition (like Sufi philosophy or Urdu poetry) as well as uncritically championing the incursive powers and qualities of a transnational recoding of culture.

This critical detachment, however, does not call for a totalization of irony in thought or a lapse into gross and indolent relativism. It simply invites a scrupulous distancing from all metaphysical truths of the "self" (of the west, as well as the east) and an examination of the very movements of relationality and incommensurability in cultural interactions. Most importantly, the task is to see these instances as part of (and not a reflection of) a flexible socialization of finance capital itself, as a process that is not *essentially and organically tied to either European-style cultural modernity or even political liberalism*. It is in this dynamic dispensation of spectacle that we frequently see attributes of a so-called tradition and those of modernity being deontologized and rendered fungible. As a result, they are removed from their old dialectical battleground of warring selves and republicized in a different realm of value as simply style and stylized information. It is precisely in such an order of metropolitan publicity that, for instance, a new age Hinduness can enter into a common ground of normativity, endearment, and comfort with the worldly works of technofinancial globalization.

The next song sequence in *Dil Se* takes place a little later in the narrative, after Amar tracks the evanescent Meghna down to her village and declares his intentions of asking for her hand in marriage. It is important to note that at this point, neither he nor the viewer has any knowledge of Meghna's identity as a terrorist. Hence, the title track sequence that follows is an anticipatory coupling of affects of violence and love, one that once again crosses an economy of subjective narration qua the point of view of the unsuspecting protagonist. The picturization of the song "Dil se re" combines different visual diagrams and motifs: the realist narrative, the steadycam shots of a CNN-style battleground reportage, a transnational consumer lifestyle of advertising, tourism, pearl necklaces, a spinning basketball on a deserted court, designer gowns, and the constantly reordered body of the woman. This is a tremulous visual style that Ratnam had also used in his previous political thrillers such as *Roja* (1992) and *Bombay* (1995). A mobile, probing, investigative camera vision that is characteristic of a transnational "on the spot" television newsgathering is "quoted" in both the films. In *Roja,* it is such a steadycam that "raids," with dazzling speed, the idyllic village of the countryside and reveals the den of "terror" at its heart. In *Bombay,* the "CNN style" on shoulder camera captures, in a "livewire" and "awry" fashion, the madness of the communal riots. This camera of information is thus inevitably a camera of emergency, by which the city instantly monitors and detects the objects of its worst fears and restores itself constantly into a consensual mass through measures of militarization, aid, and policing. In the title track of *Dil Se,* we see such ominous steadycam shots informing and recasting the space in which passion is lyrically declared. The simulated movements of news gathering (the feeling that the world is somehow, somewhere, out of joint) are thus foreboding devices here.

They are portentously orchestrated with touristic and infomercial set pieces. These disparate visibilities assemble together to effect a utopian transfer of the female body from the intriguing figure in black to a totem of a globalized middle-class desire. In doing that, it also secretly prepares the *affective* ambience for the pending revelation of the profile of the terrorist.

The "Dil se re" sequence invents a virtual intimate space of the couple (about to be denied by the narrative) and inserts it into the public domain of violence. Music, in deterritorializing bodies from their realist milieus, affects a virtual consolidation of desire that is already foreclosed by the ethical universe of exemplary national storytelling: the citizen cannot fall in love with the terrorist. As surreal insertion, musicality liberates signs and bodies from the axiomatic of narration to bring about what can be called a "postulated" expression of romance. I use the term "postulation" in the etymological sense of "prayer" here. It is interesting that postulation, as "prayer," becomes a secular heresy precisely because it establishes, in figural terms, an unreal desire not commensurate with an ethical substrate of nationhood. But let us examine the various ramifications of this question: Is it forbidden to fall in love with a terrorist simply because it is against the spirit of the law?

Love is an anarchic power here, because it threatens to introduce a terrible forking of paths between the destiny of the citizen and that of the state. As we know, in the Hegelian conceptions of the civil society and the rational state, human (heterosexual) love is a unifying middle term that sets up an organic bridge between spirit and substance, between the particular and general interest, and between individual reality and universal essence.[26] Love is therefore that which (as a force secondary to reason) animates a perpetually gestating ethical life in a manner that prevents it from becoming a cold universal. This is because the ethical life propounded by reason cannot merely be a formal entity; it must, at every point, be in an *organic* relation to the immanence of social processes. The vertical emergence of the modern rational state (as a formal expression of that ethical life) has to be a synthetic process of history and not the tyrannical imposition of a cold and distant architectonic. Partha Chatterjee, in his "against the grain" reading of Hegel in relation to Indian nationalism, points out that for the great German thinker, love, to that end, had to be necessarily telescoped into the modalities of the bourgeois nuclear family. He argues that an understanding of Indian nationalism on the other hand perhaps calls for a conceptualization of love in relation to the community rather than the nuclear family.[27] Apropos the particular story we are discussing, the peculiar nature of Indian nationalistic formations, by that token, would already delegitimize the couple because their nuclear desires contravene the ethics of their respective communities. In Amar's case, it is a Hindi-speaking North Indian one that dominates the pan-Indian state scenario, while for Meghna, it is one that is marginalized and outlawed from the very center stage of Indianness. Let us follow this Hegelian theme a little, as a powerful fiction of modernity that intersects with critical discourses about the nation-state and its becomings at large.

Three fundamental precepts of a modernist constitution—subject, unity, and law—are at stake here. It is useful to recall that the trial for Hegel was to absolve the spiritual union between the family and the state from the "contingencies" of legal contracts that feature in the works of Locke or Montesquieu. Law—constitutional or moral—in other words is not the ultimate question here. In the spiritual journey of self-consciousness toward a rational and organic unity of things, law is merely a contingent moment of isolation from the whole,[28] just as the constitution is a mere formalization of the covenant of the nation-state, or moral precepts in Kant and Rousseau are *externally* dictated categorical imperatives. For Hegel on the other hand, the absolute right of ethical consciousness is such that the deed will be nothing else but what it *knows*.[29] In a world devoid of oracular wisdom or Tiresian prognostications, the guilt of Oedipus must be historically foreclosed through a historical consolidation of private property, institutions of civil society, the bourgeois family, and the modern state that supersedes the tragic antinomies between human and divine law.

It would be interesting to see how this cartogram of modernity, perpetually afflicted by the duality of fallible earthly contracts and an irresistible, cosmological spirit of world history, intersects with forces and desires in the Third World cinemascape of *Dil Se*. The question we can begin with pertains to a psychobiographical baseline of ethical narration: to what extent, at each point of the story, does Amar *know* about Meghna's identity and how does that knowledge alter his moral being? Is Amar's "crime" on the same lines as Oedipus's—the result of a tragic absence of knowledge in an atomized and individuated world vision?[30]

That is clearly not the case. In Ratnam's film, Amar's manic quest for Meghna continues even after he comes to know of her secret. It is interesting to note that the only time he is ready to give up his pursuit happens early in the film when she lies to him that she is already married. After he comes to know that this is not true, he chases her till the bitter end, despite learning on the way that she is an enemy of the nation, even after the law declares him to be a collaborator with anti-national forces and disgraces his family. The prohibition of the legal order is not enough to dissuade Amar; he does not find his attraction to be "unnatural" (since it is neither incest nor a contravention of the territorial rights of another man—Meghna's fictional husband) despite being avowedly against the dictates of the state as well as the patriotic clan he comes from. We thus get a glimpse of a disconcerting new age, "urban" conjugal desire that is not afraid to cast itself against both the "not-yet modern" constitutional nation-state and the self-contained ethical universe of the feudal joint family.

The narrative of an obsessive and ultimately self-destructive quest of the citizen-professional protagonist is *affectively consolidated* in *Dil Se* through the star text of Shahrukh Khan and the lyrical–rhythmic motorization of bodies and nature in the song sequences.[31] A central motif of apocalyptic fatalism is established and thematically resonated in the lyrics of two songs in the film—the title track and the "Satrangire" (The colorful one) number. *Dil Se* is cast as a journey through the seven shades of love, as elaborated in ancient Arabic literature—*hub* (attraction), *uns* (infatuation), *Ishq* (love), *Aqidat* (reverence), *ibadat* (worship), *junoon* (obsession), and finally *maut* (death). This trajectory of lovelorn unbecoming departs from the normative diagram of the modern subject, in the process flouting state- and society-sanctioned ideas of conjugality. The latter feature becomes manifest in the film through Amar's brief flirtation with "home," in the form of his engagement with Preeti (Priety Zinta) — the girl who has been picked by his family to be his bride. This scenario of familial intimacy is, however, soon complicated by energies of love being suddenly informed by energies of war. The militant community that Meghna is a part of infiltrates this model domestic space. Meghna and one of her accomplices take advantage of Amar's infatuation and use his home and family to find temporary refuge from the law. As part of the terror plan, Meghna also exploits Amar's feelings for her to get a job as an All India Radio correspondent. On the other hand, Meghna's cold and efficient commitment to the cause of "terror" is also disturbed by the ardor of Amar's love. Her figuration in the film perpetually takes place in the realm of the inscrutable, in-between patriarchal formations of the old and the new, with signs of affection indeterminately distributed between communal love for her disenfranchised people and her sublimating desires for Amar, the yuppie innocent of the city.

I will not discuss in detail the debate that takes place when Amar finally confronts Meghna after coming to know of her true intentions. This dialectic between the historical legitimacy of the national state and the outraged search for law destroying violence by the marginal community is left suspended in the film. In the special urban sensibility that governs *Dil Se,* there can neither be a theodicy nor a wholesome late coming of the secular state to affect a final unity between the dialogic word of the law and an aspired, singular ontology of justice. After the unfinished interaction, conjugality can only proceed fatally, in the stark landscape of the pre/postpolitical, where god is neither absolute nor has he achieved a modern death; he has simply stopped speaking. Hence, in *Dil Se,* love consummates itself through an obstinate voluntarism of death, when Amar and Meghna blow themselves up with the explosives originally intended for the terror act. The illegitimate couple thus overcomes the fear of demise that is presumed by most modern political philosophies based on constitutive contracts or self-other dialectics of lordship and bondage. Suicide, as a perverse, yet supreme achievement of *modernism* (as Benjamin would say), deterritorializes a unitary cosmology predicated on a behavioral/cultural logic of modernity and an economic-governmental one of modernization.[32] It prevents the encounter between law and life and takes love "elsewhere." Death, in other words, becomes the utopian outlet that Amar searches for when, after coming to know of Meghna's identity, her past, and her ironclad filial obligations, he pleads that the two should run away to a place distant from the violent geopolitics of the nation-state and the proprietorship of the community.

An impossible love thus sublimates in the cleft that perpetually opens up between a universalizing discourse of modernity and a sovereign principle of exception. Amar naïvely pleads to Meghna to disarm and remove herself elsewhere, *when her identity itself is constructed by the national state in terms of a fundamental relation of war.* Indeed, it can be recalled that a totality of the Hegelian rational diagram invoked earlier comes with a necessary rejoinder—Meghna cannot be loved within the scope of an egalitarian homogeneity that constitutes *peopleness;* as a minoritarian presence, she can only be an object of *tolerance* and *suspicion.* She can, of course, be granted civil rights (which are always contractual and contingent) pertaining to representation and juridical forms, but *ethically* speaking, she can never be a citizen.[33] Like the Quakers, Anabaptists, and Jews of the Prussian state devoutly desired by Hegel, in her case, a civil recognition by law as an entity to be preserved or punished does not amount to an entry in the ethical family–state composite. Meghna is always foreclosed from entering the former as a site for individual love, as well as the latter as the repository of patriotic love. This pertains to a paradox that occupies the very heart of political liberalism—it seems that in the last instance, there can be no "universal" principle of sovereignty without one of majoritarian normativity. It is this latter organic unity that, in the Hegelian universe, dialectically presides over a force field of interests and finally renders ethics as *custom*. Meghna's legal rights can ensure her inclusion into the national fold only through a process of tolerated, differential exclusion.[34] Her aspect of terror unfolds at the very liminality of that tolerance, when her shadowy presence and insidious homeless*ness* make her drop out of the monitoring radar of a malfunctioning population state.[35] As a result, the question of law cannot be mitigated here by a benign unfolding of everyday lives and everyday desires, for it can never be *customary* to be in love with Meghna. The question of sovereignty, as far as her profile is concerned, is always of the rule of exception. The preserving/establishing violence of the law can never be extinguished for her or for her community. However, had Amar married the familial citizen Preeti, there could have been, in terms of a unitary national–communal spirit, the real possibility of diffusing the formal inclemency of law. That is, of not only rendering love legal, but also making it indistinguishable from life itself.

Love in *Dil Se* thus remains a tragic pathology in terms of narration as ethical instantiation. In the course of the baroque death drive that unfolds in the realistic storytelling, the song sequences open up luminous intervals for the visual consolidation of an unremitted desire, a picture of ardor that is an otherworldly life without political status. The nondirectional lyrical pathos of these sequences informs the dramatic buildup of events, infusing the latter process with the anarchic semiosis of an *intolerable* love that can manifest itself only musically in a prosaic world. The body of the woman, perpetually crisscrossed by contesting patriarchal forces, lends itself to various catachrestic geotelevisual ensembles of signs. It is motorized as part of a perpetually altering and forking assemblage of desire that is a mythical "outside"; this outside is a pure and immanent visual utopia that can come only *after* national geopolitics. There is, however, more to this escape. The woman, as an expressive animation of boundless desire, seems to be figurable only when it enters image diagrams of value in and as of itself. That is, only when her body is temporarily absolved of its location in unhappy history and terror, and claimed, in a state of supreme lightness of being, by pure specular relations of global commoditization. In other words, the ethically impossible picture of the terrorist as beloved becomes apparent only as *cinema-as-spectacle,* which is indeed capital accumulated to the point of image.[36] The woman-in-cinema thus assumes the form of unbridled, immanent production values (the dancing body, the fetish body, and the fashion body) in a mise-en-scène no longer weighed down or mediated by statements and realities of a historically defined situation. The song sequences exert an ontological pull that removes images of desire from an embattled geopolitical milieu of the nation-state, but this removal to an "outside" can be seen to become manifest only as a newer arcade of life*style* signatures. The *potential* that lies in a utopian friendship with terror is curtailed and telescoped into a picture of possessive individualism and a naïve catholicity of capital/nature. The pathos of a relentless conflict over the founding of civil law is offset by a nostalgic romance that unites natural law with a delirious freedom of a supply-side imagism. Commodities and vectorized time-space modules appear without historical procedures of labor and production, and an agonistic process of *becoming* tends to be flattened into a vision of a posthistorical freedom to consume that is always arriving.

However, it could be wrong to conclude that such "groundless" recoding of historical bodies and locations into batches of spectacles and ideologemes completely exhaust the semiotic energy of these interludes. They, in other words, are not simply formations that repress, gloss over, or exploit historically disenfranchised bodies like Meghna's; in strange ways, the sequences are also enabling in their very disruptive inscrutability. As modules of information and advertising power, these assemblages create realities, they produce and transform, and they are often capable of destroying sedentary and enervating pieties of the already given. In the melodramatic dispensation of *Dil Se,* the song sequences do not just bring into a critical proximity the sublime and terrifying aspect of love and the tragic naïveté of a perpetually becoming metropolitan subjectivity. Their affective and intellectual dimensions also help us think about despair and boredom in themselves as political and historical categories. In the "Satrangi re" sequence, the militarized grounds of Ladakh are transformed by nomadic assemblages of travel cinematography, exotic, a nonobligatory eroticism of dance movements, and urban motifs of bondage and ritualistic masochism. The sequence ends with the dancing figures of Amar and Meghna striking the posture of Michelangelo's *Pietà,* with Meghna as the Virgin Mary and Amar as the martyred Christ.

Perhaps, as we have briefly indicated earlier, the so-called indifference and nonobligatory nature of song sequences need to be thought in terms of *disjunctive* relations with the narrative. That is, as qualitative and expressive entities that *affect* narration through diffuse semiotic flows (as a system of signs), rather than through an overarching, synthesizing movement of semiology (as a system of language). Let us quickly try to illustrate this postulate using a couple of moments from Ratnam's two other films on political conjugality—*Roja* (1992) and *Bombay* (1995). In the first film, the "Rukmini Rukmini" ("Hey Rukmini Rukmini") sequence effects a comic disjunctive synthesis between a new-city sexuality and what Prasad has called the monitoring gaze of a not-yet modern, but no longer feudal moral guardianship.[37] The zone of privacy for the newly wed couple is a precarious, "not-yet" space in the rural milieu in which *Roja* begins, where the agrarian feudal community is shown to be dominant.[38] The latter is not narratologically refuted, but loosened from its earthly moorings and spectacularly deterritorialized in the realm of affect. We see the young and old of the village gossip, dance, and sing to celebrate the nuptial night. The traditional bodies of middle-aged village "matrons" are unhinged from ethical dictates and localized memories of the folkish earth and transmuted by an expressive power of urban musicality and laughter. They are republicized as bodies in kinetic oscillation between the discursive poles of tradition and modernity. In becoming chaosmic figures caught in the limbo between the communal body and the individuated persona, the dancing elders create the affective grounds for the nuclear couple to emerge in the narrative in the realm of pure spectacle, in which attributes of the feudal (the profile and attire of the village woman) and those of the modern (the pelvic thrust and the techno beats) are not historically resolved, but indeterminately synchronized. Musicality is thus precisely that which resonates and closes the gap between the priestly statement of the absolutist country and the clamorous prose of the liberal city. It is only after this rite of passage that the couple can cut the kinship chords and leave for Kashmir, which is, at once, an earthly paradise for honeymoon as well as a professional battleground for combating terror.

We see a similar movement in *Bombay*. The newly wed couple is at first besieged by communitarian obligations, which require them to put up a bunch of kids from a visiting family inside their bedchamber. It is only after this comical delay that the neighbors themselves take the initiative to isolate them for the bridal night. The politically sensitive interreligious marriage between the Hindu boy and the Muslim girl (who have eloped from their rural, familial moorings to the urban anonymity of the big city) is consummated in an interesting manner. The figure of the woman had hitherto been constructed in the narrative as a furtive, *burkha*-clad figure who hails from a conservative rural family. In contrast to that, in the "Humma humma" ("Hubba hubba") number we are discussing, the depiction of conjugality inside the bedroom is interspersed with a carnivalesque and libertine dance number that takes place in the neighborhood premises, now magically transformed into a pure stage of the MTV musical. The seductive techno beat rises to a crescendo and claims not just the bodies of the dancers— who are dressed in a mishmash of styles, assembling the *purdah* to ostensibly "sexy" dance costumes of an "alien" kind—but also that of Shaila Banu, the young bride. The body of the Islamic-rural woman begins to sway intermittently to the music, as part of a playful, precoital overture, and is gradually "demarked" of its attributes of tradition—the psychobiographical qualities of coyness, "lack of exposure" due to a strict "Islamic" upbringing in the rural backwaters, and sociological ones of body language and attire. It is thus the deterritorializing affect of music that carries her over to an urban ground of being where a picture of private, "consensual," and secular sex relation becomes possible. She undresses as a musical automaton and lets her body be impelled by a new urban sexuality. The mating ground between religions is thus secured not through a dialectical war of historico-political propositions and their resolution in a realm of Kantian cosmopolitanism, but in a virtual realm for *consuming* the music of metropolitan globalization. Shaila Banu, in other words, *is,* because she consumes. Like her husband, her neighbors, and the bawdy visitors from the nearby red light district, she discovers an originary plane of being capable of holding the temporalities of the ancient as well as the modern regimes. A premodern tribalism of religious conflicts and prejudices is thereby offset by an emphatic *primordialism* of consumer desire. The latter arrives disjunctively, in an instant when it reveals itself to be an always, already there technology of the self that can be activated without graduated historical measures of enfranchisement, education, or cultivation of taste. Subsequently, as Shaila Banu settles into domesticity and motherhood, her figural presence in the film lends itself to a "metro-normativity" that is defined by naturalized practices of urban Hinduization. She no longer wears the *burkha* and stops eating meat.

The moment of geotelevisuality is thus not one in which the image, in a progressive dialectical transfer, draws from the repository of a so-called organic memory and then worlds itself in an international stage. It is instead one in which figuration is not of the subject, but of combinatory movements of information particles in of themselves (of which the bodies like those of Amar and Meghna are undeniably important components). The image, to use a Heideggerian metaphor, is thus always *worked* by a technology of cinema between the nation as familial memory and horizon of the earth and the expansive, animated televisual sky of the global. It is always in the process of being overwritten or underwritten through a fluid, haphazard dynamic of language itself, where language is not an instrument of subjectivity or being, but that productive dimension in which subjectivity itself is born and inheres. This is precisely why the geotelevisual image is that which worlds the body in a manner that has the betrayal of the "self" (as a national–local precept of being) as its limit. Such images should not be judged simply on the grounds of what they "communicate," in terms of propositions or baseline addresses; instead, it would be critically rewarding to understand them in ways in which they problematize communicability itself in our political universe.[39] Indeed, if geotelevisual bodies set to music and dance in popular Indian cinema are at all subject to a playing of the cinematic, they are so as toys (as Barthes would have said), as entities cast outside a contextually rooted sociology of the *given,* that are amenable to the many global fictions they flow into.

Notes

1   See Lalitha Gopalan, *Cinema of Interruptions: Action Genres in Contemporary Indian Cinema* (London: BFI, 2002), 136.

2   Ram Gopal Varma expresses a similar modernist anxiety about an "incomplete" participation of Indian cinema in a transnational urban aesthetic. In his 2002 film *Darna Mana Hai* (Fear is Forbidden), Varma revolted against what can be called the "dictatorship of the distributor" and decided to withhold the song sequences from the final cut of the film. The musical

track of the film was thus marketed independently through audiocassette and CD sales, whereas the film (a thriller) was released in theaters without song numbers.

3 Gopalan, *Cinema of Interruptions,* 179.

4 Ibid., 180.

5 Ravi Vasudevan, "Shifting Codes, Dissolving Identities: The Hindi Social Film of the 1950s as Popular Culture," *Journal of Arts and Ideas* 23/24 (January, 1993): 60–6. See also Georg Lukács, *Theory of the Novel: A Historico-philosophical Essay on the Forms of Great Epic Literature,* trans. Anna Bostok (Cambridge, Mass.: MIT, 1971), and Erich Auerbach, *Mimesis: The Representation of Reality in Western Literature,* trans. Willard Trask (New York: Doubleday, 1957).

6 Elsewhere, Vasudevan suggests that the pleasure of visual entertainment can be seen to be operative precisely in a zone of "in-betweenness" amidst narratological propositions: "Etymologically, entertainment means 'holding between'. The cinema's work of representation performs just such an operation; its skills are used to generate fantasy spaces for its audience, spaces which are literally 'held between' phases of routine domestic and working life." See Ravi Vasudevan, "The Cultural Space of a Film Narrative: Interpreting Kismet (Bombay Talkies, 1943)," *The Indian Economic and Social History Review* 28, no. 2 (1991): 172.

7 Vasudevan, "Shifting Codes," 72.

8 Of course Gopalan's critical energies are directed toward a dismantling of this very normative of cinema. She uses "interruption" as a trope rather than as a positive concept.

9 See the three essays of Tom Gunning, " 'Primitive' Cinema: A Frame-Up? Or the Trick's on Us," in *Early Cinema: Space, Frame, Narrative,* ed. Thomas Elsaesser (London: BFI, 1990), 95–103; "Non-Continuity, Continuity, Discontinuity: A Theory of Genres in Early Films," in *Early Cinema,* 86–93; and "The Cinema of Attractions: Early Film, Its Spectator and the Avant-garde," in *Early Cinema,* 56–62. See also Miriam Hansen, *Babel and Babylon: Spectatorship in American Silent Film* (Cambridge, Mass.: Harvard, 1991).

10 Bhaskar Chandravarkar, "Growth of the Film Song," *Cinema in India* 1, no. 3 (1981): 16–20.

11 Ashok Ranade, "The Extraordinary Importance of the Indian Film Song," *Cinema Vision India* 1, no. 4 (1981): 4–11.

12 See Geeta Kapur, "Mythic Material in Indian Cinema," *Journal of Arts and Ideas* 14/15 (1987): 38–41, and the two seminal essays of Ashish Rajadhyaksha on early Indian cinema: "The Phalke Era: Conflict of Traditional Form and Modern Technology," *Journal of Arts and Ideas* 14/15 (1987): 47–78; and "Neo-traditionalism: Film as Popular Art in India," *Framework* 32/33 (1987): 20–67.

13 See Madhava Prasad, *Ideology of the Hindi Film: A Historical Construction* (New Delhi: Oxford, 1998).

14 Consider, for instance, the formal description of the popular Indian film forwarded by Arun Kaul and Mrinal Sen in the *Manifesto of the New Cinema Movement:* "... a mechanical business of putting together popular stars,

gaudy sets, glossy colour, a large number of irrelevant musical sequences and other standard meretricious ingredients." *Close Up* 1, no. 1 (July 1968): 37. Speaking about Shankar's 1994 film *Indian,* Theodor Bhaskaran categorically states that "The flow of the film would not be affected in the least if song sequences were excised, wholly or partially." Quoted in Gopalan, *Cinema of Interruptions,* 128.

15 Power in such a sense becomes immanent only in movements and perpetually forming and deterritorializing architectures. It is not founded with its own mythical big bang and the subsequent creation of a universe that it can command.

16 I am talking about a densification and globalization of such tendencies. Segmented distribution has always existed in the Indian film industries, through outlets like All India Radio, gramophone records, and audiocassettes. The standard commercial feature is made by assembling together self-contained segments of spectacle, drama, music, action, and other attractions into a loose formation whose components are not always under the vertical control of the narrative. See Prasad, *Ideology of the Hindi Film,* 42–51.

17 See Georg Lukács, "Reification and the Consciousness of the Proletariat," in *History and Class Consciousness* (New Delhi: Rupa, 1993), 83–222.

18 See Fredric Jameson, "Cognitive Mapping," in *Marxism and the Interpretation of Culture,* ed. Cary Nelson and Lawrence Grossberg (Chicago: University of Illinois Press, 1988), 347–57.

19 That is, information has acquired a socialized value in of itself. It is not a reflection of capital, but circulation of capital itself.

20 See Anustup Basu, "The Human and His Spectacular Autumn, or, Informatics after Philosophy," *Postmodern Culture* 14, no. 3 (May 2004), http://muse.jhu.edu/login?uri=/journals/postmodern_culture/v014/14.3basu.html, for a greater elaboration on the theme of geotelevisuality in an electronic age.

21 See Gilles Deleuze, *Cinema 1: The Movement-Image,* trans. Hugh Tomlinson and Barbara Habberjam (Minneapolis: University of Minnesota Press, 1986), 108–11.

22 Prasad, *Ideology of the Hindi Film,* 64.

23 I am grateful to Sangita Gopal for pointing out to me that this "geotelevisual" character is largely restricted to big-budget, A-line films in mainstream Indian cinemas. A large part of India's voluminous cinematic output consists of the so-called B- and C-grade films that offer an interesting and minoritarian visual repertoire that is remarkably different from the images I have been describing. The opening up of the visual universe in the 1990s has also resulted in complex transformations in regional film cultures. Abhijit Roy, in "The New Popular and the Bhadrolok" (unpublished essay), provides us with insightful leads about the increasing "Hindi-ization" of Bengali cinema after the 1970s, primarily inaugurated by Bombay-based filmmakers such as Shakti Samanta and Pramod Chakraborty. I am thankful to Anindya Sengupta for pointing out that this "Hindi-ization" of Bengali cinema can be said to be borrowed largely from the 1980s' "preglobalization" Hindi film.

24 In that sense, the narrative of *Dil Se* is different from various "threat-of-the-nation" stories of the 1960s and 1970s that came especially in the wake of the wars with China and Pakistan. Classic examples would be Dev Anand's *Prem Pujari* (1970) and Ramanand Sagar's *Aankhen* (1968).

25 See Gilles Deleuze and Félix Guattari, *A Thousand Plateaus: Capitalism and Schizophrenia,* trans. Brian Massumi (Minneapolis: University of Minnesota Press, 1987). Also Gilles Deleuze, *Foucault,* trans. Seán Hand (Minneapolis: University of Minnesota Press, 1997).

26 See G. W. F. Hegel, *Phenomenology of Spirit,* trans. A. V. Miller (New York: Oxford, 1977), 265–74. Also see Hegel, *Lectures on the Philosophy of World History: Introduction,* trans. H. B. Nisbet (Cambridge: Cambridge University Press, 1975), 99–100.

27 Partha Chatterjee, *Nation in Fragments: Colonial and Postcolonial Histories* (Princeton, N.J.: Princeton University Press, 1993), 230–1.

28 Hegel, *Phenomenology,* 259–61.

29 Ibid., 281.

30 Interestingly, it is an epic compact between a mythical process of justice and a primordiality of the blood relation (that does not allow one to inadvertently fall in love with a long-lost sister) that wards off the possibility of incest in popular Indian "lost and found" film narratives. See Raj Khosla's *Bambai Ka Babu* (The gentleman from Bombay, 1960) and Ravi Chopra's *Zameer* (Conscience, 1975).

31 The star persona of Shahrukh Khan was developed in the 1990s in films such as *Baazigar* (Trickster, Abbas-Mastaan, 1993), *Darr* (Fear, Yash Chopra, 1994), and *Dilwale Dulhania Le Jayenge* (The braveheart will take the bride, Aditya Chopra, 1996). This is affected through a coming together of a primordial innocence (the serial killer deprived of motherly love in *Baazigar*) that, in hyperexpanded field of desires, can schizophrenically recode both an unmitigated transgression of customs (the stalking of a married woman in *Darr*) and a supranormal adherence to them (as in *Dilwale*).

32 Fredric Jameson, in a valiant attempt to resuscitate modernity as a trope of political polemisa, rather than as a concept, makes similar distinctions in *A Singular Modernity* (London: Verso, 2002).

33 G. W. F. Hegel, *Philosophy of Right,* trans. T. M. Knox (New York: Oxford, 1967), 168.

34 I am alluding to Georgio Agamben's brilliant study of modern sovereignty in *Homo Sacer: Sovereign Power and Bare Life,* trans. Daniel Heller-Roazen (Stanford: Stanford University Press, 1998).

35 The "birth of biopolitics" as such presumes the population state, rather than the territorial one. See Michel Foucault, "The Birth of Biopolitics," in *Essential Works of Foucault 1954–1984,* vol. 1, *Ethics: Subjectivity and Truth,* ed. Paul Rabinow (New York: The New Press, 1997), 73–5; and "Security, Territory, and Population," in *Essential Works of Foucault,* 67–71. In the field of security and law, the organic composite of the "people" thus had to be disassembled into populations and sectors in order for policing to emerge as a historical function of the state during the nineteenth century.

36 Guy Debord, *Society of the Spectacle,* trans. Donald Nicholson-Smith (New York: Zone Books, 1995), 24.

37 Prasad, *Ideology of the Hindi Film,* 53–113.

38 This is established earlier in the film through a meticulous depiction of the rituals and protocols that go into the finalization of the arranged marriage. The only prenuptial meeting between the hero and his originally intended bride (she secretly confides to him that she is in love with another person; the hero chooses to marry her sister instead in order to save social embarrassment for all) is presided over by the entire community.

39 See Giorgio Agamben, *Means without End: Notes on Politics,* trans. Vincenzo Binetti and Cesare Casarino (Minneapolis: University of Minnesota Press, 2000), for an understanding of the cinematic as a politics of gesturality.

Part 2

Eccentric Orbits

6. Intimate Neighbors

Bollywood, *Dangdut* Music, and Globalizing Modernities in Indonesia

Bettina David

There has been little research on the nature of the relationship between commercial Hindi film music and imagery, and the Indonesian popular music genre *dangdut*, a hybrid pop music extremely popular among the lower classes that incorporates musical elements from Western pop, Hindi film music, and indigenous Malay tunes. Although the strong influence of Hindi film music in the emergence of *dangdut* as a distinct genre in postindependence Indonesia has been noted by most academic and mass media accounts of *dangdut,* it is usually mentioned only in passing. For example, in their recent article about contemporary developments in Indonesian popular music following the fall of President Soeharto in 1998, Barendregt and van Zanten point out that "musically, the genre [*dangdut*] is a mix of Hindustani film music, Malay *joged* dance music, and lately a strong emphasis on reggae-like bass patterns."[1] Thus, although the influence of Hindi film music on *dangdut* is acknowledged, deeper explorations of the transnational cultural dynamics of Bollywood films and their music and the emergence of regional hybrid popular music genres such as *dangdut* are still lacking, be it from a musicological, sociological, or cultural/postcolonial studies point of view.

My inquiry represents a preliminary foray into this still largely unexplored field. In describing the transnational travel of Bollywood music and its ongoing reception and cultural transformation in multiethnic, postindependence Indonesia, I will primarily be drawing on the discourses surrounding Bollywood and *dangdut* as conducted in the Indonesian mass media. I will examine the two positions that Bollywood occupies in the Indonesian "mediascape": the films themselves and Bollywood song and dance as a major musical and visual horizon that shaped the emergence of the local popular music genre *dangdut*.[2]

I will map the distinct yet overlapping cultural space assigned to both Bollywood music and *dangdut* in Indonesia's mediascape. After a preliminary sketch of the position of Bollywood films in Indonesia as well as the historical and contemporary impact of Hindi film songs on the emergence of *dangdut* as a distinct Indonesian popular music genre, I will draw attention to the dynamic upward mobility that both genres experienced in Indonesian mass-mediated "public culture" in the 1990s.[3] This development is remarkable since *dangdut* and Bollywood have traditionally been devalued as "low-class" entertainment by the more Western-oriented Indonesian urban elite. *Dangdut*'s growing acceptability among upper classes in Indonesia can be tracked alongside a marked revival in Bollywood's popularity in recent years set in motion by the extraordinary success of the film *Kuch Kuch Hota Hai* (Something is happening, Karan Johar, 1998, henceforth *KKHH*) in Indonesia. Hindi films have always enjoyed a fan base among marginalized urban lower classes, but *KKHH* was a middle-class phenomenon that created a frenzy for all things Bollywood in the Indonesian mass media. While this craze might coincide with Bollywood's new popularity in the so-called West, I suggest that the changing fortunes of Bollywood films and *dangdut* music at the turn of the millennium need to be viewed in the context of Indonesia's ongoing relationship with Indian popular culture. Analyzing the positions assigned to Bollywood films and *dangdut* in Indonesian mass-mediated discourses, I contend that the current popularity of these transnational, hybrid cultural artifacts has to be interpreted within the context of Indonesia's ongoing multiethnic contestations about possible local, national, and global identities and the emergence of different notions of what it means to be "modern," "Indonesian," "Asian," and "Muslim" in our rapidly globalizing world.

Indian cultural influence on Indonesian societies can be traced back to the beginning of the fifth century. Since then, Indian cultural elements have been incorporated in a highly syncretic way into local cultures. Even after the Islamization of the Malay Archipelago, Indian cultural heritage continued to play an integral role in core sociocultural institutions. The *Ramayana* and the *Mahabharata* and the adventures of their heroes and heroines remain to this day part of a collective imaginary landscape in modern Indonesia. Hence, it is not surprising that the broadcast of the Indian television serials *Ramayana* and *Mahabharata* in 1991 and 1992, respectively, by the private Indonesian television station TPI achieved remarkably high Nielsen ratings that ranged between 48 and 60. In fact, the supervisor for the airing of Indian films at TPI, Rahmat Suardi, traced this success to the long-standing notion of an assumed "cultural similarity" between India and Indonesia.[4] Yet while the historical, cultural, and religious impact of India on the emergence of local religious, political, and cultural structures has been thoroughly examined and depicted by archaeologists, historians, and anthropologists, the modern, postcolonial transnational flows of mass-mediated cultural forms between India and Indonesia remain under-investigated. Although there has been considerable research into modern Indonesian popular culture, at least since the 1990s, the impact of transnational flows of modern mass culture between two non-Western countries is still to be explored. Too often, globalization has been under-stood mainly as North American cultural domination or, at best, as a process where Western influences are appropriated and negotiated in local terms. However, Indian influence on Indonesian society is not merely a thing of the past. The continuing presence of Bollywood films in Indonesia and the recent surge in their popularity enable us to grasp the new circuits of distribution and consumption through which non-Western societies participate in globalization.

Bollywood in Indonesia

Commercial Indian films were first imported into Indonesia by the allied armies in 1945, in the aftermath of Indonesia's declaration of independence, as entertainment for the Indian troops that were part of the English contingent. Though Indian mainstream cinema has been part of Indonesia's media culture ever since, its main audience has been the lower classes and the urban poor. Indonesian film historians have argued that Indian (and Chinese) films served as an important model for the national film industry established in the 1950s.[5] Thus, prominent Indonesian director Jamaluddin Malik not only made imitations of Indian films but also imported an Indian director and several techni-cians to make movies in his PERSARI studio.[6] Asrul Sani, an influential Indonesian writer and poet of *Angkatan '45* (Generation '45) who also directed some films himself, has argued that the rise of the star system in

Indonesia could be traced back to the entry of Indian filmmakers into the Indonesia's national film industry.[7] These early domestic products were also addressed to lower-class audiences and could not compete against Indian imports. Though, in the mid-1950s, the import quota for Indian (as well as Malayan and Filipino) films was reduced in order to strengthen the local industry, the domestic film product continued to struggle. Berated by the upper classes as imitative and escapist, these films were shown in second- and third-class theaters, while the A-grade exhibition spaces were reserved for American and Western cinema. There seems to be considerable overlap between the audiences for Indonesian and Indian films. Though not all moviegoers could read the Indonesian subtitles, they nevertheless could follow the formulaic story-lines and enjoyed the song and dance sequences that offered light and sensual musical interludes, speaking directly to one's emotions and even allowing the audience to spontaneously sing along with their film idols.

However, the recent surge in the popularity of Indian films is often linked to the screening of the Indian television series *Ramayana* and *Mahabharata,* whose success laid the foundations for the current Bolly-wood boom in the Indonesian media. TPI continued broadcasting Indian films after 1991, targeting those film fans who had traditionally watched Bollywood films in lower-class cinemas.[8] In 1996, a second television station, Indosiar, began broadcasting Indian films over the weekend. Both television stations were also among the first to broadcast live *dangdut* shows as well as *dangdut* music videos, which they have been doing since the late 1980s and early 1990s. This development owes much to the spread of television in Indonesia in the 1990s. Although still a major luxury item, television now reaches over 90 per-cent of the population. These drastic demographic changes account for the inclusion of "low-class" entertainment forms in television program-ming. Thus TPI, among the first channels to promote *dangdut* and Hindi films, is often mockingly referred to as "Indonesian Housemaid Television" (*Televisi Pembantu Indonesia*) or even "Indian Film Televi-sion" (*Televisi Pilem India*), reflecting the anxieties of class evoked by a more democratic mass medium. Though Hindi films were being shown on television, it was *KKHH*'s enormous box-office success that launched Bollywood as a major phenomenon in Indonesia's rapidly globalizing mediascape. At the end of July 2001, *KKHH* was aired by Indosiar at prime time and inaugurated what the prestigious national newspaper *Kompas* called "Indian film fever" and "Shahrukh Khan fever."[9]

In reaction to the *KKHH* craze, most television stations followed Indosiar's lead and began broadcasting Indian films and Bollywood infotainment shows. New programs were created as television stations vied with each other to capitalize on the Bollywood craze. The moderators/VJs often displayed some "Indianness," mostly by wearing Indian-style costumes and makeup.[10] "Exotic" Indian fashion became one of the latest trends, ranging from silk saris and salwar kameezes to Indian-style anklets and bracelets and, of course, the obligatory bindi. In January 2003, the newspaper *Republika* stated that "Bollywood films are now shown almost around the clock on national television channels: not only in the mornings, but also in the afternoons and evenings."[11] In February 2002, the first issue of the new tabloid *Bollywood Indonesia* came out in Jakarta with thirty-five thousand copies and had to be reprinted.[12] In mid-2004, its circulation reached sixty thousand.[13] The World Wide Web is another source for information and interactive discussions about Bollywood. Indonesian fans are served with the latest gossip, film reviews, and song lyrics at *Taman Bollywood* (Bollywood garden). The postings in the guestbook, most of them written by Indonesians (the site is bilingual, English and Indonesian), use an English replete with hip slang and spellings characteristic of Internet and chat-room youth language. This suggests that users are consciously positioning themselves in a globalized form of modernity that is both highly Americanized and draws on characteristic local cultural influences. Though this relation to Bollywood is clearly mediated by global consumer culture and new technologies such as cheap and easily reproducible video compact discs (VCD) and the World Wide Web, Bollywood's resurgence in Indonesia owes much to ongoing regional cultural dynamics. Indonesians are usually not aware of Bollywood's salience in the West. For them, Bollywood still seems to represent something similar to their own culture in being distinctively non-Western.

The sense of a deep familiarity with Indian films goes back to the very beginnings of the cinema industry and leisure culture in postindependence Indonesia, where Indian films together with *dangdut* music have been associated with the uneducated urban working classes and the people of the *kampung* (village or slum) and their "backward" (*kampungan,* "in the style of the *kampung*") way of life. Although Bollywood as well as *dangdut,* as nontraditional mass culture genres, were clearly "modern," they were perceived as a failed, distorted attempt to be "modern" by uneducated, "backward" people. This "bastard" modernity of

Bollywood and *dangdut* was highly embarrassing to the more educated, Western-oriented elite. But the new Bollywood film of the *KKHH* variety excised these associations. In eschewing the slum aesthetics that the aspiring, upward mobile new middle classes want to distinguish themselves from, films such as *KKHH* and *Kabhi Khushi Kabhie Gham ...* (Sometimes happiness, sometimes sadness, Karan Johar, 2001) represent in fact a new kind of familiarity. *KKHH* exemplifies the new "romantic family drama."[14] A "clean" film, it was a far cry from the brutal action scenes of the typical *masala* film of the 1970s and 1980s. It depicted affluent characters, surrounded by Western status symbols and international designer fashion, but well attuned, nonetheless, to traditional values such as arranged marriages and the central role of the family. The highly modern and fashionable, yet thoroughly "Indian" and melodramatic, world of films such as *KKHH* might have addressed the deep desires, anxieties, and fantasies of its Indonesian audience, especially the newly emergent urban middle classes who are still searching for a distinct identity as they try to reconcile Western-style consumer modernity with local concerns over family, sexuality, morality, and tradition. Indian films like *KKHH* assure viewers that they can be Western-educated, at home in the globalized world of modernity and consumerism, yet still distinctively "Indian" (and as such, "Indonesian") in their loyalty to local traditions and non-Western standards of morality. In this message lies the potential of these "new" Bollywood films to appeal to cross-class audiences and in particular to capture the emotions, desires, and fears of the newly emerging middle classes. This affinity is rhetorically captured in an article in *Kompas* entitled "Our Intimate Neighbour Called 'Indian Films,' " which claims that "Indian films are now just about to become our 'neighbours', who are going to be our intimate friends."[15] However, there are two kinds of neighbors in Indonesia, especially if seen from middle- and upper-class perspectives: those you explicitly "recognize" as equals and the "masses" that are just out there, the poor, who live across the street or behind one's house. While many Bollywood films of the 1970s and 1980s reminded one of these "unacknowledged" neighbors, clean family films like *KKHH* can easily be seen as "equals," respectable neighbors dwelling in one's own "imagined community"—worlds away from the slum. These trends and events point toward mostly local dynamics in the ongoing relationship between Bollywood films and their Indonesian audience, as the preference for melodramatic family romances suggests that it so easily appeals to local emotional aesthetics.

Bollywood Film Songs and the Emergence of Indonesian *Dangdut* Popular Music

Dangdut can be considered a hybrid musical genre that incorporates influences from traditional Malay tunes and popular Hindi film songs, as well as Arab and Middle Eastern elements and Western popular music styles.[16] Sen and Hill characterize *dangdut* as "an instance of a particular localisation of codes circulating in global cultural markets."[17] *Dangdut* eventually emerged in the early 1970s from the so-called *orkes melayu* (Malay orchestra, often abbreviated to OM) that played tunes popular among their multiethnic audiences in the urban centers of Java and Sumatra. These ranged from traditional Malay folk tunes to adaptations of Western songs, popular Chinese melodies, and Hindi film songs.

One of the first *dangdut* songs "Boneka dari India" ("Doll from India," 1956) by Jakarta-born star Ellya Khadam (born 1938) dates back to a time when the term *dangdut* as referring to a distinct genre was yet to be created. The title of the song already points toward India as a major referent. It is a cover of the Hindi film song "Samay hai bahar ka" ("Time of spring," *Ashiana*, T. Trilochan, Nest, 1952).[18] Ellya Khadam developed what is usually referred to as a "very Indian" style of performing—imitating the costumes, dancing styles, gestures, and facial expressions typical of Indian film song sequences at that time. She acted in musical films and did stage shows and radio broadcasts. Her melodramatic facial expressions and flirtatious gestures taken from Indian film song and dance sequences resonated deeply with a fan base comprising mostly migrants to the city and the urban working classes. In 2000, Ellya Khadam was awarded the TPI Dangdut Award by the television channel TPI for her major role in the development of *dangdut* as a newly emerging musical genre.[19] An article about her on the Indonesian music Web site www.tembang.com is entitled "Ellya Kadam: The Real Dangdut Diva!"[20] and she is justly regarded as the "grandmother" of *dangdut* by many of *dangdut*'s senior stars. Elvy Sukaesih (born 1951), who began as a child singer in the 1960s and who is often referred to as the unrivalled

"Queen of Dangdut" since the 1970s, told the readers of the newspaper *Suara Merdeka* that "Tante Ellya" considered her a rightful successor. Elvy Sukaesih also pointed toward the "Indian" inspiration that lay behind her later career as a *dangdut* singer:

> Actually, I did not only like to sing, I also enjoyed dancing. Near my home, there was the cinema "Gembira" that screened Indian films. I loved to sing Indian songs. My mother said, "when you were a child, you often draped a towel around your head, so that it would look like long hair, or you put on a sarong and danced like in those Indian films." The sarong was said to be an Indian sari.[21]

Since the early days of Ellya Khadam's *orkes melayu* hits, *dangdut* music has continued to incorporate various new influences while, developing its own distinct character as a form of Indonesian popular music that was eventually, around 1972 or so, labeled *dangdut*—named rather derogatively on account of the distinct syncopated drum beat of the *gendang* (a tabla-style drum): dang-dang-dut.

In the early 1970s, Rhoma Irama (born 1947) transformed the older-style Malay orchestral music into a more up-tempo sound by incorporating, among other elements, Western rock music. Rhoma soon emerged as the unrivalled superstar of this new genre and is regarded as the "creator" of *dangdut* in its current form.[22] His career began in 1973 with the formation of his band *Soneta*. He proclaimed *dangdut* as "The Sound of Islam," explicitly positioning the music within a religious framework. In fact, many of his songs are commonly labeled *dangdut dakwah* (proselytizing *dangdut*). From 1976 onward, he also had huge box-office successes with his *dangdut* films that might be called "musical films" similar to Bollywood films.[23]

Though Islamic in "flavor," some of Rhoma's greatest hits include adaptations of Hindi film songs—the song "Sifana," for example, draws on "Jeeye to jeeye kaise" ("How am I to live under these conditions") from the film *Saajan* (Beloved, Lawrence D'Souza, 1991).[24] He even collaborated with Indian diva Lata Mangeshkar in an album featuring Indonesian covers of Hindi songs.[25]

Rhoma's role in publicizing *dangdut* cannot be underestimated. *Dangdut* became, after *kroncong*,[26] the second "national" popular music genre that was neither a pure adaptation of foreign influences (like the genre called *pop Indonesia* that is usually totally "Western" in musical terms) nor restricted to local ethnic idioms (like some forms of local ethnic pop music styles, *pop Sunda* and *pop Jawa*). Sung in the national language, Bahasa Indonesia, *dangdut* uses a simple, direct (and at times even vulgar) style of lyrical language. In particular, it has been its lively rhythm that, as people say, automatically makes one *goyang* (swinging one's hips) that has made *dangdut* the most popular Indonesian dance music.

Through the 1980s, Hindi film songs continued to be one of the major melodic sources for the creation of "new" *dangdut* songs. Particularly, senior stars such as Ida Laila, Meggi Z., Hamdan ATT, Muchsin and Ali Alatas, and Mansyur S. have quite regularly adapted Hindi film song melodies without necessarily acknowledging the original source. Many of the male *dangdut* singer-songwriters such as A. Rafiq, Latief Khan, Fazal Dath, and Tommy Ali are part of the wider Arab-Indian diaspora in Jakarta, where Indian films have always played a significant role.[27] Camelia Malik, one of the "senior stars," is in fact the daughter of early Indonesian film director Jamaluddin Malik who produced local imitations of popular Bollywood films in the 1950s.

With the emergence of the music video and special television programs featuring *dangdut* music videos in the late 1980s and early 1990s, the "Indian" element associated with this genre found new expression. In some music videos, an exoticized "Indian" element is mixed freely with what could be called "Arabian" styles closely resembling oriental "1001 Nights" fantasies. However, this visual reference to an imaginary "Indian" or "Oriental" setting is not necessarily connected with the lyrical content of the song. In terms of its musical as well as visual practice, *dangdut* is "citational," constituting an Indonesian version of what Homi Bhabha terms "vernacular cosmopolitanism," characterized by "performative, deformative" translations.[28]

In the late 1990s, *dangdut* and the *KKHH*-inspired Bollywood fever came together when Kerala-born *dangdut* star Ashraff's duet of the theme song to *KKHH* with Iis Dahlia, sung in Hindi, became one of the top-hit *dangdut* songs of the new millennium. Ashraff and Dahlia went on to re-record the entire sound track in Hindi. Yet the media, now familiar with the original, mocked this exercise as inauthentic. In an article about the widespread practice of "pirating" foreign music, especially with regard to *dangdut,* the author notes:

> Recently some singers were not even ashamed of imitation, singing Indian songs that are currently popular. Iis Dahlia, for example, sings

the soundtrack of "Kuch Kuch Hota Hai" in her own way, although her pronunciation of Hindi is still very faltering. Ah, there still seem to be singers in our country who feel more proud if they can imitate the work of other people, instead of creating their own original work.[29]

The "KKHH" song was also covered in numerous local cover versions and adaptations, sung in different Indonesian versions and in regional languages such as Javanese, Sudanese, and Buginese of South Sulawesi.[30] Although these cover versions clearly attempt to capitalize on the massive popularity of the "KKHH" tune, open adaptation and covering is, nevertheless, usual practice in Indonesia and a song's popularity can be measured by the various cover versions of it.[31] In most cases of the *dangdutization* of Hindi film songs, the original source and composer are not mentioned on the cassette covers. For example, on Ashraff's cassette

A typical VCD karaoke compilation of pirated *dangdut* video clips from other albums. The album by Tommy Ali and Anita features the song "*Anita Namaku*," one of the Indonesian cover versions of the "*Kuch Kuch Hota Hai*" theme song. Ashraff's song "Sarmila" is the *dangdut* cover version of "Aankh Milate Darr Lagta."

and VCD "Best of the Best Ashraff,"[32] most of the ten songs are clearly Indonesian cover versions of Hindi film tunes, yet it is Ashraff who is cited as the composer of the songs. In quite a few cases, the Indonesian audience is not aware that a particular *dangdut* song has a foreign source. The melody of the hit disco *dangdut* song of the early 1990s, "Mabuk dan judi" ("Alcoholism and gambling"), for example, is—unknown to most Indonesians—taken from the Bhangra hit "Gurh nalo ishq mitha" ("Love is sweeter than sugar") by Malkit Singh.[33]

Another very important development is the omnipresence of Hindi song-dance sequences in the Indonesian music video landscape. In particular, *Bollywood Hits,* broadcast by television station Lativi since May 2002, is dedicated to music videos while also offering information about playback singers. Even Jakarta-based MTV Indonesia (launched in May 2002) started showing four to five music videos of Bollywood song and dance sequences per day in the programs *Nonstop Hits* and *MTV Land*.[34] Furthermore, in 2001, the recording company Duta Cahaya Utama Records obtained the audio license for Indian music from four Indian recording companies.[35] Hindi film songs are also increasingly played on special private radio stations. The song-dance sequence as an autonomous source of viewing pleasure is underscored by Rahmat Suardi of TPI:

> The audience seems never to be bored. If they already know the story of the film, they still enjoy watching the film again and again because they like to see the dances and to hear the songs of the film. That's the reason why films like Milan and Boby [*sic*], starring Raj Kapoor and Rishi Kapoor, are still popular, even if they have been rerun several times. Its songs like Sawan Ka Mahina Sawane Ka Re Sor [*sic*] are hits, as well as Kabhie Kabhie [*sic*] that was presented by Amitabh Bachchan.[36]

This new widespread visibility in the mass media of Bollywood films might well enhance the Indonesian audience's awareness of the origin of some *dangdut* songs in Hindi films. But this exposure does not necessarily protect these songs from reproduction. The Hindi original version will have to share its position with countless localized cover versions and adaptations in different music genres. For in Indonesia, songs are not only there to be listened to but also there to be sung. Karaoke is a hugely popular leisure activity, and new technologies, such as karaoke VCDs, are adapted to deep-rooted oral orientations typical for many non-Western collective cultures. Thus, songs are reformulated and recreated to become part of a collective repertoire. However, Western-educated Indonesians are increasingly sensitive to notions of "authorship" and "copyright," giving rise to an uneasy awareness of the distinction between the original piece and "cheap" and "bad-quality" imitations like Iis Dahlia's version of the "KKHH" song. With Bollywood's new popularity in Indonesian television and the commercialization of all things Bollywood, "traditional" citational practices are increasingly confronted with the global dynamics and rules of commodity culture. The current Bollywood trend is thus changing *dangdut*, both in practice and in location, within the Indonesian mediascape. Indonesian music critic Bre Redana, writing in *Kompas*, stated that after the success of *KKHH*,

> [t]he situation has already changed. Indian songs are now entering the Indonesian market through networks of big companies, bound to clear legal conditions. This means that piracy is not as easy as it was before, if one does not want to get into legal problems. In the era of Kuch Kuch Hota Hai, the presence of Indian songs thus shifts the goalposts for the local music industry, not only regarding the legal aspects, but also regarding creativity. The latter is particularly challenging for dangdut music as it has to find its own colour, originality, identity and character. Dangdut cannot indulge in just dancing away.[37]

Goyang India, Goyang Dangdut

The rather "intimate" relationship between Bollywood films, its music, and *dangdut* is materialized by the close and, at times, overlapping position that both occupy in Indonesian mainstream media discourse. Here they are in fact "neighbors," inhabiting the same "district." For example, the monthly magazine *Dangdoet Plus* covers the usual gossip about *dangdut* stars and music, but under the rubric *Goyang India* (Indian hip-swinging), it offers star gossip and news about Bollywood films. This affinity between both Bollywood music and *dangdut* is also apparent in the infotainment show *Gondangdia*, that is, *go*ssip, *dang*dut, and In*dia*, on the private television station SCTV. In an advertisement for this show in the tabloid *Bollywood Indonesia*,[38] presenter Anya Dwinov sports a stylized bindi and henna decorations. The byline tells readers that *Gondangdia* is about "Gosip India [sic], Gosip Dangdut [sic], Making Film Bollywood."[39]

Advertisement for the infotainment show *Gondangdia* with presenter Anya Dwinov.

This discursive allocation of both *dangdut* and Bollywood as adjacent in the Indonesian collective imaginary needs further examination. What are the assumed "similarities" of both genres that make this "intimate neighborhood" so seemingly "natural" to Indonesians? Bollywood films and their music are "freely mixed" with *dangdut* in musical and discursive terms. Both have been historically stigmatized as lowbrow, cheap, and escapist entertainment. *Dangdut* has long served as a shorthand for *kampungan*. The tasteless aesthetics that upper-class Indonesians ascribe to *dangdut,* particularly with regard to the stage shows, evoke Ashis Nandy's identification of the urban slum as the right metaphor for Indian popular cinema. His characterization of Bollywood aesthetic of excess as a "mix of the comic and the tragic, spiced with elements borrowed indiscriminately from the classical and the folk, the East and the West"[40] might well describe the stage shows of Rhoma in the 1970s and 1980s, which might appear kitschy, and yet, as Frederick points out, neither Rhoma

nor his audiences viewed the various elements being melded together as anything but complementary. Reality and fantasy carried and strengthened each other, and the impetus they built together moved dangdut beyond music in the narrow sense. Theatrics seemed, in short, to fit the dynamism of dangdut and make of it a comprehensive whole that was somehow larger than its parts.[41]

This slum aesthetic of excess—in its musical mix of genres, in the tragic pathos of many a song lyric, in the display of the erotically dancing female body on stage, in its costumes and accessories, and in the audience's pleasure in letting itself be totally absorbed by the irresistible rhythm and the sensually charged atmosphere—conveys contradictory meanings on various levels of signification.[42] Thus, *dangdut*'s appeal to the masses, crossing ethnic and, increasingly, social barriers, and as such representing a highly integrating potential with regard to the politics of the nation-state, led to its conscious incorporation into populist national politics. In election campaigns, the performances of national *dangdut* stars are one of the highlights. *Dangdut*'s mass appeal was acknowledged in 1995 by former Secretary of State, Moerdiono, who proclaimed *dangdut* as being "very, very Indonesian" music: "This country [is] of the people, by the people, for the people. And so is dangdut of the people, by the people, and for the people."[43] At the same time, as *dangdut* migrated to television, the media predicted that it would become acceptable to the upper classes and would "go international," especially after the success of *dangdut* concerts in Japan.[44] *Dangdut*, if cleansed of the "vulgar" erotic dancing style typical for the female singers on *kampung* stages and given more "sophisticated" lyrics, would be Indonesia's answer to internationally acclaimed genres such as reggae and salsa. Yet, even today, most educated urban Indonesians seem to remain uneasy about *dangdut*—they are reluctant to admit that they like it, but they also insist on its gentrification.[45] *Dangdut* has in fact been entering upper-class hotel bars and clubs, yet social stigma is still quite pervasive if one considers *dangdut* in general. It retains the taint of the masses.

Additionally, *goyang* as an essential feature of both Bollywood (especially in the form of the song-and-dance sequences) and *dangdut* accounts for the overlapping position that both occupy in modern Indonesia and the rather ambiguous pleasures they offer—at once "low-class" and "cheap" but, nonetheless, highly seductive. The shared rhythmic pleasure of both genres as well as the dynamic of imitating and at the same time creatively localizing foreign influences is readily apparent from the lyrics of an early *dangdut* song that was extremely popular in the 1970s entitled "Terajana," sung by Rhoma Irama. In its lyrics, it refers to the Hindi film song "Tera jana" ("Your departure"), sung by Lata Mangeshkar in the film

Anari (The Simpleton, Hrishikesh Mukherjee, 1959), but at the same time, it is said to be a typical *dangdut* song, praising the distinct pleasure that *dangdut* music offers its audience: its irresistible seducing rhythm that automatically makes people swing their hips:

Tera jana	**Tera jana**
pernah aku melihat, musik di Taman Ria	Once I saw a music performance in a public park
iramanya melayu duhai sedap sekali	the Malay rhythm oh so nice to listen to
sulingnya suling bambu,	the flute the bamboo flute,
gendangnya kulit lembu	the gendang drum made of cow skin
dangdut suara gendang	the gendang drum sounding "dangdut"
rasa ingin berdendang	I feel like singing along

Ref:	**Ref:**
terajana . . . terajana . . .	terajana . . . terajana . . .
ini lagunya, lagu India	this is the song, the Indian song
hai merdunya . . . hai merdunya . . .	oh how sweet and melodious . . .
merdu suara hai penyanyinya	the melodious sound of the singer's voice
serasi dengan lincah gayanya	in harmony with her lively performance
karena asiknya aku,	I am so absorbed in fascination
hingga tak ku sadari	that I just find myself
pinggul bergoyang-goyang,	with hips swinging to and fro
rasa ingin berdendang	I feel like singing along

Goyang—long associated with *dangdut*—became the subject of a fierce national debate in 2003 when the scandalous drilling hip gyrations (labeled *goyang ngebor,* "drilling *goyang*") of *dangdut* shooting star Inul Daratista seemed to test the limits of publicly acceptable behavior. While orthodox Muslim clerics together with Rhoma Irama declared Inul's *goyang* as transgressing the limits of proper morality and thus as *haram,* calling for a ban, others stressed the fact that "dangdut tanpa goyang, ibarat sayur tanpa garam" ("*dangdut* without *goyang* is like a vegetable dish without salt"). In *Kompas,* an article dedicated to the evolution of "*goyang* through the times" repeatedly stressed the link with "Indian" (that is, Hindi film) style of dancing. It quoted Munif Bahasuan of

Orkes Melayu Kelana Ria as saying that *goyang* became popular after people had watched dancing scenes in Indian films.[46]

Similar to the *KKHH* boom, which led to the creation of all sorts of infotainment around Bollywood, Inul became the television superstar of 2003, with numerous new programs created especially for her and her dancing style, as well as featuring infotainment regarding her and *dangdut*. The "slum" had returned onto the national stage, both in a tamed and cleansed form (a "clean" *dangdut* as well as "clean" Bollywood films) and in the shocking "drilling" buttocks of Inul and the erotic song and dance sequences that are a part of the otherwise "clean" Bollywood films. While sexuality in Hollywood films is often criticized as "amoral" and deemed unacceptable to Indonesian moral standards, the acceptance of the sensual song and dance sequences, even among fans who often wear the Islamic headscarf as a sign of their new pious Muslim consciousness, is interesting. I suggest that it is precisely the relegating of the erotic dimension into a special domain, that is, the song and dance sequences, that makes them more acceptable. Eroticism is an important part of the visual and emotional spectacle Bollywood films offer their audience, but it does not threaten the overall patriarchal family-oriented moral framework of the film narrative as such. In contrast to Hollywood films, Bollywood song and dance sequences simultaneously communicate the excitement of female sexuality and formally contain it. Through this relegation into a distinct realm, it does not threaten the wider sociosymbolic order of society. However, Inul represented such a threat, as she transgressed the border and "drilled" her buttocks outside the usual *kampung* stages on national television, leading to fierce debates and contestations about *dangdut*'s proper position within Indonesian national culture.

Dangdut, Bollywood, and Indonesia's Globalizing Mediascape

The highly emotional controversy surrounding Inul and the "proper" form of *dangdut* has been the climax so far in *dangdut*'s transition from the shadows to the limelight in Indonesia's mass-mediated hegemonic public culture. The reception of Bollywood cinema has a similar timeline—it was not until *KKHH*'s phenomenal success that Bollywood became an explicitly acknowledged feature of Indonesia's mediascape. Particularly after former president Soeharto's fall in 1998 and the end of his so-called New Order regime that had regulated public expression for more than thirty years, Indonesia has increasingly opened itself up to the globalizing dynamics of transnational cultural flows. The same holds true for internal processes as hegemonic culture is increasingly faced with the challenge of incorporating its other. The recent phenomenon of both Bollywood films and *dangdut* becoming an integral part of Indonesia's public culture has to be seen within the wider context of the ongoing diversification of the globalizing influences on Indonesia's contemporary mass media landscape. Besides Hindi films, Brazilian telenovelas have been very popular, and recently there has been a boom in East Asian television dramas, such as the extremely popular Taiwanese serial *Meteor Garden* in 2002 and 2003, which had a great deal of influence on local metropolitan youth culture. The Indonesian film industry, barely alive in the mid-1990s with an average production of about five films per year,[47] has apparently profited from these fresh new impulses in the post-Soeharto mediascape. With charming, upbeat films whose storylines often evolve around the life and problems of well-off urban high-school students, a new generation of young directors succeeded in making local productions attractive even to upper-class Indonesians. *Ada Apa Dengan Cinta?* (What is up with love? Rudy Soedjarwo) was a huge success in 2002 and broke box-office records. Another powerful and increasingly dominant force has been the widespread appeal that new orthodox readings of Islam exert on Indonesian Muslims, especially students and the new middle classes, reshaping Indonesian public life as can most clearly be seen in the growing number of mostly middle-class women and female students who consciously choose to wear the Muslim headscarf. This dynamic globalization of non-Western cultural images and narratives points toward the emergence of new local identifications that imagine communities beyond the nation-state, such as the Southeast Asian pan-Islamic identity associated with the new trend of the so-called *nasyid* music and the "East Asian" form of trendy urban youth culture propagated by serials such as *Meteor Garden*. Contemporary Indonesian public culture increasingly reorients itself, looking to other non-Western social, cultural, and religious forms as alternatives in the struggle to define a modern identity without becoming totally "Westernized."

Bollywood films, while usually experienced as representing a world that bears great "cultural similarity" to Indonesia, are still foreign enough that their visual images and narratives, evolving around the key issues of modernity, love, sexuality, and the family, can function as unthreatening projections that enable Indonesians to view some of their own anxieties, fantasies, and desires screened in new ways. Larkin has argued similarly for the Nigerian context, linking the popularity of Indian films in Hausa society with the "parallel modernity" these films offer: "a way of imaginatively engaging with the changing social basis of contemporary life that is an alternative to the pervasive influence of a secular West."[48] Both Bollywood and *dangdut* music, having constituted a central feature of Indonesian "popular culture" (with all its original low-brow connotations) for a long time, have now found their way into Indonesia's modern, mass-mediated hegemonic television landscape, where they reach far wider audiences than ever before in their history. They are now acknowledged as occupying legitimate positions within the dynamics of a "national" and at the same time increasingly globalizing Indonesian public culture, thus taking an active part in the ongoing public contestations about different notions of what it means to be "modern," "Indonesian," "Asian," and "Muslim". Music plays a crucial role in these processes of identification, as has been stressed by Anderson who pointed out the "special kind of contemporaneous community" constituted by language, in particular in the forms of poetry and song:

> No matter how banal the words and mediocre the tunes, there is in this singing an experience of simultaneity. At precisely such moments, people wholly unknown to each other utter the same verses to the same melody. The image: unisonance.[49]

The "KKHH" theme song was heard and sung virtually everywhere in Indonesia. One gets the feeling that there does indeed seem to be "something happening" in today's Indonesia. At least, the newspaper *Kompas* proudly entitled interviews with young Indonesians regarding the question of their participation in the Bollywood fashion trend at the height of the *KKHH* craze: "We are already able to choose."[50]

Notes

I would like to thank Sangita Gopal and Sujata Moorti for providing valuable comments on earlier versions of this essay. I am also very grateful to Keith Snailham, who checked the language.

1 Bart Barendregt and Wim van Zanten, "Popular Music in Indonesia; Mass-Mediated Fusion, Indie and Islamic Music since 1998," *Yearbook for Traditional Music* 34 (2002): 77.
2 Arjun Appadurai, *Modernity at Large: Cultural Dimension of Globalization* (Minneapolis: University of Minnesota Press, 1996).
3 Arjun Appadurai and Carol A. Breckenridge, "Why Public Culture?" *Public Culture* 1, no. 1 (1988): 5–9.
4 CP/BRE, "Tetangga Dekat Bernama Film India," *Kompas*, October 13, 2002, http://www.kompas.com/kompas%Dcetak/0210/13/latar/teta14.htm (accessed April 5, 2003).
5 For a detailed history of the Indonesian film industry, see Karl G. Heider, *Indonesian Cinema: National Culture on Screen* (Honolulu: University of Hawai'i Press, 1991); Salim Said, *Shadows on the Silver Screen: A Social History of Indonesian Film* (Jakarta: The Lontar Foundation, 1991); and Krishna Sen, *Indonesian Cinema: Framing the New Order* (London: Zed Books, 1994).
6 *Shadows*, 41–2.
7 Ibid., 102.
8 CP/BRE, "Tetangga Dekat Bernama."
9 CP, "Sekarang Masanya Shahrukh Khan," *Kompas*, November 3, 2002, http://www.kompas.com/kompas-cetak/0211/03/hiburan/seka19.htm (accessed April 5, 2003).
10 CP, "Videoklip Lagu India: Pokoknya Sang Bintang Mesti Bergoyang," *Kompas*, May 11, 2003, http://www.kompas.com/kompas-cetak/0305/11/hiburan/306369.htm (accessed January 15, 2004).
11 *Republika*, "Bollywood Merambah Dunia," January 10, 2003, http://www.republika.co.id/cetak_berita.asp?id=109720&kat_id=145&edisi=Cetak (accessed March 31, 2003).
12 Pantau, "Menjual India," *Tahun* III, no. 033 (January, 2003), http://www.pantau.or.id/txt/33/18.html (accessed January 15, 2004).
13 Zoel Fauzi Lubis, e-mail, July 28, 2004.
14 Patricia Uberoi, "Imagining the Family. An Ethnography of Viewing *Hum Aapke Hain Koun...*!" in *Pleasure and the Nation: The History, Politics, and Consumption of Public Culture in India*, ed. Rachel Dwyer and Christopher Pinney (New Delhi: Oxford University Press, 2001), 309–51.
15 CP/BRE, "Tetangga Dekat Bernama."
16 For a detailed description of *dangdut*'s historical origins, see William H. Frederick, "Rhoma Irama and the Dangdut Style: Aspects of Contemporary Indonesian Popular Culture," *Indonesia* 34 (October 1982): 103–30.
17 Krishna Sen and David T. Hill, *Media, Culture, and Politics in Indonesia* (Melbourne: Oxford University Press, 2000), 176.
18 Bre Redana, "Goyang India di Mana-mana," *Kompas,* November 5, 2000, http://www.kompas.com/kompas-cetak/0011/05/latar/goya13.htm (accessed April 28, 2005).
19 Joko, "Ellya Kadam: Diva Dangdut Yang Sesungguhnya!" *Tembang*, http://www.tembang.com/profil/default.asp?i=139 (accessed November 19, 2003).
20 Ibid.

21 Tresnawati, "Elvy Sukaesih: Sudah Lama Jatuh-Bangun," *Suara Merdeka,* May 5, 2002, http://www.suaramerdeka.com/harian/0205/05/bincang1.htm (accessed November 25, 2003).

22 For a detailed description of Rhoma Irama's role in the emergence of *dangdut* and his position as one of Indonesia's first popular culture "superstars," see Frederick.

23 For reasons unknown, Sen in her analysis of post-1965 Indonesian cinema does not mention Rhoma Irama's hugely popular musical films.

24 *Denpasar Post,* "Hau Siang Hau Siang Jadi Lagu Dangdut Jawa," May 8, 2002, http://www.denpasarpost.tv/2002/05/08/hiburan1.htm (accessed June 24, 2003).

25 Ibid.

26 See, for example, Judith Becker, "Kroncong, Indonesian Popular Music," *Asian Music* 7, no.1 (1975): 14–19.

27 Zoel Fauzi Lubis, e-mail, July 30, 2004.

28 Homi Bhabha, *The Location of Culture* (London: Routledge, 1994), 241.

29 *Denpasar Post,* "Hau Siang Hau Siang."

30 I am grateful to Andy Sutton for sharing his Buginese version with me. The "KKHH" theme song has also, among others, been incorporated into local comedy recordings, for example, in a recording entitled "Kuch Kuch Hota Hai (Versi Cirebon: Dikuchek-Kuchek Matae)" in the local Cirebon dialect of northwestern Java. The Cirebon song lyrics are in a humorous style about poor people's problems to get the delicious meal they are dreaming of. On the same comedy recording, Ashraff's already dangdutized version of "Aankh milate darr lagta," "Sarmila," has been further Cirebonized in a song called "Saritem" (a traditional Javanese female name with strong rural and low-class connotations) (Dian Records, 20056-105).

31 Shown by Yampolsky's study of the pop Indonesia hit "Hati yang luka" ("Wounded heart," 1988) and its subsequent numerous adaptations into other Indonesian pop genres. See Philip Yampolsky, "Hati Yang Luka, an Indonesian Hit," *Indonesia* 47 (1989): 1–18.

32 HP Record.

33 *Denpasar Post,* "Hau Siang Hau Siang."

34 CP, "Videoklip."

35 CP, "Videoklip." The recording companies are T-Series, Tips, HMV Saregama, and RPG.

36 CP, "Sekarang Masanya."

37 Bre Redana, "Goyang India."

38 "Bollywood," *Edisi 63,* April 21–27, 2003, 21.

39 Like the other Bollywood infotainment shows that were produced in the midst of the Bollywood craze, *Gondangdia* is not shown anymore. It was broadcasted weekly fifty-two times until it ended on July 6, 2003 (Zoel Fauzi Lubis, e-mail, July 28, 2004).

40 Ashis Nandy, "Introduction: Indian Popular Cinema as a Slum's Eye View of Politics," in *The Secret Politics of Our Desires: Innocence, Culpability, and Indian Popular Cinema,* ed. Ashis Nandy (London: Zed Books, 1998), 2.

41 Frederick, 112.

42 For a detailed account of the erotic spectacle at kampung-style *dangdut* performances, see Ceres Pioquinto, "Dangdut at Sekaten: Female Representations in Live Performance," *RIMA* 29 (1995): 59–89; and Susan Browne, "The Gender Implications of Dangdut Kampungan: Indonesian 'Low-Class' Popular Music" (Monash University Working Paper 109, Monash University, Melbourne, Victoria, 2000). For a culture-sensitive analysis of the Javanese audience's distinct pleasure in dancing away to sad lyrics sung by erotic female singers, see Bettina David, "The Erotics of Loss: Some Remarks on the Pleasure of Dancing to Sad Dangdut Songs," in *Sonic Modernities: Popular Music and New Social Formations in the Malay World,* ed. Wim van Zanten and Bart Barendregt (Leiden: KITLV Press, forthcoming).

43 Lana Simatupang, "The Development of Dangdut Music and Its Meanings: A Study of Popular Music in Indonesia" (master's thesis, Department of Anthropology and Sociology, Monash University, 1996), 58.

44 See, for example, the interview with senior *dangdut* singer Camelia Malik, "Saya Ingin Dangdut Go International," *Republika,* December 24, 2000.

45 Browne, "The Gender Implications of Dangdut Kampungan."

46 LOK/XAR, "Goyang dari Masa ke Masa," *Kompas,* February 9, 2003, http://www.kompas.com/kompas-cetak/0302/09/latar/121501.htm (accessed April 28, 2005).

47 Marselli Sumarno, "Menuju Sinema Indonesia Baru," *Kompas,* April 2, 2000, http://www.kompas.com/kompas-cetak/0302/09/latar/121501.htm (accessed April 28, 2005).

48 Brian Larkin, "Indian Films and Nigerian Lovers: Media and the Creation of Parallel Modernities," *Africa* 67, no. 3 (1997): 434.

49 Benedict Anderson, *Imagined Communities* (London: Verso, 1983), 132.

50 Lala Amalia, "Kita Sudah Bisa Memilih," *Kompas,* December 20, 2002, http://www.kompas.com/kompas-cetak/0212/20/dikbud/kita41.htm (accessed March 31, 2003).

7. The Ubiquitous Nonpresence of India

Peripheral Visions from Egyptian Popular Culture

Walter Armbrust

[I]t struck me, suddenly, that there was nothing I could point to within his world that might give credence to my story—the remains of those small, indistinguishable, intertwined histories, Indian and Egyptian, Muslim and Jewish, Hindu and Muslim, had been partitioned long ago.
> —Amitav Ghosh, *In an Antique Land*

Egyptian popular culture is conventionally thought of in one of two ways: first, as a national tradition developing out of the internal dynamic of Egyptian society and tied economically to the entire Arabic-speaking world; second, as a national tradition corrupted by the West, to the detriment of the healthy development of a sovereign identity. Both ways of thinking are products of the nationalist "partitioning" invoked in the epigraph from Amitav Ghosh's *In an Antique Land*. Often negative views of mass-mediated Egyptian popular culture—the opinion that it is nothing but a bad copy of a Western model—take for granted the domination of the Egyptian periphery by a Western metropole. Therefore, the only influence acknowledged on Egyptian cinema is "vertical" insofar as the dominant metropole is imagined to be "higher" in a hierarchy of political and economic power than the local, or peripheral, film industry.

One commonly promoted antidote to unsatisfactory nation-centered analyses is the adoption of a transregional, or "globalized," framework. This too is not without its problems. In the end, a transregional perspective is just that, a perspective—a way of thinking about how culture gets produced that should be applicable to many different contexts. These contexts include historical ones that are by no means limited to the past few decades in which digitization and contemporary forms of capitalism called into question the solidity of national borders that were themselves of recent historical provenance. A transregional understanding of popular culture in any society should not be mistaken for an unprecedented *cultural condition*. People, things, cultural practices, information, and economic resources have always moved across previously established borders. The patterns of such movements have never been stable.

The pattern I examine here is a minor current among the various elements that created the Egyptian cinema: the image of India in Egyptian films and fan magazines. India was not a central preoccupation of the Egyptian cinema. By looking at the cinema through the lens of how it dealt with India and other non-Western cultures, I will be taking an oblique view of Egyptian popular culture. But often a view from the edge of a larger cultural phenomenon is the best way to illuminate the whole.[1]

India has had a long, though not always welcome, presence in Egyptian film culture. Egyptian filmmakers and most elites disparage Indian cinema, and this is consistent with the more generalized attitude about things Indian. "Hindi" in everyday language labels things that are strange, silly, or just plain dumb. When someone acts as if you do not know what you are doing, you can say *fakirni Hindi*? (you think I am from India or something?). *Film (i) Hindi* means "an Indian film," but also is synonymous with "a silly thing." Conceivably, the current linguistic usage of *Hindi* in the sense of "strange" or "stupid" came about at least to some extent through the introduction of Indian films and the eventually antagonist stance against it taken by the elites. My assumption in this essay, at any rate, is that the current meaning of "India" in Egyptian popular culture and linguistic usage has a history.

An emerging cultural hierarchy can be discerned in occurrences of Indian themes in Egyptian films and fan magazines and in their subsequent disappearance. I will discuss such occurrences mainly from the 1930s, though I will also allude briefly to the 1950s when Indian films entered the Egyptian market. It will become evident that in Egyptian popular culture, India was not always unambiguously a symbol of peculiarity or idiocy. But I also want to suggest that the history of modern Egyptian representations of India may, in some ways, run counter to Ghosh's narrative of willful amnesia: that the history of Indian cinema in Egypt is one of growing familiarity, albeit a familiarity that breeds contempt in some quarters.

India in the 1930s

My main textual source for this essay is the fan magazine *al-Kawakib* (The stars). It was first published from 1932 to 1934 by Dar al-Hilal, which was one of the largest and oldest publishing houses in Egypt. From 1934 to 1949, *al-Kawakib*'s cinema function was assimilated by Dar al-Hilal's variety magazine *al-Ithnayn*. Then in 1949, when cinema had greatly expanded its production capacity, *al-Kawakib* was revived as a primarily film-oriented magazine. It continues to this day, though the production standards since the late 1950s have greatly declined.[2]

The first attempt in *al-Kawakib* to put "India" and the Egyptian cinema in the same context came early on.[3] A woman in a sari was depicted on the cover of this issue. She was Aziza Amir, an important figure in early Egyptian cinema. Whether or not her clothes and general demeanor would have been convincing to an Indian audience, her intention in the photograph absolutely is to give the impression that she is Indian. The film that the cover advertises is *Kaffari 'an Khati'atik* (Atone for your sin). Aziza Amir was the star of the film, its producer, and the director. Inside issue number eight, a two-page spread showed more stills and described the plot for *al-Kawakib* readers.[4] Articles in *al-Kawakib* made, perhaps, extravagant claims about the ability of Amir to impersonate an Indian woman. One article was titled "'An Indian princess acts in Egypt!': What a foreign newspaper has to say about 'Aziza Amir." The text is as follows:

> An amusing mistake happened recently [in an] English article that 'Aziza Amir sent to us for us to have a look at and give our opinion. It had been written by one of the English correspondents resident in Egypt to the *Indian Mail* newspaper, which is published in India.
>
> The article was written under the title "An Indian princess acts in Egypt," and with the article was published the picture of a young Indian girl who is not linked to 'Aziza Amir in any way, and we believe that of its own accord the newspaper decided to use her to decorate the article or to shore up the writer's strange story.

The author says in his long article is summarized here:

> It appears that some Indian princesses love the cinema and love to appear on the silver screen before the public, so as to keep up with the stars of Hollywood. They have not found in their own country a field in which it is appropriate to work, and to achieve their desires. So they

Cover of *Al-Kawakib*, volume eight, May 16, 1932. The cover text reads, "Aziza Amir in one of the scenes from her new story, *Atone for Your Sin*, a synopsis of which appears in this issue on pages 8 and 9."

have left their country and have gone in search of another land in which they will find the means to facilitate these hopes.

Today, we have seen in one of Cairo's cinema houses an Indian film in which the Indian heroine falls in love with a young Egyptian who is famous in sports circles. She received tremendous acceptance and acclaim, especially because a young Egyptian had the lead in it and won a boxing match against his opponent!"

This hilarious correspondent says, after talking about the story and its great success among Egyptians, "This actress is very young and is the daughter of an Indian prince [amir]," and he is amazed that her father would allow himself to join her in standing before the camera, as this departure from Indian custom would have, in his opinion, the greatest effect on the success of acting and its spread among the princely classes in India![5]

The film's plot revolves around the visit of an Indian family to Egypt so that the father of the family can be treated in the mineral baths of Helwan (a spa located just south of Cairo). With him are his daughter "Mahatagumi," played by Aziza Amir, and a drunkard son, played by Zaki Rustam (a stage actor of considerable fame by that time).[6] There are various other characters, one of whom is played by an Indian actor identified as Yusuf 'Arfani. The characters most prominently mentioned in the magazine are Amir, Rustam, and an Egyptian boxer, Mahmud Salah al-Din. In the course of the film, the Indian daughter of this elite family falls in love with the boxer. According to a published synopsis, the girl and the boxer elope. The father dies in her absence, and her drunkard brother kidnaps her. He sentences her to atone for her sin of running away with the boxer. She is about to kill herself just as the boxer returns to try to save her. The last few lines give a good idea of what sort of India was being presented in this film:

> The brother has sentenced his sister to atone for her sin, and her family has left her to consider an appropriate punishment. She goes to a closet, and gets some poison. Going out to the garden, she throws herself at the feet of the Buddha, asking for pardon, and then takes the poison. Before she draws her last breath the boxer enters to save her, but is prevented from doing so by an iron door. The girl falls lifeless upon the ground, having atoned for her sin

The story was saturated with pure Indian atmosphere. Likewise, all the costumes and sets were greatly detailed and very beautiful, especially the Indian elements. This makes one appreciate the effort they have expended to create an atmosphere suitable to this strange story. Its point was defense of Indian honor in general, and it was completely Oriental.[7]

Perhaps, having a suicidal Hindu woman throw herself at the feet of a Buddha statue was a plot device somewhat lacking in ethnographic authenticity, had the film been viewed by Indian audiences. There may indeed have been little in *Kaffari 'an Khati'atik* that would qualify as an accurate representation of anything Indian. In fact, the film was heavily based on European stereotypes. Just before the opening, 'Aziza Amir revealed where the story came from:

> I wanted to make a modern film that tells a story of the East and could be shown in many foreign countries as a testimonial of our modern revival. For this I called upon "Monsieur" Albert Bodriuz, the artistic director of the German Company Sharikat Juumuun. He gave me the story kaffari 'an Khati'atik. He had borrowed it from an Italian. I liked the story, hired some actors, and returned to my country to make the film.[8]

The same article contained an excerpt from the film's story. It is a scene in which the Egyptian boxer waits for an audience with his Indian lover.

> I was alone in that strange Indian atmosphere, with the scent of musk mixing with the air and inspiring both terror and splendor. The room had statues of Indian gods spread about. In the middle was a huge realistic elephant, with treasures on its back. At its feet a statue of Buddha in his famous sitting pose.[9]

The plot does indeed read like a German story stolen from an Italian and adapted to the screen by an Egyptian director. One must nonetheless ask: why make a film featuring Indian characters at all? One reason is that Eastern themes were a potentially marketable alternative to Western-dominated cinemas.

In 1932, when the Egyptian cinema was becoming an organized industry, Hollywood was inescapable. *Al-Kawakib* frequently featured photographs of Western stars such as Marlene Dietrich, whose *Mata Hari* film was making the rounds at the time.[10] At this point, the magazine was trying to sell both the medium and the idea that Egyptian filmmakers could utilize it. Selling the medium meant, to some extent, selling Hollywood. A typical example is the article "Our Stars and Their Stars." It tells the reader the following:

> When new stars rise in Hollywood the publicists tell everything about them. A recent star in the capital of art is Sari Maritza, who signed with Paramount. Though not yet 21 the American papers have been writing about the things that distinguish her. She carries a small brass elephant given to her by the Chinese imperial family, which is

supposed to protect her from evil. She's obsessed with long backless dresses. She doesn't drink alcohol, but loves to smoke, and uses a long black cigarette holder given to her by Edgar Wallace, the famous English writer.

If we were to talk about our stars the same way, we would say that Aziza Amir carries a tiny Quran in a small gold box. And Bahiga Hafiz wears a head covering and wide Arab earrings that give her a special Eastern charm.[11]

Much of the information on the activities of *non-European* actors was mediated by Hollywood. A prominent example was Anna May Wong. Though not Indian, her presentation in *al-Kawakib* is nonetheless a good example of how the non-Western was sometimes plucked out of Hollywood press release material. In the early 1930s, Wong, a relatively minor figure in Hollywood, was featured in *al-Kawakib* at least as much as any other foreign actress.[12] Her relative ubiquity was undoubtedly connected to the fact that in 1932 Wong visited Cairo, where she was already well known due to her breakthrough role—in Egypt and, indeed, throughout the world—as a slave girl in the 1924 version of *The Thief of Baghdad*. Also, in 1932, she had just costarred with Marlene Dietrich in *Shanghai Express*.

Al-Kawakib always presented Wong as a Chinese actress, even though she in fact was born in California and acted only in Western films. But her Chinese ancestry crucially determined her place in Hollywood; it guaranteed that she would spend a career in mostly stereotyped roles despite her widely recognized talent. Indeed, in *Shanghai Express*, she earned $6,000 to Dietrich's $78,000, though many thought Wong's performance in the film was superior to that of her higher-paid costar.[13] She never cashed in on her success. On the contrary, *Shanghai Express* was the high point of Wong's career. Articles about her in *al-Kawakib* quite unselfconsciously played up Western stereotypes. In an article, presumably translated from a foreign source, she was quoted as follows:

> East is East and West is West, as the poet of the British Empire Rudyard Kipling said. But I say it's not true. I was born and raised in the East and then lived in the West. I see the West in the East, and the East in the West.
>
> Have you read the Somerset Maugham story, *The Moon and Sixpence*? It's about a painter named Gauguin who rebels when he realizes that he'll die without ever enjoying love. Leaving his wife, he goes to a

South Pacific Island where he loves a black woman and spends the rest of his days happy with her.[14]

Such frankly Orientalist cant was surely translated directly from a press release provided by an American studio, suggesting that on one level *al-Kawakib* looked at the world straightforwardly through Hollywood's eyes. At the same time, a process of selection is evident. In 1932, *al-Kawakib* made Anna May Wong more prominent not just than her costar Marlene Dietrich, but also than Greta Garbo, Joan Crawford, and many other Western actresses who were surely marketed more extensively by their studios than was Anna May Wong.

Selling a vision of the East as an alternative to Hollywood was clearly marked in "Rise of the Cinema in India," a feature on the Indian cinema published in 1932:

India began producing this modern art after WW I in the Punjab with "Hindukiyya" historicals, or fictional stories taken from 1001 Nights. The actors were common people or from the class of professional women singers who performed in cafés. Later they were replaced by educated men and women. The cinema flourished anew and was able to expand until there were 75 national companies working with private capital. This year alone three companies were formed in Lahore with huge capital resources. Up to now these companies have produced a thousand films, including both talkies and silents.[15]

This cannot be from a Hollywood press release. The article describes some of the Indian actors, emphasizing those who are Muslim, such as Iftikhar Rasool: "He is a Muslim and earned a law degree in England . . . a master of all types of Eastern dance."[16] At least some Indian companies must have wanted to market their films to Arab audiences, as a photo published with the article of a man in Bedouin costume suggests. The text also identifies an actress named Zubayda—presumably a Muslim—as a pious and good woman:

Zubayda is a famous actress who has worked in dozens of Indian films, both talkies and silents. She is very decent. Once she was asked, "What do you love?" Her answer was "prayer and sleep." She absolutely will not work in a film that includes kissing.[17]

The article presents Indian cinema as an ideal to be emulated. Though much of the non-Western imagery was filtered by Hollywood, the tendency of *al-Kawakib* was to select materials that broadened the field of cinematic representation. This is not to say that the magazine or the films themselves never constructed images that pointedly opposed their own society to the West. Indeed, decadent foreigners, usually Europeans, often appeared in Egyptian films. The first Egyptian talkie, *Sons of Aristocracy*, made in 1932 by the theater and cinema legend Yusuf Wahbi, was inspired by the real-life murder in London of an Egyptian playboy by his French wife. An issue of *al-Kawakib* featured a photo of a femme fatale played by a French actress, shown sprawled across Wahbi's lap.[18] But if Europeans made good villains, and sometimes good buffoons, it is also true that they were rarely depicted extensively. More commonly, the presence of Europeans was elided. If they appeared in Egyptian films, it was only briefly. Egyptian film narratives of all periods have been more concerned with various forms of hybridity composed of the emergent categories of "Egyptian" and "Foreign"—or alternatively, with characters viewed as culturally-compromised boundary straddlers— than with the categories themselves. The categories themselves, while always in fact changing, were unremarkable; the perception of the boundaries having been transgressed was an entirely different matter.

Kaffari 'an Khati'atik suggests that in some Egyptian popular culture of the 1930s, the category of "Indian" could be provisionally assimilated with that of "Egyptian." But such a conflation still could not pass without justification. In this vein, one other film from the 1930s must be mentioned, namely the comedy *Salama fi Khayr* (Salama is fine), made in 1937, and starring Nagib al-Rihani, one of the most popular comedians of his day.[19] Al-Rihani plays Salama, an aging Effendi. "Effendi" refers to a Western-educated office worker and is often glossed by historians as "middle class," though such a designation obscures considerable historical complexity.[20] But Salama seems destined to never fulfill his class destiny, remaining perpetually stuck at the status of *farrash* (errand boy) in a large textile company called "al-Hindawi"—a name with intriguingly Indian overtones (*al-hind* is the Arabic word for India, and "Hindawi" is a personal adjectival form denoting ancestry or origin, hence "al-Hindawi" is a person from India). Salama's boss is Khalil al-Hindawi, always referred to as *al-khawaga* (plural *khawagat*), a term nominally meaning "foreigner." In twentieth-century Egypt, some *khawagat* were long-time fixtures (for example, Egyptianized Greeks, Jews, and sometimes even Christians). But *khawaga* by this time was also acquiring derogatory overtones linked to an emerging sense of national identity. Hindawi is presented as a completely affable, if slightly bumbling, Christian *khawaga*. There are, however, plenty of much more foreign *khawagat* in the film. *Salama fi Khayr* has less to do with *khawaga* Hindawi than with the arrival of Kandahar, the Amir (prince) of Bludistan, a nation somewhere between India and Afghanistan (obviously where Pakistan would come into being ten years later). Through a series of mishaps, the humble errand-boy Salama ends up in a luxury hotel, where a stunning bevy of quite exotic *khawagat* eagerly await the arrival of the Indian prince. When Kandahar arrives, he bumps into Salama before anyone is aware of his presence and realizes that they bear an uncanny resemblance to each other. The crowd at the luxury hotel—a blend of sycophants and gold diggers—bores the prince, so he permits them to think that Salama is Kandahar. With the spotlight of celebrity directed at others, the prince prolongs the mistaken identity. Al-Rihani's performance as the prince is a gem. He is, to put it mildly, not up on the protocol of the official state visits over which he finds himself presiding. The real prince meanwhile uses his anonymity to strike up a relationship with an attractive Egyptian servant girl who is completely unaware of his true identity and hence obviously sincere in her affection for the incognito Kandahar.

Salama fi Khayr provides a social index of Egyptian society, ranging from the native-born Egyptian Effendis to an exceedingly odd world of luxury hotels, foreign languages, and glamorous women. In this galaxy of social types, Salama's boss, *khawaga* Khalil Hindawi, is interesting. Despite the *khawaga* appellation, Hindawi's textiles business bears a great resemblance to the industrial enterprises of Muhammad Tal'at Harb. Harb was the leader of the Misr group, a series of interlocking businesses that aspired to a monopolistic control of the national economy. One of the projects of Tal'at Harb's Misr group was Studio Misr—Egypt Studios—which produced this film.[21] In many ways, *Salama* is a thinly disguised advertisement for the Misr group. It promotes the ideal of trade between British protectorates, unhindered by colonial interference. At one point in the film, Salama, standing in for Kandahar, listens to a foreign businessman make a pitch to supply textiles made in his factory from cotton supplied by his Egyptian partner to the soon-to-be-formed army of Bludistan. The factory owner in *Salama fi Khayr* expresses an official narrative of local capitalists competing with foreign investors for industrial contracts—a narrative that was eclipsed in the 1950s and 1960s by a new story that saw efforts at local capitalist development as essentially doomed to failure, with the notable honorable exception of Tal'at Harb, who was interpreted as the ancestor of postcolonial statism, and thus by default the nationalist antidote to less

Hollywood advertisements, by contrast, were a regular occurrence in every single issue. Some features from *al-Kawakib* of the 1950s seem as positive about Indian cinema as the aforementioned article from the 1930s. Here is an excerpt from a text:

> The ties that bind Egypt and India are deep-rooted, marked by strong contacts in politics, commerce, and culture. Recent history is also marked by shared attitudes. When the Egyptian revolution of 1919 occurred under Sa'd Zaghlul, a similar revolution occurred in India under Ghandi. When India raised the banner of peace and positive non-alignment in Asia under Nehru Egypt was raising the same banner in the Arab East and the nations of Africa under the leadership of Gamal Abd al-Nasir.

There are similarities in the customs and traditions of the two peoples, such as honor and protectiveness toward women. The secret to the success of Indian films in Egypt is that they portray a common life of both the Indian and the Egyptian, with only trivial differences attributable to environmental factors. The music in these films moves us and lifts our spirits because it springs from the same source: the magic of the East and its spirituality.[25]

Although this 1950s article asserts "strong contacts in politics, commerce, and culture," it, like those of the 1930s, urges Indo-Egyptian friendship on the basis of rather vague similarities. But the tenor of this passage nonetheless differs significantly from similar rhetoric of the 1930s:

> It is incumbent on our politicians to strengthen the ties between ourselves and the great Indian people who have stood with us through the darkest times. And there are Egyptians who believe that nationalism requires that they act as unofficial ambassadors by developing commercial and spiritual ties between the two countries through cultural exchange that is represented by Indian films.[26]

One such unofficial citizen ambassador is mentioned by name:

> Ustaz Ahmad Darwish, owner of the Indian-Egyptian Agency for Film Distribution (*al-wikala al-Misriyya al-Hindiyya li-Tauzi'al-Aflam*), has taken up this calling. He has previously brought the best Indian films to Egypt, and now he continues his calling by bringing five of the best

films that Indian studios have produced for the new Egyptian film season. The films that have been selected are those that best fit the Egyptian environment, the Eastern character, and Arab characteristics.[27]

What looks like an article in terms of layout is in fact an "infomercial" published by Ahmad Darwish's company. The actual marketing of Indian films by this and perhaps other companies resonated with the high politics of the Non-Aligned Movement, of which Nasser and Nehru were key figures. At the same time, in the commercial popular magazines where secondary narratives elaborated those depicted on screen, a different and somewhat ambivalently exoticized image of India began to emerge. For example, one often-repeated theme was the notion that "Indian dance is worship." The idea was, on the surface, presented respectfully. As one text put it, "The origin of dance is worship. India has made it a means for expressing the most exalted human feelings."[28] Dance as worship is, of course, a dubious sentiment for textual canonists and certain kinds of modernists. It might have made sense in some strains of Sufism, but Sufism per se scarcely ever featured in the pages of *al-Kawakib*. Sufism had suffered a long decline in the face of modernist rationality and, in other contexts, Islamist disapproval. In any case, this "dance is worship" feature had nothing to do with Sufism. It depicted a dancer in Indian dress illustrating various "Indian" dance postures. The dancer, however, was a known quantity. She was Tahiyya Karioka (the stage name for Badawiyya Muhammad Karim), an "Oriental" dancer who performed both live and on-screen. In the magazine feature, Karioka's poses ostensibly illustrated particular sentiments. The captions on the photographs read "begging God's forgiveness," "supplication," and "thanks." Conceivably, Karioka's mimicking of Indian dance is evidence of the growing presence of Indian films in the market. But India was only one style of foreign identity that could be "tried on" vicariously through consuming *al-Kawakib*. Karioka, an eminently recognizable public figure who appeared in films, on stage, in cabarets, and in advertisements, was wearing an "Indian" pose (as the text described it) just as she wore the latest French hairstyles—as another element of her continually changing exoticism, which she had been cultivating throughout her career. Indeed, she had adopted the stage name of "Karioka" from the faux-Brazilian "Carioca dance" performed in the Fred Astaire–Ginger Rogers vehicle *Flying Down to*

The article "Indian Dance Is Worship," *Al-Kawakib,* May 1949, 95. The main text on this page reads, "The origin of dance is worship. India has made it a means for expressing the most exalted human feelings, and its purpose is refinement of the soul. Here is the dancer Tahiyya Karioka demonstrating types of Indian dance." The text in the center reads, "Submissiveness and humility—this is what Tahiyya conveys by these Indian dances." The text below the bottom photographs (left to right) reads, "thanks," "supplication," and "asking forgiveness."

Rio, which had been made in 1933 and marketed intensively in Egypt in 1934; hence by 1935, Badawiyya Muhammad Karim had become Tahiyya Karioka.

Trying on national styles was in fact common in late 1940s issues of *al-Kawakib* and other magazines, as was the tendency for these styles to become more distinctively national. A typical instance was an *al-Kawakib* feature titled "National Dances,"[29] which displayed a model in various national dresses: "Franco-Arab dance, used in East and West alike—a dance that mixes eastern and Western movements" (the model appears in a suitably hybrid "oriental" costume, with bare midriff, long dress, and a puffy semiblouse on one shoulder); "The Hungarian Hulahula dance, well known to the peoples of the Balkans without exception" (model in a short skirt, full blouse, one leg and one arm raised); "French dance, which greatly resembles the Italian dance in its movements" (elegant white dress, bare arms, leaning forward with one leg raised behind her in a semiballet pose); "Moroccan-Eastern dance, performed with lightness and elegance that express the magic of the East" (outfit identical to the "Franco-Arab" dance). The model, once again, is not a foreigner, but the well-known Egyptian dancer Naima 'Akif. Such features simultaneously promoted both national stars and the differentiation of national types. One can see a clear line connecting these pictorials and the 1930s Indian–Egyptian film narratives described above. At the same time, national differentiations were sharpening and were being applied equally to the "Eastern" and "Western" models. Later, the playful impersonation of other national types by Egyptian stars became relatively rare. For example, a 1957 pictorial article recycling the title "Dance Is Worship"[30] used Indonesian models. It was emblematic of a general tendency to stop using Egyptians to masquerade as other nationalities; nations must represent themselves. At the same time, Ahmad Darwish's infomercials, with their obviously self-interested appeal to cultural commonalities between Egypt and India, hawked an Indian product. The point was no longer to extol the idea of India as a worthy model to be emulated in the common struggle against Europe, as it had been in the 1930s, despite official rhetoric in the wake of the Bandung Conference. Political ties at the official level were insistently proclaimed even as simultaneously a still more insistent process of "othering" was applied to things (Far) Eastern. Ultimately between 1957 and the early 1990s, when I first became aware of the presence of Indian films in Egypt, "Indian" became a term of scorn. A social consensus developed around the idea that for a thing to be Indian was to be different, strange even, and quite possibly inferior in most respects to things Egyptian. This was perhaps already starting to become true when, in 1957, the most natural way to portray Indians was with pictures of Indians, rather than pictures of Egyptians masquerading as Indians.

My essay began with a quote from Amitav Ghosh—an Indian anthropologist who did fieldwork in Egypt. I return to him again briefly in my conclusion. One of the things that immediately struck me about *In an Antique Land,* his antinationalist ethnographic travelogue-cum-historical meditation on Mediterranean–Indian relations, was the studiously constructed nonpresence of Indian cinema in Egypt. The book makes one brief reference to a poster of the Hindi actor Raj Kapoor hanging in a barbershop.[31] This was far less engagement than I had expected with the *contemporary* connection of Egypt and India (as opposed to the historically effaced medieval connection explored in Ghosh's book). India is by no means the distant rumor in Egypt that Ghosh implies. Indeed, when Ghosh's modern Egyptian informants began referring to him in the text as "Amitab," I had to consciously remind myself that this was probably a simple consonant shift (Arabic has no "v") or perhaps because Ghosh had introduced himself as "Amitab." It was surely not because they were thinking of Amitabh Bachchan, one of the stars of the Hindi cinema and a hugely popular figure in Egypt.

Bachchan's popularity is not at all apparent at the official level, where Indian cinema is usually treated with scornful silence, but it should have been apparent to Ghosh, because below the radar of legitimate culture the presence of India is palpable. Everyone knows that Indian films are in the market. Anyone can tell a curious anthropologist that the appeal of these films is to the poor and uneducated. From a Cairene perspective, "poor and uneducated" is often conflated with "rural." Although my interest in how India and Indian films are seen in Egypt developed long after my initial period of fieldwork in Egypt, I do remember incidents that showed the presence of India among precisely this section of the population.

For example, one urban legend circulating in the early 1990s was that a plane carrying Amitabh Bachchan touched down briefly in the Cairo airport for refueling. Word got out about the Hindi star's presence, and tens of thousands of people came to the airport hoping to catch a glimpse of him. I saw a more concrete example of Bachchan's presence in the displays of vendors in a popular market near downtown

Cairo. Some of these vendors sold tee shirts emblazoned with the face of Bachchan. A poster of Bachchan was also the prize of a game of skill set up on the fringes of a *mulid* (Islamic "saint's" festival) I once attended. It was the *mulid* of Husayn, grandnephew of the Prophet Muhammad, and one of the largest celebrations of its kind in Egypt. *Mulids* and the charismatic figures they commemorate occupy a conspicuous place in Ghosh's narrative. Toward the end of the book, he goes to visit the tomb of Sidi Abu-Hasira, a saint venerated by both Jews and Muslims. His curiosity in this site lands him in the Damanhour police station, where he is taken for questioning by curious officers of the law. Ghosh makes it into an occasion for postcolonial meditation:

> I was sitting at that desk [in the police station] now because the mowlid of Sidi Abu-Hasira was an anomaly within the categories of knowledge represented by those divisions [between past and present, Hindu and Muslim, Jew and Muslim etc.]. I had been caught straddling a border, unaware that the writing of History had predicated its own self-fulfillment.[32]

Given Ghosh's concern with saints' festivals, and his interest in challenging the dictates of nationalist history, it is curious that the presence of Indian commodities valued by precisely the same people who attend such festivals is effaced in his narrative. While my sources for the 1930s are more concrete (though not easily contextualized in relation to audiences), I think the presence of an Amitabh Bachchan poster as a *mulid* carnival prize is significant. The *mulid* of Husayn, at which I saw the poster, is notable precisely because it draws people to Cairo (where the celebration takes place) by the hundreds of thousands *from the countryside*. The source of value, Arjun Appadurai tells us in a well-known essay, is exchange and not the other way round.[33] Clearly, this poster of Amitabh Bachchan, valueless in and of itself (indeed, actively devalued by Egyptian elites), derived its prizeworthiness from exactly the sorts of people with whom Amitav Ghosh lived in Egypt: people from the countryside. It seems incontrovertible that any thorough understanding of the social life of this particular thing (which happens to be emblematic of India) would have to take into account the social context of the countryside.

Paradoxically, Ghosh—a postcolonial writer whose book is best read as a polemic against nationalism—has effaced the contemporary presence of India in Egypt as surely as the nationalist historians who aim to construct a "purely" Egyptian-imagined community. The reality is that contacts between colonial societies were formed not just through the colonial period, but right into the subsequent period of nation-building. In some ways, Ghosh's cosmopolitan narrative does just as much violence to history as the nationalist narrative. Frequent references to India early in the history of Egyptian cinema, and later the subterranean presence of Indian films in Egyptian society, do suggest that flows of culture and capital can be looked at outside concerns for national film traditions and anxieties about the degree to which national identity may have been polluted by Western influences. But a cosmopolitan globalism does not necessarily right the balance; it also constructs its own version of history at the expense of other versions.

Finally, it should be emphasized that there is an ethnography of India in Egypt still waiting to be written. India is a ubiquitous nonpresence in modern Egypt. Its persistence suggests that nationalist modes of thinking can be problematized through more immediate contexts than Ghosh's contrast with the medieval Mediterranean world. The ubiquitous nonpresence of India in Egypt cries out for someone to approach it directly rather than as I have done—as a postfieldwork afterthought.

It was a young woman in Cairo who first made me think about Indian films. Although she was more or less middle class, and therefore undoubtedly fully complicit in the sentiment that a *film (i) Hindi* is a strange and silly thing, she was also quite capable of talking about Indian films with completely unselfconscious enthusiasm. Just before Ramadan in 1990, she told me with great excitement that the state-run television was going to give them a treat for the holiday: an Indian film broadcast on television every evening of the month (*"film (i) Hindi kull (i) yaum. KULL (i) YAUM"*). She could barely contain herself. Unfortunately, either her information was wrong or the state lied. In the end, only one Indian film was broadcast. But if the prospect of an Indian film every night had such a grip on a young woman's imagination as recently as 1990, I have to believe that her enthusiasm was only the tip of an iceberg.

Notes

1   Richard Bulliet, *Islam: The View from the Edge* (New York: Columbia University Press, 1994), 12.
2   For an in-house history of Dar al-Hilal, see Ahmad Husayn Tam'awi, *Al-Hilal: 100 Am min al-Tanwir wa-al-Tahadduth* (Cairo: Dar al-Hilal, 1991).

3   *Al-Kawakib,* May 16, 1932, 1.
4   "*Kaffari 'an Khati'atik*!! Film Jadid Tukhrijuhu al-Sayyida 'Aziza Amir" [Atone for your sins!! A new film directed by madame 'Aziza Amir], *al-Kawakib,* May 16, 1932, 8–9.
5   "Amira Hindiyya Tumaththil fi Misr! Ma Taquluhu Sahifa Ajnabiyya 'an 'Aziza Amir" [An Indian princess acts in Egypt! What a foreign paper said about 'Aziza Amir], *al-Kawakib,* February 27, 1933, 11.
6   "Fi Kaffat al-Mizan: Kaffari 'an Khati'atik 'ala al-Sitar al-Fadhi" [In the balance: atone for your sins on the silver screen], *al-Kawakib,* February 6, 1933, 6–7.
7   Ibid., 6.
8   "Sa'a fi al-Hind" [An hour in India], *al-Kawakib,* August 1, 1932, 14.
9   Ibid.
10 *Al-Kawakib,* December 12, 1932, 2; and *al-Kawakib,* December 19, 1932, 24.
11 "Kawakibna wa Kawakibhum," *al-Kawakib,* September 19, 1932, 8.
12 *Al-Kawakib,* April 4, 1932, 8; *al-Kawakib,* May 16, 1932, 23; *al-Kawakib,* May 23, 1932, 1; *al-Kawakib,* June 27, 1932, 24; and *al-Kawakib,* October 24, 1932, 2.
13 Wikipedia, "Anna May Wong," http://en.wikipedia.org/wiki/Anna_May_Wong (accessed June 23, 2006).
14 "Al-Sharq wa al-Gharb wa al-Hubb wa al-Zawaj—fi Nazhar Ana May Wung" [East, West, love, and marriage in the view of Anna May Wong], *al-Kawakib,* September 5, 1932, 5.
15 "Nahdat al-Sinima fi al-Hind" [Rise of the cinema in India], *al-Kawakib,* October 24, 1932, 12–13.
16 Ibid., 12.
17 Ibid., 13.
18 *Al-Kawakib,* April 4, 1932, 20. For more on the media sensation that inspired *Sons of Aristocracy,* see Shawn Lopez, "Media Sensations, Contested Sensibilities: Gender and Moral Order in the Egyptian Mass Media, 1920–1955" (PhD diss., University of Michigan, 2004), chapter 3. On Wahbi, see Walter Armbrust, *Mass Culture and Modernism* (Cambridge: Cambridge University Press, 1996), 201–3.
19 For more on Nagib al-Rihani, see Armbrust, *Mass Culture,* 71–81; Walter Armbrust, "The Golden Age before the Golden Age: Commercial Egyptian Cinema before the 1960s," in *Mass Mediations: New Approaches to Popular Culture in the Middle East and Beyond,* ed. Walter Armbrust (Berkeley: University of California Press, 2000), 292–327; and Laila Abou Saif, "The Theater of Naguib al-Rihani: The Development of Comedy in Modern Egypt" (PhD diss., University of Illinois, 1969).
20 See Lucie Ryzova, "Egyptianising Modernity: Social and Cultural Constructions of the Middle Classes in Egypt under the Monarchy," in *Reenvisioning the Monarchy,* ed. Arthur Goldshmidt, Amy Johnson, and Barak Salmoni (Cairo: American University in Cairo Press, 2004), 324–59.
21 For more on Tal'at Harb, see Eric Davis, *Challenging Colonialism: Bank Misr and Egyptian Industrialization, 1920–1941* (Princeton, N.J.: Princeton

University Press, 1983). An alternative analysis of Egyptian capitalism in the colonial period can be found in Robert Vitalis, *When Capitalists Collide: Business Conflict and the End of Empire in Egypt* (Berkeley: University of California Press, 1995). On Tal'at Harb's role in establishing a film industry in Egypt, see Hasan Ilhami, *Muhammad Tal'at Harb: Ra'id Sina'at al-Sinima al-Misriyya* (Cairo: al-Hay'a al-Misriyya al-'Amma lil-Kitab, 1986); Munir Muhammad Ibrahim, "Studiyu Misr: Madrasat al-Sinima al-Misriyya" [Studio Misr: School of the Egyptian cinema], in *Misr, Mi'at Sana Sinima,* ed. Ahmad Ra'fat Bahjat (Cairo: Matbu'at Mahrajan al-Qahira al-Sinima'i al-Dauli al-'Ishrin, 1996), 158–66; and Walter Armbrust, "Egyptian Cinema On Stage and Off," in *Off Stage/On Display: Intimacy and Ethnography in the Age of Public Culture,* ed. Andrew Shryock (Stanford: Stanford University Press, 2004), 69–98.

22 Vitalis, *When Capitalists Collide,* 29–60.

23 Robert Vitalis, "American Ambassador in Technicolor and Cinemascope: Hollywood and Revolution on the Nile," in *Mass Mediations: New Approaches to Popular Culture in the Middle East and Beyond,* ed. Walter Armbrust (Berkeley: University of California Press, 2000), 269–91, 286.

24 Ibid., 283–6.

25 "Khatawat Jadida Tuqawwi al-Rabt Baynana wa Bayna Ahl al-Hind" [New steps to strengthen ties between us and the people of India], *al-Kawakib,* November 5, 1957, 16.

26 Ibid.

27 Ibid.

28 "Al-Raqs al-Hindi 'Ibada" [Indian dance is worship], *al-Kawakib,* May 1949, 95.

29 "Raqasat Qawmiyya" [National dances], *al-Kawakib,* April 1949, 80–1.

30 "Al-Raqs 'Ibada" [Dance is worship], *al-Kawakib,* November 13, 1957, 20–1.

31 Amitav Ghosh, *In an Antique Land: History in the Guise of a Traveller's Tale* (New York: Vintage, 1994), 181.

32 Ibid., 340.

33 Arjun Appadurai, "Introduction: Commodities and the Politics of Value," in *The Social Life of Things,* ed. Arjun Appadurai (New York: Cambridge University Press, 1988), 3–63, 56.

8. Appropriating the Uncodable

Hindi Song and Dance Sequences in Israeli State Promotional Commercials

Ronie Parciack

Two well-known figures that Israeli audiences would immediately recognize as representing political and cultural polarities appear on screen. Yet during a series of thirty-second commercials, they embody harmony. They dance and frolic with each other in an empty studio, blue skies, and a rainbow serving as the backdrop. The mere appearance of these figures—Yossi Sarid and Rubi Rivlin, Shulamit Aloni and Eli Hanna, and Emanuel Halperin and Eli Hanna, who represent opposing ends of the political spectrum—raises issues regarding the fate of the state of Israel and its boundaries, as well as cultural questions regarding the country's orientation: pro-Western or pro-Eastern? While these issues are presented merely through the juxtaposition of the characters, two at a time, the pairs move as if they were dancing and playing to the beat of the Hindi film song "Mera naam Chin-Chin-Chu." This song entered the Israeli public sphere through Mira Nair's *Salaam Bombay* (1988), a non-Bollywood production that cited this song, in turn, from the film *Howrah Bridge* (Shakti Samanta, 1958). This chapter examines the channeling of Hindi music sequences to an unexpected arena: a series of promotional commercials for Bezeq, the Israeli National Telecommunications Corporation, which were produced and aired by the Israeli state and commercial television channels during 1996. In particular, I explore how Hindi song and dance sequences traveling under the sign of Bollywood gain salience in late twentieth-century Israel.

The use of Bollywood song sequences in state promotional commercials is surprising for a number of reasons: With a few exceptions, there was no commercial distribution in Israel of movies from the Bombay/Mumbai film industry since the 1970s, and the commercial distribution of coproductions such as Nair's movie was a rare event.[1] The Indian film industry in general, and Bollywood in particular, was therefore not part of the Israeli cultural sphere. What resonance can a song from an unknown—not to say excluded—industry have in commercials for an Israeli *national* corporation? Furthermore, why would a series of commercials intended to promote national unity make use of a song from another, relatively unfamiliar culture, sung in a foreign language and in a performative style that refers to unfamiliar vocal conventions? In addition, given the pro-Western tendency of many power hubs within the Israeli population (and in its mass media), a tendency that usually dictates the use of Western signifiers as models—how can the use of an element from Indian popular culture be interpreted? In the analysis that follows, I will reveal a process of layered alienation whereby a Hindi song turns the "home" (that is, Israel) unhomely in order to articulate a new cultural image.[2]

I examine Hindi song as a pivotal element in a strategy within which Israeli culture eschews its own symbols and deprives itself of the ability to fill its representations with its own cultural resources. The proposed reading of the Bezeq commercials draws a portrait of a conflicted national culture that appropriates the other—a Hindi song—positions it within itself, and assigns it (and the whole of Bollywood culture at large) the role of an undecipherable pseudocomic signifier. In the analysis that follows, I modify Fiske's understanding of "encoding" to apprehend the obscure and incomprehensible use of a Hindi song in Israeli state commercials. I term this practice "the uncodable" because Hindi song in this instance serves to articulate the inaccessibility of Israeli culture toward itself. The Hindi song becomes a crucial element in a strategy through which Israeli culture unconsciously articulates the failure of the homogenizing and harmonizing processes that these commercials attempt to promote, as well as the articulation of the inaccessibility—the uncodability—of Israeli society to itself.

The Commercials: Cast, Set, and Aspirations

Bezeq Corporation employed the Fogel-Levin advertising agency to create a commercial campaign that would help (re)present it as a company that bridges the gaps and polarities within Israeli society, creating homogeneity and harmony according to the dominant code calling for national and cultural unity.[3] The commercials produce harmony structurally by presenting two figures that represent political and/or cultural polarities within Israeli society. These pairs are then shown as singing or dancing to the sounds of "Mera naam Chin-Chin-Chu":

Mera naam [hai] Chin-Chin-Chu	My name is Chin-Chin-Chu
Chin-Chin-Chu, baba,	Chin-Chin-Chu, Mister,
Chin-Chin-Chu,	Chin-Chin-Chu
Raat, Chandni, main aur tu,	Night, moonlight, you and me
Hello, Mister: How do you do?	Hello, Mister: How do you do?

The commercials ended with the slogan: "Talking on the one hand, listening on the other," which was immediately replaced with the National Telecommunications Corporation's logo.

The Cast/Personae

Richard Dyer's concept of *polysemy* and Robert Deming's understanding of *television archives* help us comprehend the choice of public figures or celebrities in these commercials. Dyer and Deming underscore the contexts in which audiences make meanings and the ways in which known figures become imprinted in public consciousness.[4] Polysemy is the multiple but finite meanings and effects that a star image signifies, and television archives are our memories of past programs and surrounding discourses.[5] Thus, the image of John Wayne can be charged with his bigness, his association with the West, his support for right-wing politics, his masculine style, and other signifiers.[6] In an analogous manner, the Bezeq commercials used the partisan affiliations of several of the figures and their cultural connotations—tapping into viewer's archives—in order to represent the conflicted Israeli scene.

In one commercial, Yossi Sarid, at that time a Labor Party politician, appeared with Rubi Rivlin, a politician associated with the right flank of the central/right-wing party Likud. In a second commercial, Shaul Yahalom, a member of a religious-nationalist right-wing party, the Mafdal, appeared with Uzi Baram, a member of the left-leaning secular Labor Party. A third commercial featured another left-wing politician, Yael Dayan, along with a right-wing activist, Meir Uziel. Other commercials presented aspects that do not relate directly to the map of

Israeli political parties. These commercials starred Emanuel Halperin, a journalist and television persona representing highbrow culture and European manners, and Eli Hanna, the winner of numerous body-building contests in Israel and abroad. While Halperin personifies the culturally problematic representation of a fragile feminine physicality and Western intellectualism, Hanna's sturdy and robust physique comes to stand in for a corporeal masculinity identified as Eastern. Another commercial features Eli Luzon, a singer of popular Eastern music, and Yvgeny Shapovalov, an opera singer. While Luzon represents lowbrow culture, Shapovalov is representative of highbrow culture typically associated with the West. In other instances, these commercials brought together political and cultural figures. For instance, Shulamit Aloni, at that time the leader of the left-wing party Meretz and known for her radical positions, was paired with the corporeal masculinity of Eli Hanna. As mentioned earlier, the commercials imagine these characters as singing and dancing in an idyllic harmony that seemed to echo and amplify the utopian elements of Hindi song and dance sequences. As in song and dance sequences, the imagined harmonic existence generated a spiritual elevation that does away with all divides, polarities, and failures that are known all too familiar in reality—a conflictual reality that is well known to the viewers and is torn by questions of identity and cultural orientation (between West and East) and a political arena that is above all divided by the Palestinian question. This reality, which serves as the basis of these commercials, is both known and yet denied because of both the mutual childish play and the set design.

The Set

The set is identical in all the commercials: an empty and closed studio with a blue background on which is painted a rainbow. The use of an identical set in the commercials for all the characters' activities generates homogeneity and a semblance of unity across the political and cultural maps. This harmony is also conveyed through the mise-en-scène that treats all the characters similarly if not identically, using two shots that contain the pair within one space, thus containing the contradictions and conflicts within the culture. The identical treatment of the pairs representing a whole spectrum of political and cultural stances produces the aspiration to an accumulated containment of the contradictions and conflicts they embody: conflict upon conflict, all contained within an imaginary space, all identical, as if losing their edge and dissolving into an imaginary unified existence.

However, this semblance of unity and harmony seems to dissolve upon a closer look at the designed space. The commercials, which deal with a very Israeli, local, and topical issue, were shot against an artificial backdrop that shies away from any concrete aspect of the place or its culture. The blatant artificiality of the set produces a statement regarding the identity of the place that is referred to in the commercials while lacking reference to its physicality. Not only is Israel devoid of itself, it is also disconnected from anything that might establish its physicality, that is, its reality. The set's artificiality and removal from actuality emphasize the stifling artificiality of the situation itself and of the effort to mask Israel's own contradictions and conflicts.

From another perspective, the set resonates with the biblical context of the promise for peace and prosperity after the mythical deluge.

> And it shall come to pass, when I bring a cloud over the earth, that the bow shall be seen in the cloud: And I will remember my covenant, which is between me and you and every living creature of all flesh; and the waters shall no more become a flood to destroy all flesh. And the bow shall be in the cloud; and I will look upon it, that I may remember the everlasting covenant between God and every living creature of all flesh that is upon the earth.[7]

The biblical reference, which is well known to the Jewish majority in Israel—the target audience of these commercials—was displaced, reproduced, and set in the local present. It acts as an admission to the cultural turbulence of Israeli culture, its conflicts and gaps, which are externalized in these commercials. The ruptures within Israeli society are compared, to a certain extent, with the mythical deluge, and the telecommunications corporation presents itself as the unifier. At the same time, the set also serves to evade the ominous content: the artificial, non-naturalistic painting of a rainbow creates a childish and seemingly happy background; the props, one for each commercial, create a humorous context—Sarid and Rivlin sitting on a swing, as if they were children; and a heavyweight whom the fragile Halperin lifts effortlessly.

What is it that allows the simultaneous existence of these contradictions and gaps, of the acknowledgment of the failure on the one hand

and the semblance of harmony on the other? The explanation might be found in the aesthetics of the song and dance sequences.

The Aesthetics of Song and Dance Sequences

As already mentioned, the celebrities in Bezeq's commercials dance and play together, some even move their lips to the lyrics of the song as if they were dubbing it. All these elements—dance, coordinated choreography, lip movement to the lyrics of the song, and the musical sound track that dictates and generates the situation—are all well-known aesthetic aspects of Hindi song and dance sequences.[8] I argue that the commercials use them to make a statement regarding the reality they are based upon and the reality they strive to create. The layered structure of the Hindi song and dance sequence makes possible multiple meanings. While the narrative structure of the movie often addresses the noncinematic reality of caste, class, and gender-based conflicts, the song and dance sequences celebrate an idyll or utopia, breaking away from these realities. Aesthetically, the move from the conflictual layer to the harmonic/utopian one occurs as the move from speech (which dominates the narrative sphere) to song and music. The song defines the space as emotive—amplifying and celebrating the harmony and utopia that is being experienced at that moment. In the words of Sanjeev Prakash, the musical moment is perceived as a sublime moment, and this moment is identical to the raison d'être of the movie—that is, the most powerful and effective moments of the cinematic experience.[9] Das Gupta assigns to the music the role of creating a harmony of wholeness, which is in contrast to the fragmentation of the narrative.[10] Furthermore, he assigns it an orgasmatic-erotic function.[11] This function can be related directly to the erotic content that is depicted in many Hindi song and dance sequences, but it can also be treated metaphorically as a climax or denouement. The Bezeq commercials draw upon the ability inherent in the song and dance sequences to create alternative spaces, with the option of appeasement that cannot exist anywhere else. Within this space, there is room for an expression of the conflictual aspects within culture, as well as for resignification.[12]

In the Bezeq commercials, the narrative layer seems to be missing, but it actually exists in the clear identity of the participants, their anchoring within Israeli reality, and the use that is made of their characters and their identification with a political party, a political context, or a cultural/ political context. This relation between the narrative and musical layers was clarified unequivocally by the pairings, which represented polarities that directly refer to the Israeli national ethos and its failures.

Israel: Ethos versus Conflictual Reality

As with other countries, the Israeli ethos wishes to establish and maintain a homogenous and stable unified national subject, but its failure resonates profoundly through major conflicts. Schematically, one is able to explain these conflicts along two lines. The first is related to the question of cultural identity and cultural orientation, which is split between Western and Eastern orientations. This division is rooted in the structure of Israeli society: it is a society of immigrants, heterogeneous in its nature with a structural cultural diversity. This diversity can be explained as the structural and genealogical tension between populations that immigrated from "Western" countries (mainly from eastern Europe) and from the "East" (Arab countries and Islamic countries, Northwest Africa in particular). Interestingly, the communities of Indian immigrants have not been associated with the struggle over the cultural orientation in Israel, perhaps due to the fact that they have not acquired political and public power.[13] This polarity in geographical origins generates the struggle over the character of the culture itself, reproducing Orientalist and Occidentalist dynamics and colonialist and postcolonialist structures in group relations.[14] It also recapitulates Israel's relations with other countries in the Middle East and most significantly between Jewish and Palestinian populations. The second conflict within Israeli society concerns the different cultural factions' response to the domination of the Palestinian people and possibilities for conflict resolution, which includes territorial concessions. According to the religious/national/right-wing position, Israel is a sacred territory and concessions of parts of it would be considered a breach of the covenant with God ("In the same day the Lord made a covenant with Abram, saying, Unto thy seed have I given this land, from the river of Egypt unto the great river, the river Euphrates").[15] The secular left adopts a humanist position where territorial concessions are a political necessity and required to redress human rights violations stemming from the occupation.

In popular Israeli consciousness, cultural orientation and political party association are linked. In the first decades since Israel declared independence in 1948, the hegemony was identified with the Labor Party (and its previous forms as "Ma'arach" and "Mapai"), a secular centre/left-wing party that was identified with Ashkenazi bourgeoisie and a pro-Western tendency, which reproduced Orientalist positions vis-à-vis Eastern populations. The Likud party, a centre/right-wing party focusing on nationalistic and traditionalist issues and identified with Eastern populations and the working class came into power in 1977, shook the formal map of power relations and brought an Occidental leaning within the dominant discourse. Since 1977, political power has been traded between the two parties and their positions alternately gain center stage in the public discourse and in the mass media.[16] These two parties disagree on internal cultural issues as well as in their attitude toward the conflictual aspect that is turned "outward." These disagreements occur in the context of cultural and physical border instability, within a society that is both postcolonial (independence after "two thousand years in exile") and a colonizer (the occupation of the Palestinian population).

The National Telecommunications Corporation commercials were, therefore, addressing directly issues of cultural identity. They were deeply rooted within the discourse of the nation, relating to central conflictual aspects that give rise to ruptures internally and externally. In this context, the National Telecommunications Corporation emerges as the entity that promotes and strengthens a unified ethos. Because the company sells products that facilitate speech, dialogue, comment, and reaction, the commercials claimed it fosters national harmony, unifying oppositions and bridging differences. But it was not speech or dialogue that was heard in these commercials but rather fragments of a partly intelligible song. Paradoxically, the deployment of the Hindi song highlights the displacement of Israeli culture from itself as well as the imaginary harmony constituted by the infiltration of a foreign element.

Pourquoi Bollywood

The notion of home is central to Israeli national culture—it is the historical narrative of moving from "home" to "diaspora" and back "home," a two thousand-year exile that began with the "Destruction of the Temple" ("The Home of Worship" or "The Home" for short are

Hebrew names for the Jewish Temple) and created a mythic narrative that longs for the return "home." One would expect a state commercial to accentuate the local and make an explicit identification between the local and the national. The insertion of a Hindi song in state commercials is thus a surprise. The commercials address a specific national and local issue, yet at its center exists a foreign element.

What does local consciousness have to gain from the use of a foreign element? In "The Local and the Global," Stuart Hall addresses the structure of feeling that is replicated in the Israeli commercials. Hall analyzes the modes through which a national consciousness comes to see itself as natural, stable, and homogenous.[17] A national consciousness presents itself as distinct by using symbols from other cultures. National discourses manage its borders by creating a system of self and other and by defending themselves from the threat of unstable and fluid boundaries.[18] In what seems to be a paradox, other nationalities can be an integral part of the national discourse. Thus, it might be no surprise to discover elements from a foreign culture within national promotional commercials.[19] Is this the strategy that underlies the use of a Bollywood song and dance sequence in Israeli commercials? Is "Mera naam Chin-Chin-Chu" part of the strategic system of negation, which, let us say, highlights an imagined attribute as a negation of all that is Israeli? Or, does the sequence use the foreign to point out the firmness or stability of the Israeli self? A close examination of the Bezeq commercials reveals a surprising picture: these commercials do not offer a system of negation. On the contrary, they locate the foreign in the core of the self. In addition, they use the aesthetics of Hindi cinema to promote an interpretation of the seeping of the foreign into the national as harmonious and idyllic. This actually contradicts the nationalist claim for an essentialist definition of the nation. What the Bezeq commercials elucidate is that Israeli national identity is in need of a foreign element (while camouflaged by the protective aspect of the musical aesthetics). Furthermore, the foreign element is crucial for the sake of creating a semblance of national harmony and national homogeneity.

The use of a Bollywood song sequence in the Bezeq commercials might be considered unexpected for other reasons as well. Since the 1970s, there has been no commercial distribution of films from the Bombay/Mumbai industry, and the distribution of a coproduction such as Nair's *Salaam Bombay* was a rare event. This has changed marginally since the late 1990s, with two experiments in the commercial distribution of Hindi films, a cable pay-channel showing two Bollywood movies every week and other cable/satellite channels airing movies periodically. I discuss this change, as it is relevant to understanding how Hindi song came to occupy cultural space in Israel.

In 1992, Israel and India established full diplomatic relations. Since then, India has become a popular destination for thousands of young Israelis who have completed their military service. These Indian sojourns have come to signify a ritual journey in Israeli culture. On these travels, most youth embark in homogeneous groups to fixed destinations, creating outposts or enclaves of Israelis in India. They keep to themselves, and the foreign territory often serves as a mere backdrop to their activities. Anthropologists and cultural studies scholars have interpreted this young Israeli trajectory as an attempt to escape the tensions of military service and as a peculiar rite of passage into Israeli society.[20] Notwithstanding the phenomenological nature of these trips to India, it is worth noting that many Israeli youth are exposed to Hindi movies on these journeys.

This motivated Israeli distributors of Indian films to bring Hindi movies to commercial theaters, targeting the thousands of youth travelers and the fifty thousand-odd immigrants of Indian origin. The distributors assumed that the tens of thousands of travelers returning from India each year would flock to movie theaters. However, this did not happen and the distributors faced major financial losses. These losses repeated themselves in numerous cases: the commercial distribution of *Dil To Pagal Hai* (The heart is crazy, Yash Chopra, 1997; a single copy was screened in 1998 in Tel Aviv, Israel's cultural center) and Sanjay Leela Bhansali's version of *Devdas* (2003; six copies were screened in major cities) failed, and one-time screenings of these and other movies (*Virasat,* Heritage, Priyadarshan, 1997; *Khamoshi—The Musical,* Silence, Sanjay Leela Bhansali, 1996) in cinematheques during 1998 failed as well. Thus, Indian cinema, particularly Hindi movies, was not part of the Israeli cultural sphere. However, Hindi films circulated in a different circuit. Small distributors who did not own theaters continued to supply an older audience from Maharashtra with a series of box-office hits, including some Raj Kapoor films from the 1950s and 1960s and a few Amitabh Bachchan hits from the 1970s. The monopolization of foreign film distribution, however, drove these distributors out of business. Consequently, since the 1970s, bootleg cassettes of Hindi movies were regularly distributed through informal channels in the small community of immigrants from Maharashtra and in Arab centers.

Airing of Hindi films on television is a bit different, as commercial television channels have a stronger financial backing and are not dependant on revenues from individual films. Also, as opposed to film theaters that have to draw audiences, cable channels are available in peripheral areas where most of the immigrants of Indian origin live, and the cost is cheaper (including pay-channels) than the cost of a trip to a commercial movie theater and the purchase of tickets. As mentioned earlier, at the moment when the Bezeq commercials were produced, Bollywood movies were not aired on commercial channels. Although Bollywood was excluded from Israeli public sphere and its existence was denied and concealed, apart from the Bezeq commercials, Thelma Noodles also aired advertisements based on the theme song from *Dil To Pagal Hai*.[21]

My claim that this industry was excluded from the dominant cultural sphere is supplemented by the image that was associated with this industry in pro-Western, Orientalist Israeli consciousness: an inferior work not worth distribution. Israeli film critics, Shohat notes, tended to view films produced in Third World cultures through the distorted lens of ethnocentric prejudices, guided by an internalized Western ego ideal.[22] Operating from a neocolonialist position,[23] popular films from large Eastern film industries, such as Iran and India, were rejected and continue to be ill-received.[24] Apart from these structural obstacles to Indian popular culture, the pro-Western cultural orientation dominant in the field of advertising also makes Bezeq's choice intriguing. Cultural studies scholars in Israel report the dominance of a pro-Western identification in advertisement, which manifests itself in the widespread use of "American" signifiers.

An analysis of commercials aired in the past decade in the mass media reveals the wide-spread use of American signifiers for the sake of marketing a range of commodities. Israeli American products that originate in Israel, the US or in European countries, market themselves via referencing America one way or another; by quoting its values, symbols, landscape or lifestyles. America has therefore turned into the epitome of the marketing message for various products. . . .[25]

And while national unity is not a commodity, America is situated in mass culture and in the advertising industry as a model. Thus, why did the Israeli advertiser choose to use a culture that is such a far cry from what is considered a model in the advertising field?[26]

An analysis of the specific song with its aesthetic elements raises a few questions as well. In Israel, "Mera naam Chin-Chin-Chu" was not known to anyone who had not seen *Salaam Bombay*. The song could be perceived by Israeli audiences as strange and bizarre because it was not part of the popular music collection. More significantly, it is sung in a foreign language. Apart from its last sentence—"Hello, Mister: How do you do?"—the commercials use the Hindi song without subtitles.[27] The song carries the imprint of an excluded cultural/cinematic expression and cannot be deciphered. It also uses musical conventions unfamiliar to Israeli audiences. As with many other Hindi songs, "Mera naam Chin-Chin-Chu" follows the characteristics and musical schemes of Western pop music and is influenced by it. This might make it accessible to a Western or pro-Western audience such as the Israeli audience, and yet the singing voice is a very high-pitched feminine one, which to an untrained ear might seem a mockery, artificial, and affected, a kind of falsetto.

How did a musical sound track that is totally foreign and bizarre become an establishing element in commercials that present themselves as mending ruptures and failures within Israeli society? I have argued that the foreignness itself, as well as its unfamiliar cultural context, the inaccessible language that does not get explicated by subtitles, and the vocal conventions that might appear artificial and affected have a crucial role here. They serve to make the song a signifier of otherness and to create another layer of encoding. This is a radical encoding that makes all the set elements inaccessible. This creates a message not about Bollywood itself, but about the inaccessibility of the culture that channeled it into its television commercials.

The Uncodable

Cultural studies scholars stress the importance of media culture and its crucial role in the formation of national and cultural identities. Among the wide range of mass communication, the medium of television has become one of the most powerful: it is a hegemonic state apparatus. Understanding the narrative and visual codes of media is therefore crucial to those who wish to understand how the medium of television became a political arena that conveys and strengthens dominant ideologies.

Moreover, using a deconstructivist reading that relies on the fissures of the representational act can reveal how this medium is also the arena where failures of this ideology are externalized and at the same time become, to use Hall's words, "an arena of consent and resistance."[28]

In his article "Some Television, Some Topics, Some Terminology," John Fiske elaborates on the claim that all elements of mass communication and mass culture in capitalist societies are recruited to serve and reinforce the values and interests of the dominant ideology. Fiske presents a wide variety of encoding layers that are implemented by television. Each and every element in the fabric of mass media is encoded and thus serves as a vehicle of ideology. The first encoding layer uses social codes that are associated with reality: appearance, dress, makeup, environment, behavior, speech, gesture, expression, sound, and more. These go through electronic encoding using technical codes of representation: camera, lighting, editing, music, and sound, which carry the conventional representational codes and form the basis for the apparatus of representations—narrative, conflict, character, action, dialogue, setting, casting, and more. This forms the third layer, ideology, which is organized into coherence and social acceptability by the ideological codes. Fiske therefore divides the television apparatus into very detailed encoding layers.[29] He paves the way to understand the encoding systems as those that create a world that is ideologically bound and thus calls for a deconstructive reading that has the power of extracting television from its oppressive subjugation to the chains of ideology. I wish to build upon Fiske's notion to propose another layer—the uncodable—to understand the way Hindi music functions in Israeli consciousness. But before that, I wish to focus on the interpretation of the encoded world.

Roughly speaking, an encoded world is one that is symbolically organized and appears understandable. It is a fictitious world to make the cultural reality intelligible, a world whose creators wish to make of it, as Fiske puts it, "an appropriate cultural text for its audience"—a text that is ideologically accepted by the masses; a text that helps create an imaginary order, as stable a representation as possible of its culture and values.[30] American television tends to signify its heroes by using signifiers identified with the White Anglo-Saxon Protestant (WASP), while the bad guys are signified by subtle and not so subtle cues as non-American.[31] Thus, it helps to define the boundaries of a culture and the values of those who belong to it. It offers a symbolically ordered world, where organized representations of the self and the other are formed on the basis of values that the self ascribes to itself and those it rejects by virtue of assigning them otherness. The world delineated in this framework might be distorted, but it bestows a sense of order that the world is comprehensible or, to be precise, that the world seems comprehensible.

In apparent contrast to the forms of expression and the various signifiers that Fiske presents in order to show how the medium might construct an encoded, ordered, and comprehensible world, "the uncodable" refers to a signifier that seemingly remains obstructed and unattainable. It is a signifier that apparently does not allow any reading or evaluation. It is a locked door, with no key in sight, and no access path.

Using Dyer's concept of polysemy, we may take into account the multiple meanings and effects that Hindi music might signify in Israeli consciousness: its linguistic foreignness, its musical/vocal and cultural otherness, and its relation to an unfamiliar context that seemingly expropriates it from any kind of context. All those might assign the Hindi song and Bollywood music in general the role of the uncodable in Israeli consciousness. Though it is impossible to claim that the Bollywood song sequence, or any other signifier for that matter, is obstructed, one could argue that it is encoded as the uncodable—to create an interpretive framework in which it serves as obstructed and as the representation of that which cannot be deciphered. In Israeli popular consciousness, therefore, the Hindi song serves as the uncodable: foreign and bizarre; it allows the Israeli consciousness to use it symbolically as that which represents the idea of incomprehensibility in general. The Israeli identification of the Hindi song with the uncodable was reinforced by another commercial that was produced in 2000, which used a segment of the theme song from *Dil To Pagal Hai*. In this instance, the advertisement was for Asian-style noodles and not for a national corporation. Although the Thelma Noodles advertisement was not intended to foster national values, it can shed light on Israeli modes of encoding Hindi song.

The commercial depicted a box of noodles being consumed by different people in diverse backgrounds. While the music was extracted from the film's sound track, the vocals did not belong to the original singer, Lata Mangeshkar, nor were the lyrics original. Instead, the Thelma Noodles advertisement converted the Hindi words of the song into gibberish. Though Hindi is a language not understood, by using gibberish, the commercial's creators emptied the song of all meaning, ascribing incomprehensibility not just to the language of the song but to its essence. The noodles commercial summarized what is ascribed to

Bollywood in Israel: it is a signifier of fundamental incomprehensibility, a paradoxical code of "The Uncodable."

Apparently, all that is associated with Bollywood in Israel would serve to explain its irrelevance as a signifier, not its turn toward becoming an intense and present signifier located in the heart of the discourse over Israeli identity. What allowed the advertiser to make use of it in this context? Any attempt at an answer brings up a dual ambivalence—toward Bollywood and toward Israel itself. On the one hand, it is a cinematic tradition that is excluded and repressed; on the other, it is a possible signifier of a trendy travel destination and a youth culture that paradoxically serves as one of the steps toward Israeliness. From another angle, Bollywood functions as a metonymy for Indian culture and can thus symbolize Easternness.

As mentioned above, Easternness is one of the options of choice for an Israeli identity. However, Indian Easternness is not really part of the struggle over the cultural character of Israel. Thus, the Easternness signified by symbols from Indian culture does not threaten but remain in the realm of fantasy. Perhaps it is the fantasy of the colonizer who does not wish to deal with the colonized; or perhaps the fantasy of young Israelis to flee from harsh reality; or perhaps the fantasy and desire for an existence devoid of reality, separated from materiality, resembling the set where the Bezeq commercials take place.

It is thus that the Bollywood song penetrates the Bezeq commercials that convey the fractures and ruptures within Israeli society, functioning as a mediator between Israel and itself. The Bollywood song, the signifier of that which is incomprehensible and uncodable, is the dominant voice on the set. To its sounds well-known personae dance, and lips synch to its lyrics. The Bollywood song is therefore what establishes and defines the acts on the set and the national Israeli self in general. The Bollywood song is what infuses it with meaning, dictating and outlining it via the image that it received in the culture that appropriated it. The uncodable colors the set as a whole with its signifiers, eventually trespassing borders with its fundamental incomprehensibility. It is Israeli society itself that is signified by it, and its appropriation marks the failure to that which the commercials attempted to portray and promote: dialogue and idyllic harmony.

The Bollywood song, as the dominant element on the set, speaks of the profound incomprehensibility of Israeli society toward itself, its inaccessibility to itself, and its inability to bridge the gaps within it. The lyrics, which cannot be understood, speak of a mute conversation, forever sterile, that is going on between Israeli populations, which brings Israel again and again to cultural and political situations that it cannot solve both internally and externally. The artificiality that is attributed to the feminine vocals, a falsetto of sorts, speaks of the artificiality of the situation in which oppositions act out a semblance of amused and reciprocal harmony. The apparent jest of the characters that entertain each other is seemingly dictated by the foreign and bizarre song; yet it is a foil that seeks to diffuse the threat in admitting that the notion of a unified ethos has failed.

The use of a Bollywood song creates an act of displacement in regard to Israeli culture. The Bollywood song, not an Israeli song, or a patriotic one, controls the apparatus that disconnects culture from itself, ascribing dominance to the other, the foreign and the bizarre, and through it shapes culture in terms of otherness. The foreign has become dominant internally, at home, and this—typical of cultures in a post-colonial situation—creates another layer in a hybrid Israeli subject. A hybrid, due to its nature, due to the fact that the national self is in a constant process of formation, and due to the fact that the processual, in the words of Bhabha, namely, the dynamic and fluctuating course of private histories, forever overpowers the pedagogical (the narrative that seeks to stabilize people as entities of historic origin). An essential ambiguity becomes therefore the basis for the national space, the space that is forever split, and this split inevitably dictates the way nations are formed. In Bhabha's words, "the conceptual ambivalence of modern society becomes the site of writing the nation."[32]

It is through the mediation of the Bollywood song that the Israeli place is created, on a set devoid of concreteness; this space embodies what Bhabha calls "the Third Space"—a forever-ambivalent liminal space that

> makes the structure of meaning and reference an ambivalent process, destroys this mirror of representation in which cultural knowledge is customarily revealed as integrated, open, expanding code. Such an intervention quite properly challenges our sense of the historical identity of culture as homogenizing, unifying force, authenticated by originary Past, kept alive in the national tradition of the People.[33]

It is the same space that Bhabha named "the unhomely," where the border between the home and the world is undermined, where the anxiety caused by the liminal works to cover up what national consciousness regards as a threat thus finds fictitious comfort for itself through the

Hindi song. It is as if the use of this signifier cancels out what is derived from the Israeli situation specifically and the dynamics of histories in general, as if the impossibility of encoding annuls the control it exerts upon its space, and as if the national home is not expropriated from itself.

> [But] [t]he home does not remain the domain for domestic life, nor does the world simply become its social or historical counterpart. The unhomely is the shock of recognition of the world-in-the-home, the-home-in-the-world.[34]

The commercials of the Israeli National Telecommunications Corporation, "Mera naam Chin-Chin-Chu," the personae that dance and frolic to its sounds—all these articulate and reiterate the Israeli sense of unhomeliness and the extraterritorial and cross-cultural experience through the Hindi song that has become both its signifier and its producer.

Notes

1 It is important to note that Nair's film is not a Bollywood movie and was not created according to the narrative and aesthetic codes of Bollywood cinema.
2 See Walter Armbrust's essay in this volume, which explores Indian cinema's mediation of Egyptian national identity.
3 For a condensed summary of the relations between dominant ideology and cultural homogeneity, see Richard Dyer, *Stars* (London: BFI Publishing, 1998), 2–3.
4 Robert H. Deming, "*Kate and Allie*: The 'New Woman' and the Audience's Television Archives," in *Private Screenings: Television and the Female Consumer,* ed. Lynn Spigel and Denise Mann (Minneapolis: University of Minnesota Press, 1992), 206–7.
5 Ibid., 207.
6 Dyer, *Stars,* 63–4.
7 Genesis 9:14–16.
8 It is also true for the Hollywood musical. However, the rise of the playback singer points to the huge difference between the two industries. For a detailed discussion of these elements see "Introduction," this volume.
9 Sanjeev Prakash, "Music, Dance and the Popular Films: Indian Fantasies, Indian Repressions," in *Indian Cinema Superbazaar,* ed. Aruna Vasudev and Philip Langlet (New Delhi: Vikas Publishing House, 1983), 115.
10 Chidananda Das Gupta, *The Painted Face: Studies in India's Popular Cinema* (New Delhi: Roli Books, 1991).

11 Ibid., 67.

12 See Sangita Shresthova's essay in this volume on how the song picturization is resignified as it migrates from screen to stage.

13 The terms "West" and "East" are put in quotes since this is not necessarily a geographical distinction. For more on the Israeli use of these categories, see Ella Shohat, *Israeli Cinema: East/West and the Politics of Representation* [in Hebrew] (Tel Aviv: Breirot Press, 1991).

14 The use of the terms "Orientalist" and "Occidentalist" derives from Saidian terminology. As established in Shohat's works, the Ashkenazi society in Israel tended to exert an Orientalist dynamic upon the populations from Arab/Islamic countries and their cultural heritage. The use of the term "Occidentalism" in this context relates to an essentialist and binary reading of the Occident by populations from the East or from Third World countries (Carrier names this ethno-Occidentalism). See Rhoda E. Howard, "Occidentalism, Human Rights and Obligations of Western Scholars," *Canadian Journal of African Studies* 29, no. 1 (1995): 111; and James G. Carrier, "Occidentalism: The World Turned Upside-Down," *American Ethnologist* 19, no. 2 (1992): 198.

15 Genesis 15:18.

16 The Likud was in power for seven years. In 1984, due to an electoral tie, a national unity government was created and it lasted two years. During 1986–1988, another national unity government was created, and during 1988–1990, the two parties joined together in a coalition. In 1990, the Likud came back to power for two years. The Labor governed during 1992–1996 and the Likud during 1996–1999. The Labor came back to power during 1999–2001, and since then, the Likud is in power.

17 Stuart Hall, "The Local and the Global: Globalisation and Ethnicity," in *Dangerous Liaisons: Gender, Nation, and Postcolonial Perspectives,* ed. Ann McClintock, Aamir Mufti, and Ella Shohat (Minneapolis and London: University of Minnesota Press, 1997), 174–5.

18 I intentionally refrain from dealing with the possibility to actualize such stability and refer only to the national discourse's wish, which is the foundation of the aforementioned commercials, while the deconstructive reading that is presented here assumes and externalizes its gaps and failures.

19 Note that popular culture in India relies heavily on the use of the other to enforce the Indian self. The commercials of the Indian company Siyaram's, a manufacturer of suitings and shirtings, aired circa India's fiftieth Independence Day (1997) strove to present the company as a promoter of national goals, similar to the Bezeq commercials. In Siyaram's case, the targeted goal was the war against the immigration of young, educated, and successful Indians to other countries. The commercials portrayed successful Indian professionals talking to an imaginary viewer, apparently a man just like them, who lives abroad, evoking yearnings for the local culture and calling him to return home, to India. The self is reinforced via the opposition, but also by evoking the other and making it present. This trend is very prominent in Bollywood cinema. See *Sangam* (The Confluence, Raj Kapoor, 1963); *Purab Aur Pachhim* (East and West, Manoj Kumar, 1970); *Dilwale Dulhania Le Jayenge* (The Braveheart will

take the Bride, Aditya Chopra, 1995); *Pardes* (American Dreams Indian Souls, Subhash Ghai, 1997); and many others. See also Homi K. Bhabha, "The Other Question: Difference, Discrimination, and the Discourse of Colonialism," in *Black British Cultural Studies: A Reader,* ed. Houston A. Baker Jr., Manthia Diawara, and Ruth H. Lindeborg (Chicago and London: University of Chicago Press, 1996), 87–106.

20 Darya Maoz, "My Heart Is in the East—the Journey of Israeli Young Adults to India" [in Hebrew] (master's thesis, The Hebrew University of Jerusalem, 1999). Maoz is currently working on her PhD dissertation devoted to this very subject.

21 Following the use of the song in the commercial and as the opening song for a documentary series about Israelis traveling through India came the commercial distribution of *Dil To Pagal Hai.* The film was a box-office failure and did not cover the costs of its Israeli distribution.

22 Shohat, *Israeli Cinema*, 20.

23 Ella Shohat and Robert Stam, *Unthinking Eurocentrism: Multiculturalism and the Media* (London and New York: Routledge, 1994), 17.

24 As mentioned, in recent years, some Bollywood movies received commercial distribution in Israeli theaters, but they have not been successful. Films like those of Deepa Mehta and Mira Nair that adhere to Western cinema aesthetics tend to fare better.

25 Anat First and A. Abraham, "My Heart Is in the West While I am at East's End: The American Image in Israeli Advertisement," in *Communication as Culture* [in Hebrew], vol. 1, ed. Miri Talmon and Tamar Liebes (Tel Aviv: Open University Press, 2001), 340.

26 From another angle, one can find the use of exotic imagery in Western advertising; so, perhaps, the Israeli advertiser was influenced by this impulse.

27 Although some Indian immigrants in Israel do understand Hindi, it is not the language of the majority. The community of Indian immigrants in Israel counts about fifty thousand and they are from the west and south of India.

28 Stuart Hall, "Notes on Deconstructing 'the Popular,' " in *People's History and Socialist Theory*, ed. R. Samuel (London: Routledge and Kagan Paul, 1981), 239.

29 John Fiske, "Some Television, Some Topics, Some Terminology," in *Communication as Culture* [in Hebrew], vol. 1, ed. Miri Talmon and Tamar Liebes (Tel Aviv: Open University Press, 2001), 77.

30 Ibid.

31 Ibid., 81.

32 Homi K. Bhabha, *The Location of Culture* (London and New York: Routledge, 1994).

33 Ibid., 37.

34 Homi K. Bhabha, "The World and the Home," in *Dangerous Liaisons: Gender, Nation, and Postcolonial Perspectives*, ed. Ann McClintock, Aamir Mufti, and Ella Shohat (Minneapolis and London: University of Minnesota Press, 1997), 445.

Part 3

Planetary Consciousness

9. Dancing to an Indian Beat

"Dola" Goes My Diasporic Heart

Sangita Shresthova

*The distance of 10,000 miles between Berkeley and
Bollywood was bridged in two and a half hours on the
evening of February 5th at the Palace of Fine Arts in
San Francisco by eight college teams from California.
These teams came together to participate in Bollywood
Berkeley: the Fourth Annual Intercollegiate Hindi Film
Dance Competition.*

—Hindustan Times, February 10, 2005

*This is not your run-of-the-mill boy-meets-girl story.
It's boy meets girl to the beat of half a dozen songs plus sixteen
dancing friends, multiplied by 1,000 cheering fans. The fourth
annual Hindi Film Dance Competition comes to San Francisco
this Saturday, riding a wave of global popularity for the
world's biggest film industry.*

—SF Gate, February 4, 2005

Organized by the Indus Council, the annual Berkeley Hindi Film
Dance Competition provides a powerful testimony to the growing popularity of Bollywood, dance and its emergence as a recognized category
emulated on stages and classes across the world. While film-inspired
dance classes like, those run by Shiamak Davar's Institute for Performing Arts (SDIPA), are an increasingly frequent occurrence in the urban
centers in India, the proliferation of Bollywood dance is most prominent outside India, where its study and performance is fast becoming
an expression of Indian identity and an emergent marginal chic.
Bollywood dance classes have sprung up in cities such as London,
Boston, Sydney, and New York in response to the enthusiasm expressed

by audiences to learn and perform movements they may have seen in films. In London, schools like Honey Kalaria's Dance Academy specialize in the "tantalizing fusion of Indian classical, filmi, Punjabi, salsa, Arabic, hip-hop, street, jazz, and many other styles of dance, performed to the latest funky Bollywood tracks."[1] In New York, Pooja Narang's Bollywood Axion classes claim to impart the "timing, rhythm, energy ... and movement that are the ingredients to becoming a bollywood dancer."[2]

The growing enthusiasm for Bollywood dance is perhaps most evident on U.S. college campuses, where staged versions of Hindi (and, to a lesser extent, other Indian) film dances dominate South Asian and Indian cultural shows. While the time investment and professional execution of these cultural shows, showcasing South Asian (often interpreted as Indian) performance traditions, vary, they are invariably extremely popular events, often sold out weeks in advance. Student teams representing specific years (sophomore or seniors), regional origin (Gujarati or Tamil), or a specific performance tradition (classical or recent Bollywood) form groups to choreograph, learn, and perform specific dances. Even as organizers usually make an active effort to include Indian classical dance forms like Bharat Natyam, based on my own observations I would argue that Bollywood dances account for a majority of the acts performed.

Today, Bollywood dance has become a term used by film professionals, amateur performers, and audiences to reference dances choreographed to Hindi, and to a lesser extent other regional Indian, language film songs. What constitutes Bollywood dance, however, remains debated in both movement and text. In classes, Bollywood dance movement varies in quality and style from song to song, from instructor to instructor, and choreographer to choreographer.[3] On cultural show stages, choreographies may be based on, but do not limit themselves to, movements and spatial arrangements contained in films. Costume choices often reference "traditional" or "contemporary" Indian trends through bangles, headscarves, jewelry, embroidered Rajasthani blouses, and miniskirts. Facial expressions, gestures interpreting song lyrics, "*jhatkas* and *matkas*" (percussive "emphasi[ze] ... pelvic movement"), wrist whirls, and turns, all set to film music, could be identified as essential ingredients of Bollywood dance.[4] Yet, all these descriptions only skim the surface of what constitutes Indian film dance.[5] First, it is necessary to establish an analytical distinction between *Bollywood dance* as a description of choreography and movement inspired by Hindi films taught in dance classes and performed on stages and *Hindi film dance* as a reference to song and dance sequences contained in the films themselves. This distinction between dances in films and their reinterpretation in classes and performances is a crucial first step in moving toward a more nuanced understanding of Bollywood dance in the context of what Vijay Mishra identifies as the relationship between Hindi films and nostalgia among geographically dislocated Indians.[6] Therefore an investigation of what Bollywood dance is must begin with a comparative analysis between dances as they exist in films and the interpretive processes surrounding their "reincarnation" into performed compositions.

The ubiquitous presence and continued popularity of film dances raises many questions about why these dances emerged as key ingredients of Hindi commercial films, how these dances are received and reinterpreted by audiences outside India, and, finally, how the dances' choreographic and cinematic content facilitate these interpretations. In fact, it is the cyclical migration of film dance from staged performance to film and back to the stage—from a medium influenced by existing performance traditions to a medium that influences performed expressions of "Indianness"—that raises questions about the relationship between the film dances as song visualizations and their reception by audiences and reinterpretation in performed venues.

Through a case study of one dance sequence, I will begin to unravel the migration patterns of Bollywood form and content. I focus on the "Dola re dola" (The sway [of the heart]) song dance sequence featured in Sanjay Leela Bhansali's commercially successful remake of the film *Devdas* (2002) and examine the way the dance was restaged at a South Asian cultural event at the Massachusetts Institute of Technology (MIT) in April 2003. Through an analysis of the dance at these two sites and the transformations that occur, I seek to identify the multiple meanings associated with Hindi film dance. Foregrounding choreography both in film and on stage as "a tradition of codes and conventions through which meaning is constructed in dance,"[7] I approach Bollywood dances in performance among Indian diasporic populations as interpretive sites of Hindi film reception to argue that part of the search for understanding Bollywood dance and its enduring popularity lies within the imaginary spaces created by these performances and dance sequences in the films themselves.

Investigating Hindi Film Dance

In 2002, Saroj Khan received *Filmfare*'s "Best Choreography Award" for her choreography of "Dola re dola." Established in 1953, *Filmfare* Awards are recognized as one of the most prestigious honors in popular Hindi cinema and are decided by a poll of magazine readers. A testimony to the growing influence of choreographers in popular Hindi cinema, the "Best Choreography Award" was created in 1988; Saroj Khan took home the prize that year for her choreography of "Ek do teen" (one, two, three) in *Tezaab* (Acid, N. Chandra, 1988). While the scale of a film's budget, visibly achieved through star casting and publicity, may sway public opinion when it comes to voting, the fact remains that *Filmfare* Awards provide public recognition for original dance choreography in popular Hindi films and the award remains an acknowledged benchmark for achievement in the Hindi film industry.

Despite recent developments, song and dance sequences continue to be an important part of popular Hindi cinema. Dances appeared in Indian films soon after the introduction of film technology to India in 1896. The few silent films[8] that have survived of the approximately "1313 silent films produced in India" between 1912 and 1934" suggest that rhythmically choreographed sequences existed even in those early experiments.[9] It was, however, the introduction of sound to cinema heralded by *Alam Ara* (Light of the world, Ardeshir Irani, 1931) and the emergent importance of songs that introduced dance as an integral element of Hindi film narrative structure.

For spectators "used to a linear narrative style," dances in Hindi films may initially "look as if they have no connection to the substance of the film."[10] However even a cursory examination reveals varied, yet distinct, narrative conventions in how dances are deployed. Ravi Vasudevan identifies popular Hindi films as narrative systems that include attractions such as song and dance sequences and comedic subplots.[11] Lalitha Gopalan builds on this to argue that songs and dances need to be recognized as parts of an alternative narrative system: a system of interruptions.[12] Gopalan argues that "the most persistent narrative form found in Indian popular cinema includes several interruptions bearing a more or less systematic relationship to the narrative."[13] Gopalan expands on these narrative theories to propose specific kinds of interruption: the comedy, the interval, and, perhaps most importantly for this discussion, song and dance sequences. However, she stops short of analyzing how song and dance sequences interrupt the narrative and how this practice is rooted in indigenous performance traditions.

From their inception, film dances drew on a variety of Indian sources and performance traditions. In their discussion of the early influences of Indian popular cinema, Dissanayake and Gokulsing identify "two celebrated epics—the Ramayana and the Mahabharata," "Classical Indian Theater," "Folk Theater" (including the "*Yatra* of Bengal," "*Ram Lila* and *Krishna Leela* of Uttar Pradesh," and "*Tamasha* of Maharashtra"), and "Parsi theater of the nineteenth century."[14] The first Indian film *Raja Harischandra* (King Harischandra, Dadasaheb Phalke, 1913) was "based on the Ramayana and since then scores of filmmakers have mined this and the Mahabharata for plots and themes."[15] Dissanayake and Gokulsing postulate that a close analysis of Parsi theater with its "lilting songs, bawdy humour … sensationalism and dazzling stagecraft … designed to appeal to a broad mass of people" and Indian popular films would reveal "remarkable similarities" in terms of "themes, narratives, … and styles of presentation."[16] Other aspects of Indian theater adopted by popular films include extensive use of frontal address (soliloquy), recurring characters based on Hindu mythology, prominence of gesture and exaggeration of facial expression, and perhaps most significantly, the "idea of drama" as "inseparably linked with song, dance and music."[17]

At the same time, it is also important to recognize that just as Indian film dances drew on indigenous cultures, they borrowed and continued to adapt material from non-Indian movement vocabularies. For example, historian V. A. K. Ranga Rao observes the non-Indian influences on Uday Shankar's *Kalpana* (Imagination 1948) and states that the "Man-Machine sequence from Charlie Chaplin's *Modern Times* (1936) depicting the assembly line" and "Uday Shankar's Labour and Machinery number in *Kalpana*" are "too close for comfort."[18] Although foreign influences on Hindi cinema do not constitute the focus of this discussion, it is important to recognize that Hindi film dance continues to adapt content from non-Indian performance traditions.

The integration of Indian performance traditions into early films was supported by the documented migration of performers and other artists from performance traditions that had fallen into disrepute during British colonial rule.[19] The involvement of acclaimed dancers such as Gopi Krishna, Sitara Devi, Lacchu Maharaj, Roshan Kumari, and Madame Simkie, Uday Shankar's student, in the film industry further linked Hindi film dance to debates and processes surrounding the emergent distinction between "classical" and "folk" Indian performance in postcolonial India.[20]

Importantly, Indian performance traditions went through a period of significant reconstruction in pre- and postcolonial India. The selective adaptation of tradition by film dance is therefore significant. In her article "Dance in India," Rajika Puri situates the postcolonial focus on distinguishing between "folk" and "classical" traditions in the need "to create ... a sense of national identity" as a key motivation for the "oversimplified notion of common heritage." This agenda "looked for similarities in the tremendous diversity of beliefs and practices" in an attempt to present India as "an integral whole."[21]

Reconstruction efforts surrounding Sadir dance (Bharat Natyam) historically practiced by *Devadasis*, or temple dancers, in South India greatly influenced the further evolution of other Indian dances.[22] By forging a historically, scripturally substantiated connection between Bharat Natyam and spirituality, Rukmini Devi Arundale and several contemporaries in the early twentieth century sought to resignify Bharat Natyam as a "respectable," and therefore worthy of being a practice distinct from other more secular dance forms. The process of codification initiated by Bharat Natyam "set particular standards for incorporating Sanskrit and vernacular works of high literary value, traditional music associated with piety and devotion, introduction of a movement technique and *mudras* (hand gestures) and body positions codified in the Natyashastra."[23] Compliance with high standards prescribed in the traditional texts became a prerequisite for a dance form to be accepted and recognized as a 'classical' " and, therefore, refined art form.[24]

As members of the intelligentsia rallied to define "classical" dance in the Indian context, "folk" was being simultaneously defined. Government-sponsored folk dance troupes exposed Indians (and foreigners) to the "richness and range" of national performance traditions. Indian "folk traditions" were presented as diverse vernacular "testimonies" of communal and social solidarity. Shah explains:

> With the establishment of the National and State Academies, "culture" in India became formally "institutionalized" in the Euro-American sense of the term; unlike the traditional past, the interrelated major disciplines of artistic practice such as dance, drama and music became

recognized as separate categories; this division was also furthered by the sub-categories of the "classical," "folk," "tribal", etc.[25]

This process of institutionalization established "India's classical arts" as "a distillation of their highest and best cultured self" and the "folk arts … correspondingly … as imbued with 'vitality', 'variety' and 'indigenous color.' "[26] This separation of the "folk" from "classical" has a key influence on the development of Hindi film dance as identifiable dance movements; themes and costumes are adapted strategies for character development. Complementary to definitions of classical dance, folk dance forms became associated with specific costumes, group formations, gestures, and movements. Signifiers associated with both classical and folk performance traditions and non-Indian dance styles have been selectively adopted in Hindi film dances and allowed the choreography to deploy, yet simultaneously evade and even transgress these constructed classification systems.

For example, in the film *Guide* (Vijay Anand, 1965), the performances that establish the success of Rosie, the heroine (played by Waheeda Rehman), as a professional dancer reference several "classical" dance forms including Kathak, Bharat Natyam, and Manipuri. The director's choice to cut between several styles rather than focus on Rosie's mastery in a particular regionally specific dance form attempts to infuse the heroine with a pan-Indian identity, a feature that scholars have identified as a recurring feature in the immediate postindependence cinema. The almost-obsessive dances performed by Sridevi as Anju the heroine of the film *Chaalbaaz* (Cleverness, Pankaj Parashar, 1989), a woman violently abused by her relatives, draw heavily on Bharat Natyam gestures and movements to draw attention to her honorable character and tragic situation. Anju communicates her respectability through her classically inflected dance, whereas her twin sister communicates her emancipation through Madonna's music video-inspired choreography. Here, culturally coded movement choices are deployed as signifiers central to the films' narratives.

Dance also functions in some instances as shorthand for character development. In *Madhumati* (Bimal Roy, 1958), the simplicity and innocence of the heroine, Madhumati (played by the South Indian danseuse Vyjayanthimala), are underlined through her participation in a folk dance with the other villagers. Sumita Chakravarty points to *Junglee* (Wild one, Subodh Mukherji, 1960), starring and featuring dances by Shammi Kapoor, known for his freestyle rock and roll-like move-ments, as a film that "signaled the change from the deglamorized hero-ism of Raj Kapoor's Indianized Chaplin to the more cosmopolitan, rambunctious personality of the sixties hero."[27] In *Kabhi Khushi Kabhie Gham* ... (Sometimes happiness, sometimes sadness, Karan Johar, 2001), dance functions to reaffirm an immigrant Indian's adherence to traditional family values. A chorus line of dancers dressed in Bharat Natyam costumes execute *adavus* (abstract movement sequences) as they accompany Raj (Hrithik Roshan) upon his arrival in London. In this instance, the use of a classical dance form serves as a symbol of India's cultural heritage.

As evinced from these examples, dance in popular Hindi films ref-erences broader cultural contexts through culturally coded choreo-graphic choices. Hence, it becomes necessary to ask: *why* the dance happens, what motivates specific characters to dance, what does the dance achieve in the broader narrative context, and *how* the choreo-graphic content allows the dance to achieve these objectives.

"Dola Re Dola": Hindi Film Dance

Adapted from Sarat Chandra Chatterjee's novel, *Devdas* has been adapted to film at least five times. This tragic love story revolves around a love triangle involving Devdas, his childhood sweetheart Paro (or Parvati), and Chandramukhi, a courtesan with whom he develops a relationship. Though they love each other, Paro and Devdas are pre-vented from marrying by Devdas's family because Paro's mother traces her ancestry to a lineage of courtesans. Instead, Paro is married to a wealthy, widowed landowner and Devdas turns to alcohol for comfort. He meets Chandramukhi in her *haveli* and she falls in love with him. Though Devdas eventually accepts Chandramukhi's affections, he is not able to reciprocate her feelings. In the final scenes, he journeys to Paro's new home to die at her doorstep, with her on the other side of the locked gate, unable to reach him.

Though dances, particularly those performed by Chandramukhi, have always played an important role in the filmed versions of *Devdas*, Bhansali's version with its nine song and dance sequences foregrounds dance more than any of its predecessors. Early in the film, Paro dances in the privacy of her home as she anticipates Devdas's return from his studies abroad. Later, Paro's mother performs a dance on behalf of her daughter for Devdas's family. Chandramukhi performs two dances in her *haveli* and Devdas takes part in a drunken celebratory dance. But the most prominent dance is the shared public performance by Paro (Aishwarya Rai) and Chandramukhi (Madhuri Dixit) to the song "Dola re dola," as a culmination of their meeting.[28] Significantly, this meeting and dance did not occur in previous filmed versions of *Devdas,* including Bimal Roy's 1955 Hindi version and Dilip Roy's 1979 Bengali-language version.

In Bhansali's film, this dance acquires a pivotal status in the narrative as it establishes a relationship between Chandramukhi and Paro outside of the social restrictions that otherwise dictate their lives. The dance validates Chandramukhi's love for Devdas and enables her to confront the hypocrisy surrounding her profession. In terms of narrative flow, the dance foreshadows Devdas's demise and postpones the inevitability of the tragic events to come.

The dance becomes more than spectacle as it engenders an alternate expressive realm at once connected to and distinct from the film's narrative. Here, Madhava Prasad's analysis of dances in films as sites of "temporary permission" is particularly compelling.[29] Distinguishing between the private and the public and what is acceptable in Hindi films, Prasad proposes ways in which dance sequences provide glimpses of the otherwise hidden private sphere. Though his analysis focuses on representations of sexuality in the context of strict censorship, the discussion nevertheless points out that dance performs the important function of creating a temporary permissive, even transgressive, expressive realm. For Paro and Chandramukhi, "Dola re dola" creates a temporary space that permits the expression of their friendship and shared love for Devdas.

"Dola re dola" takes place in the home of Paro's in-laws at a celebration of Durga Pooja. As a courtesan, Chandramukhi transgresses social norms by attending the celebration and Paro breaks conventions by asking her to attend. In the context of the film, public dancing is associated with the questionable reputation of dancing girls and courtesans. Though Paro dances earlier in the film, these dances take place in the privacy of her own home or in dream sequences. However, earlier in the film, Paro's mother is humiliated for performing publicly on behalf of her daughter at Devdas's house. By dancing together, Paro and

Madhuri Dixit and Aishwarya Rai in *Devdas*. Courtesy of Eros International.

Chandramukhi complicate the polarity of respectability central to perceptions of public dancing.

Significantly, the movement content of "Dola re dola" differs from Chandramukhi's earlier courtesan dances performed for male audiences. As a courtesan, Chandramukhi represents a recurring character in popular Hindi films. Like other filmic courtesans, such as those in *Pakeezah* (Pure of Heart, Kamal Amrohi, 1971), *Mughal-E-Azam* (The great Mughal, K. Asif, 1960), and *Umrao Jaan* (Muzaffar Ali, 1981), Chandramukhi belongs to a tradition of women trained in the dance of "refined" seduction. Chakravarty describes the courtesan as a historical character and cinematic spectacle who remains "one of the most enigmatic figures to haunt the margins of Indian cultural consciousness."[30] As a courtesan, Chandramukhi commands a certain power in society: she is respected for her mastery of singing and dancing, yet her profession as an entertainer and her association with prostitution place her on the margins of society. Her tragedy is confirmed through her impossible longing for respectability and the unattainable love of Devdas. Chandramukhi's dances, choreographed by Kathak Pandit Birju Maharaj, demonstrate her skills as a performer as well as her unrequited love. The opulent setting and movement content of Madhuri Dixit's performances in this role differ from Chandramukhi's dances in previous filmed versions of *Devdas* (1955, 1979), which tended to stress the seductive elements of the courtesan's dance. Dixit's technical mastery of complex rhythms are accented through rhythmically coordinated camera cuts; her ability to emote through facial expression and gesture is emphasized through close-ups. These dances codify Chandramukhi as a skilled performer in control of her performance and its viewership. This attention to her skills marks Dixit's rendition of Chandramukhi different from the previous representations, particularly the one portrayed by Vyjayanthimala in the 1955 version of the film.

The intention of the "Dola re dola" choreography and cinematic arrangement distinguishes itself from both Chandramukhi's and Paro's mother's earlier performances. In "Dola re dola," Chandramukhi and Paro perform for each other. The audience becomes a secondary witness to the danced presentation of their friendship. The dance opens with Paro urging a hesitant Chandramukhi into a space already occupied by dancers. Paro and Chandramukhi are dressed in identical white saris with red borders and each wears gold jewelry. Their costumes seemingly erase differences in status and background. After the initial entry, the camera cuts abruptly to Paro, who faces the camera as she executes a series of moves that intersperse sharp pose-like movements interspersed with quick turns and level changes. On the down beats, Paro faces the camera directly. This unapologetic frontal address establishes Paro's dominating presence in the space. She rotates a slightly raised leg and leans forward, then snaps her fingers as if inviting the audience and Chandramukhi to join her. Paro's invitation alludes to the courage she demonstrated on other occasions in the film, including the moment when she initiated contact with Chandramukhi and when she visited Devdas's home in the middle of the night, urging him to elope with her.

Chandramukhi enters the performance space by posing with her left leg raised to the side with the knee bent, her arms straight and pointing to her right diagonal. She then rotates her arms in figure-eight movements as she moves front without her eyes following the movement pattern of her arms. She repeats the initial pose, reminiscent of

Durga and Shiva Nataraj poses used in Indian "classical" dances to communicate valor and courage. The camera cuts to a close-up of her face as she focuses off to the diagonal and lip-synchs "Oh maahi" (Oh lover). The movement vocabularies and expressions used to introduce Paro and Chandramukhi are qualitatively different. Paro's entrance is an indirect playful invitation; Chandramukhi's is direct and pierces the space. The camera cuts to Paro fronting a group of chorus dancers and follows them as they run toward the right to join Chandramukhi. The two dancers claim and define ownership of the dance space by moving in four directions. They establish their space and enter the performance space to establish their friendship through unified movement.

The lyrics play an important role in determining the meaning of the dance. During the recurring refrain, the two women execute a series of movements in unison to the lyrics: "Hey dola re dola re dola re dola" (Hey, I swayed, I swayed, I swayed), "Haai dola dil dola mann dola re dola" (Oh, my heart swayed, my spirit swayed). The movements incorporating a gentle sway of the hips from side to side, with one arm behind the head and a look off to the diagonal, stress that the sway of the women's hearts, caused by their love for Devdas, is the pretext for this performance. Their movements are echoed by female dancers in the foreground and male dancers in the background as the "dola" or "sway" of the heart motivates their dance. This recurring movement establishes unity between the two women as they compare the depth of their affection for Devdas.

As Paro sings, "Maathe ki bindiya mein voh hai" (He is in the bindi of my forehead), Chandramukhi responds, "Palkon ki nindiya mein voh hai" (He is in the sleep of my eyelashes). They then shift their attention to recognizing each other's love. Paro remarks to Chandramukhi, "Tere to tan mann mein voh hai" (He is in your body and mind). Chandramukhi makes a similar observation about Paro when she states, "Teri bhi dhadkan mein voh hai" (He is even in the beat of your heart). The most significant reciprocity, however, emerges when Chandramukhi, walking around Paro, communicates her gratitude, "Tumne mujhko duniya de di" (You have given me the world). The camera zooms into a close-up of the two women's upper torsos focusing on their facial expression.

Paro responds by tracing her fingers through Chandramukhi's hairline, continuing to her head in a gesture that validates Chandramukhi's love for Devdas and asserts an equality between the two women. As she sings, "Tumse kabhi na hona door" (May I never be far from you), Paro uses gestures to symbolically hand over Devdas to Chandramukhi. Through use of gesture and movements corresponding to the song's lyrics, accented through movements of the chorus dancers, the two women establish a realm that allows them to validate their love for Devdas.

The chorus dancers reinforce the imaginary and physical space in which the performance takes place. Composed of women in the foreground and men in the background, the chorus dancers also underscore the performance as female. The female chorus dancers' movements echo and react to the communication between Chandramukhi and Paro.

As the song progresses, the camera cuts, with increasing frequency, to Paro's brother-in-law, Kalibabu, who is waiting to reveal Chandramukhi's identity. His presence imbues the entire performance with a temporal fragility. Leading up to the climax, Paro and Chandramukhi repeat a variation on Chandramukhi's entrance. With the right leg straight and raised slightly off the ground and their arms out to the sides, they both walk to the side. They then repeat the step to the other side, this time keeping one arm bent at chest level with palms flexed and facing up, as if to stop someone from advancing. With their finger on their shoulder and their arms raised, they shift their weight between their hips pausing briefly on the fourth beat. In this way, they summarize their shared experience and once again assert their space. As the music moves to its final crescendo, the dancers whirl into a circular configuration and execute a series of movements as the camera spins around them at a rhythmically synchronized pace. With the last beat of music, the dance ends with a full body shot of the dancers in a circle with Paro and Chandramukhi still protected in their midst.

Kalibabu interrupts the applause to reveal Chandramukhi's identity. Although Chandramukhi confronts his hypocritical behavior as she leaves Paro's house, the temporary expressive permission allowed by the song and dance sequence is shattered. However, it is not forgotten. Paro displays her determination to keep its memory alive when she stops her mother-in-law from extinguishing the oil lamp she burns for Devdas.

The choreography executed by Paro and Chandramukhi in "Dola re dola" alludes to a more abstract and transient realm that permits the expression of subconscious, or hidden, emotions and desires in ways that influence plot development. As the temporary realm that allowed a courtesan to perform with a married woman disintegrates, both women retain a degree of stoicism in the face of the adverse consequences of their public display. Bhansali's decision to add the "Dola re dola" sequence helps create an empowering exclusively female imaginary space.

Hindi Film Dance in Performance

This allusion to an imaginary space unmoored from existing social distinctions took on a different form at MIT's Annual South Asian cultural show in April 2003 where a performance to the song "Dola re dola" facilitated an expression of perceived cultural identities experienced through Hindi films. As Vijay Mishra argues, Hindi films have become "crucial determinant[s] in globalizing the deterritorializing link[s] between the imagination and social life."[31] In the diaspora, films become mediators of "key translatable signs" that are "crucial in bringing the 'homeland' into the diaspora as well as creating a culture of imaginary solidarity across the heterogeneous linguistic and national groups that make up the South Asian (Indian) diaspora."[32] Inspired by song and dance sequences in Hindi films, performed versions of these dances dominate in South Asian cultural shows on college campuses in the United States.

These performances "showcase definitions of what constitutes 'Indian culture' ... for second generation college students" through "theatrical displays of idealized ... culture."[33] As Sunaina Marr Maira points out, these cultural shows also "provide a medium for the performative aspects of symbolic ethnicity in the second generation, creating a formally organized occasion for enacting ethnic identity at the event and during rehearsals." Maira points to the "mimetic" quality of many of the performances featured at cultural shows as "site[s] for packaging and performing cultural nostalgia" that simultaneously "highlight some of the contradictions of the ideology of ethnic authenticity."[34] While Maira's focus on the "mimetic" elements of Bollywood dance performances at cultural shows provides a useful entry into analyzing film dance in performance, her exploration stops short of accounting for the ways in which film dances are reinterpreted for the stage and how these changes affect communicated meanings.

Sunita Mukhi's exploration of a staged performance of the "Choli ke peeche kya hai" (What is behind the blouse?) song and dance sequence demonstrates how a close analysis of translations from film to stage can contribute to appreciating Bollywood dance as cultural expression.[35] Appalled by the "sexual innuendo and explicit ... dance gestures" in "Choli ke peeche kya hai" the Indian Central Bureau for Film Certification, threatened to block the release of the film *Khalnayak* (Villain, Subhash Ghai, 1993) "until this song was edited out."[36] The film was an overnight success once it was released unedited. Mukhi describes the song's restaging at the forty-seventh Indian Independence Day Parade in New York City, where the dance was performed by Preeti, a seven-year-old girl.

Mukhi observes that though Preeti took over many of the original steps, including "gyrations of her hips" and a "flirtatious facial expression," the potential vulgarity of her performance was consciously constrained. Her as yet "sexually ambiguous" body was clothed in a more "modest" costume and Bharat Natyam-like movements were added to the original choreography.[37] These adjustments allowed Preeti to "reposition" her performance:

> They [the audience] recall Madhuri's performance in the fantasy that is the Hindi film as they watch the child ... In dancing *Choli Ke Peeche,* audience and performer acquire glamour and talent of the Hindi film, its star, its multi-layered narratives, and a vernacular Indianness.[38]

Preeti presents herself as a child of middle-class parents living in the United States, respectfully in touch with her Indian heritage.

Like Preeti, student choreographers and dancers who prepare cultural shows on college campuses in the United States interpret and adapt the original versions of the dances they encounter in films. These adaptive processes lie at the heart of what Jane Desmond calls the "stakes" or underlying ideologies of movement.[39] The ways that dance movements and narrative contexts are maintained, or adapted, between film and stage help us understand Hindi film reception through dance.

The annual cultural show organized by MIT's South Asian American Students (SAAS) is one of the biggest South Asian events on campus. Performed predominantly by second-generation Indian MIT undergraduates, the audience tends to be overwhelmingly South Asian, as many friends and parents journey to see the performance. Participation in the cultural show is by audition only, and students spend a considerable amount of time and effort preparing and rehearsing the dances and other acts. Although the organizers make an explicit effort to include excerpts from Indian "classical" music and dance traditions,

Hindi film-inspired performances tend to dominate the cultural show repertoire.

In 2003, SAAS chose "Sapne," or dreams, as its theme and stressed the show's function as a space for expressing imagined Indian–American identities. The 2003 cultural show program notes stated:

> we wish to present to you a glimpse into the world as we may dream of it…Our dreams, the dreams of previous generations, and the dreams of future generations all contribute to the rich and diverse cultures of South Asia that we are given the opportunity to experience.[40]

The SAAS program notes clearly identify the act of making visible the dreamed yet physically experienced nature of the cultural show as a primary focus of this event. The expression of these dreams created by the cultural show is, in many ways, reminiscent of Prasad's formulation of song and dance sequences in films as permissive realms that allow for public expression of otherwise private dreams and desires.

The way in which temporary imaginary spaces are created through Bollywood dance becomes apparent through an examination of a performance of "Dola re dola" at "Sapne" where Chamak, MIT's Indian fusion dance troupe, integrated the song into their composition, choreographed by Payal Kadakia. In the program notes, Chamak described the group's "use [of] skill, grace, and energy to create a masterpiece that conveys a perfect compilation of Indian and American vibe[s]."[41] This description explicitly identifies Chamak's effort to engage with rather than mimic Hindi film dance. Through dance content from *Devdas* collaged with other movement vocabularies, the group used the performative space created by the cultural show to assert their perception of what it means to be second-generation Indians living in the United States.

Introduced by a digital voice countdown ("4, 3, 2, 1, hit it"), the "Dola re dola" portion of the dance began with ten dancers running forward in successive groups. The first two groups move down the diagonals. The third group approached the audience. The group then moved in unison to remixed excerpt from "Silsila yeh chaahat ka," (With all my heart) a song and dance sequence from *Devdas*. With an abrupt cut to the music and a hip-hop one liner, the audio then transitions to "Dola re dola." During the transitioned sequence, five of the dancers kneeled upstage as the other five dancers faced the audience. With an exaggerated hip swing and chest undulation, the five dancers walked confidently toward the audience. With sharp accented movements, they sliced the space with their right and left arms. They then hugged themselves and looked down and up.

Facing the audience directly, they point at the audience as they lip-synched "I am a girl at the party, look at that body shaking that thing like you never did see." In a total blackout, the music transitioned abruptly to a speeded up version of the "Dola re dola" sequence. During "Dola re dola," the dancers' movements became more contained. Importantly, Chamak's interpretation of the "Dola re dola" sequence omitted all implied differences between the courtesan and the married woman, which was central to the filmed version. Chandramukhi's nuanced use of expression to communicate her hesitation about performing in a public space gave way to a celebration of a perceived cultural identity and an "Indianized femininity" mediated through film dance. The dialogue between Chandramukhi and Paro through distinctive movements gave way to unison movements and complex group formations with rhythmic staggering and spatial symmetries, contrasted with coded American ges-tural vocabularies and combinations. Alternating subgroups of dancers broke away to gesture specific lyrics directly to the audience. After their lyrics, they rejoined the group. This focus on the group, rather than on the individual, further flattened interpretations of social differences.

At the same time, Chamak's performance consciously referenced the recurring movement from the original sequence incorporating a gentle sway of the hips, with one arm behind the head and a look off to the diagonal. Similarly, Chamak's dancers mimicked the movements of the two film protagonists, as they gestured to their ankles in changing duet configurations to the "Baandhke main ghunghroo, pahenke main paayal" lyrics. In addition to referencing the film choreography as source, Chamak deployed gestural vocabularies associated with Indian classical dance techniques to express the lyrics. Dancers placed a stylisti-cally cupped hand close to their forehead as they looked to the diago-nals in "search" of their loved one. While the red and white colors of the Chamak dancers' costumes referenced Paro and Chandramukhi, they also accented the performers' shared Indian–American identities. The red sequined wraparound trousers, the white sleeveless scarf blouse, and the red hair band helped Chamak's costumes stress the group's uniform, up-to-date identity.

As in Preeti's performance of "Choli ke peeche kya hai," these mul-tiple references allowed Chamak's performers and audience members to share their experience of an imagined Indian culture mediated through

Hindi films. Yet, unlike Preeti's performance, which sought to redignify "Choli ke peeche kya hai" through the insertion of recognizable classical dance movements, Chamak's performance collaged Indian classical dance and American hip-hop movements as it simultaneously referenced the libidinal space created through Chandramukhi and Paro's performance. This selective intertextual referencing of movement and film allowed the dancers to "position" their performance of "Dola re dola" as more than a celebration of "Indianness" and "femininity" at a cultural event outside India.

Though the imaginary realm created through Chamak's performance to "Dola re dola" differed from the filmed version, it still established a temporally limited expressive space. This space allowed the dancers to interpret their own experience of the film and their performance became a display of the dancers' perceptions of their Indian–American identities and of their cultural heritage. Significantly, Chamak's performance did not adopt any movement from Chandramukhi's courtesan dances, but did borrow from Paro's earlier dances in the film, suggesting that the assertive space presented by the group was not devoid of cultural norms for respectability.

This selective referencing of the film choreography raises important questions about what is "remembered," "forgotten," and "replaced" in the process of interpreting the dances from film to stage. The "three-sided relationship of memory, performance, and substitution" and the related process of "surrogation" proposed by Joseph Roach in *Cities of the Dead* provide a useful framework for analytical inquiry.[42] For Roach, "surrogation" is the process by which "culture reproduces and re-creates itself."[43] If we accept Hindi film dances as a form of "memory" and their staging at cultural venues as "performance," then the selective interpretation involved in translating dances from film to stage becomes a process of "surrogation." Chamak's decision to retain the unison movement between the two women, omit movements specific to the characters' social and narrative status, and substitute with assertive movement, drawing on gestures associated with American hip-hop and Indian classical dance, is significant. Chamak's performance did not strive to create an imagined realm for the expression of a friendship despite social differences. Rather, the performance sought to establish a temporary space that stressed Hindi film as an idealized heritage affirmed through assertive movements specific to the performers' location in the United States.[44] Chamak's performance did not replicate or mimic the filmic "Dola re dola" experience. Rather, it deployed the filmed version as a visual and movement archive to evoke the cultural memory of an imagined Indian heritage. Chamak's choreographic relationship to Hindi film dance was selectively citational as it enabled the dancers to articulate their utopic position through the temporary realm created by their performance.

Unpacking Chamak's choreography reveals how Hindi film dances provide source material for Indian cultural show performances on college campuses. By preserving, adapting, substituting, and forgetting movements, staged versions of Hindi film dances participate in the process of surrogation. By privileging choreography, my analysis asked why and how dances occur in the films and how these movements are in turn interpreted at cultural events outside India to demonstrate that the temporary spaces created by dances in films, encourage creative translations of dances from film to performance. Understood in this way, Bollywood dance becomes a site of film reception; its public display becomes a "performance of cultural identity," forcing us to acknowledge Hindi film dance as a form of cultural memory, Bollywood dance an emerging, expressive, and inherently hybrid vernacular movement tradition, and Hindi film-inspired performances as more than diasporic nostalgia on display.[45]

Notes

An earlier version of this article appeared in *Dance Research Journal* 36, no. 2 (Winter 2004).

1 http://www.honeykalaria.com/, 2005.
2 http://www.bollywoodaxion.com/, 2005.
3 "Silsila yeh chaahat Ka" (*Devdas,* 2002) may be taught through an explicit reference to "classical" dance, whereas "Sharara" (*Mere Yaar Ki Shaadi Hai,* My friend's wedding, Sanjay Gadhvi, 2002) mixes references to several Indian and "western" dance styles.
4 Nasreen Munni Kabir, *Bollywood: The Indian Cinema Story* (London: Channel 4 Books, 2001), 189.
5 It is important to acknowledge the definitional slippage underlying the usage of "Bollywood dance" outside India, sometimes used interchangeably with the term *filmi* dance in India. Though dances in popular films produced by language-specific regional cinemas are sometimes also colloquially labeled Bollywood dances and share some similarities with dances contained in Hindi films, they also often retain a degree of regional specificity.
6 In as constitutive of the Indian diaspora, Vijay Mishra identifies two "quite distinct moments in the history of capital". He explains that the "… first

moment (of classic capitalism) produced the movement of indentured labor to the colonies ... The second moment (of late modern capital) is largely a post 1960s phenomenon distinguished by the movement of economic migrants (but also refugees) into the metropolitan centers of the former empire as well as the New World and Australia." My discussion in this essay focuses mostly on this latter "Indian diaspora" and its "descendants."

7   Susan Foster, "Choreographies of Gender," *Signs* 24, no. 1 (1998): 1–33, 5.

8   V. A. K. Ranga Rao estimates that "in the 13 or so films that exist at the NFIA (only two or three are complete; others are truncated to various degrees), there must be a few [dances].... There is one silent example extant in the NFAI from *Lankadahan* (1917) of Dadasaheb Phalke, which clearly shows that a trick sequence must have employed the technique of music dictated movement...." See V. A. K. Ranga Rao, "Dance in Indian Cinema," in *Rasa: The Indian Performing Arts in the Last Twenty-Five Years*, ed. Sunil Kothari and Bimal Mukherjee (Calcutta: Anamika Kala Sangam Research and Publications, 1995), 301.

9   Yves Thoraval, *The Cinemas of India* (New Delhi: Macmillan India Limited, 2000), 5.

10 Ibid., 64

11 Ravi Vasudevan, "Bombay and Its Public," *Journal of Arts and Ideas* 29 (January 1996): 45–66.

12 Lalitha Gopalan, *Cinema of Interruptions: Action Genres in Contemporary Indian Cinema* (London: BFI Publishing, 2002).

13 Ibid., 18.

14 Wimal Dissanayake and K. Moti Gokulsing, *Indian Popular Cinema: A Narrative of Cultural Change* (Chester, UK: Trentham Books, 1998).

15 Ibid., 17.

16 Ibid.

17 Erik Barnouw and S. Krishnaswamy, *Indian Film* (New York: Columbia University Press, 1963), 71.

18 Rao, "Dance in Indian Cinema," 305.

19 In their historical analyses, Anne Marie Gaston, *Bharata Natyam from Temple to Theater* (New Delhi: Manohar, 1996), and Pallabi Chakravorty, "Choreographing Modernity: Kathak Dance, Public Culture and Women's Identity in India" (PhD diss., Temple University, 1999) explore the relationship between colonial rule and specific Indian performance traditions.

20 Rao, "Dance in Indian Cinema," 305.

21 Rajika Puri, "Dance in India," *Journal of Arts and Ideas* 3 (1983): 21–32.

22 Anne Marie Gaston defines *devadasis* of South India as "dancers who belonged to the *isai vellala* community ... [of] hereditary performing artists ... The *devadasi* and her dance were important adjuncts to both religious and secular occasions". Gaston, *Bharata Natyam*, 15.

23 Purnima Shah, "National Dance Festivals in India: Public Culture, Social Memory and Identity" (PhD diss., University of Wisconsin–Madison, 2000), 20.

24 Ibid.

25 Ibid., 25.

26 Uttara Asha Coorlawala, "Classical and Contemporary Indian Dance: Overview Criteria and Choreographic Analysis" (PhD diss., New York University, 1994), 5.

27 Sumita Chakravarty, *National Identity in Indian Popular Cinema 1947–1987* (Austin: University of Texas Press, 1993), 205.

28 The spectacular draw of Aishwarya Rai as Paro and Madhuri Dixit as Chandramukhi, two extremely popular Hindi film actresses, dancing together in the fast-paced, glitzy sequence cannot be underestimated. Named Miss World in 1994, Aishwarya Rai is recognized as an unofficial cultural ambassador for India. Madhuri Dixit is respected for her refined acting abilities. Both female stars have been recognized for their dancing skills, and their "classical" dance training is often cited as testimony of their professionalism in film-related media. "Dola re dola" dominated the film's publicity efforts, press reviews, and theatrical trailers.

29 Madhava Prasad, *Ideology of the Hindi Film: A Historical Construction* (New Delhi: Oxford University Press, 1998).

30 Chakravarty, *National Identity,* 269.

31 Mishra, *Bollywood Cinema,* 237.

32 Ibid.

33 Sunaina Marr Maira, *Desis in the House: Indian American Youth Culture in New York City* (Philadelphia, Pa.: Temple University Press, 2002), 120–1.

34 Ibid.

35 *Khalnayak* (1993) is a film about a seemingly incorrigible criminal whose erroneous ways are finally tamed by Ganga, a brave and morally righteous policewoman who gains his trust through her disguise as a dancing girl. Ganga, acted by Madhuri Dixit, intrigues the villain through her performance in the "Choli ke peeche kya hai" song and dance sequence. See Bhattacharjya and Mehta's essay in this anthology for an extended discussion of the "scandal" associated with this song.

36 Sunita S. Mukhi, *Doing the Desi Thing: Performing Indianness in New York City* (New York: Garland Publishing Inc., 2000), 119.

37 Ibid., 121.

38 Ibid., 122.

39 Jane C. Desmond, "Embodying Difference: Issues in Dance," in *Meaning in Motion: New Cultural Studies of Dance,* ed. Jane C. Desmond (Durham: Duke University Press, 1997), 32.

40 MIT SAAS, *Culture Show 2003—Sapne* (Cambridge: MIT SAAS, 2003), 3.

41 Ibid.

42 Joseph Roach, *Cities of the Dead* (New York: Columbia University Press, 1996), 2.

43 Ibid.

44 See Zumkhawala-Cook's essay in this anthology for an understanding of the identifications fostered by desi audiences in the United States.

45 Desmond, "Embodying Difference," 31.

10. Food and Cassettes

Encounters with Indian Filmsong

Edward K. Chan

By 2004, mainstream American popular culture had finally recognized Bollywood. Indeed, there has been a full-fledged "Bolly-chic" afoot, echoing an earlier "Indo-chic" in the world of publishing.[1] Bollywood's elaborate musical sequences have even been spoofed on *The Simpsons*, the all-seeing eye of American popular culture. We might read the spoof as either satire or homage, yet the spoof is less about Bollywood cinema itself and more about Bollywood's move from subculture to mainstream, in much the same way that Jackie Chan, Tsui Hark, and John Woo became "hip" before attaining mass-market appeal. Is this simply a Cinderella story, in which "nontraditional Bollywood consumers" (NBCs) in the United States—that is, those without a direct cultural tie to Bollywood—are now ready to see Bollywood and filmsong on its own terms?[2] Perhaps, but there is something more fundamental at stake. Filmsong's reception in the United States provides an exemplary text for diagnosing how liberal democratic humanism manages social difference.

Western appreciation of Bollywood and Hong Kong action cinema is qualitatively different from the admiration devoted to a Satyajit Ray or a Wong Kar Wai, who both reside and circulate within the left-hand side of the high art/mass culture split and not as "illegitimate" kitsch. The reception of high art or classical legitimacy lends itself to an exoticization that is ultimately sterilized by universalism. But an exoticization marked by kitsch has become the reigning sentiment that governs the NBC's encounter with Bollywood over the years:

> Counting among its initial meanings the act of collecting junk from the street, kitsch has been identified for well over a hundred years with all that is superfluous and degraded in our culture.... Tacky, gaudy,

schlock in English; *cursi, naco, picúo* in Spanish, kitsch can easily win any contest for the most disreputable term that can be ascribed to an object, a style, or even a person. Secure in this belief, different social groups have used the term "kitsch" as an infallible weapon against their adversaries.[3]

Kitsch maps a symbolic economy of cultural capital, through which subjects are located and locate themselves in social space.[4] Thus, it makes sense that Bollywood had to first travel through underground popular culture, which has the ability to reclaim bad taste as kitsch by making it "cool" or "hip."[5] But kitsch has also come to signify excess: an overabundance of emotion, "a surplus of signs," and a repetition of endless copies.[6] Traditionally, this excess was associated with the masses and mass culture. With Bollywood, however, the excess also encompasses cultural differences that reside outside the logic of mainstream American popular culture. Undoubtedly, it is the "shock" of Bollywood's racially encoded excess that enables filmsong's transformation into kitsch. Even in attempts to celebrate filmsong, the kitsch response must be worked through, and we are still left with the remainder of cultural difference. However, as we rush to "legitimize" Bollywood, are we ignoring or glossing over this difference in affect between high art canonization and mass culture "kitschification"?[7]

At first glance, this might seem to be simply a Third-World-to-First-World narrative about exoticization and kitschification—a narrative that in and of itself suggests the geopolitical inequalities inherent in the global circulation of popular culture. However, the opposition embedded in this encounter also reenacts what David Theo Goldberg calls "the irony of modernity." Goldberg is not the first to identify the contradiction at the heart of liberal democracy. His account, however, specifically casts that contradiction in relation to racial—and by extension cultural, since culture is often racialized—difference. Goldberg tracks race alongside the evolution of modernity and the rise of liberalism as its dominant ideology. While modernity and liberalism perpetually aspire to abstraction from social particularity, race

> pretends to universality in undertaking to draw otherwise disparate social subjects together into a cohesive unit in terms of which common interests are either found or fabricated. Nevertheless, race undertakes at once to furnish specific identity to otherwise abstract and alienated subjectivities.[8]

This contradiction within the liberalist deployment of race hints at the larger structural instability at the heart of liberal democracy. Race, as a particularity, is anathema to a sociopolitical system based on abstraction from particularity, what Vivian Sobchack calls "a culture that has lost its equivalent of proprioception and no longer feels the lived body intimately."[9] For Goldberg, the development of modernity produces both this insistence on abstraction and a progressive institutionalization of racial difference in science and in the nation-state (imperialism, segregation, apartheid, and so on). Thus, what he calls "the irony of modernity" and "the liberal paradox" amounts to an inability to cope with racial difference: "The more ideologically hegemonic liberal values seem and the more open to difference liberal modernity declares itself, the more dismissive it becomes and the more closed it seeks to make the circle of acceptability."[10]

As the timeline in part one of this essay shows, the reception history of Indian filmsong in American culture plays out this irony/paradox. The liberal desire for abstraction from particularity condemns NBCs to a spastic anxiety as we encounter Indian filmsong: what do we *do* with this excess of cultural difference? In the arena of cultural exchange, the desire for abstraction produces a desire for what I call "pristine consumption": subjects abstracted from social particularity consuming objects similarly abstracted from social particularity. Instead, we need to reembody these transactions. Luce Irigaray cautions against the desire for abstraction:

> The dream of dissolving material, corporeal or social identity leads to a whole set of delusions, to endless and unresolvable conflicts, to a war of images or reflections and to powers being accredited to somebody or other more for imaginary or narcissistic reasons than for their actual abilities.[11]

If we refuse these delusions, we must then acknowledge that the transcultural consumption of difference will forever be stained and dirty.

For despite the permeability of cultural boundaries and the inevitably hybrid nature of musical forms, I will insist that the borders separating one cultural logic from another still maintain influence over our consumption while being sufficiently porous to allow for appropriation across those borders. Paul Willemen characterizes this process in a very useful way:

> [I]n art and media studies, insufficient attention is paid to the deter-
> mining effects of the geographically bounded state-unity, and this
> encourages a kind of promiscuous or random form of alleged interna-
> tionalism, which I would prefer to call an evasive cosmopolitanism
> masking imperial aspirations. Another, more polemical way of putting
> this is to say that the discourse of universalist humanism is in fact an
> imperial and a colonising strategy. If we accept that national bound-
> aries have a significant structuring impact on national socio-cultural
> formations (please note that I have written "a significant impact" and
> not that these boundaries are the only determinations, nor necessarily
> the most important ones in all circumstances: merely they are real and
> significant), this has to be accounted for in the way we approach and
> deal with cultural practices from "elsewhere."[12]

Willemen's parenthetical caution is important. It is enough to say that
national/cultural borders are "merely ... real and significant," making
cultural borders impossible to ignore—this even despite the American
ideology of multiculturalism within a nationalist postnationalism.[13] I
contend that whatever crosses these borders is forever stained with cultural difference. As Graham Huggan claims, "[e]xchange ... at both
literal and symbolic levels is always uneven, as are the structures of economic development that underpin the global circulation of designated
'exotic' goods."[14] Overdetermined by global capitalism, liberalism, and
Eurocentrism, the movement of Third World culture to the First World
seems inevitably trapped within a model of consumption understood in
terms of kitsch, exoticism, and/or food; food especially drives home the
significance of the body in these transactions.

As such, the anxieties about cultural difference presiding over the
American encounter with Bollywood force us to confront a tension
between "dirty" and "pristine" consumption. Framing the consumption
of cultural difference as dirty acknowledges the messiness of difference
and its subcutaneous influence over our everyday practices, like dirt
under fingernails. Without this acknowledgment, discourse surrounding the consumption of Bollywood will inevitably replay these anxieties
again and again. The problem is that acknowledging difference often
leads to an unacceptable exotification of, or discrimination against, that
difference. The desire for pristine consumption tries, on the other hand,
to transcend difference and allows us to confront cultural objects as
abstract individuals. This desire typically leads to an emphasis on structure and form, whereby cultural difference is either converted into

"expertise" or erased altogether. What the urge toward abstraction and transcendence must repress is that cross-cultural consumption will always be dirty—a messiness that liberal democracy cannot allow for as it tries to manage social difference.

A Timeline

The following annotated timeline chronicles the appearance of filmsong in American culture.[15] Though not exhaustive, I offer it as representative of the process. My texts include some of the compact discs (CDs) and films that played a role in presenting filmsong to NBCs. Filmsong entered into American popular culture (at times via England and Europe) through underground music culture. Much of that trajectory reflects NBCs' inability to encounter filmsong as anything other than exotic kitsch (even if beloved): condescending, uncomprehending, and superficial. The songs that are highlighted tend to be those lending themselves readily to kitschification, such as "Jaan pehechan ho (Lets get to know each other)" and "Dum maro dum." We should note, as well, that consumption of filmsong by NBCs is divorced from its "native" contexts, in several ways. There is the cultural context: a different language, non-Western instrumentation, and so on. Moreover, the act of consumption concentrates on *song* and generally excludes *image and narrative sequence* (though film posters and sound track packaging are also consumed). It is not that listening to filmsong as a disembodied commodity is wrong, as if we need to verify the authenticity of consumption; however, we do need to consider how filmsong is reembodied and given social meaning.

As the timeline shows, there are a number of other recurring tropes and themes that accompany NBCs' reception of filmsong. The most striking is perhaps the reversion to food and eating as the appropriate metaphors for consumption. But the most important is the anxiety with which we encounter cultural difference—an anxiety rooted in liberal democratic ideology—leading us to simultaneously highlight and negate that difference.

1983

Channel Four in England produced Jeremy Marre's documentary *There'll Always Be Stars in the Sky: The Indian Film Music Phenomenon.*

Pantheon released the companion book *Beats of the Heart: Popular Music of the World* in the United States in 1985, and Shanachie Records released the videotape in 1992.[16] A section of this documentary looks at the brotherly duo of musical directors Kalyanji and Anandji Shah (credited as "Kalyanji, Anandji") whose music figures in the kitsch-driven compilations *Bombay the Hard Way* (1998) and *Bombay 2* (2001). Marre introduced NBCs to filmsong through the context of "world music," which has become a distinct market for music consumption in the West.

1990

The British label Ace Records put out three volumes of *Golden Voices from the Silver Screen: Classic Indian Film Soundtrack Songs from the Television Series "Movie Mahal,"* the sound track to a series directed by Nasreen Munni Kabir for Channel Four.[17] The CDs span the 1940s through the 1980s and do not purposely emphasize filmsong as kitsch (though volume three does contains "Jaan pehechan ho").[18]

1992

David Byrne's label, Luaka Bop, released *Dance Raja Dance: The South Indian Film Music of Vijaya Anand* as the first in the Asia Classics series, which markets over-the-top exoticness.[19] Yale Evelev, who compiled *Dance Raja Dance,* explains his discovery of Anand:

> Some friends of ours … had come back [from India] with a cassette of some really cool Indian film music that I imagined had been made by some young guy in a basement studio with some samplers. They bought the tape in Mysore and it was a very hand done cover that said *Vijaya Anand Dance Raja Dance*. I had heard quite a bit of "filmi," but this music was different. Much more current-sounding, with the wonderful kitsch amalgamations of different musics, including electronic dance music.[20]

Several notable themes emerge here. The ready availability of culture throughout the world enables both a deterritorialized consumption and a constant traffic of cultural goods from one place to another, exemplified by a touristic memento like the Anand tape. The wandering Western expatriate "discovers" a curiosity in an exotic land. The curiosity is rendered primitive: the "hand done cover" and the supposed cottage industry from which the curiosity originated (especially ironic, given Anand's star status in a full-fledged industry). The primitive quality is converted into kitsch value and appropriated as "cool." Most notably, cultural difference masquerades as kitsch.

1994

On a tiny independent label, Amarillo Records, "Heavenly Ten Stems," an obscure underground rock band, put out a 7-inch record that includes two filmsong covers: "China Town" and "Jan pehechan ho [*sic*]."[21] What is notable about the latter recording is that it sounds, in Borgesian fashion, almost exactly like the original. The song had already appeared on volume three of *Golden Voices* (1990) and again on the compilation *Doob Doob O'Rama* (2000), and it reappeared in the film *Ghost World* (2004).

1995

Daisy von Scherler Mayer's *Party Girl* appeared using a song from Anand's *Dance Raja Dance* called "Desire soars up high."[22] In the film, the song signifies the exoticization/eroticization of Mustafa (Omar Townsend), a *Lebanese* falafel vendor, by Mary (Parker Posey). The sequence shows Mary approximating a belly dance in her kitchen while emitting a high-pitched nasal "singing" as the song plays in the background. At one point, Mary picks up a washcloth to use as a makeshift veil. The shots of Mary's dance are interspersed with shots of Mustafa slowly taking his jacket off to reveal his naked torso. The mise-en-scène of the latter shot is dark; Mustafa's falafel cart sits in the foreground with white steam from it pluming around him. Although the Anand song plays a very minor role in the film as a whole, its pan-ethnic usage demonstrates the signifying power of filmsong in American culture to conjure up a generalized oriental exotic. It also reinforces "indie cred" for the film and its director. Scherler Mayer went on to direct *The Guru* (2002), another cross-cultural tale about an Indian immigrant's seemingly inevitable positioning as a cultural stereotype.

1997

The British group Cornershop produced "Brimful of Asha" (on Luaka Bop), a second-generation tribute to filmsong through the iconicity of

Asha Bhosle (or Bhonsle).[23] Although the song has more meaning in its original British context, it did achieve some success in the United States also, appearing on college radio (if not mainstream alternative) playlists.

1998

The American independent label Motel Records put out *Bombay the Hard Way: Guns, Cars & Sitars* featuring songs composed by Kalyanji-Anandji for what the CD's producers call "Brownsploitation" flicks—that is, Indian films from the 1970s that drew upon Blacksploitation sound track classics.[24] The original filmsongs are remixed by Dan "the Automator" Nakamura, a prominent Bay Area hip-hop producer, with additional drum tracks provided by the trip-hop artist DJ Shadow. As part of the package, the producers crafted song titles such as "The Good, the Bad and the Chutney," "Ganges a go-go," "Fists of Curry," and "Fear of a Brown Planet."

2000

Q. D. K. Media, a German record label, put out *Doob Doob O'Rama: Filmsongs from Bollywood*.[25] "Jaan pehechan ho" is again featured, clearly having become the predominant metonym for Bollywood cinema as a whole in underground music culture. The cover of *Doob Doob O'Rama*, taken from an Indian billboard, features the cartoon image of an Indian woman with a quizzical expression confronting the phallic contours of a snake.

2001

This was a watershed year, seeing the release of several Bollywood-related items, including three films: *Ghost World*, *Moulin Rouge*, and *Monsoon Wedding*.[26] As we move toward the mainstream of American popular culture, the presence of Bollywood also becomes visual. And by showing the elaborate costuming and dancing, the films increase even further the notion of Bollywood as excess. Zwigoff's *Ghost World* is particularly important in defining Bollywood as kitsch. It opens with a musical dance sequence featuring "Jaan pehechan ho" from the film *Gumnaam* (Nameless, Raja Nawathe, 1965), described in the original film's trailer

Interpellating the hipster consumer: cover of *Doob Doob O'Rama* compact disc. Courtesy of Thomas Hartlage.

as "India's first horror thriller."[27] As in *Party Girl*, the filmsong's narrative role is quite marginal. However, the sequence in *Ghost World* sets the tone for Enid's (Thora Birch) later appropriation of two instances of race: an old blues song by Skip James and an old, racist logo for a fast-food chicken chain.[28] Here again, the filmsong functions as a marker of hipness, both *in* the film for the characters and *for* the film as an independent production. The filmsong clip's purpose in *Ghost World* is often read as one element Zwigoff uses to establish the outsider status of the main character, Enid.[29] The *Gumnaam* sequence is perfect in setting up the encounter with cultural (racial) difference in the film (presumably unintentional). In *Ghost World*, the filmsong configures the management of difference into either debased kitsch or fascinating authenticity (to some degree erotically desirable, as in *Party Girl*).

Several more filmsong compilations appeared in 2001. The punny song titles continue in *Bombay 2: Electric Vindaloo* by Kalyanji-Anandji:

"Basmati Beatdown," "T. J. Hookah," and "Sexy Mother Fakir."[30] According to the sleeve notes, the original music is derived from films of the 1980s, and because much of the music existed only in thirty-second sound bites, the producers hired DJs to transform them into full-fledged songs. *Doob Doob O'Rama 2: More Filmsongs from Bollywood* also appeared featuring "Mera naam Chin-Chin-Chu (My name is Chin-Chin-Chu)" sung by Geeta Dutt and "Ankhen meri maikhana" sung by Asha Bhosle.[31] The songs again promote a kitschy "otherworldliness"—from low-sound quality to the humor in what sounds like nonsensical words (for example, Kishore Kumar and chorus chanting "Ina mina dika") to the reinscription of Western simulations of "the Orient" in "Sayonara" to wah-wah guitars to the childish-sounding vocals in "Ezhupaalam kadamnu" to R. D. Burman's comical vocals in "O meri jaan main ne kaha."

We also see the appearance of the compilation *Mondo India: Featuring A. R. Rahman*, one of the new giants of Bollywood music.[32] Notably, Rahman is a more current music director than R. D. and S. D. Burman, who were responsible for many of the older songs appearing on NBC compilations. Like the other compilations, *Mondo India* plays out the tension between difference and abstraction, as the back cover makes clear: "By incorporating western production styles and sensibilities to Indian traditions, Rahman has created a music that is universal even as it is distinctly Indian." It is likely that the shift from R. D. Burman to Rahman marks a larger cultural shift not only in filmsong's reception in a nontraditional Bollywood market, but also at home. R. D. Burman is of a generation for whom using Western musical forms signaled "unclean" appropriation, whereas Rahman can freely appropriate Westernism and be celebrated on both sides of the cultural divide.[33] Yet, despite his talent and deftness, Rahman's brand of filmsong still contains the residues of cultural difference, which are still subject to an anxiety over how to characterize that difference, "universal even as it is distinctly Indian."

Another filmsong compilation, *The Kings and Queens of Bollywood: Classic Sixties Indian Film Themes*, appeared in 2001 from the British Nascente label in collaboration with the Demon Music Group (another British underground label).[34] It compiles songs from films such as *Kismet* (Fate, Gyan Mukherjee, 1943), *Mr. X in Bombay* (Shantilal Soni, 1964), and *Talash* (The search, O. P. Ralhan, 1969)—again, the older, kitsch-ready styles prevail. The CD packaging also plays up the

Bollywood as kitsch: cover of *The Kings and Queens of Bollywood* compact disc.

kitschiness in its choice of imagery and the brash and playful fonts, creating an intentional amateurism.

2002

At this point, we get not only Andrew Lloyd Weber and Rahman's *Bombay Dreams* and *Lagaan*'s Land Tax, Gowariker nomination for the Oscars, but also *The Rough Guide to Bollywood: The Glitz, the Glamour, the Soundtrack* compiled by DJ Ritu, BBC Radio host, cofounder of Out-caste Records, and owner of two "legendary London Bollywood nightclubs" in collaboration with Bhagwant Sagoo, the Scotland-based head of Asian Network at BBC Radio.[35] This CD compiles songs mostly from 1970s films such as *Hare Rama Hare Krishna* (Dev Anand, 1971)—"a kitsch classic"—and *Caravan* (Nasir Hussain, 1971), as well as more recent films such as *Kuch Kuch Hota Hai* (Something is happening, Karan Johar, 1998) and *Kaho Naa ... Pyaar Hai* (Say this is love, Rakesh Roshan, 2000).

Also appearing in 2002 was Brazilian-born, British electronica musician Amon Tobin's *Out From Out Where*, put out by Ninja Tune, an independent trip-hop label.[36]

Food and Cassettes

An archetypal scene emerges in the discovery of filmsong by NBCs in the United States. That scene was the Indian restaurant or sometimes the grocery store often located next door—part of what Laura Marks calls, borrowing Paul Rodaway's term, the "sensuous geographies whose monuments are grocery stores, places of worship, coffee and tea shops, and kitchens."[37] NBCs could hear the sounds of Bollywood while dining or pay two bucks for a dusty cassette of Lata's greatest hits. In one scenario, a non–South Asian patron walks into the restaurant, at which point a member of the staff immediately changes the music from beat-driven filmsong to the meditative Indian classical music. Erik Davis corroborates my own experience of this:

> I first heard filmi music when I opened the door to an empty Indian restaurant on East Sixth and walked into a swirl of peppy tablas, harmonium, and sugary vocals. In five seconds flat the waiter slapped on the ragas, which he must have figured conformed more to my notion of Orientalism.[38]

In another scenario, the "adventurous" NBC ventures into the grocery store often located next door to the Indian restaurant, maybe thinking to get frozen samosas or garlic naan, two metonymical mainstays of the non-Indian diner. At the store, the NBC would come across a wall or perhaps a large box haphazardly filled with hundreds of cassettes selling for two or three dollars.

There seems to be an inevitable correlation between eating and the transpositioning of filmsong. Commenting on the use of Roy Orbison's song "Oh, Pretty Woman" for the film *Kal Ho Naa Ho* (Tomorrow may never come, Nikhil Advani, 2003),[39] Orbison's wife Barbara observes

> Here's a song written and recorded such a long time ago, and then Roy passes on, and then we have a movie called *Pretty Woman....* And now

all of a sudden I get a call from India, which is so far away from our culture. It gives another lifetime to our copyright.[40]

In the renewal of the Orbison estate's copyright, there is no question that music ultimately circulates as intellectual property. However, there is also a cultural exchange happening. India—"so far away from our culture" not just geographically but also culturally and aesthetically—consumes not merely Orbison's intellectual property, but also the specific cultural flavor that his song connotes. "Oh, pretty woman" invokes an upbeat, feel-good America projected through the visual image of Julia Roberts. And, as if to make clear the role of "spice" in the cultural transaction involving the song, Barbara Orbison tells us that the songwriter "would be tickled": "'Roy's favorite food was Indian,' she exclaims, adding that she plans her first trip to India—'a date with destiny'...."[41] The relationship between food and ethnicity/culture has been a standard trope for literary and film studies for some time now, and "[o]ne could call 'food porn' a film that reduces cultural rituals around food and eating to a consumable, visual image."[42]

Indeed, Huggan has specified the encounter between India and the West as a process of "consuming India": special issues of *The New Yorker* and *Granta* celebrated the Golden Jubilee of India's independence through "that Western exotic staple, 'Eastern cuisine.'"[43] Along with ethnic performances and carefully crafted tour packages, eating Indian cuisine becomes a literalization of "the mutual consumption of the other."[44] And neither the trope of consuming the other nor the second-level trope of ethnic dining issues from only one side. In its promotional campaigns, the India Tourist Office invites visitors to eat India, such that "India ... is more available than ever for consumption; and more prevalent than ever are the gastronomic images through which the nation is to be consumed."[45] The NBC's consumption of filmsong does not stray from these established tropes and exhibits "a sensorium of the commodity," in which multiple senses are brought to bear on the cultural particularities of the commodities we consume.[46] There is an incredible consistency in the way that we can see the cultural difference in the music we hear, taste its "spices," and either value it or, if you will, throw it up.

I, myself, first became conscious of filmsong as a desirable commodity during a visit in the late 1980s to the Amok bookstore in Los Angeles (now called Koma Books), known for its stock of obscure, and thus ultrahip, merchandise: the mystical roots of Nazism, biographies of serial murderers, explorations of drug culture, and so on. Hearing filmsong in this context made perfect sense since it traveled a significantly different consumer circuit than "poco lit": not a path of literary prestige but of hipster alternativism. Filmsong had already begun to seep into my subconscious while eating at Indian restaurants and while channel surfing past television programs like "Namaste America." My first cassette featured the title *Rare Punjabi Old Songs Selection* not photocopied but mimeographed onto plain orange construction paper, in stark contrast to the color film stills on most of the other cassettes.[47] In the absence of actual knowledge, cassette covers provided my criteria for purchasing.

In my continuing quest for filmsong, the next major find was an S. D. Burman double-feature cassette of songs from *Talash* (The search, O. P. Ralhan, 1969) and *Ishq Par Zor Nahin* (Cannot control love, Ramesh Saigal, 1970).[48] Another find was *Cha Cha Cha* (Chandrashekhar, 1964) with music by Iqbal Qureshi.[49] I happened to come across volume two of *Golden Voices from the Silver Screen* and eventually tracked down volumes one and three. Another interesting discovery was Vijaya Anand's *Dance Raja Dance,* found in a bin of castoff one-dollar CDs.

We must keep in mind that the availability of cultural goods relates also to those consumers not usually interpellated by the commodity— that is, "poachers." This might suggest that cultural borders have broken down sufficiently to no longer be a factor in the consumption of commodities from elsewhere. And though "the continued salience of the nation-state as the key arbiter of important social changes"[50] is certainly disturbed, those borders still nevertheless enact the drama of desire between the self and the other. In relation to filmsong, American taste seems only able to encounter itself as transmuted through filmsong in terms of kitsch—thus, the popularity of a song like "Jaan pehechan ho" with its surf/secret-agent musical stylings. What truly titillates for NBCs in the United States might very well be the quaint echo of the American past reflected back with excess. Even as I try to approach filmsong without the condescension implicit in kitsch, I cannot deny that an "ethnification" of kitsch, as well as a "kitschification" of ethnicity, has taken place.

This intersection between kitsch and cultural difference is precisely where filmsong tends to enter the American market. As the timeline shows, one of the main trajectories into American popular culture for filmsong in addition to world music was through underground music subculture. Filmsong also fits nicely in the tradition of "exotica" music. Exotica saw a resurgence in popularity during the 1990s at roughly the same time that filmsong started to emerge in American culture. In short, filmsong fits very nicely with hipster consumers rediscovering exotica.

Davis was a relatively early commentator on the reception of filmsong in the United States. In a 1992 article for *The Village Voice*, he writes:

> Neither "universal" nor "exotic," the unabashed melodrama of Lata, Asha, and Geeta Dutt invigorates the thousands of miles of cultural difference that lie between Bombay and my living room the way that eyes flirting across a room break down distance while maintaining it at the same time. When Asha Bhosle slides up to a note, she seduces the ear the way a sitar does. When she starts in with the hiccups, coos, and raspy breaths, she just seduces.[51]

Davis appropriately characterizes his encounter with filmsong as an invigoration of cultural difference *and* its denial, the collapse of distance *and* its maintenance. I would agree that this process is *neither* universal nor exotic—paradoxically, it is both. The difference remains, whether as cultural presence (sitar) or converted into desire (sensuality). Huggan provides another way to understand this spatialization of difference:

> These "new" exotic products (African statues, Pacific Island necklaces, Indonesian batiks, and so forth) are characterised, not by remoteness but by *proximity*—by their availability in a shop or streetmarket or shopping-mall somewhere near you....[52]

Filmsong has taken its place among these products. It became available to NBCs in the United States first as cheap cassettes, then as CD compilations, and eventually in British and American cinema. However, the collapsing of distance never fully banishes cultural difference.

Drawing on Michael Taussig's work, Will Straw argues that

> the Third World and its objects are in a global perspective generally seen as permanently "recently outdated," a reservoir of First World hand-me-downs and sleepy-eyed memories of its earlier consumer items.[53]

This outdatedness structures the relationship of American hipster consumers to filmsong in terms of kitsch. It is no accident that most compilations of filmsong directed at the NBC contain the older songs.

Following in the tradition of Arjun Appadurai, Michael Thompson, and others, Straw draws our attention to the global circuits traveled by cultural objects and answers, in part, the question, through what channels in the cultural system of popular music does filmsong infiltrate American popular culture?

Americans had already encountered Indian music in the form of the sitar through the British invasion (for example, the Beatles's "Tomorrow Never Knows"[54] and the Rolling Stones' "Paint It Black"[55]). And who can forget the look of collective ecstasy written on Micky Dolenz's face, jumping out of his seat to applaud Ravi Shankar at the Monterey Pop Festival? What sets the more recent encounter with filmsong apart from these earlier encounters is that filmsong cannot be consumed with the supposed dignity of spirituality and authenticity. As I have suggested, Indian classical music and filmsong often vie for dominance within the archetypal space of the restaurant. Filmsong has been constructed quite differently than classical music: as outlandish, excessive, and kitsch. However, it would be a mistake to reduce the fetishization of filmsong simply to an example of exotic kitschification. The problem is not that the cultural difference embedded in filmsong is fetishized. That difference will always be there, subject to exoticization and kitschification. The more significant problem arises when we try to avoid the ineluctable messiness of difference—that is, when we follow the path of abstraction. The question is whether a Westerner can relate to non-Western music abstractly (and vice versa). This is possible only if we believe that the consumption of cultural difference can be clean, pure of the sticky residue of that difference. And it is not only naïve forms of consumption that are implicated here. Even if we are vigilant and mindful, the consumption will always be dirty. The liberal democratic model requires a consensual amnesis about the remainder resulting from the relocation of cultural particularity from one context to another. When confronting the exotic, there are several possible reactions. We might dismiss outright the exotic excess as inferior to our own culture and, therefore, not worthy of our attention. Or we might celebrate the excess while still defining it as inferior, in which case it becomes kitsch. If we celebrate the excess while defining it as *superior* to our culture, we participate in an equally problematic "reversal" (to borrow a term from the field of intercultural communication). Yet another way we might embrace cultural difference seemingly escapes a judgment of comparative value: "it's just different," we might say, neither bad nor good. This seemingly value-neutral gesture attempts to neutralize difference, erasing it from our consideration altogether (even if it might affect us subconsciously).

If exoticism, as decadent objectification, is an inappropriate response to cultural difference, a universalism that relies on abstraction is unrealistic because it presumes that there exists a clean way to consume commodities across that difference. To the contrary, purity will never occur until there is the possibility of equal exchange in the "aesthetics of decontextualization" (Appadurai). Since it is unlikely that cross-cultural consumption can, or even should, be avoided—and this would be true from whichever direction—the question becomes, what do we do with cultural difference during the process of consumption? Do we disavow it? Do we ignore it? Do we pretend it does not exist?

Introducing Bollywood and Forgetting the Remainder

In a special issue of *Film Comment* devoted to Bollywood, David Chute remarks:

> Most of us have experienced this alternate universe of cinema in puzzling fragments, perhaps as a grainy video image running on the big-screen TV in a Punjabi restaurant. (What's the first image that comes to mind? Pudgy lovers in disco shirts dancing around trees?) Now for the first time, in the new wave of subtitled DVD releases…, we *firangis* have a golden opportunity to turn in our tourist visas and "go native," to become resident aliens of Bollywood.[56]

This desire to go native is one that certainly has its roots in Western imperialism and Orientalism. As a figure of speech, it casts a particular light on the NBC's encounter with Indian film (song). It is not simply an extension of the commodification and consumption of the exotic other, though it is certainly both of those. More importantly, it suggests a desire to encounter the exotic other outside the terms of difference, that is, on the level of abstraction. For Chute:

> it is possible for us *firangis* to have a direct and personal relationship with these films. And in an odd way it seems to be the stylized unreality of the conventional Hindi movie that makes this immediate experience possible

for us, because no matter how strange these spectacles seem on the surface, you still get a sense of the hospitable human beings who were hard at
work behind the scenes, pulling the strings for our pleasure.[57]

What would a direct and personal relationship entail? Was there ever any
doubt that hospitable human beings were behind the scenes, as if the perceived cultural outlandishness in Bollywood film suggests the inhuman,
the alien? (The answer is probably yes.) Chute must revert to abstract uni-
versality in order to manage the anxiety of difference: "human beings."
Regardless of intention, difference very simply and inevitably exists.

I do not mean to be unduly flippant with Chute's remarks. His are
sincere questions and I would presume many of us share similar sentiments or at least hope that an acceptable way to engage with "the
exotic" exists. Chute's remarks are merely a convenient opportunity
through which to understand the larger encounter between American
popular culture and Indian film (song). We all reside in difference, after
all, and yet we yearn for that uncorrupted condition, which might be
more appropriately thought of in terms of antisepsis or even prophy-
laxis: we want to be able to neutralize the alien microbes of difference so
that we can penetrate the membrane that separates us from the exotic
other without harm to either party. In other words, this is a condition
where the social complications evoked by difference are not in play, a
moment of abstraction as hypothesized by liberal democracy.

Critical race theory attempts to reembody the law to save it from
liberal colorblindness, naming a problem inherent in the history of the
United States, which has always needed to accommodate racial (and
sexual) difference while figuring its constituency as abstract, and thus
equal, citizens.[58] And as Lauren Berlant suggests

> it is possible to see the history of the Constitution as a record of the
> nation's gradual recognition that it needs officially to theorize an ideal
> relation between its abstract "citizen" and the person who lives,
> embodied, an everyday life.[59]

It is precisely the embodiment of racialized difference that becomes the
problem when encountering exotic cultural objects.

Slavoj Žižek's analysis of democratic abstraction is particularly useful
in thinking about the messiness of difference.[60] In the process of abstraction, as we disavow our social particularity, something remains as a "stain"
forever marking the event. The production of this stain is coextensive

with democracy itself; the latter cannot exist without the former. Even as we participate in democracy as abstract citizens without particularity, this "remainder" (Žižek's term) haunts us and becomes available for reinscription. The remainder, in fact, requires reinscription in order for the ideological fantasy of abstraction to work. Often, we inscribe the remainder as a form of racial otherness: the black, the Jew, the Arab, and the Oriental. The remainder is what prevents cross-cultural consumption from ever being clean; it is always dirty, smeared with difference.

In place of some pristine encounter with cultural difference, I would offer one that is inevitably sullied, dripping with clinging residues—those complicated chains of meaning, power, and history that constitute cultural difference—something more akin to what Maithili Rao suggests about Bollywood's reception in the West: "an unacknowledged visceral response to the lurid seductions of an unclassifiable genre that glories in its excesses with naïve unself-consciousness, and takes for granted an astonishing level of stylization."[61] I would take this even further and suggest we need to consider our experience with cultural objects not only in terms of Sobchack's "cinesthetic" subject, but also what Marks calls "the skin of the film": "Audiovisual images call up conscious, unconscious, and nonsymbolic associations with touch, taste, and smell, which themselves are not experienced as separate."[62] We also need to take a question Rao raises to heart: "can't [Indian] song-and-dance melodramas infiltrate *firangi* sensibilities shaped by Hollywood genres and European art cinema?"—infiltrate, that is, rather than being "either condescendingly dismissed or seen as a cultural curiosity, a species of Oriental exotica or a Third World artifact to be deconstructed by academics exhausting yet another post-colonial territory."[63] But would infiltration really deliver us from either exotica or academic opportunism? And if infiltration does somehow indicate a more acceptable encounter with Indian film (song), how would it be different? I fear it would be more pristine, floating above difference.

Jacob Levich gives us another caveat:

> It's zany, extravagant, kitschy. It's delightfully (or fabulously) cheesy (or tacky). It's mad, wild, wacky, over-the-top. Campy. Exotic. Transgressive. Liberating. Et cetera. Et cetera. Et cetera.
>
> Film critics always reach into the same bag of breathless adjectives when trying to sell Bollywood movies to non-Indian audiences. If the words ring a bell, it's because you're hearing the vocabulary of cult-movie special pleading, equally handy for touting direct-to-video

horror, chopsocky extravaganzas, and all-midget musical Westerns. It's the language of bad faith. We use it to hedge our bets when we're not confident that our particular obsessions will stand up to serious critical scrutiny. At the same time, we use it to praise ourselves: Aren't we special for loving this unconventional, demotic, multicultural stuff? And aren't we, well, ever so slightly *superior* to it?[64]

Levich is right, and his remarks apply equally to filmsong. Part of my purpose here has been to interrogate how NBCs consume filmsong in the United States, which is to say my own consumption. There is an element of exotic fascination involved that implicates me in the dirt and residue of cultural difference. To avoid bad faith, Levich appraises the equivalence of Golden Age Bollywood films with those of Hollywood. Thus, Guru Dutt's *Kaagaz Ke Phool* (Paper flowers, 1959) is as good as Vincente Minnelli's *The Bad and the Beautiful* (1952), P. C. Barua's *Devdas* (1935) is as good as *Citizen Kane* (1941), and so forth. But placing Bollywood in the context of high art is no better. I would not argue with Levich's claims, but is it more a matter of incommensurability than equivalence? Equivalence would require that difference can be cut off from both object and consumer and that the two can interact in the abstract space of liberal democracy. Is liberal democratic humanism the best model for understanding the NBC's encounter with filmsong? I would say no. It is as much a mistake to ignore or splice out difference as it is to exoticize that difference. The question to ask is, are we ever really clean?

The encounter with filmsong by NBCs elicits an anxiety over what to do with the cultural difference filmsong embodies, an anxiety that is encouraged by the intersection of liberal democratic humanism, global capitalism, and the desire for multiculturalism. The anxiety simultaneously highlights and negates difference by provoking an impulse not only to exoticize cultural difference but also to negate its messiness through abstraction. If we are able to reject the desire for pristine consumption, this leaves us needing a model of consumption that can account for cultural difference in all its messiness.

I also want to resist slipping into a model of hybridity that can fall too quickly into an easy commingling of differences. What we need—and I am afraid I must end by articulating a desire instead of a solution—is a model of consumption that (1) takes seriously the physicality involved in consuming cultural difference through food or artifact (a cultural phenomenology), (2) acknowledges the positioning of subjects in (geo)social space à la Bourdieu (a critical sociopolitics), and (3) is self-conscious about the subjective and objective terms of evaluation (a reflexive aesthetics). In order to move beyond liberal democratic abstraction, we must edge ever closer to an acknowledgment of filthy embodiment. Charles Johnson describes how this might look in terms of race:

> as a black, [I am] seen as a stained body, as physicality, basically opaque to others—a possibility that, of course, whites themselves have in a room of blacks.... My world is epidermalized, collapsed like a house of cards into the stained casement of my skin.[65]

We also see it in the feminist theory that tries to rescue the body by way of phenomenologically inclined Continental philosophy; for Elizabeth Grosz, corporeality is inextricable from difference: "Alterity is the very possibility and process of embodiment."[66] Sobchack's construction of a cinesthetic film theory draws on a more general desire:

> It is not only personally but also politically important that we inform critical thought and cultural studies with a phenomenological understanding of the body that includes and resonates with our ownbodies— that is, bodies not merely objectively beheld but also subjectively lived. Unlike the beheld body, this lived body provides the material premises for meaning—giving ethical gravity to semiotic and textual production and circulation.[67]

If we accept all these pleas to ground our epistemology in the body— inevitably a dirty, messy process—it is incumbent upon us to apply this understanding to the consumption of cultural difference, whether as image, text, sound, or food. We need to reconcile ourselves to the inevitable stains that mark the consumption of filmsong and to move toward a critical practice that can move beyond the fantasy of liberal democracy's abstractions.

Notes

1   Graham Huggan, *The Postcolonial Exotic: Marketing the Margins* (New York: Routledge, 2001), 59, 67.
2   Although Bollywood is a supremely global phenomenon, I am here concerned with a mainstream American consumer who does not grow up with Bollywood as a cultural legacy.
3   Celeste Olalquiaga, "The Dark Side of Modernity's Moon," *Celeste's World* (1992), http://celesteolalquiaga.com/moon.html. In addition to its early

origins in the mid-1800s, the term became important in attempts to define the authenticity of art during the 1930s by Hermann Bloch and Clement Greenberg and in the 1960s by Umberto Eco and Susan Sontag: kitsch is, respectively, "earthly, not cosmic"; a product of "industrialisation and massification, capitalism and consumer culture"; "passing for real art"; and "stultifying." However, kitsch was also reclaimed by Walter Benjamin as allowing "a more intense experience of the world," and more recently, the same has been done in alternative subcultures. See also Celeste Olalquiaga, *The Artificial Kingdom: A Treasury of the Kitsch Experience* (New York: Pantheon, 1998).

4 Pierre Bourdieu, *Distinction: A Social Critique of the Judgment of Taste*, trans. Richard Nice (Cambridge, Mass.: Harvard University Press, 1984), 6.

5 Ibid., 62, 282.

6 Celeste Olalquiaga, "The Pandemoniac Junk Shop of Solitude: Kitsch and Death," *Celeste's World* (1993), http://celesteolalquiaga.com/solitude.html.

7 For another reading of Bollywood as kitsch, see Dudrah's essay in this collection.

8 David Theo Goldberg, *Racist Culture: Philosophy and the Politics of Meaning* (Cambridge, Mass.: Blackwell, 1994), 4.

9 Vivan Sobchack, *Carnal Thoughts: Embodiment and Moving Image Culture* (Berkeley: University of California Press, 2004), 196–97. Proprioception is "that sixth and grounding sense we have of ourselves as positioned and embodied in worldly space, that sense that could be said to provide us our body image but for the fact that such an image emerges not from the objective sight of our bodies (or directly from vision) but from the invisible and subjective lived feeling of our material being" (192).

10 Goldberg, *Racist Culture,* 6.

11 Luce Irigaray, *I Love to You*, quoted in Pheng Cheah and Elizabeth Grosz, "On Being-Two: Introduction," *Diacritics* 28, no. 1 (1998): 14.

12 Paul Willemen, *Looks and Frictions: Essays in Cultural Studies and Film Theory* (Bloomington: Indiana University Press, 1994), 210–11.

13 Frederick Buell, "Nationalist Postnationalism: Globalist Discourse in Contemporary American Culture," *American Quarterly* 50, no. 3 (1998). Buell claims nationalism reasserts itself in a seemingly postnationalist context (550–53, 557–62).

14 Huggan, *The Postcolonial Exotic,* 16.

15 See Bhattacharjya and Mehta's essay for another reading of this timeline.

16 *There'll Always Be Stars in the Sky*, VHS, 1983, dir. Jeremy Marre (London: Harcourt Films/Shanachie, 1992).

17 Compiled by Ben Mandelson, Ace Records, CDORBD 54, 56, 59, copyright 1990, three compact discs.

18 As pointed out elsewhere in this collection, *Golden Voices* interpellates a diasporic audience living in England but nostalgic for Bollywood rather than NBCs, who consume it nevertheless.

19 Asia Classics Volume 1, Luaka Bop/Sire Records/Warner Bros, 9 26847-2, copyright 1992, compact disc.

20 Luaka Bop, "Label," http://www.luakabop.com/label/index.php3.

21 Amarillo Records, AM 597, 1994, 7-inch record.

22 Toronto, Canada: Lions Gate, 1995.

23 *When I Was Born for the 7th Time*, Luaka Bop/Warner Bros, 9 46576-2, copyright 1997, compact disc.

24 Prod. Dan the Automator, Motel Records, Room 3, copyright 1998, compact disc.

25 Prod. Stephen Abry and Rudy Burr, Q. D. K. Media/Normal, CD 033, copyright 2000, compact disc.

26 *Ghost World,* DVD, dir. Terry Zwigoff (Santa Monica, CA: MGM Home Entertainment, 2002). Ghost World's production date was 2000; however, it premiered in June 2001 at the Seattle International Film Festival. I have chosen not to discuss *Monsoon Wedding* and *Moulin Rouge* since they are discussed at length elsewhere in this collection.

27 *Gumnaam*, DVD (London: Eros Multimedia, 2000). (Music by Shankar-Jaikishan.)

28 Thanks to Sangita Gopal and Sujata Moorti for pointing this out to me.

29 See the reviews of the film by David Germain, "At the Movies: 'Ghost World,' " *Associated Press*, July 17, 2001, and Carla Meyer, "Clueless but Trying Hard to Connect," *San Francisco Chronicle*, February 8, 2002, D10.

30 Prod. Adrian Milan and Christina Bates, Motel Records, Room 5, copyright 2001, compact disc.

31 *Doob Doob O'Rama 2: More Filmsongs from Bollywood* (compilation), prod. Rudy Burr, Q. D. K. Media/Normal, CD 036, copyright 2001, compact disc.

32 The Mondo Series, Ark 21, 186 850 033 2, copyright 2001. One would think that the term "mondo" stands for "the exotic," because there is nothing necessarily "mondo" in Rahman's music.

33 See chapter by Biswary Son for a different understanding of R. D. Burman's with world music.

34 Compiled by Tom Hingston, Nascente/Demon Music Group, NSCD 090, copyright 2001, compact disc.

35 World Music Network, RGNET 1074, copyright 2002.

36 Ninja Tune, 70, copyright 2002.

37 Laura U. Marks, *The Skin of the Film: Intercultural Cinema, Embodiment, and the Senses* (Durham, N.C.: Duke University Press, 2000), 245.

38 Erik Davis, "The Big Playback: Indian Film Music," http://www.techgnosis.com/playback.html (originally published in *The Village Voice*, 1992).

39 "Oh, Pretty Woman," 1964, *16 Biggest Hits*, Sony, 69738, copyright 1998, compact disc.

40 Quoted in Jim Bessman, "Orbison Goes Bollywood," *Billboard*, December 20, 2003, 64.

41 Ibid.

42 Marks, *The Skin of the Film,* 234.

43 Huggan, *The Postcolonial Exotic,* 60.

44 Ibid., 67.

45 Ibid., 82.

46 Marks, *The Skin of the Film,* 245.

47 Classic Movie Club, n.d.

48 Original motion picture sound tracks, HMV/Gramophone Company of India, STHV 42851, copyright 1988, audiocassette.

49 Original motion picture sound track, EMI/Gramophone Company of India, SPHO 44377, copyright 1990, audiocassette.

50 Arjun Appadurai, *Modernity at Large: Cultural Dimensions of Globalization* (Minneapolis: University of Minnesota Press, 1996), 4.

51 Davis, "Big Playback."

52 Huggan, *The Postcolonial Exotic*, 15.

53 Will Straw, "Exhausted Commodities: The Material Culture of Music," *Canadian Journal of Communication* 25, no. 1 (Winter 2000): 6, http://www.cjc-online.ca/viewarticle.php?id=571&layout=html.

54 *Revolver*, Capitol, CDP 7 464412 2, copyright 1966, compact disc.

55 *Aftermath*, ABKCO, 719476, copyright 1966, compact disc.

56 David Chute, "Bollywood Rising: A Beginner's Guide to Hindi Cinema," *Film Comment* 38, no. 3 (May–June 2002): 36.

57 Ibid.

58 See Kimberlé Crenshaw, Neil Gotanda, Gary Peller, and Kendall Thomas, "Introduction," in *Critical Race Theory: The Key Writings That Formed the Movement*, ed. Kimberlé Crenshaw, Neil Gotanda, Gary Peller, and Kendall Thomas (New York: New Press, 1995).

59 Lauren Berlant, *The Anatomy of National Fantasy: Hawthorne, Utopia, and Everyday Life* (Chicago: University of Chicago Press, 1991), 13.

60 The following comments are derived from *The Sublime Object of Ideology* (New York: Verso, 1989) and "Formal Democracy and Its Discontents," *American Imago* 48, no. 2 (1991): 181–98. I have also written about Žižek's treatment of the remainder as it relates to difference and abstraction elsewhere: Edward K. Chan, "Subject of Utopia" (PhD diss., University of Rochester, 2004), 59–68.

61 Maithili Rao, "How to Read a Hindi Film and Why," *Film Comment* 38, no. 3 (May–June 2002): 37.

62 Marks, *The Skin of the Film*, 222.

63 Rao, "How to Read a Hindi Film," 37.

64 Jacob Levich, "Freedom Songs: Rediscovering Bollywood's Golden Age," *Film Comment* 38, no. 3 (May–June 2002): 48 (original emphasis).

65 Charles Johnson, "A Phenomenology of the Black Body," *Michigan Quarterly Review* 32, no. 4 (1993): 606.

66 Elizabeth Grosz, *Volatile Bodies: Toward a Corporeal Feminism* (Bloomington: Indiana University Press, 1994), 209.

67 Sobchack, *Carnal Thoughts*, 187.

11. Queer as Desis

Secret Politics of Gender and Sexuality in Bollywood Films in Diasporic Urban Ethnoscapes

Rajinder Dudrah

2002 was the year of Bollywood in Britain—the celebrated product displays at Selfridges, the opening of Andrew Lloyd Weber's *Bombay Dreams,* and Bollywood-inspired fashion and accessories at Top Man, Top Shop, and H&M were all governed by an aesthetics of excess that has, by now, become synonymous with the global image of Bollywood. This stylistic excess, read as kitsch and camp, was highlighted in the commodification of Bollywood by the mainstream culture, fashion, and entertainment industries in the United Kingdom. Ironically, this very style has, until recently, disqualified Bollywood from serious consideration in Western film scholarship. Bollywood cinema was viewed as trivial and escapist, created to feed the entertainment needs of the masses.[1] While consumer culture's embrace of Bollywood style can hardly be called political, it nonetheless draws attention to this long-neglected cinema and invites us to reevaluate Bollywood style as a cultural resource.

This chapter will explore the politics of Bollywood style by looking at how this aesthetic has been appropriated by queer desis in the diaspora to read themselves back into Bollywood cinema.[2] Thus, I draw attention to the difference between camp as commodity and camp as a mode and means to cultural and political identity.[3] Bollywood's emergence as cosmopolitan style is linked to the queer use of Bollywood by its urban South Asian and diasporic audiences; while the queer appropriation enhances Bollywood's cool quotient, its commodification is apolitical. Here, I will examine how queer desis in the United Kingdom make sense of and recreate in the diaspora the politics of Bollywood as a cinema of the masses. I will also allude to how these strategies differ from white mainstream queer practices around Hollywood.

While the aesthetics of Bollywood films, particularly as inscribed in the songs and dances, are embedded in and arise out of culturally specific contexts, they are also constantly subject to slippage around issues of gender and sexuality. They warrant consideration as promiscuous and unstable texts moving in and out and in-between heteronormative and queer desires and sensibilities. Although a number of recent academic studies have theorized Bollywood in complex and interesting ways, they rarely deal explicitly with sexuality.[4] I will use readings of Indian cinema by Ashis Nandy and Madhava Prasad as a framework for thinking popular cinema's relation to politics. I will then use Arjun Appadurai's concepts of ethno- and mediascapes to track the translation that Bollywood makes from national to diasporic spaces. I will bring these studies into dialogue with a body of work that addresses queer readings of Bollywood cinema.[5] I will use this theoretical frame to offer a reading of the pleasures of gender and sexuality at a British Asian gay and lesbian club night focusing in particular on translations and recreations of song-dance sequences at these sites.

Bollywood's Secret Politics of the Everyman/woman

Let us begin with Ashis Nandy. Nandy argues that the vantage of popular Hindi cinema is that of the everyman/woman—the lower middle classes and the slum dwellers—and this accounts for the directness, vigor, and crudeness of its language and aesthetics:

> An average, "normal," Bombay film has to be, to the extent possible, everything to everyone. It has to cut across the myriad ethnicities and lifestyles of India and even of the world that impinges on India. The popular film is low-brow, modernizing India in all its complexity, sophistry, naivete and vulgarity. Studying popular film is studying Indian modernity at its rawest, its crudities laid bare by the fate of traditions in contemporary life and arts. Above all, it is studying caricatures of ourselves.[6]

Nandy's idea about a caricature of selfhood can be usefully extended to think about a notion of self-identity as constituted by the consumption of Bollywood films. He claims that not only is popular cinema implicated in and shaped by politics, but more significantly, it *constitutes the language for a new form of politics*. Bollywood thus serves as a cultural resource—supplying the semantic and visual cues for the political practice of queer desis in the diaspora. But before we get to that through Appadurai, it is important to heed the words of Madhava Prasad.

Ideology and Bollywood Cinema

Prasad draws on Marxist ideas of ideology and applies them to popular Hindi cinema.[7] He focuses on the 1970s period in India where he demonstrates that a change in social and political ideology was under way as part of the fragmentation of the postindependence national consensus, which was brought about by shifts in political alignments. For Prasad, these shifts challenged the aesthetic conventions and mode of production of the Indian film industry of the time, causing it to split into three categories: art cinema, middlebrow cinema, and commercial cinema.[8] Prasad claims that popular cinema affirmed the status quo and was complicit in reproducing existing social relations. Although Prasad can help us grasp the heteronormative ideology of Hindi cinema, we should also pay attention to how ideology is reworked and contested in and through the signs and codes that Bollywood cinema might offer us as constituting the language for a new form of politics, especially one based around the queer pleasures of gender and sexuality. Furthermore, Prasad's critique of Bollywood cinema's role in hegemonic formation also operates within the framework of the nation-state. The appearance of Bollywood songs and dances in the queer spaces of the diaspora requires a careful consideration of the relationship of the homeland and its diaspora.[9]

Bollywood and Diasporic Mediascapes

This leads us to the work of Arjun Appadurai. While Nandy and Prasad write about the Indian context, we need to think more about how their useful ideas can be incorporated and translated in the Indian and South Asian diasporic context. Appadurai offers a useful perspective for understanding the relationship between cultural texts and social experience as elaborated through the concept of the imagination. He argues that new possibilities are often suggested imaginatively through the production of, and in and through the performance of, sounds and images in texts. Moreover, he elaborates how global social flows are part of a "disjunctive" order of economies and cultural signs, which are played out between "ethnoscapes," the landscapes of living persons, and "mediascapes," "image-centred, narrative based accounts of strips of reality."[10]

The availability of mediascapes for diasporic ethnic groups in their countries of settlement is especially pertinent here. An ethnic mediascape, such as Bollywood, offers an audiovisual site where ideas of the homeland can be translated and negotiated in the places of diasporic settlement.[11] Bollywood supplies the sounds and images that constitute a diasporic imaginary. In this imaginary, the place of origin and country of settlement inform each other and the diasporic subject fashions new sensibilities of being and belonging. The diasporic imaginary becomes part of the everyday of diasporic subjects, as the sounds and images of mediascapes are integrated into the routines and rituals of daily life, as well as the struggles for settlement and belonging. Appadurai's work, then, allows us to examine the place of imagination, fantasy, and desire in everyday social practices. The imagination as expressed through dream sequences, songs, music, television, film, and stories offers a repertoire of possibilities to grasp the subjects' social world as it articulates with global ideas and cultural processes. This articulation allows for an engagement with the subjects' immediate sense of self and for the contemplation of a wider set of possible lives. Thus, Nandy, Prasad, and Appadurai provide useful frameworks for analyzing the translations of Bollywood cinema that take place in the diasporic urban ethnoscape of the British Asian gay and lesbian club night. Before moving on to an analysis of this site, let us consider some recent queer readings of Bollywood cinema to see how they engage this critical framework.

Queering Bollywood

Although East Asian cinema seemed explicitly queer in aesthetic and content, popular Indian cinema seemed to work more implicitly such that queerness emerged as queer audiences reread the heteronormative film text such that it yielded other sensibilities. Gayatri Gopinath draws on cultural theory and feminist audience studies to argue that Bolly-wood cinema provides queer diasporic audiences with the means by which to reimagine and reterritorialize the homeland by making it the locus of queer desire and pleasure. Gopinath is interested in tracing the "interpretive interventions and appropriations" made by queer dias-poric audiences of Bollywood films. She employs a "queer diasporic viewing practice" in order to see articulations of same-sex desire in par-ticular examples of popular Hindi cinema throughout the diegesis of the film, even when the film has an orthodox heterosexual ending.[12] Rather than attempt to look for gays and lesbians in Bollywood, she is more interested in "looking for the moments emerging at the fissures of rigidly heterosexual structures that can be transformed into queer imag-inings."[13] Gopinath goes on to read the possibilities offered by images that suggest gay, lesbian, and *hijra* or transgendered modes of being.

As a result of such tracings, the queer diasporic subjectivity put forward by Gopinath is the product of dominant Euro-American con-structions of gay and lesbian identity brought into dialogue with the experience of South Asian queers who negotiate between the spaces of multiple homes, communities, and nations across the cultural registers of the East and the West.[14] This is a useful formulation of the queer diasporic subjectivity, as it does not privilege a European mode of understanding or performing of queer cultural identity at the cost of its Asian counterpart, but rather asks for an analysis of the communicative dialogue that is possible when the two different sensibilities interact. Although Gopinath posits this fascinating exchange between European and Asian queer cultural identity at a theoretical level, she never really demonstrates the articulation of the two. She tends to privilege the queer diaspora and the readings that take place within it (that is, as reimagining the homeland) without due consideration to the queer pos-sibilities in the homeland or the reciprocating social flows between the homeland and its diasporas. I will address this briefly by looking, in conclusion, at Bollywood cinema's increasing attention to queer themes and representations in recent years.

Rao and Kavi analyze some of the key motifs and signifying codes of Bollywood films to show how these are interpreted by its queer audi-ences. For example, Rao describes the motifs of *yaar* (friend and/or lover) and *yaari* (friendship) as expressed in the lyrics and picturization of song sequences as recapitulated in queer subculture as a yearning for an affec-tionate same-sex relationship.[15] Kavi outlines the changing image of the male hero in Hindi films over some five decades to suggest how the contemporary male body, and in particular the semiclad and gym-fit physique of 1990s star Salman Khan, has been ambiguously paraded and eroticized on-screen such that its appeal exceeds straight pleasures.[16] Furthermore, Rao reveals the social practices of urban Indian cinema-viewing that are also made queer in the dark spaces of the cinema hall patronized largely by men. Here, close physical contact and same-sex intimacy can and does occur, and as Rao describes one of his visits to the cinema, "[a]s the lights went off, the action began, so to speak, both on the screen and off it."[17] Both, Rao's and Kavi's works, then, suggest that the formulation of Indian queer identity, and gay urban Indian identity in particular, as taking shape in relation to the hierarchy of male sexuality (where men have greater access and control to public spaces and can thus express, if implicitly, their same-sex desires). Here, subversion and a reading against the grain of the heteronormative Bollywood diegesis is often a recurring strategy of existence. Extending this work, then, does the homosocial polysemy of popular film music also permit queer identifications in Bollywood's transnational circuits?

Thomas Waugh draws on the anthropology of Lawrence Cohen's exploration of male same-sex activities in Benares, India, to examine "the profuse and rigidly ambiguous indigenous male-male sexual iconographies" in contemporary Bollywood cinema.[18] By exploring queer readings of male-buddy moments in films such as *Sholay* (Flames, Ramesh Sippy, 1975) and *Main Khiladi Tu Anari* (I am the player, you are the amateur, Sameer Malkan, 1994), Waugh outlines how the cultural devices of *khel* (play/playfulness) and *dosti* (friendship) between the on-screen heroes (which involves the use of sexual innuendos, phallic symbols, and the close proximity of male bodies in intimate postures) can be read as an implicit homosocial sphere that operates within and yet beyond the predominant heterosexual reel and real life.[19] Waugh usefully posits that devices such as same-sex *khel* and *dosti* challenge and redefine the rules of heterosexual gazes and desires as the dominant and only modes of seeing and interacting.[20] Such devices allow queer audiences to view themselves and their heroes and heroines as simultaneously visible and invisible, polyvocal, and ambiguous.[21] Elaborating on Waugh further, how does the transnational circulation of Hindi film music invest these textual ambiguities with new libidinal possibilities?

Let us now incorporate these queer readings of popular Hindi cinema within the theoretical framework of Nandy, Prasad, and Appadurai as formulated above. Gopinath's, Rao's, Kavi's, and Waugh's approach to Bollywood exemplify Nandy's hypothesis of popular Indian cinema as consisting of tacit or secret cultural politics relating to the projects of self-identity and nationhood. Such politics become more pressing and engaging as these readings insist that the queer in Bollywood needs to be included as a part of the discussion of Bollywood cinema and its audiences. Rao, Kavi, and Waugh emphasize local audiences in India and Gopinath attends to the queer diaspora. This article articulates the local and global manifestations in a reciprocal dialogue by focusing on Bollywood's song and dance sequences in particular. Developing the work of Prasad, how might we account for the reworking of the heterosexual ideology of gender and sexuality in queer Bollywood spaces? Using the insights of Appadurai, we might begin to understand the diasporic queer urban ethnoscape of the gay and lesbian club as an imaginative site and ask to what extent the social strategies and cultural devices as described by Gopinath, Rao, Kavi, and Waugh are also prevalent and translated in such spaces. Furthermore, is the homeland simply reconfigured in the queer diaspora, or does the homeland also respond to the queer diaspora, or vice versa, albeit in secret ways?[22]

The Diasporic Urban Ethnoscape of the South Asian Gay and Lesbian Club Night

The qualitative and participant observations that I draw on and outline in this section were witnessed and experienced at a particular Asian gay and lesbian club in the United Kingdom. But the description that follows could apply to any one of the growing Asian gay and lesbian club nights in Birmingham,[23] Leicester,[24] London,[25] or Manchester[26] (all U.K.-based) or even perhaps in New York[27] and elsewhere. To conceive of such a club night as a diasporic urban ethnoscape is to attend to the social and cultural interactions between people and their mediascapes.[28] These interactions draw on signs and codes from various homelands that have arrived at a new place of settlement and offer multiple, or at least new, modes of being that shift between the homeland and the place of residence. The club night thus offers an empirical template from which we can engage with some of the theoretical issues and queer textual readings put forth earlier.

An advertising banner from the Birmingham-based Saathi Night's Web site, which uses images of Bollywood stars as queer icons and aesthetics.

To describe the club night as a "gay and lesbian" one is in keeping with the way queer desi clubgoers think about these events. The term "gay and lesbian," then, is used as a shorthand to describe the club's eclectic clientele but is meant in no way to exclude the diverse peoples, sexualities, and personalities who frequent the clubs. Clubgoers include Asian drag queens, *hijras* or transgendered people, cross-dressers, bisexuals, queer-friendly straights, straight couples, and those who might just be exploring or passing through. The people who regularly attend the club where I conducted my analysis include Asians (predominantly South Asians and also other Asians), Africans and Caribbeans, and Caucasians too—a metropolitan and racially diverse mix of people indicative of the cultural and social exchanges and possibilities at this diasporic site of reception. The club is, therefore, a cosmopolitan nodal point on the transnational movement of Bollywood music. Thus, an understanding of queer desi identities in this club space needs to be located and explored through the different social registers and cultural performances of race and ethnicity, gender and sexuality as articulating together.

The particular club venue under analysis has a large square dance floor fronted by a raised stage. On the back wall of the stage is a white canvas—similar to that of a small cinema screen—on which images from Bollywood movies are projected. Opposite the stage and on the other side of the dance floor is the DJ booth that overlooks the dance space. From the center of the ceiling hangs a large shiny disco ball amid other sophisticated discotheque lighting. The club night is almost always held on a Friday, so there is a start of the weekend euphoria that is articulated with the prowess of gender and sexual pleasures. These pleasures include girls eyeing girls, girls eyeing boys, boys eyeing boys, boys eyeing girls, and more besides these, and almost everyone is overcome with a desire to dance and exalt in their bodily performances. One of the friends I was there with suggested that it was "like being at an Indian wedding party after all the official ritual and ceremonies have taken place, only this is a bit more fun, more risky"—a comment that affirmed the secret politics referred to above.[29] In fact there seems to be a continuity, here, as well as a new line of flight between the diaspora's appropriation of the homeland through Bollywood and the queer diaspora's uses of the same, because Bollywood movie clips and song and dance sequences are often used at South Asian weddings and other community gatherings such as beauty pageants. The articulation of social desires and fantasies to do with the homeland are also possibly similar—an articulation of referents from the homeland and the place of settlement professing dual or multiple cultural sensibilities. However, the issue of sexuality is often an unspoken and silent register in the enactment of cultural identities at diasporic community events and this is where the queer desi club night offers an explicit engagement with issues of gender and sexuality. The space of the club is highlighted further as a marker of gender and sexual difference within the South Asian diaspora itself.

Fashion predominates at the club as vibrant colors and South Asian dress styles coalesce with the best of Western haute couture. Seventy percent of the music is a mixture of Bollywood, bhangra, Arabic pop, rap, and Anglo-Asian fusion music, while the remainder blends R&B, ragga, and hip-hop, with the odd dash of pop thrown in for good measure; the tracks of Kylie Minogue often feature as pop classics in this club. This mélange of musical genres testifies to the clubgoers' eclectic cultural identities, and they also signify certain kinds of identities that are enabled on the dance floor through a performance of the self. These include fluid gender and sexual identities produced by some of the more promiscuous melodies and lyrics of the songs from each of the genres, and at the same time, urban and racialized identities are evoked through a singing and dancing out of some of the more urban politicized lyrics and music—British bhangra, Anglo-Asian fusion, rap, ragga, and hip-hop being cases in point.[30] Not only are South Asian gay and lesbian identities constructed and celebrated in the queer desi club space, they are also articulated with brown skins and ethnic identities that negotiate the inequalities of racism, gender, and sexuality that exist not only in heteronormative spaces but also in predominantly white gay and lesbian spaces.[31] The queer desi club is a safe space and its dance floor is an interesting outlet that allows these kinds of performances to take place. The dance floor is a site where identities are rendered mobile through a play of actual bodily movements and embodied gestures that use fantasy and the imagination to interact with the music and create a queer ambience in the club.

Amid the performance of selves on the dance floor, one can also witness some of Bollywood's key motifs of *yaar* and *yaari,* the signifying codes of the eroticized body and the cultural devices of *khel* and *dosti* as acted out and translated in this diasporic space. In order to illustrate this performance, I want to draw on three practices that I experienced and partook of at the club on more than one occasion. First, the Bollywood tracks that are frequently played, both in their original and in their remixed versions, feature lyrics professing love for one's *yaar* or the desire to be in *yaari*—for instance, "Mera yaar bura dildaara ..." ("My friend/lover is truly a braveheart"), "Tu mera yaar, tu mera pyaar ..." ("You are my friend/lover, you are my love"), and "Aaja ve mere yaar ..." ("Come on my friend/lover"). Here, the notion of *yaar* and *yaari* is clearly wrenched from its heterosexual context and recast for queer affect and the display of same-sex affection. Moreover, this rereading of *yaar/yaari* is further layered through the fusion of different musical genres (Bollywood bhangra beats and Afro-American rap). Not only is the original heterosexual version of *yaar/yaari* changed into a queer one, the queer *yaar/yaari* is further nuanced through the mixture of international music genres that signify new musical sounds and fluid social identities in the United Kingdom. Here, queer identities coalesce with and negotiate ethnic and racial identities. In this way, the homosocial polysemy of popular Hindi film music permits queer identifications that are also sensitive to and relevant for the lives of queer desis across Bollywood's transnational circuits.

The second practice involves the relationship of the dancing body to the Bollywood images projected on the white canvas on stage. On this occasion, the dance floor is packed and we are halfway through the club night. Sweating bodies infused with cologne and decorated with colorful glitter groove the night away. One track comes to an end and the other begins. The new track is "Chaiyya, Chaiyya" ("Walk in the shadow of love") from the film *Dil Se* (From the heart, Mani Ratnam, 1998). The crowd shouts in excitement and begins to mimic the dance steps of actor Shahrukh Khan and his gypsy-girl consort (Malaika Arora Khan) from the film, with hips swaying, pelvics thrusting, and arms waving about in the air—this is one of their queer performances to shout out to and to make their own.[32] A momentary lapse occurs between the on-screen mediascape in the club and the song playing over the club's sound system. The audio of the song is a few seconds ahead of its projected image.

The "Chaiyya, Chaiyya" clip on-screen has also been edited and is interspersed with songs from other Bollywood movies; of note is the flashing torso of Salman Khan gyrating. The dancing bodies on the dance floor are a few paces ahead of the dancing figures in the moving image. This moment is telling of the ways in which gender and sexual pleasures are aestheticized in different yet related ways. In the film, Shahrukh Khan is mesmerized after having just met his on-screen heroine, Manisha Koirala, and breaks into song and dance, affirming his newfound heterosexual love. In the club, the crowd also registers this filmic moment while simultaneously reclaiming and acknowledging the song as one of their queer anthems. The straight aesthetics on the screen are there to be seen as part of the literal backdrop to the club's setting, while in the foreground, club-goers both mimic and perform this song-dance number in queer ways. The singing and dancing on the dance floor is a few paces ahead of its on-screen version both literally and symbolically. The further editing of the *Dil Se* film clip with images of the naked torso of Salman Khan also deliberately queers and displaces the dominant straight aesthetics of the clip to enable new pleasures around gender, sexuality, and the dancing of the body. The physical use of the body in dance, here, plays with conventional and expected patterns of heteronormativity. Signifiers of perceived masculine and feminine traits are used by both genders, mingled with Bollywood, Westernized and black urban street moves, and queer displays of eclectic sexual identities, thereby creating a stylized camp performance. Within this performative space, a caricature of conservative heterosexual expectations of how men and women should conduct themselves sexually is put in play. Males on males, females on females, and males and females alternate with each other, playing up "butch" and "passive" body movements and dance gestures and thereby exaggerate normative gender and sexual ideologies. Through feminine and masculine screams, yells, and screeches and through the repertoire of their dress and vivid colors— almost costume-like—the club revelers also emphasize and play up their own camp performances. Caricature, in this instance, works to recreate a performance about heterosexuality and its limits in order to make way for a queer semantics and also to render a specific performativity about South Asian queerness in the club space.

The third instance exemplifies how *khel* takes place in the club and consolidates an understanding of *dosti* that is communicative in a social-cementing sense and also in terms of its queer sexual connotations. The track "Koyi Kahen" ("People will say") from the film *Dil Chahta Hai*

(What the heart wants, Farhan Akhtar, 2001) is played. This draws the dancing crowd together singing almost in unison and jumping up and down in ways that are similar to how the lead actors and actresses dance in the filmed version.[33] Boys turn to dance with boys and girls dance with girls as well as there is exchange of other gender and sexuality combinations. The *dosti* that is forged in this *khel* is commensurate with the lyrics of the song. In the movie, the singers proclaim their disavowal of rigid societal norms and elder and peer generational pressures in order to forge a new way for themselves. In the space of the queer South Asian club, the translations here are quite easy to decipher. *Dostis* are made in the *khel* about being different to straight societal norms and expectations. A cultural solidarity is exhibited in and through the *dostis* that profess gender and sexual differences on the dance floor and partake in a promiscuous *khel* wherein several bodies are up close and personal—touching, sweating, and being sexually suggestive. Yet, the *khel* is promiscuous only up to a point. Like many other devices of playfulness in South Asian cultural traditions, the *khel* here also works through suggestion and within its own boundary limits. Although there is full-on same-sex kissing and touching, it very rarely becomes X-rated. The suggestion of same-sex sexual display and affection is far more titillating and provocative than going beyond it (that is, flirtations of sexual innuendos and the close proximity of bodies in intimate postures and gestures). Also of interest here is that there is no dark room in the club, and this appears to be the case also for the other U.K. desi gay and lesbian clubs that I attended.[34] Whereas the heterosexual ideology of Bollywood is done away within the *khel* of the club, the signs and codes of how heterosexuality is coded and performed in Bollywood imposes an order of gender and sexual conduct that is reconfigured by Bollywood's queer patrons.[35] In mainstream Bollywood, one rarely sees explicit sexual exhibitionism—rather it is often laced with coyness, innuendos, and metaphors of suggestion. This is also the case in the South Asian gay and lesbian club. It appears that just as the song and dance sequence was sexualized in order to get around Indian censorship rules, so too desi queers use Bollywood song-dance to avert the censure of heteronormativity, simultaneously engaging in playfulness and same-sex sexual suggestions while maintaining a certain bodily decorum. Here lies another difference between the diasporic South Asian gay and lesbian scene and its white Western counterpart. Public displays of sexual mores that are an exploration and illustration of selfhood are deliberately coded through Bollywood conventions that provide a social etiquette through which to conduct oneself in the club space. This public etiquette stresses cultural difference in relation to other queer scenes. The Bollywood song-dance establishes the codes of excess and celebration of the sexually avant-garde and liberating performances that operate within this cultural horizon.

We must also note certain similarities between desi and the white gay and lesbian culture, which also uses mainstream pop songs and Hollywood film stars to express queerness. For example, feminist readings of Hollywood have drawn our attention to a number of extracinematic identificatory practices.[36] These include posturing, mimicry, dressing up, irony, exaggeration, performing like a star, deploying the stars' masculine/feminine qualities, using the star's sexual appeal, and relishing in how the star has excelled at surviving the social order of the day in the reel/diegetic world on the screen and perhaps even in real/actual life. Similarly, Bollywood has no limit to the number of its stars, both male and female, that have achieved demigod status in South Asia and its diasporic societies over the years. These stars have been appropriated by different sections of Bollywood's audiences, not least its gay and lesbian fans.[37]

Finally, Bollywood song and dance is a central node of pleasure for desi queers. I am drawing on the notion of pleasure as it has been widely used in the discipline of cultural studies.[38] Here, pleasure inheres in the audiences' ability to use its cultural capital to read, partake, and identify with particular forms of popular culture. The audiences' familiarity with the text's codes and conventions contributes to an aesthetic, emotional, and, in the case of dance, a physical enjoyment of the form. In the queer South Asian club space, the pleasures of the Bollywood film text are also extended and translated in terms of queer desires and sensibilities of *yaar/yaari, dosti,* and *khel* and the performativity of the eroticized body.

Is the Queer Reread in Bollywood or Is Bollywood Inherently Queer?

Let us finally consider whether the homeland is simply reconfigured in the queer diaspora or whether the homeland also responds to the queer diaspora, or vice versa, albeit in secret ways?[39] As we have seen above, the queer diaspora clearly subverts and translates Bollywood's heteronormative boy-meets-girl romances, but this is not unique to the diaspora. Queer cultures, almost everywhere, often appropriate straight social texts and discourses for their own means and thereby create a new language through which they communicate and express themselves. The "newness" in the queer South Asian diaspora is its constituting of a tacit and secret politics that is in dialogue with its Bollywood sources such that each informs and produces the other anew. But these secret politics are also becoming more visible and encoded into the workings of mainstream Bollywood that suggest a reconfiguring of the relationship between the homeland and the diaspora that is more complex. I want to conclude by suggesting two lines of inquiry for further research and analysis.

First, the aesthetic and traditional conventions of Bollywood need to be considered further as hybrid, "queer," and "camp" from their outset.[40] In particular, I am thinking of how the early development of popular Indian cinema has always been eclectic, even if it has not been acknowledged as such. Early cinema (for example, *Raja Harischandra,* Phalke, 1913) had either men playing female roles or prostitutes were hired as actresses; acting in Indian cinema was considered a social taboo for "respectable" women. Such films were paradoxically used to create and confirm a social order of heterosexuality and patriarchy, but how might one also account for the early queer desires and secret politics that were enabled by such transgressions on-screen? If such a line of thought can be developed further out of historical and contemporary inquiry, is it possible to argue that South Asian queer spaces, both in the diaspora *and* in the homeland, not only signify from and reread or appropriate Bollywood, but are and have been preexisting in the formation of Hindi cinema from its outset? Such areas of research could include the "camp" theatrical performances of early Hindu mythologicals where men dressed up to play women characters and of early heroines who played masculine and "butch" action roles.[41] The Parsi and regional theaters that included stories situated in the *khota* (courtesan houses and brothels), with their coexisting narratives of heterosexuality and lesbianism, is another possible instance.[42] Bringing the ideas of Nandy into conversation with the queer readings put forward here, then, it is possible to argue that in a caricature of selfhood queer Bollywood is not only a matter of the "queer readings" that "queer audiences" bring to the text, but rather Bollywood's investment in caricature makes it a rich cultural resource where meanings of "queer" and "camp" can be readily created and contested.[43] Thus, even the manifest heteronormative content is queered by a representational excess that marginalizes questions of authenticity (of straightness, for example) because both queer and straight are equally caricatured; they are representations of an ordered and constructed world (that is, of heteronormativity) and its slippages that make spaces for insights into new queer worlds.

The second line of thought acknowledges the shift and changes that are taking place in more recent Bollywood films in which queer themes and representations are becoming slightly more visible and perhaps more fluid, and therefore, is Bollywood listening to and in dialogue with queer South Asian cultural politics both in the homeland *and* in the diaspora? Two brief examples will suffice here. First, the queer *khel* between Aman Mathur (Shahrukh Khan) and Rohit Patel (Saif Ali Khan) in *Kal Ho Naa Ho* (Tomorrow may never come, Nikhil Advani, 2003), set in the diasporic city of New York, is wrongly interpreted by Rohit's housemaid as a gay relationship. This film sets up a heterosexual love triangle between Aman, Rohit, and Naina Catherine Kapur Patel (Preity Zinta). However, sexual innuendos between the two male characters and scenes of their bodies in close intimate proximity to each other abound in this film. The two characters also flirt with camp performativity and dance together with added suggestions

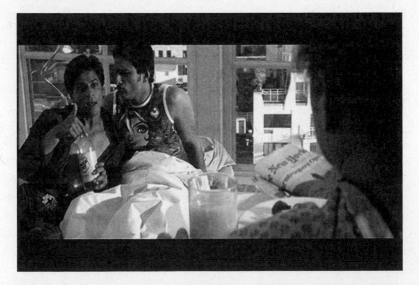

Aman (Shahrukh Khan) and Rohit (Saif Ali Khan) perform queer *khel* while the maid looks on in *Kal Ho Naa Ho*.

of homosexuality, albeit through the use of humor as a backdrop. Even the film's climax is open to a queer reading. As Aman lies dying on a hospital bed, the two male characters reach a compromise over their individual love for Naina, while holding and embracing each other closely. During this climax, Naina is seen outside of the frame of the two characters, outside of the hospital room in which Aman and Rohit make their private agreement with each other.

My second example is taken from Sudhir Mishra's *Chameli* (Scented/healing flower, 2004). In a scene in this film, Aman (Rahul Bose) and Chameli (Kareena Kapoor) get into conversation while they are sheltering from the heavy rain under the same archway in Mumbai. When Aman realizes that one of Chameli's friends, Raja, is gay and is in love with a male cross-dresser, Hasina, he initially appears surprised. During their conversation, Chameli asks Aman whether he feels that there is something wrong with two men being in a relationship. Aman hesitantly responds "no" and qualifies his response saying he has other male friends who are gay. Chameli goes on to declare that there is nothing "abnormal" about gay relationships as long as there is love in them—"bus pyar hona chayen." Reasons for such noticeable queer representations in contemporary Bollywood cinema owe much to the rise of queer politics in India and the courting of the diaspora as an audience for Bollywood. However, what needs to be investigated further is that are genuine queer possibilities opening up here or are they simply subsumed within the dominant heteronormative workings of Bollywood cinema?[44]

By way of conclusion, let us return to the opening remarks made about the Selfridges' celebration of Bollywood popular culture that has been juxtaposed with the diasporic ethnoscape of the queer South Asian club. The example of Bollywood film and music culture's translation at the gay and lesbian club is telling of the secret politics that the Selfridges store could only take on board in very subtle ways. The Selfridges' camp and kitsch that was lifted from Bollywood was not quite right. It was not sure of how to fully deal with these aspects other than through mere suggestion, and it focused more on making a profit by trying to cater to the highest-spending pound and thereby making the consumption of Bollywood safe and yet exotic. What needs to be noted is precisely how queer culture is increasingly being appropriated to market and promote consumption. Thus, what happens to camp when it turns into commodity? One is not arguing that the Asian gay and lesbian clubs are the only place for different and potentially progressive Bollywood-influenced genders and sexualities to flourish, but that they are a space in which the diasporic imaginary can shift more usefully between the place of residence or the new homeland (that is, Britain) and the originating homeland (that is, South Asia) and wherein both the homeland and the diaspora can be brought into dialogue with each other in ways beyond the exotica of Orientalism. Furthermore, the use of Bollywood in the gay and lesbian club scene illustrates one of the internal fissures within the wider South Asian diaspora where considerations of gender and sexual difference can often be marginalized or excluded.[45] The direct enactment and performance of gender and sexuality in the queer club space forces the nation and its diaspora to confront such issues. In these ways, the social interactions that take place at the gay and lesbian club appropriately draw on, flaunt, and recreate the original queer and hybrid aesthetic and traditional forms of the popular Hindi cinema in ways that are yet to be fully researched.

Notes

This chapter is a revised version of, and draws on material from, chapter 5 from Rajinder Dudrah, *Bollywood: Sociology Goes to the Movies* (London: Sage, 2006).

1 For an example of such film criticism, see David Cook, *A History of Narrative Film* (New York: Norton, 1996), 861.
2 The term "desi" is used by diasporic South Asians from the South Asian vernacular to refer to themselves as having sociocultural attachments to their respective homelands.
3 Throughout this chapter, "queer" is used as an umbrella term, exploring the social construction and performance of different gender and sexual identities such as gay, lesbian, bisexual, and heterosexual. It also involves a critique and displacement of heteronormative structures and predominantly straight desires.
4 See Arjun Appadurai, *Modernity at Large: Cultural Dimensions of Globalisation* (Minneapolis and London: University of Minnesota Press, 1996); Sumita Chakravarty, *National Identity in Indian Popular Cinema: 1947–1987* (New Delhi: Oxford University Press, 1996); Rachel Dwyer, *All You Want Is Money, All You Need Is Love: Sex and Romance in Modern India* (London: Cassell, 2000); Fareed Kazmi, *The Politics of India's Conventional Cinema: Imaging a Universe, Subverting a Multiverse* (London: Sage, 1999); Vijay Mishra, *Bollywood Cinema: Temples of Desire* (London and New York: Routledge, 2002); Ashis Nandy, *The Secret Politics of Our Desires: Innocence, Culpability, and Indian Popular Cinema* (London: Zed

Books, 1998); Madhava Prasad, *Ideology of the Hindi Film: A Historical Construction* (New Delhi and Oxford: Oxford University Press, 1998); Ashish Rajadhyaksha, "Indian Cinema," in *The Oxford Guide to Film Studies,* ed. John Hill and Pamela Church Gibson (London: Oxford University Press, 1998), 535–40; Ravi Vasudevan, ed., *Making Meaning in Indian Cinema* (New Delhi: Oxford University Press, 2000); and Jyotika Virdi, *The Cinematic Imagination: Indian Popular Films as Social History* (New Brunswick: Rutgers University Press, 2003).

5 Gayatri Gopinath, "Queering Bollywood: Alternative Sexualities in Popular Indian Cinema," *Journal of Homosexuality* 39, nos. 3 and 4 (2000): 283–97; Ashok Row Kavi, "The Changing Image of the Hero in Hindi Films," *Journal of Homosexuality* 39, nos. 3 and 4 (2000): 307–12; R. Raj Rao, "Memories Pierce the Heart: Homoeroticism, Bollywood-Style," *Journal of Homosexuality* 39, nos. 3 and 4 (2000): 299–306; and Thomas Waugh, "Queer Bollywood, or I'm the Player You're the Naïve One: Patterns of Sexual Subversion in Recent Indian Popular Cinema," in *Key Frames: Popular Cinema and Cultural Studies,* ed. Matthew Tinkcom and Amy Villarejo (London and New York: Routledge, 2001), 280–97.

6 Nandy, *Secret Politics,* 7.

7 Prasad, *Ideology.*

8 Ibid., 118.

9 The term "diaspora" refers to a social condition that brings into play the coordinates of the place of origin and the place of settlement and a diasporic consciousness that is created and shifts between these two places through actual and imagined cultural movements. I am less interested in nostalgic understandings of and attachments to the homeland through Bollywood cinema and am more interested in exploring the possibilities for new social and cultural formations that render problematic any simple formulations of the homeland and its diaspora. This encourages us to make a point of departure, a new line of flight as it were.

10 Arjun Appadurai, "Disjuncture and Difference in the Global Cultural Economy," in *Global Culture,* ed. Mike Featherstone (London: Sage, 1990), 298. See also Appadurai, *Modernity.*

11 Homi Bhabha, *Nation and Narration* (London: Routledge, 1990).

12 Gopinath, "Queering Bollywood," 284.

13 Ibid.

14 Ibid.

15 Rao, "Memories," 304–5.

16 Kavi, "Changing Image," 308–10.

17 Rao, "Memories," 304.

18 Waugh, "Queer Bollywood," 282. See also Lawrence Cohen, "Holi in Banaras and the Mahaland of Modernity," *Gender and Lesbian Quarterly* 2, no. 4 (1995): 399–424, and Lawrence Cohen, "The Pleasures of Castration: The Postoperative Status of Hijras, Jhankas, and Academics," in *Sexual Nature/Sexual Culture,* ed. Paul Abramson and Steven Pinkerton (Chicago and London: University of Chicago Press, 1995).

19 Waugh, "Queer Bollywood," 292.

20 Ibid., 293.

21 Ibid., 296.
22 Compare Gopinath, "Queering Bollywood."
23 See the Birmingham South Asian gay and lesbian club night's Web site at http://www.saathinight.com/.
24 See the Leicester South Asian gay and lesbian club night's Web site at http://www.clubishq.com/.
25 See the London South Asian gay and lesbian club night's Web site at http://www.clubkali.co.uk/.
26 See the Manchester South Asian gay and lesbian club night's Web site at http://www.clubzindagi.com/.
27 See the New York City South Asian gay and lesbian club night's Web site at http://www.sholayevents.com/. Of note here is the work of Sunaina Maira on South Asian American youth club culture in New York City. Although she acknowledges in passing the existence of separate queer desi club nights and also the existence of queer desis at predominantly heterosexual club events in New York City, she concurs that queer desi parties in North America exist as parallel to "often aggressively heterosexual bhangra remix youth subculture where queerness was invisible." Sunaina Maira, *Desis in the House: Indian American Youth Culture in New York City* (Philadelphia: Temple University Press, 2002), 47–48. The emergence of queer desi club nights in the diaspora should be understood, in part, as a call for safe spaces amid the racism and exoticization of brown bodies in predominantly white queer clubs and also as a response to (male) aggressive behavior prevalent at predominantly heterosexual Bhangra nights that were in swing from the mid-to-late 1980s.
28 Compare Appadurai, "Disjuncture and Difference," 295–310.
29 Compare Nandy, *Secret Politics*.
30 On the fusion and social possibilities of these music genres, see Sanjay Sharma, John Hutnyk, and Ashwani Sharma, eds., *Dis-Orienting Rhythms: The Politics of the New Asian Dance Music* (London: Zed Books, 1996), and Rajinder Dudrah, "Drum N Dhol: British Bhangra Music and Diasporic South Asian Identity Formation," *European Journal of Cultural Studies* 5, no. 3 (2002): 363–83.
31 For more on the formation of Asian queer identities in relation to white racism in its heteronormative and queer forms, see Russell Leong, ed., Asian American Sexualities: Dimensions of the Gay and Lesbian Experience (London Routledge, 1996).
32 In the film, this song is picturized on a moving train (that can be read as phallic) making its journey through the picturesque virginal countryside. For a further reading of the film's extensive use of Sufi mysticism as articulated within the film's narrative, and especially in its song and dance sequences, and about the struggle for love amid Indian state politics, see Ananya J. Kabir, "Allegories of Alienation and Politics of Bargaining: Minority Subjectivities in Mani Ratnam's *Dil Se*," *South Asian Popular Culture* 1, no. 2 (2003): 141–59.
33 In the film, the lead players are Aamir Khan, Akshaye Khanna, Preity Zinta, and Saif Ali Khan.

34 A "dark room" is a designated area within a gay and lesbian club, often separate from the dance floor, where people can enter and partake in or observe numerous kinds of sexual escapades.

35 See Prasad for an account of how Bollywood songs and dancing are used in the context of Indian film censorship rules as standing in for the real thing. Prasad asserts that it is patriarchal authority that is promulgated in the scopophilia of these song and dance numbers.

36 See Jackie Stacey, *Star Gazing: Hollywood Cinema and Female Spectatorship* (London: Routledge, 2003).

37 Kavi, for example, describes the queerness of Bollywood star Dev Anand as possessing "a strange effeminacy that bordered on the child-like" and "had an innocuous sensuality about him that conspired to make his heroine into an oedipal figure" (Kavi, "Changing Image," 308).

38 Stephen Regan, ed., *The Politics of Pleasure and Cultural Theory* (Philadelphia: Open University Press, 1992).

39 Compare Gopinath, "Queering Bollywood."

40 I fully acknowledge here that this line of thought is brief and highly speculative and begs the need for further research to prove or disprove the claims being put forward in this instance about early Hindi cinema. Thus, by labeling the terms "queer" and "camp" in literal and metaphoric scare quotes, I wish to draw attention to the possibilities in which these terms *can* and *might not* operate in ways that we understand their use in Western culture. This points toward a line of flight that requires us to think more about the similarities and dissimilarities of queer and camp cultures in South Asia and elsewhere.

41 I am thinking here of the films starring the stunt actress Nadia from the early 1930s onward.

42 For example, Veena Oldenburg drawing on interviews with retired courtesans in Lucknow, India, argues that most courtesans, as well as many prostitutes, practiced lesbianism (*chapat bazi*), considering heterosexuality to be work and not pleasure. Veena Oldenburg, *The Making of Colonial Lucknow 1856–1877* (Delhi: Oxford University Press, 1989).

43 See Nandy, *Secret Politics* and Gopinath, "Queering Bollywood".

44 See, for instance, the Gay Bombay Web site http://www.gaybombay.org/ (accessed June 15, 2006).

45 The recent history of the struggle of the New York-based South Asian Lesbian and Gay Association (SALGA) to be included in the India Day Parade on the streets of Manhattan is a case in point. See Svati P. Shah, "Out and Out Radical: New Directions for Progressive Organizing," http://www.samarmagazine.org/archive/article.php?id=60.

12. Bollywood Gets Funky

American Hip-Hop, Basement Bhangra, and the Racial Politics of Music

Richard Zumkhawala-Cook

If you happened to tune in the local pop radio stations in the summer of 2003, you might have gotten the impression hip-hop's executive class had just returned from spring break in South Asia and was proudly sharing its audio postcards with the world. "Mundian to bach ke" ("Beware of the Boys"), Jay-Z's collaboration with British bhangra DJ Panjabi MC, was hailed as an anthem of the summer by *Billboard Magazine* when the single and its *tumbi* and *dhol* bassline flew to the top of American and European charts. Dr. Dre's production of the Truth Hurts's track "Addictive," featuring Lata Mangeshkar's vintage Bollywood background vocals, became a staple in playlists on urban beat radio, as did the synthesized ghazal-riff of Missy Elliott's "Get Ur Freak On" and the Hindi-song sampled "React" by Erick Sermon. Indian music was all the rage, apparently, as music journalists and the rap culture industry celebrated the sounds of the subcontinent—but in ways that ultimately reflected the racist underpinnings of global America. Ethnic clichés described the songs as "spicing up hip-hop radio"[1] or as mixing "the Eastern spiritual side with the power of the bass of the West."[2] Stereotypes and cultural conflations by the artists and their audiences swelled around the music's promotion and popularity: Jay-Z's stage performances of "Beware" featured blonde belly dancers while his lyrics mention snake charmers; Truth Hurts admitted to not knowing that India was in Asia; and radio program directors worried about playing "Beware" after American bombs began falling on Iraq—the uncertainty of the song's Punjabi lyrics raised questions about their political affiliations. The ignorance of these artists and of the American pop music industry about the Indian sources that provided the very structure of the music they performed reached more egregious levels when

308

Erick Sermon's rap-a-deux with Bollywood lyrics confounded listeners who could translate the Hindi:

> *Kisiko khudkhushi*
> *ka shouk ho to*
> *kya karen hum*
> [If someone wants to commit suicide, then what can you do?]
> Whateva she said, then I'm that
> If this here rocks to ya'all, then react.

As Bishwarup Sen's essay in this anthology notes, the circulation and consumption of Hindi film aesthetics even became the subject of a copyright suit when prolific Bollywood songwriter Bappi Lahiri sued Dr. Dre's record company for including his music without credit in "Addictive."

Such oversights are undoubtedly grounded in well-worn Orientalist fantasies by Westerners of the exotic and primitive East, but the circulation of commercial Indian music in mainstream American hip-hop reflects the tenuous relationship the United States has with South Asia in a post-9/11 world.[3] In response to George W. Bush's war on terror, images of Afghanistan, Pakistan, and the rest of the Arab world have fueled intrigue about the spectacle of the brown-skinned other and have provided new cultural inspiration for artists and musicians. Although the appropriation of Asian forms in white Western pop music has thrived for decades, the stakes changed after New York's World Trade Center was felled and America's tendency for bigoted stereotypes of region, culture, and religion caused brown-skinned immigrants to suffer violent and state-sanctioned suspicion. The intensified racialization of South Asian identity and its cultural forms drew the commodification of sights and sounds associated with this region clearly into public view as evidence of the "immigration problem."[4] Meanwhile, new popular aesthetic combinations of these forms took pleasure in recalibrating South Asian identity as a dangerous element in the economy of race in America. Just as Public Enemy's canonized 1990 album title, *Fear of Black Planet,* reveled in white America's anxieties about African American advances, mainstream hip-hop has found purchase in drawing its sounds closer to the perceived racial threat of a planet turned brown.[5] Although these patterns of appropriation highlight some of the existential parallels of black and Indian identities within the color lines of

America, they are, however, ultimately articulated through techniques that either reproduce white-supremacist caricatures of the mystical, militant, and lawless East or cast Indian culture and identity wholly into the background. Bollywood's mere appearance in the context of American hip-hop does not necessarily signal a progressive collaboration but reinscribes the asymmetries of power that enable the first world to raid the cultural products of the third.

Outside of the large music culture industry, however, is another story of the Indian American hip-hop urban underground music scene. As this essay demonstrates later, young people of the Indian diaspora in the United States construct grassroots networks of collective affiliation and affect by linking antiestablishment and progressive codes of African American identity with Bollywood or classical Indian aesthetic structures. Responding to hegemonic multiculturalism's persistent denial of racism's structural effects, particularly on Asian immigrants, the adoption of African American iconography politicizes, at least temporarily, Indian racial identities by drawing attention to Asian–black connections. As Sunaina Maira argues in her study of Indian American youth culture, *Desis in the House,* for second-generation adolescents and young professionals who have grown up interpreting Bhangra and Bollywood as the sound track of their parents' traditions, hip-hop music's intricate lexicon of styles and speech functions as a means for building alternative, even oppositional, cultural spaces and political identities.[6] Especially for lower-class urban immigrants, it is a movement of radical identifications across the mainstream's chasms of race and culture. For others, the underground Asian hip-hop scene enables a largely conservative assimilatory move toward youth "cool" by merely reflecting middle-class white America's essentialist notions of black culture's authenticity, which anxiously projects fantasies of countercultural hipness, sexual liberty, and aesthetic rebellion onto black popular forms. For each, this negotiation of racial identity resists appearing too "white," a category associated with bourgeois educational and economic success that elides racial and cultural experience of Asian Americans. At the same time, it rejects the caricature of the docile Asian immigrant, such as *The Simpsons*'s Kwiki-Mart owner, Apu, or the 7-Eleven owners, Norman and Pakeeza, in Eric Bogosian's 1994 play, and subsequent film, *SubUrbia*. Although aesthetic integrations do not guarantee solidarity between black and South Asian populations, this process of making cultural identity offers the possibility of shifting the overdetermined assimilationist terrain of black/white racial polarities. At its best, the integration of hip-hop and Bollywood by South Asian Americans and immigrants has moved beyond formal syncretizations not as mere "style" or "difference," but as means for articulating political agency and identificatory solidarities against America's reactionary post-9/11 cultural landscape.[7]

The Global Routes of Indian Hip-Hop

The allure of Hindi film tracks, Bhangra, and traditional Indian music in mainstream hip-hop reveals the global character of aestheticized blackness as representations of "alien" cultures that serve to negotiate the boundaries of race and nationality. Such integrations link the oppositional aesthetics of hip-hop and the popular Indian musical forms associated with desi identities in the United States. If, as Tricia Rose argues, the transformative politics of rap as a black cultural form "involves the contestation over public space, the meanings, interpretations, and value of the lyrics and music,"[8] then the surge by the most elite names in American hip-hop to incorporate Indian forms into their music reveals a desire to lay claim on the multinational circulation of culture in the global marketplace and to exploit South Asia's valence in America as a cultural and racial threat to public life. Paul Gilroy notes that hip-hop has long been involved in the polyphonic borrowing and reinscription of transnational African traditions, from Brazil to the Congo, to acknowledge diasporic sources of counterhegemonic racial identity.[9] Now, however, Asian voices and rhythms are used to rearticulate the modes of modern African American experience invoking a cosmopolitan but racially alternative "worldliness" that redefines the popularized urban spaces of American blackness in ways that now include non-African ethnoscapes.[10] Yet, as Arjun Appadurai explains, such spaces or "ethnoscapes" are often commodified fragments, partial realities, and audience fantasies mediated by state and commercial interests of information dissemination.[11] In other words, American hip-hop's engagement with racial boundaries says as much about the corporate music industry's culture of profit and its mainstream listeners' thirst for sanitized cultural differences as it does about the identities constructed in the music itself.

Even further, these strategies of hip-hop–Bollywood integrations follow the transnational patterns of migration and movement marked by the South Asian diaspora more generally in the West. As Jay-Z's collaboration with Panjabi MC indicates, American hip-hop's use of commodified Indian musical forms undoubtedly capitalizes on earlier aesthetic negotiations of black and Indian identities that became popular in Great Britain. The proliferation since the early 1990s of Afro-Indian musical combinations and their performances in the United Kingdom by such artists as Fun-Da-Mental, Asian Dub Foundation, and Apache Indian have earned praise by scholars and journalists alike for constructing plural cultural spaces for antiracist identification and a politics of social transformation. According to Sanjay Sharma, such sonically integrative musics help "to articulate and deploy a sense of 'Asianness' that is not necessarily in opposition to notions of being Black, and though more problematically, even British. These dance musics may, then, act as a site for the translation between diasporic Asian, Black and British identifications."[12] In response to racist anti-immigrant discourse claiming true (that is, white) Englishness, "black" identity is dislodged from racial phenotype and becomes a strategic category of solidarity available to Asian, African, and Caribbean immigrants to resist white hegemony.[13] "Black" expression in public life includes recombined fusions of popular and traditional forms from various "homelands." These syncretic products unsettle dominant notions of primitivist immigrant identities and construct an antiestablishment underground scene with fecund opportunities for what Paul Gilroy hopefully identifies as alternative public spaces.[14]

As I illustrate below, the Indian textures in the music of Truth Hurts, Jay-Z, Missy Elliott, and Erick Sermon, however, provide few alternatives in the fabric of racist America. In contrast to Britain's mainly independent productions of Afro-Indian fusions, Bhangra, Lata, and Bollywood function on American corporate radio as another material ornament, or "bling," marking the entrepreneurial worth of music produced from the largest global entertainment corporations. Indian forms are collapsed into the framework of black expression, a maneuver that reflects the general inability of American racial politics to think beyond differences of black and white, especially since the practices of racial prejudice against South Asians are commonly subsumed by questions of "cultural" style rather than racial difference. The result is a derailing of meaningful public action against the lived realities of subtle or overt practices of white supremacy.[15] In other words, Indian music may participate in hip-hop's alternative public, but only insofar as this global diversity renders invisible the politics of South Asian identities in America.

Despite the evident myopia and ignorance in Erick Sermon's or Jay-Z's productions, many Indian Americans feel culturally legitimated when they hear the commercialized sounds of Bollywood or Bhangra in music produced by popular voices of black America. As New York DJ and club host, DJ Rekha explains, "I see Indian kids in a club who get so excited when these hip-hop songs come on, because for that one moment they feel visible. They don't see the misrepresentations."[16] This desire for legitimation and visibility propelled the international success of Bally Sagoo's 1994 breakthrough long playing (LP) record, *Bolly-wood Flashback* (see Edward K. Chan's essay for a detailed account of the Asian underground). Sagoo's remixed Hindi film classics like "Chura liya" (*Yaadon Ki Baraat,* 1973), with electronic dance beats, infused household "oldies" from India with Western R&B, reggae, and hip-hop cool. As was—and still is—the case in the United Kingdom, bars, discos, and underground clubs across the United States, from New York to San Francisco to Houston, host Bhangra parties and "masala nights," which feature one of the hundreds of DJs who have been mixing South Asian music into hip-hop, and hip-hop into South Asian music, for years. As the essay explains later, these locally produced sites of enunciation create a different logic of subcultural connection than those produced by Jay-Z and open opportunities for radicalizing their spaces with explicit links to critical awareness of social justice networks. The same Hindi film songs and the traditional dance forms that serve as a transnational mainline of Indian popular culture to the diaspora are rearticulated as a political gathering point through fundraisers and con-sciousness raising events to resist the socially conservative associations commonly ascribed to these forms. Strict heteronormative codes of romance, sexual purity, and female passivity, central to so many classic Bollywood ballads, for instance, become opportunities for ironic gen-der bending and expressions of sexual excess, while the fetishization of obedient middle-class consumerism and individual wealth that often serve as films' narrative backdrop are transformed into collective cele-brations and grassroots organizational efforts for cultural and political dissent. Dancehall activism engages cultural difference not as a product to be consumed, but as an event that foregrounds, mixes, and remixes aesthetic and political connections within an ongoing struggle for jus-tice and progressive equality.

Addicted to Lata

The appearance of Lata Mangeshkar's twenty-year old ballad, "Thoda resham lagta hai," on Truth Hurts's 2002 top 10 U.S. single, and the accompanying video, "Addictive," tore down the frontiers of nationality that usually associate hip-hop with the sounds and styles of the African diaspora. Mangeshkar's pronounced vocals, clearly foreign to hip-hop's main target audience, carry the first thirty seconds of the track before Truth and Rakim enter the verbal mix. An acoustic sounding bass-track of hand-drums, cymbals, and handclaps lightly amplifies the original rhythm, maintaining its tempo and its structural integrity. Hindi and Bollywood make much more than a minor appearance in "Addictive"; they provide four interrupted minutes of the track's frame, beat, and melody. It is thus no surprise that when the ninety-year-old music and film company Saregama India found no credit given to the performers, writers, or owners of "Thoda resham lagta hai" on the American editions, but they had reason to pursue a successful five-hundred-million-dollar copyright lawsuit against producer Dr. Dre and his label, Aftermath Records. *India Times* reported one lawyer as saying, "They literally superimposed their own drum track and lyrics over the beat,"[17] while the *BBC* quoted another claiming, "they didn't even try to get original with it … [They didn't] try to change it up or anything like that."[18] Despite Rakim's fitting line from "Addictive" that they "roll like they own the world," a federal judge ordered Aftermath's parent company, Universal Music Group, to halt all U.S. distribution of the album, *Truthfully Speaking,* until the names of songwriter Bappi Lahiri and Saregama India appeared on the album.

Although this example of hip-hop meeting Bollywood provides a telling illustration of the legalities of aesthetic appropriation, to reduce the issue to copyright law obfuscates its cultural and racial implications, as well as Bollywood's own history of liberal appropriation of international sounds and plotlines. Saregama, Lahiri, and Mangeshkar were erased in "Addictive" at the same time as their work was sold and pumped into the airways as background to Truth Hurts's single. Nonetheless, Lahiri's Bollywood product is far from a culturally authentic or nationally pure artifact devoid of its own hybrid transnational appropriations. Similarly, the contexts and meanings of "Thoda resham lagta hai" are certainly not given voice in a small print byline, as if cultural imperialism is no longer an issue when the law of property is maintained (despite the lawsuit, the judge did not insist that credit be given to Mangeshkar, but to her producer). More important is how Indian artistic production becomes a resource for American cultural meanings, not only in the interests of African American DJs and rappers, but to the world's largest music company Vivendi Universal, which owns both Aftermath Records and Universal Music Group. "Addictive" looks to an exoticized version of a foreign tradition to highlight Truth's and Rakim's lyrical themes of individual power through wealth, misogynist renderings of female desire, and the thrills of conspicuous consumption.

The upbeat dance beat and rap vocals of Truth Hurts's single might seem to be a hip youth vibe of progressive culture, but its narrative of a kept woman offering the praises of her man's material and sexual prowess reproduces the most retrograde male fantasies. Consistent with the tradition in hip-hop of sampling lines, rhythms, and themes from a variety of sources, "Addictive" uses the Bollywood track as a point of reference, but then resituates its meaning within a heavy drum and bass composition and the overlay of rap lyrics. Rose suggests about hip-hop's methods:

> Rap DJs and producers reshuffle known cultural formulas and themes. It is in this context that narrative originality is lodged. In the age of mechanical reproduction, these cultural formulas and themes are in the form of recorded sound, reshuffled, looped and recontextualized.[19]

The mixing may offer an original product, but these processes of cut and mix are merely tools; they still can produce decontextualized global cultural patterns, or "strips of reality," to quote Appadurai, that reinforce a socially repressive imaginary.[20]

Over the top of Mangeshkar's vocals, "Thoda resham lagta hai, ho thoda sheesha lagta" ("It takes a little silk, it takes a little glass"), Truth's chorus adoringly parallels her erotic desire to the physical dependency of drug addiction: "He's so contagious/He turns my pages/He's got me anxious, he's what I've waited for."[21] Indeed, much of the song is devoted to describing her insatiable appetite for extreme sex in proclaiming "I like it rough" and "My back is achin'/From our lovemakin'." As Mangeshkar's vocals become a sustained series of backup "ohs," Truth sings, "He treats me clean/And gives me things/He makes me scream/ … He hits the spot, he makes me hot." The voice of unbridled libido unashamedly announces her desires, as perhaps a figure of sexual liberation. But Truth's lyrics show a woman defined exclusively by these desires, which, as an addict, she cannot control, and as an oversexed and financially dependent woman, she should be grateful for. And from start to finish, the Hindi film track follows in step with Truth's lyrics, weaving in and behind her vocals, as if they were one voice in contrast to the eventual male rap vocals. At the structural center of the song, both literally and thematically, are the words of the man himself, rapped by 1980s hip-hop icon, Rakim, as Truth's and Mangeshkar's voices recede into the background. He lauds the "twisted" sex that has the lovers "speakin' in tongues," but also warns of his professional duties as a drug kingpin: "Keep it strong, but I gotta hit the streets when I'm done." His heroic sexuality intertwines with the glamorous life he dangerously earns on the streets: "You was there at half a gram/Now it's kilos and c-notes and high fashion brands/ … You just pray I don't get killed when I hit the hood/Just another hundred mil, and I'm a quit for good."

There is nothing new for pop music in this image of a sex-crazed mistress awaiting in silent patience the material spoils of her man's public achievements. Nor is any new ground broken with the fetishization of extravagant wealth. What is new, for mainstream American hip-hop anyway, is the premiere voice of India authorizing this ideology. Mangeshkar's vocals and the instrumentation of "Thoda resham lagta hai" from the film *Jyoti* (1981) at once exoticize the track by offering an indecipherable lyrical layer (to most American listeners), while also globally pluralizing the glorified female submission apparent in Truth's "addiction," as if it should be understood that Mangeshkar's aural presence articulates the same position.[22] This commonly employed white-supremacist reduction of the subservient Eastern woman ignores not only history itself, but the very meanings of the Hindi song, which, although confined by its own patriarchal contexts of Bollywood, presents a woman playfully defining the cures for love's pains on her own terms. The structural parallel between Mangeshkar's and Truth's lyrics only makes sense if viewed from a lens that elides the particulars of the sampled song or Lata's oeuvre.

These juxtapositions of intertextual and intercultural reference speak not only to the product, however, but also to the social contexts of contact and exchange within global capitalism that promote the market circulation of cultural forms. DJ Quik, who coproduced "Addictive," described his accidental first encounter with "Thoda resham lagta hai":

> I woke up one morning … I turned on the TV and landed on this Hindi channel and just turned it up real loud … There was a commercial on, and I just got up and went into the bathroom and started brushing my teeth. I'm brushing, and before I knew it, I was grooving. … [The beat] was just in my body. I went back in there and looked at the TV—there was a girl on there bellydancing, just like real fly. So I pushed record on the VCR.[23]

This allegory of commodity culture and its consumption illustrates the neat technological delivery of international differences right into our private spheres (while we brush our teeth) like an unexpected, but ultimately welcome gift. And the VCR commemorates the experience in a materially reproducible form ready for transportation and redefinition. "Addictive" is as much a creation of Zee TV and of Turner Classic Movies' Hindi film days as it is of DJ Quik or Aftermath Records.

As Michael Hardt and Antonio Negri have explained, the global marketplace produces cultural differences by constructing detailed knowledge of new territories and endlessly multiple distinctions of social life. The fluidity and portability of cultural forms may liberate culture from the old master narratives and repressive monolithic modernist social categories of the self and the other—ethnicity, region, and nationality—that might regard Mangeshkar's presence in a hip-hop song to be an unworkable combination. But such a liberation also divorces culture from other old categories such as historical contexts, local sovereignty, and political solidarities that would prevent globalization's easy flow of cultures turned into capital:

> The ideology of the world market has always been the anti-foundational and anti-essentialist discourse par excellence. Circulation, mobility, diversity, and mixture are its very conditions of possibility. Trade brings differences together and the more the merrier. Differences (of commodities, populations, cultures, and so forth) seem to multiply infinitely in the world market which attacks nothing more violently than fixed boundaries: it overwhelms any binary division with its infinite multiplicities.[24]

More than merely discovering difference, Hardt and Negri contend that this globalization produces differences, localities, and marginal spaces, not as part of the market, but as the very market itself. Culture is thus constituted within this rationality, always proliferating and constructed by market forces. In the margins lay new differences, new cultures, and new combinations of them for new consumers and new markets, all of which form the constantly shiftable boundaries of capitalism's global landscape.

Just as McDonald's and its mutton hamburgers have become Indian in the logic of globalization, so too has Bollywood become American, and for our purposes here, African American. Yet with culture as a commodity, new differences and new combinations also bring new oversights and exclusions. In the video version of "Addictive," Bollywood functions not only as the backdrop of the Truth Hurts's song, but as an anthem for America's anxieties about the Middle East. Set in a giant ornate Middle Eastern palace, Rakim performs as an affluent drug warrior surrounded by gyrating female dancers with heavily henna-stained skin, finger-cymbals, and scantily clad sequined outfits. The clichéd spectacle of the sultan and the harem visually structures the song within a setting of male pleasure and excess, wherein valuable goods and women abundantly coded as sexually "exotic" substantiate the authority of his words. In context, Rakim's lyrics about making it in a "fucked up world" take on new meaning when considering the video's release in the summer of 2002 coincided with the ongoing deployment of thousands of disproportionately black and brown American troops to an Afghan zone renowned for its opium trade. The romanticization of profit in a corrupt world in the song and video also came at a time when images of India became increasingly associated with fears of "outsourced" American labor to Asian workers.[25] Bollywood, then, becomes recontextualized as a sound track for fantasies of street-thug life and economic prowess set in the latest conquerable territory. The Middle East may be an object of fear and danger for Americans, but it is also a source for playing out desires of erotic, economic, and social conquest. And although India may not be a member of Bush's "axis of evil" (nor a part of the Middle East), the Truth Hurts video's collapse of geographic and cultural locations is the same maneuver employed by Bush's apothegm, "you are either with us, or you are with the enemy." Simultaneously a threat and an opportunity, the encroaching totalized "Third World" other functions as a site for enforcing and containing market and military profit within the cultural mixing of contemporary empire.

Market Mergers, Bhangra Style

In 2004, *The Source* magazine, a glossy monthly devoted to hip-hop culture, argued that the largest names in the industry today have made it big not as artists, but as entrepreneurs. According to writer Harry Allen, hip-hop moguls now understand that success is built through synergies of entertainment and corporate brands, as well as a diversification of strategies that bring hip-hop names to the public. As one marketing specialist explained, "Hip-hop has the uncanny ability to literally build a brand. And you have marketers who spend all day in the ivory towers of corporate America trying to do that: hip-hop artists figured it out in real time."[26] Take, for instance, Busta Rhymes's 1999 song "Pass the Courvoisier," which virtually saved the cognac industry's American market from ruin, as the drink became the alcohol of choice for African American youth who suddenly consumed 60–80 percent of the product's U.S. imports. So when Jay-Z, the rapper crowned as "the father of hip-hop" for his musical achievements and expansive business ventures (footwear, bars, clothes, and NBA teams), transformed a five-year-old Bhangra track sung by a Bollywood vocalist into an international hit, one wonders whether this is the crossover of African American and Indian aesthetic sensibilities or just another market merger.

George Lipsitz explains that for artists across the world, the "popular" functions at an intersection between commercial culture and "the emergence of a new public sphere that uses the circuits of commodity production and circulation to envision and activate new social relations."[27] Pop music's definition and profound dependence on the flows of capital, which enable the circulation of its forms, draw into question any space of "authentic" new sounds that are not already implicated in market overlaps, consumer bases, and the economic networks of distribution. Consistent with the new demands of entrepreneurship in iconic hip-hop, as Jay-Z describes his "dumbed down lyrics" (to "double his dollars"), his collaboration with Panjabi MC, where the hip-hop and Bhangra styles are offered as equals, represents both musical opportunity and shrewd business. We might thus be skeptical of Lipsitz's hopeful assertion that such moves represent any "new social relations." Not unlike Jay-Z's dozens of collaborations featuring such hip-hop elites as Notorious B.I.G., Foxy Brown, and Eminem, "Beware" taps not only the talent of an established performer, but also his or her audience. When Jay-Z heard the already popular original version in a Swiss nightclub, he contacted Panjabi MC, he cut his rap in hours, and Panjabi MC mixed it in days.[28] Unlike the Bollywood samples in American hip-hop, which seem to function as an open authorless source of a traditional culture, this collaboration is treated as the work of two artists at the progressive cusp of their respective cultural spheres; Bhangra DJs in the United Kingdom and South Asia since the 1980s have found great success remixing the "traditional" sounds of Hindi film.[29] And even though Bhangra is not Bollywood—they are very different aesthetic forms— they occupy overlapping dominant spaces in the popular Indian music scene and have enjoyed similar successes with international audiences who view them both as "authentic" Indian sounds. If "Addictive" and "React" represent the well-worn terrain of imperial cultural pillage, Jay-Z stands as the new model for global integration where flexible influence over the "new" is preferable to absolute control of the "old," international partnership is better than local authority, and new market synergies signal progress.

Of the examples of American hip-hop's foray into Indian sounds, Jay-Z's 2003 duet with Panjabi MC garnered the most widespread attention. Selling hundred thousand singles in two days, dominating the *Billboard* charts in the United States, the United Kingdom, Germany, and Italy, and earning MTV's Dance Hit of the Year, "Beware," or "Mundian to bach ke," demonstrated that mainstream Western hip-hop audiences had a hearty appetite for its signature Bhangra instrumentation and Punjabi lyrics. The opening jangling notes of the track and sampled bassline from the internationally syndicated American television show, "Knight Rider," can now be heard as background on MTV shows, "Cribs" and "The Real World," and have even become a crowd-pleasing musical staple at National Basketball Association games. As with Lata Mangeshkar's vocals on "Addictive," the prominent drum and dhol and voice of Bollywood singer, Labh Janjua, announce the piece's cultural difference before the rap lyrics of Jay-Z enter. However, what distinguishes "Beware" from other hip-hop fusions of Indian forms is not its sound, but the collaborative process between two performers in the global sphere of contemporary music; the American rapper is presented as a piece of Panjabi MC's track, rather than the total owner of it. Jay-Z's rap vocals disappear not long into the song before the Punjabi verses, which warn a young girl of the boys who notice her good looks, soar above the instrumentation for the balance of the track. And in terms of distribution, the cut never appears on any of

Jay-Z's albums, but served instead as the springboard for the subsequent release of Panjabi MC's first American album, *Beware*.

"Beware" clearly marks its Indian character with the opening musical lines, but Jay-Z's lyrics illustrate the desire for situating the song as doubly located in American and what are called "overseas" sounds. "Yes, live from the United States/Brooklyn, New York it's ya boy" goes the rap, declaring the song's origins in a largely black and brown urban community, but one that is in musical harmony with the Bhangra rhythms and Punjabi vocals ("I am simply attached to the track like a symphony") and, by extension, in social harmony with the New York City South Asian population, the largest in the United States.[30] Also articulated is the transnational space the song and its performers inhabit as voices of "the streets": "As soon as the beat drop/We got the streets locked/Overseas Panjabi MC and the Roc [Jay-Z]." "Beware" uniquely

Hip-hop's global partner: Panjabi MC, *Beware* (2003).

gives name to both collaborators, acknowledging not only Panjabi MC's talent, but also his labor. Yet Jay-Z's additions to the track indulge in some of the cultural clichés that have saturated hip-hop's "discovery" of India. Like "Addictive" and "React," the oblique reference to "overseas" denies specificity, reinforced by Jay-Z's likening himself to a "snake charmer." If, as Lipsitz explains, popular culture serves "as a site for experimentation with cultural and social roles not yet possible in politics,"[31] then "Beware" only cautiously approaches cultural solidarity in its totalized East. As both the English and the Punjabi lyrics demonstrate, it is a bond exclusively between men whose interest is to either preserve or venture across the sexual boundaries of women. Jay-Z's image of easy and available women consistent with so much of popular music ("I take one of ya chicks straight from under ya armpit/the black Brad Pitt I mack till 6 in the AM") contrasts with the Punjabi lyrics, which warn against the very male predatory advances that Jay-Z celebrates. Asia is equated with sexual purity, America is associated with sexual libertinism, and we are right back to the foundations of Orientalism's violent and reactionary constructions.

Despite the stereotypes, the release of "Beware" in March 2003, the same time as the U.S. military's invasion of Iraq, put the track in a politically charged position. As the American public sphere railed against "anti-American" political expressions and held all racialized immigrant identities in legally sanctioned suspicion, radio program directors hesitated to air "Beware" on their stations because the Punjabi language represented potential political dissent from foreign voices sounding too Middle Eastern.[32] Jay-Z may be guilty of misrepresentations, but his presence in music that even incorrectly hints at Middle Eastern aesthetics gives an affirmative valence to these sounds in a mainstream arena and authorizes African American–Middle Eastern affiliations, as well as African American–South Asian affiliations, to those who know better. In this context, the Jay-Z/Panjabi MC collaboration expresses a loose sense of social identification in a country where dark skin is read as a threat, recalling what Frantz Fanon called "the fact of blackness," or the transnational imprisonment of identity and expression by white-supremacist racial hierarchies.[33] A later remix of "Beware" answered questions about its political valence when Jay-Z rhymed throughout the song, "Leave Iraq alone," offering an oblique, but discernible voice of opposition to a conflict whose casualties on all sides remain overwhelmingly black and brown.

Nevertheless, the success of "Beware" ultimately represents only limited possibilities for cultural and political connections between South Asian and African American communities, largely because its "opposition" also panders to the same racial and cultural reductions that have functioned to divide groups of color. Jay-Z's partial embrace of Bhangra, but full embrace of its popularity in Europe, follows in step with wider patterns of global appropriation that largely offer the artifice of equal cultural understanding and unthreatening or sanitized messages of political opposition. Naomi Klein exposes this trend of transnational outreach in her study, *No Logo,* by focusing on the "Market Masala" of multicultural commodification:

> Today the buzzword in global marketing isn't selling America to the world, but bringing a kind of market masala to everyone in the world. In the late nineties, the pitch is less Marlboro Man, more Ricky Martin: a bilingual mix of North and South, some Latin, some R&B, all couched in global party lyrics. This ethnic-food-court approach creates a One World placelessness, a global mall in which corporations are able to sell a single product in numerous countries without triggering the old cries of "Coca-Colonization."[34]

The most cynical reading of Jay-Z's collaboration with Panjabi MC would claim that the main act of solidarity exists between markets: one of pop music's largest brands embraces an international audience that had already proved its taste for the original 1998 version of "Mundian to bach ke." Hip-hop's intimate relationship with a gargantuan entertainment corporation (like Truth Hurts, Jay-Z is with Vivendi) would lend credence to this view. However, the fact that many South Asian youths in the United States felt their culture legitimated by hip-hop blackness in this song, according to DJ Rekha, represents the paucity of affirmative intersections of popular black and Asian aesthetics.[35] Despite this, Jay-Z and Vivendi are not all of American hip-hop, nor do they represent all of the possibilities of social critiques of culture in hip-hop. Largely ignored by MTV and BET, African American hip-hop stars such as Dead Prez, Spearhead, Lauryn Hill, Paris, and The Coup maintain a socially active radical antiracist and explicitly anticorporate position in their music.[36] "Beware" should have us wondering what lies beyond corporate music's definition of hip-hop and the cultural mixes it offers, as well as what kind of hip-hop articulations enable radical avenues of Indian–African American musical intersections outside the "official" corporate markets.

Basement Bollywood and Radical Politics

According to the urban culture publications *Time Out* and *The Village Voice,* Basement Bhangra and Bollywood Disco have become integral to the face of New York City nightlife. Hosted by veteran DJ, DJ Rekha Malhotra, these events feature hip-hop dance music layered with a sonic and visual collage of fragments from film clips, traditional melodies, and Bollywood lyrical classics to construct a "party" space for negotiating new discursive modes of collective and diasporic identity. Continuing the tradition of hip-hop as cultural movement of racial self-identification through the vernacular of dress, dance, and "cut-and-mix" musical practices, South Asian DJs produce an affirmative and, even further, a consciously politicized environment for locals to listen to music, dance, and construct activist alliances. As Rekha claims in one of her many press interviews, she is not trying to create a community; it already exists: "It's about community-building."[37] If diasporic identity is formed by a "confluence of narratives as it is lived and relived, produced and reproduced and transformed through individual as well as collective memory and re-memory" as Avtar Brah describes in *Cartographies of Diaspora,* then dancehall music and its remixing become an avenue for more public identification for young desi "clubbers" not only with each other, but with social justice causes.

Maira notes that Indian American youth grapple with their ambivalent relationship to South Asian aesthetic traditions by infusing old forms with the codes of subcultural "cool," in essence claiming both the nostalgia for the "authentic Indian" and the modernity of "hip" America in order to positively reinvent themselves as hybrids.[38] Music serves as the nexus for forging alternative identities and new cultural alliances through shared marginal practices in America of listening, viewing, and responding to popular films and musical themes from the "homeland." With the easy availability and exchange of video and audio, as well as new Hindi film productions, popular music from India functions as an accessible means of maintaining transnational cultural connections.[39] Yet Bollywood melodies and dance sequences, which stand as the primary benefactors in this transnational exchange, are transformed by desi youth from the sound track of their parents' generation, multicultural fairs, and local samaj programs into the ground for affective identification with the personal and collective experiences of engaging with these forms. In speaking of diasporic blackness in musical forms, Paul Gilroy explains:

> [Transnational entertainment corporations'] means of distribution are capable of dissolving distance and creating new and unpredictable forms of cultural affinity between groups that dwell far apart. The transformation of cultural space and the subordination of distance are only two factors that contribute to a parallel change in the significance of appeals to tradition, time, and history.[40]

Simultaneously Indian and "Western," new music and popular style ultimately challenge the fixity of these reductive categories while also relocating the productive mechanisms of Bollywood. The music itself, as well as the process of mixing, sampling, and fusing melodies and rhythms, acknowledges the listening practices of diasporic South Asians, but also integrates these familiar chord progressions, lyrics, and beats with locally familiar sounds and the consumptive patterns of "cool" within youth culture. As one announcement for an Outernational gig promises: "hip-hop, rock, reggae, funk and bhangra into a ferocious live mix. 21st century rebel music—the baddest band this side of the revolution." Much of this "cool" manifests itself through codes of popular American blackness represented in hip-hop styles that resist assimilative codes of white middle-class propriety, like funky "Om" tattoos, baggy pants, or the adoption of urban dialect. Although born from a need for self-definition, these codes do not necessarily transcend social and political social conflicts, in particular the commodification of black culture embedded in these strategies. In other words, this appropriation can easily become what we hear from Jay-Z and Erick Sermon. Just as many suburban white youths struggle to define themselves in opposition authoritative structures through identifying with massmarketed black America, the integration of hip-hop styles for Indian American youth can remain radically distant from the lives of African Americans. At the same time, not all cross-cultural interactions are mediated by the branded versions of black identity; the lives of many South Asian American youth, especially those, like Rekha, who grew up in African American and multiethnic neighborhoods, refute tidy distinctions between African American and Asian American cultures.

Many DJs in America, however, have gone further than the party scene to make "community building" a pedagogical activity of political mobilization, linking these events to the social justice activist networks that groups of South Asians have been engaged in for some time.[41] Rekha's two-year-old Bollywood Disco and Basement Bhangra nights, which launched in 1997, as well as the number of other large club parties across the nation hosted by DJs such as DJ Siraiki, Zakhm, and Outernational, politicize their remixed versions of South Asian cinematic and musical traditions as ways of bringing the immigrant youth and young professionals together and organizing them through fundraising and awareness campaigns. Basement Bhangra, for instance, regularly devotes the first two hours of its evening to disseminate information about progressive causes and takes most of the proceeds form the door for "Your Attention Please" programs to benefit acid burn victims in Bangladesh, the South Asian Women's Domestic Violence Agency, and rallies against police brutality. Bollywood Disco has similarly dedicated its party to International Human Rights Day by advertising "a human rights look at Bollywood," as the music also, for example, mixes, fragments, and mocks the intensely gendered conventions of the romantic ballad. In 1997, Rekha and Siraiki formed the Musical Insurgency Across All Borders, or the Mutiny collective, to

"Basement Bhangra against George W. Bush" party, New York, 2004.

bring contemporary artists of the global South Asian diaspora, as well as non-Asian "local diaspora diabolics" like DJ Spooky and Portishead's Andy Smith, together to raise money for independent films and antiracist campaigns in the United States and in the United Kingdom.[42] Besides hosting these parties, which have brought widely multiracial audiences over a thousand strong, these DJs also appear as musical guests at social justice events like Voices Rising, the National Day of Solidarity with Muslim, Arab, and South Asian Immigrants, university conferences on defending immigrant rights, and Books not Bombs protests. San Francisco DJs likewise formed the Ahimsa Music Tour to address the post-9/11 backlash against South Asians, Muslims, and Arabs by developing memorials for victims of racist murders and helping to reconstruct Hindu temples that were burnt down.[43]

If any group has been closed out of the media, the entertainment industry, and popular culture markets, it would be groups of color who openly express their political agendas such as the Black Radical Congress, the South Asian Women for Action (SAWA), or the Brown Berets of Aztlan. Networks of affiliation and affect are constructed in this South Asian underground of dancehall activism through practices of political organization and action, which are mediated by the spaces of musical cultural experimentation. These charged spaces force entertainment to engage discourses that critically negotiate race and imagine ways to address white-supremacist violence and cultural subordination. Being South Asian, dancing to Bhangra, and viewing clips from classic Bollywood films cease to be epiphenomena of everyday life or matters of "personal taste" and become acts of direct engagement with America's social dynamics of racism, patriarchy, and state power. And for the broad multiracial audience that attends these events, the sounds and rhythms of Bollywood and Bhangra cease to be sites for mere consumption of the Indian other, but a space for participation in counterhegemonic politics. At the same time, these solidarities are built through alternative desires for public and performative acts of political unity and cultural expressions of resistance wholly unavailable in mainstream cultural venues, but encoded in the music and dance.

With a newly energized cultural conservatism in the United States, the stakes are high in recognizing and addressing the oppressive patterns in the commodification and consumption of cultural differences. The brand name hip-hop that incorporates Indian and Asian forms into its music and performance certainly demonstrates an inability to move

328 | RICHARD ZUMKHAWALA-COOK

beyond the tired racist and sexist images that have dogged South Asians for decades. However, when current American policy is dictated by "us and them" proclamations, the music of Jay-Z and others adopts forms that align themselves, although clumsily, against conventional versions of the white suburban American cultural "us." This, of course, does little to think beyond race as only black and white experiences, but at best foregrounds the limited number of representations of hip-hop's many moves across racial and cultural lines, where participatory and grassroots resistance to the centralization of power and wealth has demanded a formal and collective voice. Even further, the trip to India by corporate hip-hop requires a better recognition of the lived black–Asian relationships in the United States and around the world that have constructed democratic, rather than exploitative, alliances in their integrations of cultural traditions. This is DJ Rekha's hope for "community building" in organizing beyond the "Addictive" consumption of differences toward affirmative and productive identifications with a fluent but critical combination of a variety of popular Bollywood and hip-hop sounds and the desires to transform America's white-supremacist politics.

Notes

1 Jim Farber, "Indian Flavor Worth Currying," *New York Daily News,* May 20, 2003, 36.
2 Panjabi MC as quoted in Phillip Zonkel, "Global Hip-Hopping," *Long Beach Press-Telegram,* September 8, 2003.
3 See Edward Said, *Orientalism* (New York: Vintage, 1978).
4 See Jasbir K. Puar and Amit Rai, "Monster, Terrorist, Fag: The War on Terrorism and the Production of Docile Patriots," *Social Text* 20, no. 3 (Fall 2002): 117–48.
5 The 1998 album *Bombay the Hard Way* by remixers DJ Shadow and Dan the Automator undoubtedly had these politics in mind with their track, "Fear of a Brown Planet." For more on such albums, see Edward K. Chan's essay in this anthology.
6 Sunaina Maira, *Desis in the House: Indian American Youth Culture in New York City* (Philadelphia: Temple University Press, 2002), 66–7.
7 See Rajinder Dudrah's essay for the specificity of queer identifications enabled by these cut-and-mix practices.
8 Tricia Rose, *Black Noise: Rap Music and Black Culture in Contemporary America* (Middletown, Conn.: Wesleyan University Press, 1994), 124.
9 Paul Gilroy, *The Black Atlantic: Modernity and Double Consciousness* (Cambridge: Harvard University Press, 1993), 107–8.

10 Since the writing of this essay, big hits have also been scored by hip-hop artists who have sampled Middle Eastern instrumentation (Beyoncé Knowles's "Naughty Girl") and Chinese dancehall music (Christina Milian's "Dip It Low").

11 Arjun Appadurai, *Modernity at Large* (Minneapolis: University of Minnesota Press, 1996), 35–6.

12 Sanjay Sharma, "Noisy Asians or Asian Noise," in *Dis-Orienting Rhythms: The Politics of the New Asian Dance Music,* ed. Sanjay Sharma, John Hutnyk, and Ashwani Sharma (London: Zed Books, 1996), 40.

13 See Stuart Hall, "The Meaning of New Times," in *Stuart Hall: Critical Dialogues in Cultural Studies,* ed. David Morely and Kuan-Hsing Chen (London: Routledge, 1996), 236.

14 Gilroy, *Black Atlantic,* 83.

15 See Vijay Prashad, *Everybody Was Kung Fu Fighting: Afro-Asian Connections and the Myth of Cultural Purity* (Boston: Beacon, 2001), for a smart analysis of America's racist techniques of denying black and Asian political and cultural alliances.

16 As quoted in Tina Chadha, "Mix This," *Village Voice,* July 8, 2003, 48.

17 "Federal Court Lawsuit Claims That Hit Single 'Addictive' Borrows from Hindi Song by B. Lahiri," *India Times Online,* November 8, 2002, http://www.newsindia-times.com/2002/11/08/dias-32-fed.html (accessed January 23, 2004).

18 "Indian Composer Sues Rapper Dr Dre," *BBC Online,* October 31, 2002, http://news.bbc.co.uk/1/hi/entertainment/music/2383847.stm.

19 Rose, *Black Noise,* 88.

20 Appadurai, *Modernity at Large,* 35–6.

21 Thanks to Arti Parikh for the help with the translation.

22 This, of course, is in direct contrast to Lata's global image of feminine and national purity. See Sanjay Srivastava, "The Voice of the Nation and the Five-Year Plan Hero: Speculations on Gender, Space, and Popular Culture," in *Fingerprinting Popular Culture: The Mythic and the Iconic in Indian Cinema,* ed. A. Nandy and V. Lal (New Delhi: Oxford University Press, 2006), 122–55.

23 As quoted in Gil Kaufman, "Judge Rules Truth Hurts' Album Must Be Pulled or Stickered," *MTV News Online,* February 4, 2003, http://www.mtv.com/news/articles/1459838/20030204/truth_hurts.jhtml.

24 Michael Hardt and Antonio Negri, *Empire* (Cambridge, Mass.: Harvard University Press, 2000), 150.

25 My thanks to the editors for this insight.

26 As quoted in Harry Allen, "Poppin Tags," *Source* 177 (January 2004): 29.

27 George Lipsitz, *Dangerous Crossroads: Popular Music, Postmodernism, and the Poetics of Place* (London: Verso, 1994), 12.

28 Farber, "Indian Flavor Worth Currying," 36.

29 Sharma, "Noisy Asians or Asian Noise," 33.

30 Maira, *Desis in the House,* 16–17.

31 Lipsitz, *Dangerous Crossroads,* 17.

32 Steve Jones, "Jay-Z Remix Spices Interest in Panjabi MC," *USA Today,* May 20, 2003, 1D.

33 Frantz Fanon, *Black Skin, White Masks* (New York: Grove Press, 1967), 112–13.

34 Naomi Klein, *No Logo* (New York: Picador, 2002), 116.

35 Chadha, "Mix This," 48.

36 See Michael Eric Dyson, *Open Mike: Reflections on Philosophy, Race, Sex, Culture, and Religion* (New York: Basic Books, 2003) 293–5.

37 "Exclusive Interview with DJ Rekha," *EthnoTechno*, April 10, 2002, http://www.ethnotechno.com/int_rekha_print.php.

38 Maira, *Desis in the House,* 196–7.

39 See Peter Manuel, *Cassette Culture: Popular Music and Technology in North India* (Chicago: University of Chicago Press, 1993), for a study of the circulation of Indian popular culture through personal and informal reproductions of cassette copies. The exchange of musical styles, he argues, may generate cultural relations across disparate geographic locations, but this process ultimately homogenizes the landscape of popular music in marginalizing local products.

40 Gilroy, *Black Atlantic,* 194.

41 See Vijay Prashad, *The Karma of Brown Folk* (Minneapolis: University of Minnesota Press, 2000), for an insightful long history of radical politics in South Asian American communities.

42 "About Mutiny," *Mutiny: Musical Insurgency across All Borders,* http://www.mutinysounds.com/theclub/aboutmutiny.php3. Much of the energy in the United States for politicized South Asian hip-hop and reggae forms has been inspired by the broad emergence of groups in the 1990s such as Fun-Da-Mental and Asian Dub Foundation in the United Kingdom, both of which have been likened to England's answer to Public Enemy. See Sharma et al., *Dis-Orienting Rhythms.*

43 Anmol Chaddha, "South Asian DJs Throw It Down in the Bay Area," *Hardboiled* 5.2, http://www.hardboiled.org/5.2/52-15-dj.html (accessed November 20, 2003).

Acknowledgments

Thanks are first due to our contributors for making this project exciting and fulfilling for us. Several reviewers provided astute criticism and suggestions that helped sharpen the arguments and focus of this collection; we are most grateful for their input. We also wish to thank Helen Abadzi for making available her research findings and a wonderful photo archive of Hindi cinema's reception in Greece. Our appreciation goes out to N. Pushpamala who gave us permission to use her Bollywood-inspired artwork and to the staff at the National Film Archive of India, especially Kiron Dhiwar, Lakshmi Iyer, Urmila Joshi, and Aarti Kharkhanis, who tracked down, with their typical ingenuity, obscure films and other materials.

As is usual with any edited anthology that has evolved over a period of time, we have accumulated more debts than we can possibly acknowledge here.

Nevertheless, the following must be thanked for graciously sharing ideas and suggestions: Moinak Biswas, Sumita Chakravarty, Gayatri Chatterjee, David Chute, Corey Creekmur, Jigna Desai, Rachel Dwyer, Bishnupriya Ghosh, Lalitha Gopalan, John Hutnyk, Priya Jaikumar, Priya Joshi, Suvir Kaul, Ann Kibbey, Amitava Kumar, Brian Larkin, Philip Lutgendorf, Neepa Majumdar, Ashis Nandy, Tejeshwini Niranjana, Prashant Pandya, Madhava Prasad, Amit Rai, Bhaskar Sarkar, Timothy Taylor, Ravi Vasudevan, and Mimi White.

A number of colleagues and students at Middlebury College, Old Dominion University, and the University of Oregon helped us through various stages of the project; we thank them all.

Andrea Kleinhuber, formerly at the University of Minnesota Press, enthusiastically supported this project in its early days. Jason Weideman and his colleagues at the Press provided invaluable feedback and timely assistance while Satishna Gokuldas and her team have been spectacular in helping us wade through the minutiae of the publication process.

Above all, we must thank our families for encouraging us and for the good cheer with which they have borne many a late-night confabulation. Of course, it goes without saying, that the seductive power of Chitrahaar and Vividh Bharati, reminiscences about filmsong by strangers from Istanbul to Lima, and dancehalls in the diaspora are the catalysts that resulted in this anthology.

Sangita Gopal and Sujata Moorti

Contributors

Walter Armbrust is the Albert Hourani Fellow of Modern Middle East Studies, St Antony's College, and a university lecturer at the University of Oxford. He is the author of *Mass Culture and Modernism in Egypt* and editor of *Mass Mediations: New Approaches to Popular Culture in the Middle East and Beyond*.

Anustup Basu is an assistant professor at the University of Illinois, Urbana-Champaign. His essays have been published in *Critical Quarterly*, *Postmodern Culture*, and *Postscript*.

Nilanjana Bhattacharjya is assistant professor of music at Colorado College, where she teaches ethnomusicology, popular music, and music theory.

Edward K. Chan is assistant professor of English at Kennesaw State University in Georgia. His research and teaching interests include twentieth-century American literary, film, and cultural studies, particularly race in the utopian imagination and the reception of texts across cultures.

Bettina David is a freelance writer and translator for Malay and Indonesian. Affiliated with the Department of Austronesian Studies at Hamburg University, she is completing a PhD thesis on globalization and moral panic in post-1998 Indonesia.

Rajinder Dudrah is a senior lecturer in screen studies at the University of Manchester. He is founder and coeditor of the journal *South Asian Popular Culture* and author of *Bollywood: Sociology Goes to the Movies*.

Sangita Gopal is assistant professor of English at the University of Oregon.

Shanti Kumar is associate professor in the Department of Radio-Television-Film at the University of Texas, Austin. He is the author of *Gandhi Meets Primetime: Globalization and Nationalism in Indian Television* and coeditor of *Planet TV: A Global Television Reader*.

Monika Mehta is assistant professor of English at Binghamton University. She is completing a book manuscript that examines film censorship of sex.

Sujata Moorti is professor of women and gender studies at Middlebury College.

Anna Morcom is Research Council UK academic fellow in the music department of Royal Holloway College, London University. She is the author of *Hindi Film Songs and the Cinema.*

Ronie Parciack is a lecturer in East Asian studies at Tel Aviv University. Her PhD dissertation focuses on the unique aesthetics of Hindi films.

Biswarup Sen teaches popular culture and globalization in the School of Journalism at the University of Oregon. He is author of *Of the People: Essays in Indian Popular Culture.*

Sangita Shresthova is a scholar, filmmaker, and choreographer trained in classical Indian and Nepali dance.

Richard Zumkhawala-Cook is associate professor of English at Shippensburg University, where he teaches postcolonial and British literature and cultural studies.

Index